SYNOPSIS

OF THE

Books of the Bible

SYNOPSIS

OF THE

Books of the Bible

By J. N. DARBY

Volume III

MATTHEW—JOHN

LOIZEAUX BROTHERS, PUBLISHERS
19 WEST 21st STREET
NEW YORK

Revised Edition, 3,250 .... May, 1942

PRINTED BY THE

L. B. PRINTING CO., INC.
19 West 21st Street
New York City

PRINTED IN THE U.S.A.

CONTENTS

SYNOPSIS

OF THE

Books of the Bible

INTRODUCTION
TO THE NEW TESTAMENT

The concentration and expansion of divine light and the immense importance of the truths in the New Testament

IN pursuing these Scripture studies, it is with a certain kind of fear that I approach the New Testament, great as may be the blessing attendant on so doing. The concentration and at the same time expansion of divine light in this precious gift of God, the immense reach of the truths contained in it; the infinite variety of the aspects and true applications of one and the same passage, and of its relations with the whole circle of divine truths; the immense importance of these truths, whether considered in themselves or with reference to the glory of God or in relation to the need of man; the manner in which they reveal God and meet that need—all these considerations, which I can but imperfectly express, would cause any humble-minded person to retire from the pretension of giving a true and (even in principle) adequate idea of the purpose of the Holy Ghost in the books of the New Testament. And the more truth itself is revealed, the more true light shines, the more one's incapacity to speak of it must be felt, and the more one must fear to darken that which is perfect. The more pure the truth is with which we have to do (and here it is truth itself), the more difficult is the endeavor to lay it before others without in some respects injuring its purity; and the more fatal also is this injury. In meditating on such or such a passage, we may communicate, for the profit of others, the measure of light granted to us.

7

But in attempting to give an idea of the Book as a whole, all the perfection of truth itself, and the universality of the purpose of God in the revelation He has made of it, present themselves to the mind; and one trembles at the thought of undertaking to give a true and general idea, if it be not a complete one, which no really Christian person would pretend to do.

In the Old Testament God has spoken, but in the New Testament God manifests Himself

The Old Testament may perhaps appear more difficult to some persons than the New, and with respect to the interpretation of certain isolated passages it may be so; but, although the inspired writers of that part of Scripture reveal the mind of God as communicated to them by Him (and we can admire the wisdom there unfolded), yet God Himself was still hidden behind the veil. We may mistake or overlook the meaning of an expression, and we suffer loss, for it was God who *spoke;* but in the New Testament it is God *Himself*—meek, gentle, human, on earth, in the Gospels; instructing with divine light in the subsequent communications of the Holy Ghost; yet still *God*—who manifests Himself. But if the light is brighter, both for our personal guidance and for the knowledge of Himself, it becomes a yet more serious thing to misinterpret these living communications, or to disguise by our own thoughts that which is the truth itself. For we must remember that Christ is the Truth. He is the Word. It is God who speaks in the Person of the Son, who, while truly Man, manifests also the Father.

The New Testament fulfilling and eclipsing the Old Testament and introducing what is eternal and heavenly

As regards even interpretation itself, the truth itself, the light, eternal life, being in that which is revealed to us in the New Testament, it may be looked at in so many aspects, that the practical difficulty is much greater. For this truth may be looked at in its intrinsic and essential value: we may view it as the manifestation of the eternal nature of God, or in its manifestation with respect to the glory of the Son; we may examine its connections and its contrasts with the partial communications of the Old Testament, which it fulfils and eclipses by its own brightness, with the economy of God's earthly government, which is set aside in order to introduce that which is eternal and heavenly. It may be viewed in its relations to man, for the life was the light of men, God having been pleased to manifest and to glorify Himself in man, to make Himself known to man, and to constitute him the means of the revelation of Himself to His other intelligent creatures. On every passage there would be something to say with respect to each of these aspects; for the truth is one, even as it is of God, but it shines on all things, and displays their true character.

The channels of the pure and living water

Two things, however, encourage me: first, that we have to do with a God of perfect goodness, who has given us these wondrous revelations that we may profit by them; and, in the second place, that, although the source of truth is infinite and perfect, although these revelations flow from the fulness of truth in God, and its communication to us is perfect, after the perfection of Him that made it, nevertheless it is made by means of divers instruments, in themselves of a limited capacity, of which God makes use in communicating this or that portion of truth to us. This pure and living water has been in no wise corrupted, but in each communication it has been limited by the purpose of God, in the instrument used by Him to dispense it, while still in connection with the whole, according to the perfect wisdom of Him who has communicated all truth. The channel is not infinite. The water which flows through it is infinite, but not infinite in its communication. They prophesied in part, and we know in part. The aspect and the application of truth have even an especial character, according to the vessel through which truth is communicated. The living water is there in its perfect pureness. As it exists in its source, so it gushes forth: the form of the fountain through which it flows before men is according to His wisdom who has formed it to be His instrument for that purpose. The Holy Ghost acts in man, in the vessel thereunto prepared. God had created, formed, fashioned and adapted the vessel, morally and intellectually, for such and such a service in respect to the truth. He acts in the vessel according to the object for which He has prepared it. Christ was and is the truth. Others have communicated it, each one according to that given him, and in connection with those elements with which God had brought his mind and heart into unison, and with that object for which the Holy Ghost had thus prepared him.

Leaving therefore my fears behind, I address myself confidingly to the accomplishment of this service, my heart resting on the perfect goodness of God who delights to bless us. May the just sense of my responsibility prevent my hazarding anything not according to God; and may the Lord Himself, in His grace, deign to direct me, and furnish me with that which shall be a blessing to the reader!

The character of the New Testament: the presence of God Himself as a Man among men

The New Testament has evidently a very different character from the Old. That which I have already remarked constitutes the essence of this difference. The New Testament treats of the revelation of God Himself, and shows us man brought in righteousness into glory in the presence of God. Formerly God had made promises, and He had executed judgments. He had governed a people on earth, and acted towards the nations without, having this people in view as the centre of His counsels as to earth. He had given them His law, and bestowed on them, by means of the prophets, a growing light, which announced, as nearer and nearer, *His* coming, who should tell them all things from God. But the presence of God Himself, a Man amongst men, changed the position of everything. Either man must receive, as a crown of blessing and of glory, the One whose presence was to banish all evil, and develop and perfect every element of good, furnishing at the same time an object which should be the centre of all affections, rendered perfectly happy by the enjoyment of this object; or, by rejecting Him, our poor nature must manifest itself as being enmity against God, and must prove the necessity for a completely new order of things, in which the happiness of man and the glory of God should be based upon a new creation.

Man's rejection of God the means of the fulfilment of God's eternal purposes for a new order of things

We know what happened. He who was the image of the invisible God had to say, after the exercise of a perfect patience, "Righteous Father, the world hath not known Thee." Alas, yet more than that: He had to say, "They have seen and hated both Me and My Father."

Nevertheless this condition of man has in nowise prevented God from fulfilling His counsels; on the contrary it became the means of His doing so. He would not reject man until man had rejected Him (as in the garden of Eden man, conscious of sin, being unable to bear the presence of God, withdrew from Him before God had driven him out of the garden). But now that man on his part had entirely rejected God come in mercy into the midst of his misery, God was free—if one may venture to speak thus, and the expression is morally correct—to carry out His eternal purposes. But it is not judgment that is carried into effect, as was the case in Eden, when man had already departed from God. It is sovereign grace which, when man is evidently lost and has declared himself the enemy of God, carries on its work to magnify His glory, before the whole universe, in the salvation of poor sinners who had rejected Him.[1]

But in order that the perfect wisdom of God should be manifested, even in the details, this work of sovereign grace, in which God revealed Himself, must be seen as having its due connection with all His previous dealings revealed in the Old Testament, and also as leaving its full place to His government of the world.

The four principal subjects of the New Testament

All this is the cause that (apart from the one great idea which reigns throughout) there are four subjects in this wonderful book which unfold themselves to the eye of faith.

First, the great subject, the dominant fact, is that the perfect light is manifested: God reveals Himself. But this light is revealed in love, the other essential name of God.

Christ, who is the manifestation of this light and love, and who, if He had been received, would have been the fulfilment of all the promises, is then presented to man, and especially to Israel (looked at in their responsibility),

---

[1] See Titus 1: 2; 2 Timothy 1: 9, 10, and compare Proverbs 8: 22-31, specially 30, 31, and Romans 16: 25, 26 (reading "prophetic Scriptures"), Ephesians 3: 5, 10, Colossians 1: 26. Under the law God never came out, and man could not go in. In Christianity God is come out, and man is gone in; and these things are of the essence of both. Before there was promise. These are characteristic relations.

with every proof, personal, moral, and of power—proofs which left them without excuse.

Secondly, being rejected (a rejection by means of which salvation was accomplished), the new order of things— the new creation, man glorified, the assembly sharing with Christ in heavenly glory—is put before us.

Thirdly, the connection between the old order of things upon earth, and the new, with respect to the law, the promises, the prophets, or the divine institutions on earth, is set forth; whether in exhibiting the new as the fulfilment and setting aside of that which had grown old, or in stating the contrast between the two, and the perfect wisdom of God, which is demonstrated in every detail of His ways.

Finally, the government of the world, on the part of God, is prophetically displayed; and the renewal of God's relations with Israel, whether in judgment or in blessing, is briefly but plainly stated, on the occasion of the rapture of those relations by the rejection of the Messiah.

It may be added, that everything necessary for man, as a pilgrim on earth until God shall accomplish in power the purposes of His grace, is abundantly supplied. Come forth, at the call of God, from that which is rejected and condemned, and not yet in possession of the portion that God has prepared for him, the man who has obeyed this call needs something to direct him, and to reveal the sources of the strength he requires in walking towards the object of his vocation, and the means by which he can appropriate this strength. God, in calling him to follow a Master whom the world has rejected, has not failed to supply him with all the light and all the directions needed to guide and encourage him on his way, as well as point him to the sources of strength and how to obtain the supply of it.

Every reader of the Bible will understand that these subjects are not treated methodically and separately in the New Testament. Were it so, they would be much less perfectly understood. It is in life and in power, whether that of Christ or that of the Holy Ghost in the inspired writers, that they develop themselves to our hearts.

Its divisions and their subjects

The Gospels, in general, set Christ before us as light and grace—still, though not doctrinally, as God Himself, first presented to men in this world, as well as the One in whom the promises made to Israel would be accomplished; and then openly as a divine Person in whom the purposes of the Father would be accomplished, the Jews being looked at as reprobate in their then standing. The Apocalypse—the introduction of the government of God over this world, in connection with the responsibility under which its relations to a revealed God have placed it. The writings of Paul—man's acceptance and place before God by redemption, the new creation, and the assembly according to the counsels of God, the mystery of God. Various subjects connected with these are, however, found everywhere in the Epistles, and each separate development of one of these subjects throws light upon all the rest. The writings of John, we may add, treat particularly of the manifestation of God, and of the divine life in Christ, and then in quickened man, corresponding as they must, to one another; those of Peter, of the Christian's pilgrimage, founded on Christ's resurrection, and of the moral government of the world.

Truth shining out in living manifestation of God and in living application to men

But, I repeat it, whether in the Person of Christ or in the communications of the Holy Ghost (Christ's life being, in one way or other, the light of men), the truth shines out in the living manifestation of God, and in its living application to men; and also, according to the wisdom of God, it is connected with the progressive development[2] inherent to truth when communicated to man, and adapted to the especial wants and to the spiritual capacities of the men to whom it was addressed.

No doubt the revelations of the New Testament are for the saints in all ages; but they were addressed, speaking historically, to living men, and adapted to their condition. But this circumstance weakens in no manner the truth communicated: it is of God, even as the apostle expresses it, "We are not as many which corrupt the Word of God; but as of sincerity, but as of God, in the sight of God, speak we in Christ." And again, "Not handling the Word of God deceitfully, but by manifestation of the truth commending ourselves to every man's conscience in the sight of God." He adds nothing to this

[2] It must be clearly understood that I speak here of the truth revealed in the New Testament. Its communication, *in this revelation,* became gradually more clear, the Holy Ghost having been given after the Lord was glorified. The apostle could say, when speaking of the nature of God Himself, "Which thing is true in Him [Christ] and in you, because the darkness is past, and the true light now shineth." It is a Christ who is the wisdom of God. In Him dwelleth all the fulness of the Godhead bodily. All the fulness was pleased to dwell in Him. He sanctified Himself that we'might be sanctified through the truth. The Holy Ghost, having taken the things of Christ and revealed them unto the apostles, led them into all truth. Now all things that the Father hath are Christ's: therefore He has said that the Holy Ghost should take of His, and should show it unto them.

This being the case, the question of a subsequent development is judged. Is there anything more than "the fulness of the Godhead"? anything more than "all that the Father hath"? anything clearer than the "true light"? But it is this which is revealed. If one thinks of man whose ideas originate in himself, as the spider spins a web out of its own substance, development may no doubt be spoken of; but if the question is the revelation of Christ, by the gift of the true light already come, Christ does not increase. And, assuredly, we shall find nothing good outside "all that the Father hath given Him." This is what we possess by revelation. The development inherent in the communication of truth to man, belongs to his capacity of reception (in this there is progress for each one of us), and to the manifestation of Christ, from the time of John the Baptist unto His full revelation by the Holy Ghost —a revelation which we possess in the New Testament. No tradition can add to the revelation of that which Christ is. No development can give us one new truth with respect to His fulness. But this is everything. It is thus that the lofty pretensions of man are brought to nothing.

pure wine, he does not adulterate it. That which he received flows from him as pure as he received it.[3]

The Word of God: its effect and authority

But the Word of God addressed to men has even greater reality than any mere abstract truth; it is more immediately of God. We have not men's ideas with respect to God, nor the reasonings of men's minds even with truth for their subject; nor is it even truth, as it is in God, submitted abstractedly to the capacity of men that they may judge it. It is God who addresses Himself *to* man, who speaks to him, who communicates His thoughts as being His own. For if man is to judge them, they are not the words of God proclaimed as such. "Ye received the Word of God," says the apostle, "not as the word of men, but as it is in truth the Word of God."

The effect produced on man, which causes him to own the truth and authority of the Word, has often been confounded with a judgment formed by man upon the Word as upon something submitted to him. Never can the Word thus present itself. It would be denying its own nature; it would be saying, It is not my God who speaks. Can God say that He is not God? If not, He could not speak, and say that His Word has not authority in itself.

The Word is adapted to the nature of man: the life is the light *of men*. There are many things that produce

---

[3] The statements of 1 Corinthians 2 are very striking as to this, and in these days of all importance. "Eye hath not seen, nor ear heard, neither have entered into the heart of man the things which God hath prepared for them that love Him" (that was the Old Testament state), "but God hath revealed them unto us by His Spirit;" that is revelation. "Which things also we speak, not in words which man's wisdom teacheth, but which the Holy Ghost teacheth," that is the communication of them, inspiration. Thirdly, "They are spiritually discerned:" that is the reception of them. The revelation, the inspired testimony, and the receiving them by the grace and power of the Spirit only, are all distinctly affirmed.

an effect according to the nature of the thing to which they are applied, without their being judged by that thing. It is the case in all chemical action. A medicine is administered to me; I experience its effect. It has this effect according to my nature. Thus I am convinced of this effect, and of the power of the medicine. It is not a question of my forming a judgment on the medicine as submitted to my capacity. It is the same thing, through grace, with the revelation of Christ, save that the wicked will of man opposes also and rejects it, so that it becomes a savor of death unto death. The Word of God is never judged when it produces its effect; it judges "the thoughts and intentions of the heart." Man is subject to it; he does not judge it.

The historical circumstances given of great assistance in understanding what is said

When man has, through grace, received the Word of truth, which addresses itself to him as such, he is in a condition to understand all its bearings by the help of the Holy Ghost; and, in this case, the circumstances of the persons, to whom it was addressed historically, become a means of understanding the intention of the mind of God in that part of the Word which is under consideration. These circumstances, as we have seen, do not at all affect the divine pureness of the Word; but, since God speaks to men according to their condition, this condition as set before us in the Word itself, is a very great assistance in understanding that which is said. This condition itself is only understood by the Word, and by the help of the Holy Ghost. Sometimes it is the effect of the wickedness of the human heart; sometimes it partly depends on the dispensations of God.

The light of the Word within men's reach and applicable to their condition

However this may be, grace addresses itself to men according to their condition,[4] according to the faithfulness of God to His promises, and in connection with His ways, which He has already taught them. It is not that (the true light being come) this light is dimmed or lowered to accommodate it to the darkness. Were this done, it would no longer be itself nor be capable of raising man by delivering him from the condition he is in; but it is so communicated as to be within the reach of men and applicable to their condition. It was this which they needed, it was this which was worthy of God. He alone could do it. And this is equally true as applicable to the subjects of which the Lord speaks, and to those spoken of by the Holy Ghost through the apostles. He may address Himself to Jews, converted but still attached to the Jewish system, in order to bring out the intentions of God (ever faithful to His promises) with regard to this people; as He might also, when raised on high, communicate by His Spirit all the consequences of the union of the Church with Himself in the heavenly places, outside all the dealings of God upon the earth. And to those souls that were feeding on worldly elements, contrary to this heavenly elevation, and who did not lay hold in it of that which would deliver them from this worldly and carnal tendency—to such He might display the proofs of the evil into which they were falling; and this He might do by means that would bring them into unison with the eternal truths of God, in a manner

---

[4] It is God come in grace in the midst of evil—grace adapted to man in it. It reveals God as nought else does, but is adapted to man however evil he may be, yea as evil. So that while it gives what is purely heavenly and divine, it does it, and so much the more as it is so adapted, in meeting the evil here. This, though it reveals God as He will be known in heaven, is, as to the fact of its operation, unknown in an earthly or heavenly paradise—good in the midst of evil. The angels desire to look into it. Further it is sovereignty, grace, and wisdom, what simple good cannot be, though leading into it in its highest form.

which, although elementary, would judge this carnal disposition that is found at all times in those who do not rise to the height of God's purposes. Or the Spirit might reveal the truth more simply in the elevation proper to it. He might dwell upon the essential characteristics of the nature of God, in order to judge all that pretended, under the most plausible forms, to be Christian light, but which sinned against that nature in the most simple things; and thus link the most simple and most immature souls with the most exalted qualities of God Himself, in the essence of His nature.

Apprehension of divine truth and practical truth realized in the soul

The understanding (derived from the Scriptures themselves, in which these things are found) of the position of those to whom they are addressed is of great use, under the guidance of the Holy Ghost, in apprehending the divine truth contained in them; truth which is absolute, but, by the grace of God, applied truth, practical truth, realized in the soul by the power of God working in it, and guarding it by means of this truth, from the carnal tendency of the heart to fall into those evils which were the occasion of the Scriptures that speak of them; truth that comes down to us, whatever our condition may be, not by altering its own character to accommodate itself to us, nor by taking a form according to our condition, though suited to it, but comes down to us in order to raise us up to the source from whence it came down, and from which it never separates itself (for the truth communicated to us is ever the truth in God and in Christ, in order to raise us up morally to all the height of the divine nature); "Which thing is true in Him and in us, because the darkness is past, and the true light now shineth." It is the effect of the intervention of Christ, to whom we are united by the Holy Ghost, and who is one with God the Father.

Christ the Centre of the counsels of God

This truth, that the communications of God are adapted to the position of those who historically received them, brings us into intelligence of all the counsels of God; for He reveals Himself in His authority, His wisdom, and His sovereignty, in these counsels, as He makes Himself known in His nature by the revelation of Himself in Christ. Christ is the centre of these counsels, but every family in heaven and earth is ranged under the Father of our Lord Jesus Christ. Angels, principalities, powers, Jews, Gentiles, everything that is named, shall be placed under His authority (the Church being united to Him in His glory). Now, the counsels of God with respect to us are revealed in His Word; and, although God does not speak to us in order to gratify our curiosity, many subjects, outside salvation strictly speaking, which are connected with this supremacy of Christ, are connected also with that which God sets before us for our instruction, as the development of this in His dealings here below.

The New Testament displaying the harmony of God's ways

Thus, although His intentions with regard to the Jews may naturally be much more developed in the Old Testament, yet the connection of their history with the subjects of the New, the historical transition from the old economy to the new, the reconciling the promises made to the Jews with the universality of the gospel economy—all these subjects must necessarily have a place in the New Testament if the ways of God are to be known by us. I say, the ways of God; for we have not to think of the Jews only; it is God who acts and who makes Himself known in His dealings. Thus, although the full light displays itself in the New Testament, we find there things addressed to the Jews, and to the disciples who had formed a part of that people, and which reveal the dealings of God towards them. And without these revelations, and if they did not refer to the position of that people, there would be no harmony in the ways of God; at least it would be hidden from us, and would not exist morally. This refers to doctrine, to history (that is, to the presentation of the Messiah), to prophecy, which shows the faithfulness of God, and to the judgment upon that people.

God Himself known, enjoyed and glorified

In order that we may know God—the God who has condescended to interpose in the affairs of this world—mere light is not enough. He must be known, not only as He is in His nature, although that is the essential and principal thing, but as He has revealed Himself in the totality of His ways; in those details in which our little narrow hearts can learn His faithful, patient, condescending love; in those dealings which develop the abstract idea of His wisdom, so as to render it accessible to our limited intelligence, which can trace in it things which have been realized amongst men—although entirely above and beyond all their prevision, but which have been declared by God, so that we know them to be of Him. Above all, God has been pleased to connect Himself in a special way with man in all these things; marvellous privilege of His feeble creature! Philosophy—senseless, narrow-minded, and even essentially stupid in its arguments—would have it that the world is too small for God thus to expend Himself on an impotent being like man, on that which is but a mere point in an immense universe. Contemptible folly! As if the material extent of the theatre were the measure of the moral manifestations wrought upon it, and of the war of principles which is there brought to an issue. That which takes place in this world is the spectacle that unfolds to all the intelligences of the universe the ways, and the character, and the will of God. It is for us to receive thereby, through grace, understanding, and power, that we may enjoy it, and that in us God may be glorified—not only by us, which will be true of all things, but in us. This is our privilege, through the grace that is in Christ, and by our union with Him who is the wisdom of God and the power of God. The more we are as little children, obedient and humble, the more we shall realize this glorious position. Hereafter we shall know as we are known. Meanwhile, the more Christ is objectively our portion and our occupation, the more shall we resemble Him subjectively. Thanks be to God! He has hid these things from the wise and prudent, and has revealed them unto babes. "Howbeit," says the apostle, "we speak wisdom among them that are perfect; yet not the wisdom of this world, nor of the princes of this world, that come to nought; but we speak the wisdom of God in a mystery, the hidden wisdom, which God ordained before the world unto our glory."

The order of the truths revealed in the New Testament

Let us now present a general idea of the contents of the New Testament, or rather of the order in which the truths contained in it are revealed.

We need not depart from the order in which the books are usually placed, without, however, attaching any importance to it.[5]

The first subject that presents itself is the history and Person of the Lord Jesus Himself, contained in the four Gospels.

[5] In some German Bibles, as well as in several Roman Catholic editions, and in many manuscripts, the order is different. For the proposed object this difference is of no importance. Every one knows that the arrangement of the books has nothing to do with the revelation itself.

The second is the founding of the assembly, and the propagation of the gospel in the world after His ascension. The history of this is given in the Acts of the Apostles.

Afterwards the development of the true doctrine of Christ, the care bestowed by the apostles on the assemblies and on individual souls, with the directions necessary for a walk that would glorify the Lord while waiting for His return, the refutation of errors by which the enemy sought to corrupt the faith, and the instructions needful to preserve the faithful from the seductions of the instruments of his malice. All these subjects, the first especially, include the personal glory of the Lord. We refer evidently to the contents of the Epistles.

In the last place, we find the prophecies which announce the evil that would tarnish and corrupt the testimony rendered to Christ in the world, and which, when fully developed, would lead to judgment. These prophecies reveal also the progress of God's judgments, which will end with the destruction of those enemies who will dare to rebel openly against the Lamb, the King of kings, and the Lord of lords; and likewise the glory and blessing which will succeed those judgments. This last subject links Christian teaching with the revelation of the ways of God as to the government of the world. It is largely developed in the Apocalypse; but in divers epistles its connection with the decay of the Church is exhibited.

The four Gospels presenting the various characters of Christ in a living way

We shall naturally begin with the Gospels, which give us the history of the Lord's life, and present Him to our hearts, whether by His actions or by His discourses, in the various characters which make Him precious in every way to the souls of the redeemed, according to the

measure of intelligence bestowed on them, and according
to their need—characters which, though He be seen here
in humiliation,[6] together form the plenitude of His personal glory, so far as we are capable of apprehending it
here below in these our earthen vessels.[7]

It is evident that, according to the counsels of God,
and according to the revelations of His Word, the Lord
must unite in Himself more than one character on earth,
for the accomplishment of His glory and for the maintenance and manifestation of the glory of His Father.
But, that this might take place, He must also *be* something, that He might be viewed in the light of His real
nature, as walking down here. He must needs accomplish the service which it behooved Him to render to God,
as being Himself *the* true servant; and that, as serving
God by the Word, in the midst of His people, according
to Psalm 40 (for instance, verses 8, 9, 10), Isaiah 49:
4, 5, and many other passages.

A multitude of testimonies had announced that the
Son of David should sit, on the part of God, on His
father's throne; and the accomplishment of God's counsels with regard to His earthly people is linked in the
Old Testament with Him who should thus come, and
who on earth should stand in the relation of Son of God
to the Lord God.

The Christ, the Messiah, or, which is but the same
word translated, the Anointed, was to come and present
Himself to Israel, according to the revelation and the
counsels of God. And this promised seed was to be
Emmanuel, God with the people.

But this character of Messiah, although the expectation

---

[6] Compare 1 Corinthians 2: 8.

[7] In order to be clearly understood, I should perhaps except His
relationship with the assembly—a subject which we find in the Epistles;
but I do not include, in the expression "His personal glory," this very
precious part of the doctrine of Christ. With the exception of the fact
that He would build a Church on the earth, it is only by the Holy Ghost
sent down after His ascension that He made known to the apostles and
prophets this priceless mystery.

of the Jews scarcely went beyond it—and they looked even at that in their own way, merely as the exaltation of their own nation, having no sense of their sins or of the consequences of their sins—this character of Messiah was not all that the prophetic Word, which declared the counsels of God, had announced with respect to the One whom even the world was expecting.

He was to be the Son of Man—a title which the Lord Jesus loves to give Himself—a title of great importance to us. It appears to me, that the Son of Man is, according to the Word, the Heir of all that the counsels of God destined for man as his portion in glory, all that God would bestow on man according to those counsels. (See Daniel 7: 13, 14; Psalm 8: 5, 6; 80: 17, and Proverbs 8: 30, 31.) But in order to be the Heir of all that God destined for man, He must be a Man. The Son of Man was truly of the race of man—precious and comforting truth!—born of a woman, really and truly a Man, and, partaking of flesh and blood, made like unto His brethren.

In this character He was to suffer, and be rejected; that He might inherit all things in a wholly new estate, raised and glorified. He was to die and to rise again, the inheritance being defiled, and man being in rebellion— His co-heirs as guilty as the rest.

But He was then to be the Servant, the great Prophet, though the Son of David, and the Son of Man, and therefore truly a Man on the earth, born under the law, born of a woman, of the seed of David, Heir to the rights of David's family, Heir to the destinies of man according to the purpose and the counsels of God. But in order to be this He must glorify God according to the position man was in as fallen in his responsibility, meet that responsibility so as to glorify God there, but while here bearing a prophet's testimony, the faithful witness.

But who was to be all this? Was it only an official glory which the Old Testament had said a man was to inherit? The condition of men, manifested under the law, and without law, proved the impossibility of making them partakers of the blessing of God as they were. The rejection of Christ was the crowning proof of this condition. And, in fact, man needed above all to be himself reconciled to God, apart from all dispensation and special government of an earthly people. *Man* had sinned, and redemption was necessary, for the glory of God and the salvation of men. Who could accomplish it? Man needed it himself. An angel had to keep and fill his own place, and could do no more; he could not be a saviour. And who among men could be the Heir of all things, and have all the works of God put under His dominion, according to the Word? It was the Son of God who should inherit them; it was their Creator who should possess them. He then, who was to be the Servant, the Son of David, the Son of Man, the Redeemer, was the Son of God, God the Creator.[8]

The Gospels, in general, develop these characters of Christ, not in a dogmatic manner (that of John alone having to a certain degree that form), but by so relating the history of the Lord as to present Him in these different characters, in a much more living way than if it were only set before us in doctrine. The Lord speaks according to such or such a character; He acts in the one or in the other; so that we see Him Himself accomplishing that which belonged to the different positions that we know to be His according to Scripture.

Christ revealed as a Person whom we know: the fulness of God's grace

Thus, not only is the character much better known in its moral details, according to its true scriptural import, as well as the meaning and purpose of God therein revealed, but Christ Himself becomes in these characters

---

[8] The act of creation, when not spoken of God generally, but distinguishing the Persons in Deity, is always ascribed to the Son or the Spirit.

more personally the object of faith and of the heart's affections. It is a *Person* whom we know, and not merely a doctrine. By this precious means which God has deigned to use, truths with respect to Jesus are much more connected with all that went before, with the Old Testament history. The change in God's dealings is linked with the glory of the Person of Christ, in connection with which this transition from God's relations with Israel and the world to the heavenly and Christian order took place. This heavenly system, while possessing a character more entirely distinct from Judaism than would have been the case if the Lord had not come, is not a doctrine that nullifies, by contradicting, that which preceded it. When Christ came, He presented Himself to the Jews as on the one hand subject to the law, and on the other as the Seed in whom the promises were to be fulfilled. He was rejected; so that this people, not only had broken the law, which they had done from Sinai on,[9] but forfeited all right to the promises, and promises without condition always distinguished. (See Rom. 10.) God could then bring in the fulness of His grace. At the same time the types, the figures, had their accomplishment; the curse of the law was executed; the prophecies that related to the humiliation of Christ were fulfilled; and the relations of all souls with God—always necessarily attached to His Person, when once He had appeared—were connected with the position taken by the Redeemer in heaven. Thence the door was opened to the Gentiles, and the purpose of God with respect to the assembly, the Body of the ascended Christ, fully revealed. Son of David

---

[9] It is solemn but instructive to remark that in everything God has set up, the *first* thing man has done has been to ruin it. Man himself first of all. Then Noah, the new head of the world, he got drunk. Then the golden calf when the law was given, the priesthood offering strange fire the first day. Solomon turning to idolatry and ruining the kingdom. Nebuchadnezzar making the golden image and persecuting the servants of the true God. God went on in grace, but the system was fallen. So I doubt not with the Church. All will be made good more gloriously in the second Adam.

according to the flesh, and declared to be the Son of God with power by resurrection from the dead, He was a minister of the circumcision for the truth of God, to confirm the promises made to the fathers, and that the Gentiles might glorify God for His mercy. He was the firstborn from the dead, the head of His Body the assembly, that in all things He might have the pre-eminence.

The new order of things attached to the Person of Christ glorified, setting its seal on all that preceded it

The glory of the new order of things was so much the more excellent, so much the more exalted above all the earthly order that had preceded it, that it was attached to the Person of the Lord Himself, and to Him as Man glorified in the presence of God His Father. And at the same time, that which took place puts its seal upon all that had preceded it, as having had its true place, and having been ordained of God; for the Lord presented Himself on earth in connection with the system that existed before He came.

Christ as set forth in the first three Gospels and in John

The first three Gospels give to us the presentation of Christ to responsible man, and especially to Israel. John presents to us the divine and eternal character of the Lord Himself, Israel from chapter 1 being viewed as having rejected Him, and themselves hardened and rejected, and the world as insensible to the presence of its Creator; hence effectual and sovereign grace, and being born again, and the cross as the foundation of heavenly things, come fully out in this Gospel.

MATTHEW

The distinctive character and scope of Matthew's Gospel

LET us now consider the Gospel by St. Matthew. This Gospel sets Christ before us in the character of the Son of David and of Abraham, that is to say, in connection with the promises made to Israel, but presents Him withal as Emmanuel, Jehovah the Saviour, for such the Christ was. It is He who, being received, should have accomplished the promises (and hereafter He will do so) in favor of this beloved people. This Gospel is in fact the history of His rejection by the people, and consequently that of the condemnation of the people themselves, so far as their responsibility was concerned (for the counsels of God cannot fail), and the substitution of that which God was going to bring in according to His purpose.

In proportion as the character of the King and of the kingdom develops itself, and arouses the attention of the leaders of the people, they oppose it, and deprive themselves, as well as the people who follow them, of all the blessings connected with the presence of the Messiah. The Lord declares to them the consequences of this, and shows His disciples the position of the kingdom which should be set up on the earth after His rejection, and also the glories which should result from it to Himself and to His people with Him. And in His Person, and as regards His work, the foundation of the assembly also is revealed —the Church as built by Himself. In a word, consequent on His rejection by Israel, first the kingdom as it exists now is revealed (chap. 13), then the Church (chap. 16), and then the kingdom in the glory (chap. 17).

At length, after His resurrection, a new commission,

addressed to all nations, is given to the apostles sent out by Jesus as risen.[1]

Chapter 1

The Lord's legal genealogy from David and Abraham: its object

THE object of the Spirit of God, in this Gospel, being to present Jehovah as fulfilling the promises made to Israel, and the prophecies that relate to the Messiah (and no one can fail to be struck with the number of references to their fulfilment), He commences with the genealogy of the Lord, starting from David and Abraham, the two stocks from which the Messianic genealogy sprang, and to which the promises had been made. The genealogy is divided into three periods, conformably to three great divisions of the history of the people: from Abraham to the establishment of royalty, in the person of David; from the establishment of royalty to the captivity; and from the captivity to Jesus.

We may observe that the Holy Ghost mentions, in this genealogy, the grievous sins committed by the persons whose names are given, magnifying the sovereign grace of God who could bestow a Saviour in connection with such sins as those of Judah, with a poor Moabitess brought in amidst His people, and with crimes like those of David.

It is the *legal* genealogy which is given here, that is to say, the genealogy of Joseph, of whom Christ was the rightful heir according to Jewish law. The Evangelist has omitted three kings of the parentage of Ahab, in order to have the fourteen generations in each period. Jehoahaz and Jehoiakim are also omitted. The object

[1] This was from resurrection in Galilee; not from heaven and glory, that was near Damascus.

of the genealogy is not at all affected by this circumstance. The point was to give it as recognized by the Jews, and all the kings were well known to all.

The birth of Jesus: the infinite and eternal importance of its facts

The Evangelist briefly relates the facts concerning the birth of Jesus—facts which are of infinite and eternal importance, not only to the Jews, who were immediately interested in them, but to ourselves—facts in which God has deigned to link His own glory with our interests, with man.

Mary was betrothed to Joseph. Her posterity was consequently legally that of Joseph, as to the rights of inheritance; but the child she carried in her womb was of divine origin, conceived by the power of the Holy Ghost. The angel of Jehovah is sent, as the instrument of Providence, to satisfy the tender conscience and upright heart of Joseph, by communicating to him that that which Mary had conceived was of the Holy Ghost.

We may remark here, that the angel on this occasion addresses Joseph as "son of David." The Holy Ghost thus draws our attention to the relationship of Joseph (the reputed father of Jesus) to David, Mary being called his wife. The angel gives at the same time the name of Jesus (that is, Jehovah the Saviour) to the child that should be born. He applies this name to the deliverance of Israel from the condition into which sin had plunged them.[2] All these circumstances happened, in order to fulfil that which Jehovah had said by the mouth of His prophet, "Behold a [the] virgin shall be with child, and shall bring forth a Son, and they shall call His name Emmanuel, which being interpreted is, God with us."

[2] It is written, "For He shall save His people," thus plainly showing the title of Jehovah contained in the word "Jesus" or "Jehoshua." For Israel was the people of the Lord, that is, of Jehovah.

The titles of the Lord drawing the outline that He alone could fill up

Here then is that which the Spirit of God sets before us in these few verses: Jesus, the Son of David, conceived by the power of the Holy Ghost; Jehovah, the Saviour, who delivers Israel from their sins; God with them; He who accomplished those marvellous prophecies which, more or less plainly, drew the outline that the Lord Jesus alone could fill up.

Joseph, a just man, simple in heart and obedient, discerns without difficulty the revelation of the Lord, and obeys it.

These titles stamp the character of this Gospel, that is, of the way Christ is presented in it. And how wonderful this revelation of Him by whom the words and promises of Jehovah were to be fulfilled! What a groundwork of truth for the understanding of what this glorious and mysterious Person was, of whom the Old Testament had said enough to awaken the desires and to confound the minds of the people to whom He was given!

Born of a woman, born under the law, Heir to all the rights of David according to the flesh, also the Son of God, Jehovah the Saviour, God with His people:—who could comprehend or fathom the mystery of His nature in whom all these things were combined? His life in fact, as we shall see, displays the obedience of the perfect Man, the perfections and the power of God.

The characteristic titles connected with Christ's glory in Israel

The titles which we have just named, and which we read in chapter 1: 20-23, are connected with His glory in the midst of Israel—that is to say, the Heir of David, Jesus the Saviour of His people, and Emmanuel. His birth of the Holy Ghost accomplished Psalm 2: 7 with

regard to Him as a Man born on the earth. The name
of Jesus, and His conception by the power of the Holy
Ghost, no doubt go beyond this relationship, but are
linked also in an especial manner with His position in
Israel.[3]

Chapter 2

Formally acknowledged by the Gentiles as King of the Jews

THUS born, thus characterized by the angel, and fulfilling the prophecies that announced the presence of
Emmanuel, He is formally acknowledged King of the
Jews by the Gentiles, who are guided by the will of God
acting on the hearts of their wise men.[4] That is to say,
we find the Lord, Emmanuel, the Son of David, Jehovah
the Saviour, the Son of God, born King of the Jews,
recognized by the heads of the Gentiles. This is the
testimony of God in Matthew's Gospel, and the character
in which Jesus is there presented. Afterwards, in the
presence of Jesus thus revealed, we see the leaders of the
Jews in connection with a foreign king, knowing however
as a system the revelations of God in His Word, but
wholly indifferent to Him who was their object; and this
king, the fierce enemy of the Lord, the true King and
Messiah, seeking to put Him to death.

[3] The wider relationship is more distinctively given in the Gospel of
Luke, where His genealogy is traced up to Adam; but here the title of
Son of Man is specially appropriate.

[4] The star does not lead the wise men from their own country to
Judea. It pleased God to present this testimony to Herod and to the
leaders of the people. Having been directed by the Word (the meaning
of which was declared by the chief priests and scribes themselves, and
according to which Herod sent them to Bethlehem), they *again* see the
star which they had seen in their own country, which conducts them to
the house. Their visit also took place some time after the birth of Jesus.
No doubt they first saw the star at the time of His birth. Herod makes
his calculations according to the moment of the star's appearance, which

God's providence over the Child born to Israel

The providence of God watches over the Child born
unto Israel, employing means that leave the responsibility
of the nation its full place; and that accomplish at the
same time all the intentions of God with regard to this
only true remnant of Israel, this only true source of hope
for the people. For, out of Him, all would fall and
suffer the consequences of being connected with the people.

The true Branch re-commencing Israel's history out of Egypt

Gone down into Egypt to avoid the cruel design of
Herod to take away His life, He becomes the true Branch;
He re-commences (that is, morally) the history of Israel
in His own Person, as well as (in a wider sense) the
history of man as the second Adam in relation with God:
only that for this His death must come in—for all, no
doubt, for blessing. But He was Son of God and Messiah,
Son of David then. But to take His own place as Son
of Man He must die. (See John 12.) It is not only
the prophecy of Hosea, "Out of Egypt have I called My
Son," which thus applies to this true beginning of Israel
in grace (as the beloved of God), and according to His
counsels (the people having entirely failed, so that with-

---

he had carefully ascertained from the lips of the wise men. Their
journey must have occupied some time. The birth of Jesus is related in
chapter 1. The first verse of chapter 2 should be read, "Now Jesus
having been born:" it speaks of a time already past.

I would also remark here that the Old Testament prophecies are
quoted in three ways, which must not be confounded:—"That it might
be fulfilled;" "So that it was fulfilled;" and, "Then was fulfilled." In
the first case it is the object of the prophecy; Matthew 1: 22, 23 is an
instance. In the second it is an accomplishment contained in the scope
of the prophecy, but not the sole and complete thought of the Holy
Ghost; Matthew 2: 23 may serve as an example. In the third it is
simply a fact which corresponds with the quotation, which in its spirit
applies to it, without being its positive object—chapter 2: 17, for instance. I am not aware that the first two are distinguished in our
English translation. Where the sense may require it, I shall hope to
point out the difference.

out this, God must have cut them off). We have seen, in
Isaiah, Israel the servant giving place to Christ the
Servant, who gathers a faithful remnant (the children
whom God has given Him while He hides His face from
the house of Jacob), that become the nucleus of the new
nation of Israel according to God. Chapter 49 of that
prophet gives this transition from Israel to Christ in a
striking manner. Moreover this is the basis of all the
history of Israel, looked at as having failed under the
law, and being re-established in grace. Christ is morally
the new stock from which they spring. (Compare Isaiah
49: 3, 5.) [5]

The Son of God in Nazareth of Galilee among the despised of the people

Herod being dead, God makes it known to Joseph, in
a dream, commanding him to return, with the young
child and its mother, into the land of Israel. We should
remark, that the land is here mentioned by the name that
recalls the privileges bestowed by God. It is neither
Judea nor Galilee; it is the "land of Israel." But can
the Son of David, in entering it, approach the throne
of His fathers? No: He must take the place of a stranger
among the despised of His people. Directed by God in a
dream, Joseph carries Him into Galilee, whose inhabitants
were objects of sovereign contempt to the Jews, as not
being in habitual connection with Jerusalem and Judea—
the land of David, of the kings acknowledged by God,
and of the temple, and where even the dialect of the
language common to both betrayed their practical separation from that part of the nation which, by the favor
of God, had returned to Judea from Babylon.

[5] In verse 5 Christ assumes this title of Servant. The same substitution of Christ for Israel is found in John 15. Israel had been the vine
brought out of Egypt. Christ is the true Vine.

Even in Galilee Joseph establishes himself in a place, the very name of which was a reproach to one who dwelt there, and a blot on his reputation.

Such was the position of the Son of God when He came into this world, and such the relationship of the Son of David with His people, when, by grace and according to the counsels of God, He stood amongst them. On the one hand, Emmanuel, Jehovah their Saviour, on the other, the Son of David; but, while taking His place among His people, associated with the poorest and most despised of the flock, sheltered in Galilee from the iniquity of a false king, who, by help of the Gentiles of the fourth monarchy, was reigning over Judea, and with whom the priests and rulers of the people were in connection; the latter, unfaithful to God and dissatisfied with men, proudly detesting a yoke which their sins had brought upon them, and which they dared not shake off, although they were not sufficiently sensible of their sins to submit to it as the just infliction of God. Thus is it that the Messiah is presented to us by this Evangelist, or rather by the Holy Ghost, in connection with Israel.

Chapter 3

The threefold ministry of John the Baptist

WE now begin (chap. 3) His actual history. John the Baptist comes to prepare the way of Jehovah before Him, according to the prophecy of Isaiah; proclaiming that the kingdom of heaven was at hand, and calling on the people to repent. It is by these three things that John's ministry to Israel is characterized in this Gospel. First the Lord Jehovah Himself was coming. The Holy Ghost leaves out the words "for our God," at the end of the verse, because Jesus comes as man in humiliation, although acknowledged at the same time to be Jehovah, and Israel could not be thus owned as entitled to say "our." In the second place the kingdom of heaven [6] was at hand—that new dispensation which was to take the place of the one which, properly speaking, belonged to Sinai, where the Lord had spoken on the earth. In this new dispensation "the heavens should reign." They should be the source of, and characterize, God's authority in His Christ. Thirdly, the people, instead of being blessed in their present condition, were called to repentance in view of the approach of this kingdom. John therefore takes his place in the wilderness, departing from the Jews, with whom he could not associate himself because he came in the way of righteousness. (Chap. 21: 32.) His food is that which he finds in the wilderness (even his prophetic garments bearing witness to the position which he had taken on the part of God), himself filled with the Holy Ghost.

Thus was he a prophet, for he came from God, and addressed himself to the people of God to call them to repentance, and he proclaimed the blessing of God according to the promises of Jehovah their God; but he was more than a prophet, for he declared as an immediate thing the introduction of a new dispensation, long expected, and the advent of the Lord in Person. At the same time, although coming to Israel, he did not own the people, for they were to be judged; the threshing-floor of Jehovah was to be cleansed, the trees that did not bear good fruit to be cut down. It would be a remnant only that Jehovah would place in the new position in the kingdom that he announced, without its being yet revealed in what manner it was to be established. He proclaimed the judgment of the people.

---

[6] This expression is found only in Matthew, as specially occupied with dispensations, and the dealings of God with the Jews. "The kingdom of God" is the generic term. "The kingdom of heaven" is the kingdom of God but the kingdom of God as specially taking this character of heavenly government; we shall find it (farther on) separated into the kingdom of our Father, and the kingdom of the Son of Man.

The Lord God in the midst of His people Israel

What a fact of immeasurable greatness was the presence of the Lord God in the midst of His people, in the Person of Him who, although He was doubtless to be the fulfilment of all the promises, was necessarily, though rejected, the Judge of all the evil existing among His people!

And the more we give these passages their true application, that is to say, the more we apply them to Israel, the more we apprehend their real force.[7]

Eternal necessity for repentance: the consequences of refusal of God's call to it

No doubt repentance is an eternal necessity to every soul that approaches God; but what a light is thrown upon this truth, when we see the intervention of the Lord Himself who calls His people to this repentance, setting aside—on their refusal—the whole system of their relationships with Him, and establishing a new dispensation—a kingdom which only belongs to those who hear Him—and causing at length His judgment to break forth against His people and the city which He had so long cherished! "If thou hadst known, even thou, at least in this thy day, the things which belong unto thy peace! but now they are hid from thine eyes."

---

[7] And we must remember that, besides the special promises to, and calling, of Israel as God's earthly people, that people were just man viewed in his responsibility to God under the fullest culture that God could give him. Up to the flood there was testimony but no dispensational dealings, or institutions of God. After it, in the new world, human government, calling and promise in Abraham, law, Messiah, God come in grace, everything God could do, and that in perfect patience, was done, and in vain as to good in flesh; and now Israel was being set aside as in the flesh, and the flesh judged, the fig-tree cursed as fruitless, and God's man, the second Adam, He in whom blessing was by redemption, introduced into the world. In the first three Gospels, as we have seen, we have Christ presented to man to be received; in John, man is set aside and Israel, and God's sovereign ways in grace and resurrection brought in.

Judgment impending: a new state distinguished by baptism

This truth gives room for the exhibition of another and most highly important one, announced here in connection with the sovereign rights of God rather than in its consequences, but which already contained in itself all those consequences. The people from all parts, and as we learn elsewhere especially the ungodly and despised, went out to be baptized, confessing their sins. But those who, in their own eyes, held the chief place among the people, were in the eyes of the prophet who loved the people according to God, the objects of the judgment he announced. Wrath was impending. Who had warned these scornful men to flee from it? Let them humble themselves like the rest; let them take their true place, and prove their change of heart. To boast in the privileges of their nation, or of their fathers, availed nothing before God. He required that which His very nature, His truth, demanded. Moreover He was sovereign; He was able of those stones to raise up children to Abraham. This is what His sovereign grace has done, through Christ, with regard to the Gentiles. There was reality needed. The axe was at the root of the trees, and those that did not bring forth good fruit should be cut down. This is the great moral principle which the judgment was going to put in force. The blow was not yet struck, but the axe was already at the root of the trees. John was come to bring those who received his testimony into a new position, or at least into a new state in which they were prepared for it. On their repentance he would distinguish them from the rest by baptism. But He who was coming after John—He whose shoes John was not worthy to bear—would thoroughly purge His floor, would separate those that were truly His, morally His, from among His people Israel (that was His floor), and would execute judgment on the rest. John on his part opened

the door to repentance beforehand; afterwards should
come the judgment.

The twofold baptism attributed to Jesus by John

Judgment was not the only work that belonged to
Jesus. Two things are however attributed to Him in
John's testimony. He baptizes with fire—this is the
judgment proclaimed in verse 12, which consumes all
that is evil. But He baptizes also with the Holy Ghost
—that Spirit which, given to, and acting in divine energy
in man, quickened, redeemed, cleansed in the blood of
Christ, brings him out from the influence of all that acts
on the flesh, and sets him in connection and in communion
with all that is revealed of God, with the glory into which
He brings His creatures in the life which He imparts, destroying morally in us the power of all that is contrary to
the enjoyment of these privileges.

The only good fruit recognized by John

Observe here, that the only good fruit recognized by
John, as the way of escape, is the sincere confession,
through grace, of sin. Those only who make this confession escape the axe. There were really no good trees
excepting those which confessed that they were bad.

But what a solemn moment was this for the people
beloved of God! What an event was the presence of
Jehovah in the midst of the nation with whom He stood
in relationship!

The Messiah presented as Jehovah the Judge

Observe that John the Baptist does not here present
the Messiah as the Saviour come in grace, but as the
Head of the kingdom, as Jehovah, who would execute
judgment if the people did not repent. We shall see
afterwards the position which He took in grace.

The baptism of Jesus: the Lord's presentation of Himself with His people in grace

In verse 13 Jesus Himself, who until now has been presented as the Messiah and even as Jehovah, comes to John to be baptized with the baptism of repentance. We must remember that to come to this baptism was the only good fruit which a Jew, in his then condition, could produce. The act proved itself to be the fruit of a work of God—of the effectual work of the Holy Ghost. He who repents confesses that he has previously walked afar from God; so that it is a new movement, the fruit of God's word and work in him, the sign of a new life, of the life of the Spirit in his soul. By the very fact of John's mission, there was no other fruit, no other admissible proof, of life from God, in a Jew. We are not to infer from this, that there were none in whom the Spirit already acted vitally; but, in this condition of the people and according to the call of God by His servant, that was the proof of this life—of the turning of the heart to God. These were the true remnant of the people, those whom God acknowledged as such; and it was thus they were separated from the mass who were ripening for judgment. These were the true saints—the excellent of the earth; although the self-abasement of repentance could be their only true place. It was there they must begin. When God brings in mercy and justice, they avail themselves thankfully of the former, confessing it to be their only resource, and they bow their heart before the latter, as the just consequence of the condition of God's people, but as applying it to themselves.

Now Jesus presents Himself in the midst of those who do this. Although truly the Lord, Jehovah, the righteous Judge of His people, He who was to purge *His* floor, He nevertheless takes His place among the faithful remnant who humble themselves before this judgment. He takes the place of the lowest of His people before God; as in

Psalm 16 He calls Jehovah His Lord, saying unto Him, "My goodness extendeth not to Thee;" and says to the saints, and the excellent in the earth, "All My delight is in them." Perfect testimony of grace—the Saviour identifying Himself, according to this grace, with the first movement of the Spirit in the hearts of His own people, humbling Himself not only in the condescension of grace towards them, but in taking His place as one of them in their true position before God; not merely to comfort their hearts by such kindness, but in order to sympathize with all their sorrows and their difficulties; in order to be the pattern, the source, and the perfect expression of every sentiment suitable to their position.

The Lord's association with the poor of the flock to lead them on to enjoyment of blessing

With wicked, unrepentant Isarel He could not associate Himself, but with the first living effect of the Word and Spirit of God in the poor of the flock, He could and did in grace. He does so now. With the first right step, one really of God, Christ is found.

But there was yet more. He comes to bring those who received Him into relation with God, according to the favor which rested on perfectness like His, and on the love which, by taking up His people's cause, satisfied the heart of the Lord, and, having perfectly glorified God in all that He is, made it possible for Him to satisfy Himself with goodness. We know indeed that in order to do this, the Saviour had to lay down His life, because the condition of the Jew, as that of every man, required this sacrifice before either the one or the other could stand in relation with the God of truth. But even for this the love of Jesus did not fail. Here however He is leading them on to the enjoyment of the blessing expressed in His Person, which should be securely founded on that sacrifice—blessing which they must reach by the path of re-

pentance, into which they entered by John's baptism;
which Jesus received with them, that they might go on
together towards the possession of all the good things
which God has prepared for them that love Him.

John's opposition: the true character of the Lord's action

John, feeling the dignity and excellency of the Person
of Him who came unto him, opposes the Lord's intention.
The Holy Ghost by this brings out the true character of
the Lord's action. As to Himself, it was righteousness
which brought Him there, and not sin—righteousness
which He accomplished in love. He, as well as John the
Baptist, fulfilled that which belonged to the place assigned
Him by God. With what condescension He links Himself at the same time with John—"It becometh *us.*" He
is the lowly and obedient Servant. It was thus He ever
behaved Himself on earth. Moreover, as to His position,
grace brought Jesus there, where sin brought us, who came
in by the door the Lord had opened for His sheep. In
confessing sin as it is, in coming before God in the confession of (the opposite of sin morally) our sin, we find
ourselves in company with Jesus.[8] Indeed it is in us the
fruit of His Spirit. This was the case with the poor sinners who came out to John. Thus it was that Jesus took
His place in righteousness and obedience among men, and
more exactly among the repentant Jews. It is in this
position of a Man—righteous, obedient, and fulfilling on
earth, in perfect humility, the work for which He had
offered Himself in grace, according to Psalm 40, giving
Himself up to the accomplishment of all the will of God
in complete renunciation—that God His Father fully

---

[8] It is the same thing as to the sense of our nothingness. He made
Himself nothing, and in the consciousness of our nothingness we find
ourselves with Him, and at the same time are filled with His fulness.
Even when we fall, it is not until we are brought to know ourselves as
we really are that we find Jesus raising us up again.

acknowledged Him, and sealed Him, declaring Him on
earth to be His well-beloved Son.

The heavens opened: the beloved Son: the descent of the Holy Spirit

Being baptized—the most striking token of the place
He had taken with His people—the heavens are opened
unto Him, and He sees the Holy Ghost descending on
Him like a dove; and lo, a voice from heaven, saying,
"This is My beloved Son, in whom I am well pleased."

But these circumstances demand attention.

Never were the heavens opened to the earth, nor to
a man on the earth, before the beloved Son was there.[9]
God had doubtless, in His long-suffering and in the way
of providence, blessed all His creatures; He had also
blessed His own people, according to the rules of His
government on earth. Besides this, there were the elect,
whom He had preserved in faithfulness. Nevertheless
until now the heavens had not been opened. A testimony
had been sent by God in connection with His government of the earth; but there was no object on the earth
upon which the eye of God could rest with complacency,
until Jesus, sinless and obedient, His beloved Son, stood
there. But what is so precious to us is, that it is as soon
as in grace He takes publicly this place of humiliation
with Israel—that is, with the faithful remnant, presenting
Himself thus before God, fulfilling His will—the heavens
open upon an object worthy of their attention. Ever
doubtless was He worthy of their adoration, even before
the world was. But now He has just taken this place in
the dealings of God as a Man, and the heavens open
unto Jesus, the object of God's entire affection on the

---

[9] In the beginning of Ezekiel, it is said indeed that the heavens were
opened; but this was only in vision, as the prophet himself explains.
In that instance it was the manifestation of God in judgment.

earth. The Holy Ghost descends upon Him visibly. And He, a Man on earth, a Man taking His place with the meek of the people who repented, is acknowledged as the Son of God. He is not only anointed of God, but, as Man, He is conscious of the descent of the Holy Ghost upon Him—the seal of the Father set upon Him. Here it is evidently not His divine nature, in the character of the Eternal Son of the Father. The seal would not even be in conformity with that character; and as to His Person it is manifested, and His consciousness of it, at twelve years old in Luke's Gospel. But while He is such, He is also a Man, the Son of God on the earth, and is sealed as a Man. As a Man He has the consciousness of the immediate presence of the Holy Ghost with Him. This presence is in connection with the character of lowliness, meekness, and obedience, in which the Lord appeared down here. It is "like a dove" that the Holy Ghost descends upon Him; just as it was in the form of tongues of fire, that He came down upon the heads of the disciples, for their testimony in power in this world, according to the grace which addressed each and every one in his own language.

The glory of the Lord's Person carefully guarded

Jesus thus creates in His own position as Man the place into which He introduces us by redemption. (John 20: 17.) But the glory of His Person is always carefully guarded. There is no object presented *to* Jesus, as to Saul for instance, and, in a still more analogous case, to Stephen, who, being full of the Spirit, sees also the heavens opened, and looks up into them, and sees Jesus, the Son of Man, and is transformed into His image. Jesus has come; He is Himself the object over whom the heavens open; He has no transforming object, as Stephen, or as we ourselves in the Spirit; heaven looks down at Him, the perfect object of delight. It is His relationship with

His Father, already existing, which is sealed.[10] Neither
does the Holy Ghost create His character (except so far
as, with respect to His human nature, He was conceived
in the virgin Mary's womb by the power of the Holy
Ghost); He had connected Himself with the poor, in the
perfection of that character, before He was sealed, and
then acts according to the energy and the power of that
which He received without measure in His human life
here below.   (Compare Acts 10: 38; Matthew 12: 28;
John 3: 34.)

Four memorable occasions on which the heavens open: Christ the object of each

We find in the Word four memorable occasions on
which the heavens open. Christ is the object of each of
these revelations; each has its especial character. Here
the Holy Ghost descends upon Him, and He is acknowledged the Son of God. (Compare John 1: 33, 34.) At
the end of the same chapter of John, He declares Himself
to be the Son of Man. There it is the angels of God who
ascend and descend upon Him. He is, as Son of Man, the
object of their ministry.[11]   At the end of Acts 7 an
entirely new scene is opened. The Jews reject the last
testimony that God sends them. Stephen, by whom this
testimony is rendered, is filled with the Holy Ghost, and
the heavens are opened to him. The earthly system was
definitely closed by the rejection of the Holy Ghost's
testimony to the glory of the ascended Christ. But this
is not merely a testimony. The Christian is filled with
the Spirit, heaven is opened to *him*, the glory of God is
manifested to him, and the *Son of Man* appears to him,
standing at the right hand of God. This is a different
thing from the heavens open over Jesus, the object of

[10] This is true also of us when we are in that relationship by grace.
[11] It is all a mistake to make Christ the ladder. He, as Jacob was,
is the object of their service and ministry.

God's delight on earth. It is heaven open to the Christian himself, his object being there when rejected on earth. He sees there by the Holy Ghost the heavenly glory of God, and Jesus, the Son of Man, the special object of the testimony he renders, in the glory of God. The difference is as remarkable as it is interesting to us; and it exhibits, in a most striking manner, the true position of the Christian as on earth, and the change which the rejection of Jesus by His earthly people has produced. Only the Church, the union of believers in one Body with the Lord in heaven, was not yet revealed. Afterwards (Rev. 19) heaven opens, and the Lord Himself comes forth, the King of kings and Lord of lords. Thus we see:—

Jesus, the Son of God on earth, the object of heaven's delight, sealed with the Holy Ghost;

Jesus, the Son of Man, the object of the ministry of heaven, angels being His servants;

Jesus, on high at the right hand of God, and the believer, full of the Spirit, and suffering here for His sake, beholding the glory on high, and the Son of Man in the glory, and

Jesus, the King of kings and Lord of lords, coming forth to judge and make war against the scornful men who dispute His authority and oppress the earth.

The obedient Man on earth, the Son of God, sealed with the Holy Ghost

To return: the Father Himself acknowledges Jesus, the obedient Man on earth, who enters as the true Shepherd by the door, as His beloved Son in whom is all His delight. Heaven is opened to Him; He sees the Holy Ghost come down to seal Him, the infallible strength and support of the perfection of His human life; and He has the Father's testimony to the relationship between them. No object on which His faith was to rest is presented to Him as it is to us. It is His own relation to heaven and to His Father which is sealed. His soul enjoys it through the descent of the Holy Ghost and the voice of His Father.

Heaven opened to believers by redemption

But this passage in Matthew requires some further notice. The blessed Lord, or rather what occurred as to Him, gives the place or model in which He sets believers, be they Jew or Gentile: only of course we are brought there by redemption. "I go to My Father and your Father, My God and your God," is His blessed word after His resurrection. But to us heaven is opened; we are sealed with the Holy Ghost; the Father owns us as sons. Only the divine dignity of Christ's Person is always carefully guarded here in humiliation, as in the transfiguration in glory. Moses and Elias are in the same glory, but disappear when Peter's haste, permitted to be expressed, would put them on a level. The nearer we are to a divine Person, the more we adore and recognize what He is.

The Trinity first fully revealed

But another very remarkable fact is found here. For the first time, when Christ takes this place among men in lowliness, the Trinity is fully revealed. No doubt the Son and Spirit are mentioned in the Old Testament. But there the unity of the Godhead is the great revealed point. Here the Son is owned in man, the Holy Ghost comes down on Him, and the Father owns Him as His Son. What a wonderful connection with man! What a place for man to be in! Through Christ's connection with Him the Godhead is revealed in its own fulness. His being a man draws it out in its display. But He was really a Man, but the Man in whom the counsels of God about man were to be fulfilled.

In conflict with the enemy

Hence, as He has realized and displayed the place in which man is set with God in His own Person, and in the counsels of grace as to us our relationship with God, so, as we are in conflict with the enemy, He enters into that side of our position also. We have our relationship with God and our Father, and now we have to say to Satan also. He overcomes for us, and shows us how to overcome. Remark, too, the relationship with God is first fully settled and brought out, and then, as in that place, the conflict with Satan begins, and so with us. But the first question was, Would the second Adam stand where the first had failed?—only, in the wilderness of this world and Satan's power—instead of the blessings of God —for there we had got.

The people's history closed in judgment: a new thing announced—the kingdom of heaven

Another point is to be remarked here, fully to bring out the place the Lord takes. The law and the prophets were till John. Then the new thing is announced, the kingdom of heaven. But judgment closes with God's people. The axe is at the root of the trees, the fan is in the hand of the coming One, the wheat is gathered into God's garner, the chaff burnt up. That is, there is a close of the history of God's people in judgment. We come in on the ground of being lost, anticipating the judgment; but man's history as responsible was closed. Hence it is said, "Now once in the *end of the world* He hath appeared to put away sin by the sacrifice of Himself." It has happened externally and literally to Israel; but it is morally true for us: only we are gathered for heaven, as in result the remnant then, and shall be *in* heaven. But, Christ rejected, the history of responsibility is over, and we come in in grace as already lost. Consequent on the announcement of this as imminent, Christ comes and, identifying Himself with the remnant who escape on repentance, makes this new place for man on the earth: only we could not be in it till redemption was accomplished. Still He revealed the Father's name to those He had given Him out of it.

Chapter 4

Led of the Spirit to be tempted of the devil

HAVING thus in grace taken up His position as Man on earth, He commences (chap. 4) His earthly career, being led of the Spirit into the wilderness to be tempted of the devil. The righteous and holy Man, the Son of God, enjoying the privileges proper to such a one, He must undergo the trial of those devices through which the first Adam fell. It is His spiritual condition which is tested. It is not now an innocent man in the enjoyment of all God's natural blessings, who is put to the proof in the midst of those blessings which should have made him remember God. Christ, nigh to God as His beloved Son, but in the midst of trial, having the knowledge of good and evil, and as to outward circumstances come down into the midst of man's fallen state, must have His faithfulness to this position fully tried with respect to His perfect obedience. To maintain this position, He must have no other will than that of His Father, and fulfil it or suffer it, whatever might be the consequences to Himself. He must fulfil it in the midst of all the difficulties, the privations, the isolation, the desert, where Satan's power was, which might tempt Him to follow an easier path than that which should be only for the glory of His Father. He must renounce all the rights that belonged to His own Person, save as He should receive them from God, yielding them up to Him with a perfect trust.

The enemy did his utmost to induce Him to make use of His privileges, "If Thou be the Son of God," for His own relief, apart from the command of God, and in avoidance of the sufferings which might accompany the performance of His will. But it was to lead Him to do His own will, not God's.

With the enemy in the wilderness

Jesus, enjoying in His own Person and relationship with God the full favor of God as Son of God, the light of His countenance, goes into the wilderness for forty days to be in conflict with the enemy. He did not go away from man, and from all intercourse with man and the things of man, in order (like Moses and Elias) to be with God. Being already fully with God, He is separate from men by the power of the Holy Ghost to be alone in His conflict with the enemy. In the case of Moses, it was man out of his natural condition to be with God. In the case of Jesus, it is so to be with the enemy: to be with God was His natural position.

Simple and absolute obedience, living by God's words

The enemy tempts Him first by proposing to Him to satisfy His bodily need, and, instead of waiting on God, to employ according to His own will and on His own behalf the power with which He was endowed. But, if Israel was fed in the wilderness with manna from God, the Son of God, however great His power, would act in accordance with what Israel should have learnt by that means, namely, that, "Man doth not live by bread only, but by every word that proceedeth out of the mouth of God." The Man, the obedient Jew, the Son of God, waited for this Word, and would do nothing without it.

He was not come to do His own will, but the will of Him who sent Him. This is the principle that characterizes the Spirit of Christ in the Psalms. No deliverance is accepted but the intervention of Jehovah at His own good time. It is perfect patience, in order to be perfect and complete in all the will of God. There could be no sinful lust in Christ; but to be hungry was no sin, yet it was a human need, and what harm in eating when hungry? There was no will of God to do it, and that will by the Word He came to do. Satan's suggestion was, "If Thou be the Son of God, command;" but He had taken the place of a servant, and this was not commanding: he sought to get the Lord out of the place of perfect service and obedience, out of the place of a servant.

The written Word and the character of Christ's obedience

And note here the place the written Word has, and the character of Christ's obedience. This character is not simply that the will of God is a rule; it is the one motive for action. We have a will arrested often by the Word. Not so Christ. His Father's will was His motive; He acted not merely according to, but because it was, God's will. We delight to see a child who would run off to something it delights in, stop and cheerfully do its parents' will when called to do it. But Christ never obeyed thus, never sought a will of His own, but was stopped by His Father's. And we are sanctified to the obedience of Christ. Note further that the written Word is that by which He lives and by which He overcomes. All depended here on Christ's victory, as all did on Adam's fall. But for Christ, one text, rightly used of course, suffices. He seeks no other: that is obedience. It suffices for Satan; he has no reply. His wiles are thus defeated.

The first principle of conquest is simple and absolute

obedience, living by words out of God's mouth. The next is perfect confidence in the path of obedience.

Perfect confidence in the path of obedience

In the second place then, the enemy sets Him on a pinnacle of the temple, to induce Him to apply to Himself the promises made to Messiah, without abiding in the ways of God. The faithful man may assuredly reckon on the help of God while walking in His ways. The enemy would have the Son of Man put God to the test (instead of reckoning on Him while walking in His ways) to see whether He might be trusted in. This would have been a want of confidence in God, instead of counting on God in obedience.[12] Taking His place with Israel in the condition they were in when without a king in the land, and, quoting the directions given to them in that book to guide them in the godly path there taught, He uses for His guidance that part of the Word which contains the divine injunction on this subject, "Thou shalt not tempt the Lord thy God;" a passage often quoted as if it forbade excess in trusting God; whereas it means not to distrust, and try if He is faithful. They tempted God, saying, Is God indeed among us? And this Satan would have had the Lord do.

The earthly inheritance offered the Son of Man by Satan in open hostility to God

The enemy, failing to deceive that obedient heart, even by hiding himself under the use of the Word of God, shows himself in his true character, tempting the Lord, thirdly, to spare Himself all the sufferings that awaited

---

[12] We need confidence to have courage to obey; but true confidence is found in the path of obedience. Satan could use the word in guile, but not turn Christ the Lord from it. He still uses it as the adequate divine weapon, and Satan still has no reply. To have forbidden obedience would have been to show himself Satan. As regards the place in which the Lord was dispensationally, we may remark the Lord always quotes from Deuteronomy.

Him, by showing Him the inheritance of the Son of Man on earth, that which would be His when He had reached it through all those paths, toilsome yet necessary to the Father's glory, which the Father had marked out for Him. All should now be His, if He would acknowledge Satan by worshipping him, the god of this world. This in fact was what the kings of the earth had done for only a part of these things—how often done for some trifling vanity!— but He should have the whole. But if Jesus was to inherit earthly glory (as well as all other), the object of His heart was God Himself, His Father, to glorify Him. Whatever might be the value of the gift, it was as the gift of the Giver that His heart prized it. Moreover He was in the position of tested man and a faithful Israelite; and whatever might be the trial of patience into which the sin of the people had brought Him, be the trial ever so great, He would serve none but His God alone.

The believer's attitude towards Satan

But if the devil carries temptation, sin, to the utmost, and shows himself to be the adversary (Satan), the believer has the right to cast him out. If he comes as a tempter, the believer should answer him by the faithfulness of the Word, which is man's perfect guide, according to the will of God. He does not need to see through everything. The Word is the Word of Him who does, and in following that, we walk according to a wisdom which knows everything, and in a path formed by that wisdom, and which hence involves absolute trust in God. The first two temptations were the wiles of the devil, the third, open hostility to God. If he comes as the open adversary of God, the believer has a right to have nothing to do with him. "Resist the devil, and he will flee from you." He knows he has met Christ, not flesh. May believers *resist* if Satan would tempt them by the world, remembering it is Satan's domain in fallen man!

The believer's safeguard

The believer's safeguard, morally (that is, as to the state of his heart), is a single eye. If I seek only the glory of God, that which presents no other motive than my own aggrandizement, or my own gratification, whether of body or mind, will have no hold upon me; and will show itself in the light of the Word, which guides the single eye, as contrary to the mind of God. This is not the haughtiness that rejects temptation on the ground of being good; it is obedience, humbly giving God His place, and consequently His Word also. "By the Word of Thy lips I have kept me from the paths of the destroyer," from him that did his own will and made it his guide. If the heart seeks God alone, the most subtle snare is discovered, for the enemy never tempts us to seek God alone. But this supposes a pure heart, and that there is no self-seeking. This was displayed in Jesus.

Our safeguard against temptation is the Word, used by the discernment of a perfectly pure heart, which lives in the presence of God, and learns the mind of God in His Word,[13] and therefore knows His application to the circumstances presented. It is the Word that preserves the soul from the wiles of the enemy.

Observe also that, consequently, it is in this spirit of simple and humble obedience that power lies; for where it exists, Satan can do nothing. God is there, and accordingly the enemy is conquered.

---

[13] There must be no other motive for action than the will of God, which, for man, is always to be found in the Word; because, in that case, when Satan tempts us to act, as he always does, by some other motive, this motive is seen to be opposed to the Word which is in the heart, and to the motive which governs the heart, and is therefore judged as being opposed to it. It is written, "Thy Word have I hid in my heart, that I might not sin against Thee." This is the reason why it is so often important, when we are in doubt, to ask ourselves by what motive we are influenced.

The three temptations and characters of the Lord

It appears to me that these three temptations are addressed to the Lord in the three characters of Man, of Messiah, and of Son of Man.

He had no sinful desires like fallen man, but He was an-hungered. The tempter would persuade Him to satisfy this need without God.

The promises in the Psalms belonged to Him as being made to the Messiah.

And all the kingdoms of the world were His as the Son of Man.

He always replies as a faithful Israelite, personally responsible to God, making use of the Book of Deuteronomy, which treats of this subject (namely, the obedience of Israel, in connection with the possession of the land, and the privileges that belonged to the land, and the privileges that belonged to the people in connection with this obedience; and this, apart from the organization which constituted them a corporate body before God).[14]

Satan departs from Him, and the angels come to exercise their ministry towards the Messiah, the Son of Man victorious through obedience. What Satan would have Him try God about, He has fully. They are ministering spirits for us also.

Satan met and bound for man

But how profoundly interesting is it to see the blessed Lord come down, the Son of God from heaven, and take—the Word made flesh—His place among the poor

[14] A careful examination of the Pentateuch will show that, though needed historical facts are stated, yet the contents of Exodus, Leviticus, and Numbers are essentially typical. The tabernacle was made according to the pattern shown in the mount—the pattern of heavenly things; and not only the ceremonial ordinances, but the historical facts, as the apostle distinctly states, happened unto them for types, and are written for our instruction. Deuteronomy gives directions for their conduct in the land; but the three books named, even where there are historical facts, are typical in their object. I do not know if one sacrifice was offered after they were instituted, unless perhaps the official ones. (See Acts 7: 42.)

godly ones on the earth, and, as having taken that place, owned of the Father as His Son, heaven being opened and opened to Him as Man, and the Holy Ghost coming down and abiding on Him as Man though without measure, and so forming the model of our place, though we were not yet in it; the whole Trinity, as I have said, being first fully revealed when He is thus associated with man; and then, we being slaves to Satan, going in this character and relationship to meet also Satan for us, to bind the strong man, and give man through Him this place also: only for us redemption was needed to bring us where He is.

The Lord's ministry outside Jerusalem, fulfilling prophecy

John being cast into prison, the Lord departs into Galilee. This movement, which determined the scene of His ministry outside Jerusalem and Judea, had great significance with respect to the Jews. The people (so far as centred in Jerusalem, and boasting in the possession of the promises, the sacrifices, and the temple, and in being the royal tribe) lost the presence of the Messiah, the Son of David. He went away for the manifestation of His Person, for the testimony of God's intervention in Israel, to the poor and despised of the flock; for the remnant and poor of the flock are already in chapters 3, 4, clearly distinguished from the heads of the people. He thus really became the true stock, instead of being a branch of that which had been planted elsewhere; although this effect was not yet fully manifested. The moment corresponds with John 4.

We may remark here, that, in John's Gospel, the Jews are always distinguished from the multitude.[15] The language, or rather the pronunciation, was entirely different. They did not speak Chaldee in Galilee.

[15] Called "the people" in the Gospels.

At the same time this manifestation of the Son of David in Galilee was the fulfilment of a prophecy in Isaiah. The force of that prophecy is this:—although the Roman captivity was far more terrible than the invasion of the Assyrians when they came up against the land of Israel, there was nevertheless this circumstance which altered everything, namely, the presence of the Messiah, the true Light, in the land.

The Lord's history here passed over till the death of John the Baptist

We observe that the Spirit of God here passes over the whole history of Jesus until the commencement of His ministry after the death of John the Baptist. He gives Jesus His proper position in the midst of Israel — Emmanuel, the Son of David, the Beloved of God, acknowledged as His Son, the faithful One in Israel, though exposed to all Satan's temptations; and then at once, afterwards, His prophetic position announced by Isaiah, and the kingdom proclaimed as at hand.[16]

He then gathers around Him those who were definitively to follow Him in His ministry and His temptations; and, at His call, to link their portion and their lot with His, forsaking all beside.

The strong man was bound, so that Jesus could spoil his goods, and proclaim the kingdom with proofs of that power which was able to establish it.

The proclamation of the kingdom in power: its character, nature and subjects

Two things are then brought forward in the Gospel narrative. First, the power which accompanies the proc-

---

[16] And we may remark here, that He leaves the Jews and Jerusalem, as already remarked, and His natural place, so to speak, what gave Him His name, Nazareth, and takes His prophetic place. The casting of John into prison was significant of His own rejection. John was His forerunner in it, as in his mission, of the Lord. See chapter 17: 12. The testimony of Jesus is the same as that of John the Baptist.

lamation of the kingdom. In two or three verses,[17] without other details, this fact is announced. The proclamation of the kingdom is attended with acts of power that excite the attention of the whole country, the whole extent of the ancient territory of Israel. Jesus appears before them invested with this power. Secondly (chaps. 5 to 7), the character of the kingdom is announced in the sermon on the Mount, as well as that of the persons who should have part in it (the Father's name withal being revealed). That is, the Lord had announced the coming kingdom, and with the present power of goodness, having overcome the adversary; and then shows what were the true characters according to which it would be set up, and who could enter, and how. Redemption is not spoken of in it; but the character and nature of the kingdom, and who could enter. This clearly shows the moral position which this sermon holds in the Lord's teaching.

The Lord's position in Israel: the principles of His kingdom

It is evident that, in all this part of the Gospel, it is the Lord's position which is the subject of the teaching of the Spirit, and not the details of His life. Details come after, in order fully to exhibit what He was in the midst of Israel, His relations with that people, and His path in the power of the Spirit which led to the rupture between the Son of David and the people who ought to have received Him. The attention of the whole country being thus engaged by His mighty acts, the Lord sets before His disciples—but in the hearing of the people— the principles of His kingdom.

[17] It is striking that the whole ministry of the Lord is recounted in one verse (23). All the subsequent statements are facts, having a special moral import, showing what was passing amongst the people in grace onward to His rejection, not a proper consecutive history. It stamps the character of Matthew very clearly.

Chapters 5 to 7

The divisions and contents of the Sermon on the Mount

THIS discourse may be divided into the following parts:[18]

[18] In the text I have given a division which may assist in a practical application of the Sermon on the Mount. With respect to the subjects contained in it, it might perhaps, though the difference is not very great, be still better divided thus:—

Chapter 5: 1-16 contains the complete picture of the character and position of the remnant who received His instructions—their position, as it should be, according to the mind of God. This is complete in itself.

Verses 17-48 establish the authority of the law, which should have regulated the conduct of the faithful until the introduction of the kingdom; the law which they ought to have fulfilled, as well as the words of the prophets, in order that they (the remnant) should be placed on this new ground; and the despisal of which would exclude whoever was guilty of it from the kingdom; for Christ is speaking, not as in the kingdom, but as announcing it as near to come. But, while thus establishing the authority of the law, He takes up the two great elements of evil, treated of only in outward acts in the law, violence and corruption, and judges the evil in the heart (22, 28), and at all cost to get rid of His disciples, and their state of soul—that which was to characterize it and every occasion of it, thus showing what was to be the conduct of them as such. The Lord then takes up certain things borne with by God in Israel, and ordered according to what they could bear. Thus was now brought into the light of a true moral estimate, divorce—marriage being the divinely-given basis of all human relationships—and swearing or vowing, the action of man's will in relationship to God; then patience of evil, and fulness of grace, His own blessed character, and carrying with it the moral title to what was His living place—sons of their Father who was in heaven. Instead of weakening that which God required under the law, He would not only have it observed until its fulfilment, but that His disciples should be perfect *even as their Father* in heaven was perfect. This adds the revelation of the Father, to the moral walk and state which suited the character of sons as it was revealed in Christ.

Chapter 6. We have the motives, the object, which should govern the heart in doing good deeds, in living a religious life. Their eye should be *on their Father*. This is individual.

Chapter 7. This chapter is essentially occupied with the intercourse that would be suitable between His own people and others—not to judge their brethren and to beware of the profane. He then exhorts them to confidence in asking their Father for what they needed, and instructs them to act towards others with the same grace that they would wish shown to themselves. This is founded on the knowledge of the goodness of the Father. Finally, He exhorts them to the energy that will enter in at the strait gate, and choose the way of God, cost what it may (for many would like to enter into the kingdom, but not by that gate); and He warns them with respect to those who would seek to deceive them by pretending to have the Word of God. It is not only our own hearts that we have to fear, and positive evil, when we would follow the Lord, but also the devices of the enemy and his agents. But their fruits will betray them.

The character and the portion of those who should be in the kingdom (vers. 1-12).

Their position in the world (vers. 13-16).

The connection between the principles of the kingdom and the law (vers. 17-48).[19]

The spirit in which His disciples should perform good works. (Chap. 6: 1-18.)

Separation from the spirit of the world and from its anxieties (vers. 19-34).

The spirit of their relation with others. (Chap. 7:1-6.)

The confidence in God which became them (vers. 7-12).

The energy that should characterize them, in order that they might enter into the kingdom; not however merely enter, many would seek to do that, but according to those principles which made it difficult for man, according to God—the strait gate; and then, the means of discerning those who would seek to deceive them, as well as the watchfulness needed that they might not be deceived (vers. 13-23).

Real and practical obedience to His sayings, the true wisdom of those that hear His words (vers. 24-29).

The revelation of the Father's name

There is another principle that characterizes this discourse, and that is the introduction of the Father's name. Jesus puts His disciples in connection with His Father, as their Father. He reveals to them the Father's name, in order that they may be in relation with Him, and that they may act in accordance with that which He is.

The rejection of the King: the consequent position and conduct of His followers

This discourse gives the principles of the kingdom, but supposes the rejection of the King, and the position into which this would bring those that were His; who

[19] It is important however to remark that there is no general spiritualization of the law, as is often stated. The two great principles of immorality amongst men are treated of (violence and corrupt lust), to which are added voluntary oaths. In these the exigencies of the law and what Christ required are contrasted.

consequently must look for a heavenly reward. They
were to be a divine savor where God was known and
was dealing, and would be a spectacle to the whole
world. Moreover this was God's object. Their confession was to be so open that the world should refer
their works to the Father. They were to act, on the
one hand, according to a judgment of evil which reached
the heart and motives, but also, on the other, according to the Father's character in grace—to approve themselves to the Father's character in grace—to approve
themselves to the Father who saw in secret, where the
eye of man could not penetrate. They were to have full
confidence in Him for all their need. His will was the
rule according to which there was entrance into the
kingdom.

The discourse pronounced in Israel before the kingdom is set up

We may observe that this discourse is connected with
the proclamation of the kingdom as being near at hand,
and that all these principles of conduct are given as
characterizing the kingdom, and as the conditions of entrance into it. No doubt it follows that they are suitable to those who have entered in. But the discourse is
pronounced in the midst of Israel,[20] before the kingdom is
set up, and as the previous state called for in order to
enter, and to set forth the fundamental principles of the
kingdom in connection with that people, and in moral
contrast with the ideas they had formed respecting it.

The Beatitudes: the character and portion of those in the kingdom

In examining the beatitudes, we shall find that this

[20] We must always remember that, while dispensationally Israel has
great importance, as the centre of God's government of this world,
morally Israel was just man where all the ways and dealings of God
had been carried out so as to bring to light what he was. The Gentile
was man left to himself as regards God's special ways, and so unrevealed.
Christ was a light (*eis apokalypsen ethnon*) to reveal the Gentiles.

portion in general gives the character of Christ Himself. They suppose two things; the coming possession
of the land of Israel by the meek; and the persecution
of the faithful remnant, really righteous in their ways,
and who asserted the rights of the true King (heaven
being set before them as their hope to sustain their
hearts).[21]

The disciples' position in the world

This will be the position of the remnant in the *last*
days before the introduction of the kingdom, the last
being exceptional. It was so, morally, in the days of
the Lord's disciples, in reference to Israel, the earthly
part being delayed. In reference to heaven, the disciples are looked at as witnesses in Israel; but—while the
only preservative of the *earth*—they were a testimony to
the *world*. So that the disciples are seen as in connection with Israel, but, at the same time, as witnesses on
God's part to the world (the kingdom being in view, but
not yet established). The connection with the last days
is evident; nevertheless their testimony then had, morally,
this character. Only the establishment of the earthly
kingdom has been delayed, and the Church, which is
heavenly, brought in. Chapter 5: 25 evidently alludes to
the position of Israel in the days of Christ. And in fact
they remain captive, in prison, until they have received
their full chastisement, and then they shall come forth.

---

[21] The characters pronounced blessed may be briefly noted. They
suppose evil in the world, and amongst God's people. The first is not
seeking great things for self, accepting a despised place in a scene contrary to God. Hence mourning characterizes them there, and meekness,
a will not lifting up itself against God, or to maintain its position or
right. Then positive good in desire, for it is not yet found; hungering
hence and thirsting after it, such is the inward state and activity of the
mind. Then grace towards others. Then purity of heart, the absence
of what would shut out God; and, what is always connected with it,
peacefulness and peace-making. I think there is moral progress in the
verses, one leading to the next as an effect of it. The two last are the
consequences of maintaining a good conscience and connection with
Christ in a world of evil. There are two principles of suffering, as in
1 Peter, for righteousness' and Christ's sake.

The obedient Man, the Lord from heaven

The Lord ever speaks and acts as the obedient Man, moved and guided by the Holy Ghost; but we see in the most striking manner, in this Gospel, who it is that acts thus. And it is this which gives its true moral character to the kingdom of heaven. John the Baptist might announce it as a change of dispensation, but his ministry was earthly. Christ might equally announce this same change (and the change was all-important); but in Him there was more than this. He was from heaven, the Lord who came from heaven. In speaking of the kingdom of heaven, He spoke out of the deep and divine abundance of His heart. No man had been in heaven, excepting Him who had come down from thence, the Son of Man who was in heaven. Therefore, when speaking of heaven, He spoke of that which He knew, and testified of that which He had seen. This was the case in two ways, as shown forth in Matthew's Gospel. It was no longer an earthly government according to the law: Jehovah, the Saviour, Emmanuel, was present. Could He be otherwise than heavenly in His character, in the tone, in the sense, of His whole life?

The character of Christ identified with heaven

Moreover, when He began His public ministry and was sealed by the Holy Ghost, heaven was opened to Him. He was identified with heaven as a man sealed with the Holy Ghost on earth. He was thus the continual expression of the spirit, of the reality, of heaven. There was not yet the exercise of the judicial power which would uphold this character in the face of all that opposed it. It was its manifestation in patience, notwithstanding the opposition of all around Him and the inability of His disciples to understand Him. Thus in the sermon on the Mount we find the description of that which was suitable to the kingdom of heaven, and even the assurance of reward in heaven for those who should suffer on earth for His sake. This description, as we have seen, is essentially the character of Christ Himself. It is thus that a heavenly spirit expresses itself on earth. If the Lord taught these things, it is because He loved them, because He *was* them and delighted in them. Being the God of heaven, filled as man with the Spirit without measure, His heart was perfectly in unison with a heaven that He perfectly knew. Consequently therefore He concludes the character which His disciples were to assume by these words: "Be ye therefore perfect, even as your Father in heaven is perfect." All their conduct was to be in reference to their Father in heaven. The more we understand the divine glory of Jesus, the more we understand the way in which He was as Man in connection with heaven, the better shall we apprehend what the kingdom of heaven was to Him with regard to that which was suitable to it. When it shall be established hereafter in power, the world will be governed according to these principles, although they are not, properly speaking, its own.

The remnant in the last days, I doubt not, finding all around them contrary to faithfulness, and seeing all Jewish hope fail before their eyes, will be forced to look upward, and will more and more acquire this character, which, if not heavenly, is at least very much conformed to Christ.[22]

---

[22] Those who are put to death will go up to heaven, as Matthew 5: 12 testifies, and the Apocalypse also. The others, who are thus conformed to Christ, as a suffering Jew, will be with Him on Mount Zion; they will learn the song which is sung in heaven, and will follow the Lamb whithersoever He goeth (on earth). We may also remark here, that in the beatitudes there is the promise of the earth to the meek, which will be literally fulfilled in the last days. In verse 12 a reward in heaven is promised to those who suffer for Christ, true for us now, and in some sort for those who shall be slain for His sake in the last days, who will have their place in heaven, although they were a part of the Jewish remnant and not the assembly. The same are found in Daniel 7: only, remark, it is the times and laws which are delivered into the beast's hands, not the saints.

The multitude and the Lord's power and character

There are two things connected with the presence of
the multitude, verse 1. First, the time required that the
Lord should give a true idea of the character of His
kingdom, since already He drew the multitude after Him.
His power making itself felt, it was important to make
His character known. On the other hand, this multitude
who were following Jesus were a snare to His disciples;
and He makes them understand what an entire contrast
there was between the effect which this multitude might
have upon them, and the right spirit which ought to
govern them. Thus, full Himself of what was really good,
He immediately brings forward that which filled His own
heart. This was the true character of the remnant, who
in the main resembled Christ in it. It is often thus in the
Psalms.

The salt of the earth and the light of the world

The salt of the earth is a different thing from the light
of the world. The earth, it appears to me, expresses
that which already professed to have received light from
God—that which was in relationship with Him by virtue
of the light—having assumed a definite shape before Him.
The disciples of Christ were the preservative principle in
the *earth*. They were the light of the *world*, which did
not possess that light. This was their position, whether
they would or no. It was the purpose of God that they
should be the light of the world. A candle is not lighted
in order to be hidden.

Men's opposition to the establishment of the kingdom

All this supposes the case of the possibility of the kingdom being established in the world, but the opposition
of the greater part of men to its establishment. It is
not a question of the sinner's redemption, but of the

realization of the character proper to a place in the kingdom of God; that which the sinner ought to seek while
he is in the way with his adversary, lest he should be
delivered to the judge—which indeed has happened to
the Jews.

Relationship with the Father: prayer in dependence

At the same time the disciples are brought into relationship with the Father individually—the second great
principle of the discourse, the consequence of the Son
being there—and a yet more excellent thing is set before
them than their position of testimony for the kingdom.
They were to act in grace, even as their Father acted, and
their prayer should be for an order of things in which
all would correspond morally to the character and the
will of their Father. "Hallowed be Thy name, Thy kingdom come," [23] is, that all should answer to the character
of the Father, that all should be the effect of His power.
"Thy will be done on earth as it is in heaven," is perfect
obedience. Universal subjection to God in heaven and
on earth will be, to a certain point, accomplished by the
intervention of Christ in the millennium, and absolutely
so when God shall be all in all. Meanwhile the prayer
expresses daily dependence, the need of pardon, the need
of being kept from the power of the enemy, the desire
of not being sifted by him, as a dispensation of God, like
Job or Peter, and of being preserved from evil.

The special application of "the Lord's Prayer"

This prayer also is adapted to the position of the
remnant; it passes over the dispensation of the Spirit,
and even that which is proper to the millennium as an

[23] That is, the Father's. Compare Matthew 13: 43.

earthly kingdom, in order to express the right desires, and speak of the condition and the dangers of the remnant until the Father's kingdom should come. Many of these principles are always true, for we are in the kingdom, and in spirit we ought to manifest its features; but the special and literal application is that which I have given. They are brought into relationship with the Father in the realization of His character, which was to be displayed in them by virtue of this relationship, causing them to desire the establishment of His kingdom, to overcome the difficulties of an opposing world, to keep themselves from the snares of the enemy, and to do the Father's will. It was Jesus who could impart this to them. He thus passes from the law,[24] recognized as coming from God, to its fulfilment, when it shall be as it were absorbed in the will of Him who gave it, or accomplished in its purposes by Him who *alone* could do so in any sense whatever.

Chapter 8

The beginning of the Lord's testimony in the midst of Israel

THEN, in chapter 8, the Lord begins in the midst of Israel His patient life of testimony, which closed with His rejection by the people whom God had so long preserved for Him, and for their own blessing.

He had proclaimed the kingdom, displayed His power throughout the land, and declared His character, as well as the spirit of those who should enter the kingdom.

[24] The law is the perfect rule for a child of Adam, the rule or measure of what ought to be, but not of the manifestation of God in grace as Christ was, who in this is our pattern—a just call to love God and walk in the fulfilment of duty in relationship, but not an imitating of God, walking in love, as Christ has loved us and given Himself for us.

The character of the Lord's mircles

But His miracles,[25] as well as the whole Gospel, are always characterized by His position among the Jews and God's dealings with them, till He was rejected. Jehovah, yet the Man obedient to the law, foreshowing the entrance of the Gentiles into the kingdom (its establishment in mystery in the world), predicting the building of the Church or assembly on the recognition of His being Son of the living God, and the kingdom in glory; and, while detecting as the effect of His presence the perversity of the people, yet bearing on His heart with perfect patience the burden of Israel.[26] It is Jehovah present in goodness, outwardly one of themselves: wondrous truth!

The healing of the leper: God manifest in grace and goodness

First of all, we find the healing of a leper. Jehovah alone, in His sovereign goodness, could heal the leper; here Jesus does so. "If Thou wilt," says the leper, "Thou canst." "I will," replies the Lord. But at the

---

[25] The miracles of Christ had a peculiar character. They were not merely acts of power, but all of them of the power of God visiting this world in goodness. The power of God had been often shown specially, from Moses, but often in judgment. But Christ's were all the deliverance of men from the evil consequences sin had brought in. There was one exception, the cursing the fig-tree, but this was a judicial sentence on Israel, that is, man under the old covenant when there was great appearance but no fruit.

[26] I subjoin here some MS notes, made when reading Matthew, since this was written, as throwing, I think, light on the structure of this Gospel. Matthew 5 to 7 gives the character required for entrance into the kingdom, the character which was to mark the accepted remnant, Jehovah being now in the way with the nation to judgment. Chapters 8, 9 give the other side—grace and goodness come in, God manifest, His character and actings, that new thing which could not be put into the old bottles—still goodness in power, but rejected, the Son of Man (not Messiah) who had not where to lay His head. Chapter 8 gives present intervention in temporal goodness with power. Hence, as goodness, it goes beyond Israel, as it deals in grace with what was excluded from

same time, while He shows forth in His own Person that which repels all possibility of defilement—that which is above sin—He shows the most perfect condescension towards the defiled one. He touches the leper, saying, "I will; be thou clean." We see the grace, the power, the undefilable holiness of Jehovah, come down in the Person of Jesus to the closest proximity to the sinner, touching him so to speak. It was indeed "the Lord that healeth thee." [27] At the same time He conceals Himself, and commands the man who had been healed to go to the priest according to the ordinances of the law and offer his gift. He does not go out of the place of the Jew in subjection to the law; but Jehovah was there in goodness.

Sovereign grace to a Gentile

But in the next case we see a Gentile, who by faith enjoys the full effect of that power which his faith ascribed

God's camp in Israel. It includes power over all Satan's power and sickness and the elements, and that in taking the burden on Himself, but in conscious rejection. Chapter 8: 17-20 leads us to Isaiah 53: 3, 4, and the state of things calling for the wholly following Him, giving up all. This leads to the sad testimony that, if divine power expels Satan's, the divine presence manifest in it is insupportable to the world. The swine figure Israel thereupon. Chapter 9 furnishes the religious side of His presence in grace, forgiveness, and the testimony that Jehovah was there according to Psalm 103, but there to call sinners, not the righteous; and this was especially what could not suit the old bottles. Finally, this chapter practically, save the patience of goodness, closes the history. He came to save Israel's life. It was really death when He came: only, wherever there was faith in the midst of the surrounding crowd, there was healing. The Pharisees show the blasphemy of the leaders: only the patience of grace still subsists, carried out towards Israel in chapter 10, but all found to be of no avail in chapter 11. The Son was revealing the Father, and this abides and gives rest. Chapter 12 develops fully the judgment and rejection of Israel. Chapter 13 brings Christ as a sower, not seeking fruit in His vineyard, and the actual form of the kingdom of heaven.

[27] One who touched a leper became himself unclean, but the blessed One did come thus close to man, but removed the defilement without contracting it. The leper knew His power, but was not sure of His goodness. "I will" declared it, but with a title which God only has to say, "I will."

to Jesus, giving the Lord occasion to bring out the solemn truth, that many of these poor Gentiles should come and sit down in the kingdom of heaven with the fathers who were honored by the Jewish nation as the first parents of the heirs of promise, while the children of the kingdom should be in outer darkness. In fact the faith of this centurion acknowledged a divine power in Jesus, which, by the glory of Him that possessed it, would (not forsake Israel, but) open the door to the Gentiles, and graft into the olive-tree of promise branches of the wild olive-tree in the place of those which should be cut off. The manner in which this should take place in the assembly was not now the question.

Peter's wife's mother healed: present intervention in temporal goodness and power

He does not however yet forsake Israel. He goes into Peter's house, and heals his wife's mother. He does the same to all the sick who crowd around the house at even, when the sabbath was over. They are healed, the devils are cast out, so that the prophecy of Isaiah was being fulfilled: "Himself took our infirmities and bare our sicknesses." Jesus put Himself in heart under the weight of all the sorrows that oppressed Israel, in order to relieve and heal them. It is still *Emmanuel*, who feels for their misery and is afflicted in all their affliction, but who has come in with the power that shows Him capable of delivering them.

Conscious rejection

These three cases show this character of His ministry in a clear and striking manner. He hides Himself; for, until the moment when He would show judgment to the Gentiles, He does not lift up His voice in the streets. It is the dove that rests upon Him. These manifestations of power attract men to Him; but this does not deceive Him: He never departs in spirit from the place He has taken. He is the despised and the rejected of men; He has nowhere to lay His head. The earth had more room for the foxes and the birds than for Him, whom we have seen appear a moment before as the Lord, acknowledged at least by the necessities which He never refused to relieve. Therefore, if any man would follow Him, he must forsake all to be the companion of the Lord, who would not have come down to the earth if everything had not been in question; nor without an absolute right, although it was at the same time in a love which could only be occupied by its mission, and by the necessity that brought Him there.

The storm permitted for the trial of faith and to manifest Christ's dignity

The Lord on earth was everything or nothing. This, it is true, was to be felt morally in its effects, in the grace which, acting by faith, attached the believer to Him by an ineffable bond. Without this, the heart would not have been morally put to the test. But this did not make it the less true. Accordingly the proofs of this were present: the winds and waves, to which in the eye of man He seemed to be exposed, obeyed His voice at once—a striking reproof to the unbelief that woke Him from His sleep, and had supposed it possible for the waves to engulf Him, and with Him the counsels and the power of Him who had created the winds and waves. It is evident that this storm was permitted in order to try their faith and manifest the dignity of His Person. If the enemy was the instrument who produced it, he only succeeded in making the Lord display His glory. Such indeed is always the case as to Christ, and for us, where faith is.

Now the reality of this power, and the manner of its operation, are forcibly proved by that which follows.

Divine power expels Satan's power: the divine presence insupportable to the world

The Lord disembarks in the country of the Gergesenes. There the power of the enemy shows itself in all its horrors. If man, to whom the Lord was come in grace, did not know Him, the devils knew their Judge in the Person of the Son of God. The man was possessed by them. The fear they had of torment at the judgment of the last day is applied in the man's mind to the immediate presence of the Lord: "Art Thou come to torment us before the time?" Wicked spirits act on men by the dread of their power; they have none unless they are feared. But faith only can take this fear from man. I am not speaking of the lusts on which they act, nor of the wiles of the enemy; I speak of the *power* of the enemy. Resist the devil and he will flee from thee. Here the devils wished to manifest the reality of this power. The Lord permits it in order to make it plain, that in this world it is not merely man that is in question whether good or bad, but that also which is stronger than man. The devils enter into the swine, which perish in the waters. Sorrowful reality plainly demonstrated, that it was no question of mere disease or of sinful lusts, but of wicked spirits! However, thanks be to God, it was a question also of One who, although a Man on earth, was more powerful than they. They are compelled to acknowledge this power, and they appeal to it. There is no idea of resistance. In the temptation in the wilderness Satan had been overcome. He completely delivers the man whom they had oppressed with their evil power. He could have delivered the world from all the power of the enemy, if that only had been in question, and from all the ills of humanity. The strong man was bound, and the Lord spoiled his goods. But the presence of God, of Jehovah, troubles the world even more than the power of the enemy degrades and domineers over mind and body. The control of the enemy over the heart—too peaceful, and alas, too little perceived—is more mighty than his strength. This succumbs before the word of Jesus; but the will of man accepts the world as it is, governed by the influence of Satan. The whole city, who had witnessed the deliverance of the demoniac and the power of Jesus present among them, entreat Him to depart. Sad history of the world! The Lord came down with power to deliver the world—man—from all the power of the enemy; but they would not. Their distance from God was moral, and not merely bondage to the enemy's power. They submitted to his yoke, they had become used to it, and they *would not* have the presence of God.

I doubt not that that which happened to the swine is a figure of that which happened to the impious and profane Jews who rejected the Lord Jesus. Nothing can be more striking than the way in which a divine Person, Emmanuel, though a Man in grace, is manifested in this chapter.

Chapter 9

Jehovah present in Israel with proof of His title to forgive sinners in grace

IN the following chapter (9), while acting in the character and according to the power of Jehovah (as we read in Psalm 103), "Who forgiveth all thine iniquities, who healeth all thy diseases;" it is the actual grace in itself towards and for them, in which He came, which is presented. It gives the character of His ministry, as the previous one gives the dignity of His Person and the bearing of what He was. He presents Himself to Israel as their true Redeemer and Deliverer; and, to prove His title (which unbelief already opposed) to be this blessing to Israel, and to pardon all their iniquities which raised

a barrier between them and their God, He accomplishes
the second part of the verse, and heals the disease. Beautiful and precious testimony of kindness to Israel, and at
the same time, the demonstration of His glory who stood
in the midst of His people!   In the same spirit, as He
had forgiven, and healed, He calls the publican and goes
to his house—come not to call the righteous, but sinners.

The development of opposition: the rejection of the Lord's work and Person

But now we enter on another portion of the instruction
in this Gospel — the development of the opposition of
unbelievers, of the learned men and the *religionists* in
particular; and that of the rejection of the work and
Person of the Lord.

The idea, the picture of that which took place, has
been already set before us in the case of the Gergesene
demoniac—the power of God present for the entire deliverance of His people, of the world, if they received
Him—power which the devils confessed to be that which
should hereafter judge and cast them out, which displayed
itself in blessing to all the people of the place, but which
was rejected, because they did not desire such power to
dwell among them.   They would not have the presence
of God.

The rejection of God's intervention on earth

The narration of the details and the character of this
rejection now commences.   Observe that chapter 8: 1-27
gives the manifestation of the Lord's power—this power
being truly that of Jehovah on the earth.   From verse
28 the reception this power met with in the world, and
the influence which governed the world, are set forth,
whether as power, or morally in the hearts of men.

We come here to the historical development of the
rejection of this intervention of God upon the earth.

The multitude glorify God who had given such power to a man. Jesus accepts this place. He was Man: the multitude saw Him to be man, and acknowledged the power of God, but did not know how to combine the two ideas in His Person.

God manifest in grace to sinners

The grace which contemns the pretensions of man to righteousness is now set forth.

Matthew, the publican, is called; for God looks at the heart, and grace calls the elect vessels.

The Lord declares the mind of God on this subject, and His own mission. He came to call sinners; He would have mercy. It was God in grace, and not man with his pretended righteousness counting on his merits.

New principles and new power

He assigns two reasons which make it impossible to reconcile His course with the demands of the Pharisees. How should the disciples fast when the Bridegroom was there? When the Messiah was gone, they might well do so. Moreover it is impossible to introduce the new principles and the new power of His mission into the old Pharisaic forms.

Life given to the dead, proof that Jehovah was there in grace

Thus we have grace to sinners, but (grace rejected) now comes at once a higher proof that Messiah-Jehovah was there, and there in grace. Being entreated to raise up a young girl from her bed of death, He obeys the call. As He goes, a poor woman, who already employed every means of cure without success, is instantaneously healed by touching in faith the hem of His garment.

Christ the power for dead Israel and for individual faith: the Pharisees' wickedness

This history supplies us with the two great divisions of the grace that was manifested in Jesus. Christ came to awaken dead Israel; He will do this hereafter in the full sense of the word. Meanwhile, whosoever laid hold of Him by faith, in the midst of the multitude that accompanied Him, was healed, let the case be ever so hopeless. This, which took place in Israel when Jesus was there, is true in principle of us also. Grace in Jesus is a power which raises from the dead, and which heals. Thus He opened the eyes of those in Israel who owned Him to be the Son of David, and who believed in His power to meet their need. He cast out devils also, and gave speech to the dumb. But having performed these acts of power in Israel, so that the people, as to the fact, owned them with admiration, the Pharisees, the most religious part of the nation, ascribe this power to the prince of the devils. Such is the effect of the Lord's presence on the leaders of the people, jealous of His glory thus manifested among them over whom they exercised their influence. But this in no way interrupts Jesus in His career of beneficence. He can still bear testimony among the people. In spite of the Pharisees His patient kindness still finds place. He continues to preach and to heal. He has compassion on the people, who were like sheep without a shepherd, given up, morally, to their own guidance. He still sees that the harvest is plenteous and the laborers few. That is to say, He still sees every door open to address the people and He passes over the wickedness of the Pharisees.

The patience and kindness of grace

Let us sum up what we find in the chapter, the grace developed in Israel. First, grace healing and forgiving as in Psalm 103. Then grace come to call sinners, not the righteous; the bridegroom was there, nor could grace in power be put in Jewish and Pharisaic vessels; it was new even in respect of John Baptist. He comes in reality to give life to the dead, not to heal, but whoever then touched Him by faith—for there were such—were healed in the way. He opens eyes to see, as Son of David, and opens the dumb mouth of him whom the devil possessed. All is rejected with blasphemy by the self-righteous Pharisees. But grace sees the multitude as yet as having *no* shepherd; and while the porter holds the door open, He ceases not to seek and minister to the sheep.

Chapter 10

The twelve disciples sent to the lost sheep of Israel: their message and authority

SO long as God gives Him access to the people, He continues His labor of love. Nevertheless, He was conscious of the iniquity that governed the people, although He did not seek His own glory. Having exhorted His disciples to pray that laborers might be sent into the harvest, He begins (chap. 10) to act in accordance with that desire. He calls His twelve disciples, He gives them power to cast out devils and to heal the sick, and He sends them to the lost sheep of the house of Israel. We see, in this mission, how much the ways of God with Israel form the subject of this Gospel. They were to announce to that people, and to them exclusively, the nearness of the kingdom, exercising at the same time the power they had received: a striking testimony to Him who was come, and who could not only work miracles Himself, but confer power on others to do so likewise. He gave them authority over evil spirits for this purpose. It is this which characterizes the kingdom—man healed of all sickness and the devil cast out. Accordingly, in

Hebrews 6, miracles are called "the powers of the world to come." [28]

Dependence for their need: acceptance or rejection as the King's messengers

They were also, with respect to their need, to depend entirely on Him who sent them. Emmanuel was there. If miracles were a proof to the world of their Master's power, the fact that they lacked nothing should be so to their own hearts. The ordinance was abrogated during that period of their ministry which followed the departure of Jesus from this world. (Luke 22: 35-37.) That which He here (Matt. 10) commands His disciples appertains to His presence as Messiah, as Jehovah, Himself on the earth. Therefore the reception of His messengers, or their rejection, decided the fate of those to whom they were sent. In rejecting them they rejected the Lord, Emmanuel, God with His people.[29] But, in fact, He sent them forth as sheep in the midst of wolves. They would need the wisdom of serpents, and were to exhibit the harmlessness of doves (rare union of virtues, found only in those who, by the Spirit of the Lord, are wise unto that which is good and simple concerning evil).

---

[28] For then Satan will be bound and man delivered by the power of Christ. And there were partial deliverances of the kind.

[29] There is a division of the Lord's discourse at verse 15. Up to that, it is the then present mission. From verse 16 we have more general reflections on their mission, looked at as a whole in the midst of Israel on to the end. Evidently it goes beyond their then present mission, and supposes the coming of the Holy Ghost. The mission by which the Church is called as such a distinct thing. This applies only to Israel; they were forbidden to go to Gentiles. This necessarily closed with the destruction of Jerusalem and the dispersion of the Jewish nation, but it is to be renewed at the end, till the Son of Man be come. There was a testimony to the Gentiles only, as brought before them as judges, as Paul was, and that part of his history even on to Rome in Acts, was amidst Jews. The latter part, from verse 16, has less to do with the gospel of the kingdom.

If they did not beware of men (sad testimony as to these), they would but suffer; but when scourged and brought before councils and governors and kings, all this should become a testimony unto them—a divine means of presenting the gospel of the kingdom to kings and princes, without altering its character or accommodating it to the world, or mixing up the Lord's people with its usages and its false greatness. Moreover circumstances like these made their testimony much more conspicuous, than association with the great ones of the earth would have done.

Help and encouragement

And, to accomplish this, they should receive such power and guidance from the Spirit of their Father as would cause the words they spoke to be not their own words, but His who inspired them. Here, again, their relation with their Father, which so distinctly characterizes the Sermon on the Mount, is made the basis of their capacity for the service they had to perform. We must remember that this testimony was addressed to Israel only; only that, Israel being under the yoke of the Gentiles since the time of Nebuchadnezzar, the testimony would reach their rulers.

Rejection of the message foreseen: the testimony to be resumed in Israel

But this testimony would excite an opposition that should break all family ties, and awaken a hatred that would not spare the life of those who had been the most beloved. He who in spite of all this should endure to the end should be saved. Nevertheless the case was urgent. They were not to resist, but if the opposition took the form of persecution, they were to flee and preach the gospel elsewhere, for before they had gone over the cities

of Israel the Son of Man should come.[30]   They were to
proclaim the kingdom.   Jehovah, Emmanuel, was there,
in the midst of His people, and the heads of the people
had called the master of the house Beelzebub. This had
not stopped His testimony, but it very strongly characterized the circumstances in which this testimony was to be
rendered.   He sent them forth, warning them of this
state of things, to maintain this final testimony among
His beloved people as long as possible. This took place
at that time, and it is possible, if circumstances permit,
to carry it on until the Son of Man comes to execute
judgment.   Then the master of the house will have *risen
up* to shut the door. The "today" of Psalm 91 will be
over.   Israel in possession of their cities being the object
of this testimony, it is necessarily suspended when they
are no longer in their land. The testimony to the future
kingdom, given in Israel by the apostles after the Lord's
death, is an accomplishment of this mission, so far as
this testimony was rendered in the land of Israel; for the
kingdom might be proclaimed as to be established while
Emmanuel was on the earth; or this might be by Christ's

---

[30] Observe here the expression "Son of Man." This is the character
in which (according to Dan. 7) the Lord will come, in a power and
glory much greater than that of His manifestation as Messiah, the Son
of David, and which will be displayed in a much wider sphere. As the
Son of Man, He is the heir of all that God destines for man. (See
Heb. 2: 6-8, and 1 Cor. 15: 27.) He must, in consequence, seeing what
man's condition is, suffer in order to possess this inheritance. He was
there as the Messiah, but He must be received in His true character,
Emmanuel; and the Jews must thus be tested morally. He will not have
the kingdom on carnal principles. Rejected as Messiah, as Emmanuel,
He postpones the period of those events which will close the ministry of
His disciples with respect to Israel, unto His coming as the Son of Man.
Meantime God has brought out other things, that had been hidden from
the foundation of the world, the true glory of Jesus the Son of God,
His heavenly glory as Man and the Church united to Him in heaven.
The judgment of Jerusalem, and the dispersion of the nation, have
suspended the ministry which had begun at the moment of which the
Evangelist here speaks. That which has filled up the interval since
then is not the subject here of the Lord's discourse, which refers solely
to the ministry that had the Jews for its object. The counsels of God
with respect to the Church, in connection with the glory of Jesus at the
right hand of God, we shall find spoken of elsewhere.

Luke will give us in more detail that which concerns the Son of Man.
In Matthew the Holy Ghost occupies us with the rejection of Emmanuel.

returning from heaven as announced by Peter in Acts 3. And this might take place if Israel were in the land, even until Christ should return. Thus the testimony may be resumed in Israel, whenever they are again in their land and the requisite spiritual power is sent forth by God.

The position of God's witnesses on earth: Christ the touchstone

Meanwhile, the disciples were to share in Christ's own position. If they called the master of the house Beelzebub, much more they of His household. But they were not to fear. It was the necessary portion of those who were for God in the midst of the people. But there was nothing hid that should not be revealed. They themselves were to hold nothing back, but were to proclaim on the house-tops all that they had been taught; for everything should be brought into the light; their faithfulness to God in this respect, as well as all other things. This, while it met the secret plottings of their enemies, was itself to charac-terize the ways of the disciples. God, who is light, and sees in darkness as in light, would bring all out into the light, but they were to do this morally now. Therefore were they to fear nothing while performing this work, unless it were God Himself, the righteous Judge at the last day. Moreover the hairs of their head were num-bered. They were precious to their Father, who took notice of even a sparrow's death. This could not happen without Him who was their Father.

Finally, they were to be thoroughly imbued with the conviction that the Lord was not come to send peace on the earth; no, it should be division, even in the bosom of families. But Christ was to be more precious than father or mother, and even than a man's own life. He who would save his life at the expense of his testimony to Christ should lose it; he who would lose it for the sake of Christ should gain it. He also who should receive this testimony, in the person of the disciples, received Christ, and, in Christ, Him that sent Him. God, therefore, being thus acknowledged in the person of His witnesses on earth, would bestow, on whoever received the latter, a reward according to the testimony rendered. In thus acknowledging the testimony of the rejected Lord, were it only by a cup of cold water, he who gave it should not lose his reward. In an opposing world, he who believes the testimony of God, and receives (in spite of the world) the man who bears this testimony, really confesses God, as well as His servant. It is all that we can do. The rejection of Christ made Him a test, a touchstone.

The judgment of the nation decided

From that hour we find the definitive judgment of the nation, not indeed as yet openly declared (that is in chapter 12), nor by the cessation of Christ's ministry, which wrought, notwithstanding the opposition of the nation, in gathering out the remnant, and in the still more important effect of the manifestation of Emmanuel; but it is unfolded in the character of His discourses, in the positive declarations which describe the condition of the people, and in the Lord's conduct amid circumstances which gave rise to the expression of the relations in which He stood towards them.

Chapter 11

John the Baptist's question: the Lord's true testimony as to Himself

IN chapter 11, having sent His disciples away to preach, He continues the exercise of His own ministry. The report of the works of Christ reaches John in prison. He, in whose heart, notwithstanding his prophetic gift, there

still remained something of Jewish thoughts and hopes,
sends by his disciples to ask Jesus if He is the One who
should come, or if they were still to look for another.[31]
God allowed this question in order to put everything in
its place. Christ, being the Word of God, ought to be
His own witness. He ought to bear testimony to Himself
as well as to John, and not to receive testimony from the
latter; and this He did in the presence of John's disciples. He healed all the diseases of men, and preached
the gospel to the poor; and John's messengers were to
set before him this true testimony of what Jesus was.
John was to receive it. It was by these things men were
tested. Blessed was he who should not be offended at the
lowly exterior of the King of Israel. God manifest in
the flesh did not come to seek the pomp of royalty, although it was His due, but the deliverance of suffering
men. His work revealed a character much more profoundly divine, which had a spring of action far more
glorious than that which depended on the possession of
the throne of David—than a deliverance which would
have set John at liberty, and put an end to the tyranny
that had imprisoned him.

To undertake this ministry, to go down into the scene
of its exercise, to bear the sorrows and the burdens of
His people, might be an occasion of stumbling to a carnal
heart that was looking for the appearance of a glorious
kingdom which would satisfy the pride of Israel. But was
it not more truly divine, more necessary to the condition
of the people as seen of God? The heart of each one
therefore would be thus tested, to show whether he belonged to that repentant remnant, who discerned the ways
of God, or to the proud multitude, who only sought their
own glory, possessing neither a conscience exercised before
God, nor a sense of their need and misery.

---

[31] His sending to Jesus shows full confidence in His word as a prophet,
but ignorance as to His Person; and this is what is brought out here
in its full light.

The Lord's witness to John and his testimony to the coming kingdom

Having set John under the responsibility of receiving this testimony, which put all Israel to the test, and distinguished the remnant from the nation in general, the Lord then bears witness to John himself, addressing the multitude, and reminding them how they had followed the preaching of John. He shows them the exact point to which Israel had come in the ways of God. The introduction, in testimony, of the kingdom made the difference between that which preceded and that which followed. Among all that are born of women there had been none greater than John the Baptist, none who had been so near Jehovah, sent before His face, none who had rendered Him a more exact and complete testimony, who had been so separate from all evil by the power of the Spirit of God—a separation proper to the fulfilment of such a mission among the people of God. Still he had not been in the kingdom: it was not yet established; and to be in the presence of Christ in His kingdom, enjoying the result of the establishment of His glory,[32] was a greater thing than all testimony to the coming of the kingdom.

The kingdom announced and preached but not yet established

Nevertheless from the time of John the Baptist there was a notable change. From that time the kingdom was announced. It was not established, but it was preached. This was a very different thing from the prophecies that spoke of the kingdom for a yet distant period, while recalling the people to the law as given by Moses. The Baptist went before the King, announcing the nearness

---

[32] This is not God's assembly; but the rights of the King as manifested in glory being established, the foundation being laid, Christians are in the kingdom, although in a very peculiar and exceptional manner, because they are in the kingdom and the patience of Jesus Christ, who is glorified but hidden in God. They share the destiny of the King, and will share His glory when He reigns.

of the kingdom, and commanding the Jews to repent that they might enter into it. Thus the law and the prophets spake on God's part until John. The law was the rule; the prophets, maintaining the rule, strengthened the hopes and the faith of the remnant. Now, the energy of the Spirit impelled men to force their way through every difficulty and all the opposition of the leaders of the nation and of a blinded people, that they might at all costs attain the kingdom of a King rejected by the blind unbelief of those who should have received Him. It needed —seeing that the King had come in humiliation, and that He had been rejected—it needed this violence to enter the kingdom. The strait gate was the only entrance.

John as the Elias who should come

If faith could really penetrate the mind of God therein, John was the Elias who should come. He that had ears to hear, let him hear. It was in fact for those only.

Had the kingdom appeared in the glory and in the power of its Head, violence would not have been necessary; it would have been possessed as the certain effect of that power; but it was the will of God that they should morally be tested. It was thus also that they ought to have received Elias in spirit.

The character of "this generation" manifested by its rejection of Jesus

The result is given in the Lord's words which follow, that is, the true character of *this generation,* and the ways of God in relation to the Person of Jesus, manifested by His rejection itself. As a generation the threatenings of justice, and the attractions of grace were equally lost upon them. The children of wisdom, those whose consciences were taught of God, acknowledged the truth of John's testimony, as against themselves, and the grace, so necessary to the guilty, of the ways of Jesus.

The Lord's righteous rebuke of their folly given in warning

John, separate from the iniquity of the nation, had, in their eyes, a devil. Jesus, kind to the most wretched, they accused of falling in with evil ways. Yet the evidence was powerful enough to have subdued the heart of a Tyre or Sodom; and the righteous rebuke of the Lord warns the perverse and unbelieving nation of a more terrible judgment than that which awaited the pride of Tyre or the corruption of Sodom.

But this was a test for the most favored of mankind. It might have been said, Why was the message not sent to Tyre, ready to hearken? Why not to Sodom, that that city might have escaped the fire that consumed it? It is that man must be tested in every way; that the perfect counsels of God may be developed. If Tyre or Sodom had abused the advantages which a God of creation and of providence had heaped upon them, the Jews were to manifest what was in the heart of man, when possessing all the promises and made the depositaries of all the oracles of God.

They boasted of the gift, and departed from the Giver. Their blinded heart acknowledged not and even rejected their God.

The people's contempt felt by the Lord but accepted as His Father's will

The Lord felt the contempt of His people whom He loved; but, as the obedient Man on earth, He submitted to the will of His Father, who, acting in sovereignty, the Lord of heaven and earth, manifested, in the exercise of this sovereignty, divine wisdom, and the perfection of His character. Jesus accepts the will of His Father in its effects, and, thus subject, sees its perfection.

God's revelation to the lowly: the glory of God's counsels

It was befitting that God should reveal to the lowly all the gifts of His grace in Jesus, this Emmanuel on earth; and that He should hide them from the pride that sought to scrutinize and to judge them. But this opens the door to the glory of God's counsels in it.

The truth was, that His Person was too glorious to be fathomed or understood by man, although His words and His works left the nation without excuse, in their refusal to come unto Him that they might know the Father.

Jesus, subject to His Father's will, although thoroughly sensible of all that was painful to His heart in its effects, sees the whole extent of the glory that should follow His rejection.

The revelation of the Son to faith and the revelation of the Father by the Son

All things were delivered unto Him of His Father. It is the Son who is revealed to our faith, the veil that covered His glory being taken away now that He is rejected as Messiah. *No one* knoweth Him but the Father. Who among the proud could fathom what He was? He who from all eternity was one with the Father, become Man, surpassed, in the deep mystery of His being, all knowledge save that of the Father Himself. The impossibility of knowing Him who had emptied Himself to become Man, maintained the certainty, the reality, of His divinity, which this self-renunciation might have hidden from the eyes of unbelief. The incomprehensibility of a being in a finite form revealed the infinite which was therein. His divinity was guaranteed to faith, against the effect of His humanity on the mind of man. But if no one knew the Son, except the Father only, the Son, who is truly God, was able to reveal the

Father. No man has ever seen God. The only-begotten
Son, who is in the bosom of the Father, has revealed
Him. No one knows the Father but the Son, and he to
whom the Son will reveal Him. Wretched ignorance that
in its pride rejects Him! It was thus according to the
good pleasure of the Son that this revelation was made.
Distinctive attribute of divine perfection! He came for
this purpose; He did it according to His own wisdom.
Such was the truth of man's relations with Him, although
He submitted to the painful humiliation of being rejected
by His own people, as the final test of their, of man's
state.

The door opened to the Gentiles

Observe also here, that this principle, this truth, with
regard to Christ, opens the door to the Gentiles, to all
who should be called. He reveals the Father to whomsoever He will. He always seeks the glory of His Father.
He alone can reveal Him—He to whom the Father, the
Lord of heaven and earth, has delivered all things. The
Gentiles are included in the rights conferred by this title,
even every family in heaven and earth. Christ exercises
these rights in grace, calling whom He will to the knowledge of the Father.

Those who refused the Revealer left in total
   ignorance

Thus we find here the perverse and faithless generation;
a remnant of the nation justifying the wisdom of God as
manifested in John and in Jesus in judgment and in
grace; the sentence of judgment on the unbelievers; the
rejection of Jesus in the character in which He had presented Himself to the nation; and His perfect submission,
as Man, to the will of His Father in this rejection, giving
occasion for the manifestation to His soul of the glory
proper to Him as Son of God—a glory which no man

could know, even as He alone could reveal that of the Father. So that the world who refused Him was in total ignorance, save at the good pleasure of Him who delights in revealing the Father.

The disciples' mission to Israel continues until the coming of the Lord in judgment

We should also remark here, that the mission of the disciples to Israel who rejected Christ continues (if Israel be in the land) until He comes as the Son of Man, His title of judgment and of glory as Heir of all things (that is to say, until the judgment by which He takes possession of the land of Canaan, in a power that leaves no room for His enemies). This, His title of judgment and glory as Heir of all things, is mentioned in John 5, Daniel 7, Psalms 8 and 80.

Sovereign grace: the place of perfect rest to the heart

Observe too, that in chapter 11, the perverseness of the generation that had rejected John's testimony, and that of the Son of Man come in grace and associating Himself in grace with the Jews, opens the door to the testimony of the glory of the Son of God, and to the revelation of the Father by Him in sovereign grace—a grace that could make Him known as efficaciously to a poor Gentile as to a Jew. It was no longer a question of responsibility to receive, but of sovereign grace that imparted to whomsoever it would. Jesus knew man, the world, the generation which had enjoyed the greatest advantages of all that were in the world. There was no place for the foot to rest on in the miry slough of that which had departed from God. In the midst of a world of evil Jesus remained the sole revealer of the Father, the source of all good. Whom does He call? What does He bestow on those who come? Only source of blessing and revealer of the Father,

He calls all those who are weary and heavy laden. Perhaps they did not know the spring of all misery, namely, separation from God, sin. He knew, and He alone could heal them. If it was the sense of sin which burdened them, so much the better. Every way the world no longer satisfied their hearts; they were miserable, and therefore the objects of the heart of Jesus. Moreover He would give them rest; He does not here explain by what means; He simply announces the fact. The love of the Father, which in grace, in the Person of the Son, sought out the wretched, would bestow rest (not merely alleviation or sympathy, but rest) on every one that came to Jesus. It was the perfect revelation of the Father's name to the heart of those that needed it; and that by the Son; —peace, peace with God. They had but to come to Christ; He undertook all and gave rest. But there is a second element in *rest*. There is more than peace through the knowledge of the Father in Jesus. And more than that is needed; for, even when the soul is perfectly at peace with God, this world presents many causes of trouble to the heart. In these cases it is a question of submission or of self-will. Christ, in the consciousness of His rejection, in the deep sorrow caused by the unbelief of the cities in which He had wrought so many miracles, had just manifested the most entire submission to His Father, and had found therein perfect rest to His soul. To this He calls all that heard Him, all that felt the need of rest to their own souls. "Take My yoke upon you, and learn of Me," that is to say, the yoke of submission to His Father's will, learning of Him how to meet the troubles of life; for He was "meek and lowly in heart," content to be in the lowest place at the will of His God. In fact nothing can overthrow one who is there. It is the place of perfect rest to the heart.

Chapter 12

The nation's rejection plainly shown: a new position in sovereign grace

AT length the rejection of the nation, in consequence of their contempt of the Lord, is plainly shown, as well as the cessation of all His relations with them as such, in order to bring out on God's part an entirely different system, that is to say, the kingdom in a particular form. Thus this last chapter is the great turning-point of the whole history. Christ is a divine witness to Himself, and John Baptist has so to receive Him, as another would. He stood no longer as Messiah witnessed to, but as Son of God, but gives His full testimony to John. But the nation had rejected God manifested in warnings and grace alike: only there was a remnant. Wisdom was justified of her children. Then comes His submission to His rejection, evil as it might be, as the Father's will; but this leads Him out into the consciousness of His personal glory, the real ground of that rejection. All things were delivered to Him of His Father. *None* could know Him, nor any the Father unless He revealed Him. The whole world, tested by His perfection, was found lying in wickedness (though with a spared remnant), but man was universally away from God. He looked down from heaven to see, as we read, but they were *all* gone out of the way, none righteous, no, not one. So Jesus, as He walked on the sea, stood alone in a judged world, judged by His rejection, but now in the sovereign grace of the Father, as the Son revealing Him, and calling to the revelation of this grace in Himself. This is just now the new position. He had tried man. The very thing that He was, hindered their receiving Him. Now he that was weary must come to Him who stood thus alone, and He would give them rest. They must learn of Him who thus had absolutely submitted, and they would have rest as to the world and everything here. So with us: where we wholly bow, we come into the conscious possession of our privileges as disowned, on the heavenly and higher ground.

The Son of Man as Lord of the Sabbath

The first circumstance that brought forward the question of His Person, and of His right to close the dispensation, was the disciples' plucking the ears of corn and crushing them in their hands to satisfy their hunger. For this the Pharisees rebuke them, because it was on a Sabbath day. Jesus sets before them that the king, rejected by the malice of Saul, had partaken of that which was only given to the priests. The Son of David, in a similar case, might well enjoy a similar privilege. Besides God was acting in grace. The priest also profaned the Sabbath in the service of the temple; and One greater than the temple was there. Moreover, if they had really known the mind of God, if they had been imbued with the Spirit which His Word declared to be acceptable to Him —"I will have mercy and not sacrifice," they would not have condemned the guiltless. In addition to this, the Son of Man was Lord even of the Sabbath. Here He no longer takes the title of Messiah, but that of Son of Man —a name which bore witness to a new order of things, and to a more extended power. Now that which He said had great significance; for the Sabbath was the token of the covenant between Jehovah and the nation (Ezek. 20: 12-20); and the Son of Man was declaring His power over it. If that was touched, it was all over with the covenant.

The Pharisees' persistent hatred: the Lord's position

The same question arises in the synagogue; and the Lord persists in acting in grace, and in doing good, showing them that they would do the same for one of their sheep. This only excites their hatred, great as was the proof of His beneficent power. They were children of the murderer. Jesus withdraws from them, and great

multitudes follow Him. He heals them, charging them
not to make Him known. In all this, however, His doings
were but the fulfilment of a prophecy which clearly traces
out the Lord's position at this time. The hour would
come when He should bring forth judgment unto victory.
Meanwhile He retained the position of entire lowliness,
in which grace and truth could commend themselves to
those who appreciated and needed them. But in the
exercise of this grace, and in His testimony to the truth,
He would do nothing to falsify this character, or so to
attract the attention of men as to prevent His true work,
or which could make it even suspected that He sought
His own honor. Nevertheless the Spirit of Jehovah was
upon Him as His beloved, in whom His soul delighted;
and He should declare judgment to the Gentiles, and
they should put their trust in His name. The application of this prophecy to Jesus at that moment is very
evident. We see how guarded He was with the Jews,
abstaining from the gratification of their carnal desires
respecting Himself, and content to be in the background,
if God His Father was glorified; and glorifying Him perfectly Himself on the earth by doing good. He was soon
to be declared to the Gentiles; whether by the execution
of the judgment of God, or by presenting Himself to them
as the One in whom they should trust.

This passage is manifestly placed here by the Holy
Ghost, in order to give the exact representation of His
position, before laying open the new scenes which His
rejection prepares for us.

The blindness of the religionists: the power of Beelzebub: sealing their own condition

He then casts out a devil from a man who was blind
and dumb—a sad condition, truly depicting that of the
people with respect to God. The multitude, full of admiration, exclaim, "Is not this the Son of David?" But
the religionists, on hearing it, jealous of the Lord, and

hostile to the testimony of God, declare that Jesus wrought this miracle by the power of Beelzebub, thus sealing their own condition, and putting themselves under the definite judgment of God. Jesus demonstrates the absurdity of what they had said. Satan would not destroy his own kingdom. Their own children, who had the pretension to do the same, should judge their iniquity. But if not the power of Satan (and the Pharisees admitted that the devils were really cast out), it was the finger of God, and the kingdom of God was among them.

He who had come into the strong man's house to spoil his goods had first to bind him.

The unpardonable sin: deciding their own fate

The truth is that the presence of Jesus put everything to the test; everything on God's part was centred in Him. It is Emmanuel Himself who was there. He who was not with *Him* was against Him. He who did not gather with *Him* scattered. Everything now depended on Him alone. He would bear with all unbelief as to His own Person. Grace could not remove that. He could pardon all sin; but to speak against and blaspheme the Holy Ghost (that is, to *acknowledge* the exercise of a power, which is that of God, and to attribute it to Satan) could not be pardoned; for the Pharisees admitted that the devil was cast out, and it was only with malice, with open-eyed deliberate hatred to God, that they attributed it to Satan. And what pardon could there be for this? There was none either in the age of the law [33] or in that

---

[33] Take notice of this expression. We see the manner in which the Holy Ghost passes on from the time then present to the Jews, which would soon end, to the time when the Messiah would set up His kingdom, their "world [age] to come." *We* have a position outside all this, during the suspension of the public establishment of the kingdom. The apostles even did but preach or announce it; they did not establish it. Their miracles were "the powers of the age *to come.*" (Compare 1 Peter 1: 11-13.) This, as we shall see by-and-by, is of great importance. Thus also, with regard to the new covenant, of which Paul was the minister; and yet he did not establish it with Judah and Israel.

of the Messiah. The fate of those who thus acted was
decided. This the Lord would have them understand.
The fruit proved the nature of the tree. It was essentially
bad. They were a generation of vipers. John had told
them the same. Their words condemned them. Upon
this the scribes and Pharisees asked for a sign. This
was nothing but wickedness. They had signs enough.
It was only stirring up the unbelief of the rest.

The Pharisees' request granted: the sign of judgment given: their condemnation by the Gentiles

This request gives the Lord occasion to pronounce the
judgment of this generation.

There should be only the sign of Jonah for this evil
generation. As Jonah was three days and three nights
in the belly of the fish, so should the Son of Man be
three days and three nights in the heart of the earth.
But then, lo, Christ was already rejected.

The Ninevites by their conduct should condemn this
generation in the day of judgment, because they repented
at the preaching of Jonah; and a greater than Jonah was
here. The queen of the south likewise testified against
the wickedness of this perverse generation. Her heart,
attracted by the report of Solomon's wisdom, had led her
to him from the uttermost parts of the earth; and a greater than Solomon was here. Poor ignorant Gentiles understood the wisdom of God in His Word, whether by the
prophet or the king, better than His beloved people, even
when the Great King and Prophet was among them.

Israel's judgment pronounced

This was then His judgment: the unclean spirit (of
idolatry) which had gone out of the people, finding no
rest away from Israel (alas, its true house, whereas they
ought to have been the house of God), should return

with seven spirits worse than itself. They would find the house empty, swept, and garnished; and the last state should be worse than the first. What a solemn judgment of the people was this—that those among whom Jehovah had walked should become the habitation of an unclean spirit, of a superabundance of unclean spirits; not merely of seven, the complete number, but together with these (who would incite them all to madness against God and those who honored God, thus leading them to their own destruction) that other unclean spirit also, who would draw them back into the wretched idolatry from which they had escaped! Israel's judgment was pronounced.

Natural bonds publicly broken: new ones acknowledged

In conclusion, Jesus publicly breaks the bonds that naturally existed between Himself and the people after the flesh, acknowledging those only which were formed by the Word of God, and manifested by doing the will of His Father which was in heaven. Those persons only would He acknowledge as His relations, who were formed after the pattern of the Sermon on the Mount.

Chapter 13

A new position, a new work as the Sower to produce fruit

HIS actions and His words after this bear witness to the new work which He was really doing on the earth. He leaves (chap. 13) the house and sits beside the lake. He takes a new position outside, to proclaim to the multitude that which was His true work. A sower went forth to sow.

The Lord was no longer seeking fruit in His vine. It had been requisite according to God's relations with Israel that He should seek this fruit; but His true service, He well knew, was to bring that which could *produce* fruit, and not to *find* any in men.

It is important to remark here, that the Lord speaks of the visible and outward effect of His work as a Sower. The only occasion here on which He expresses His judgment as to the inward cause is, when He says, "They had no root;" and even here it is a matter of fact. The doctrines respecting the divine operation needed for the production of fruits are not here spoken of. It is the Sower who is displayed, and the result of His sowing, not that which causes the seed to germinate in the earth. In each case, except the first, a certain effect is produced.

The Lord is then here presented as commencing a work which is independent of all former relation between God and men, bearing with Him the seed of the Word, which He sows in the heart by His ministry. Where it abides, where it is understood, where it is neither choked nor dried up, it produces fruit to His glory, and to the happiness and profit of the man who bears it.

Distinction made between the remnant and the nation: the reason for the Lord's use of parables

In verse 11 the Lord shows the reason why He speaks enigmatically to the multitude. A distinction is now definitely made between the remnant and the nation: the latter was under the judgment of blindness pronounced by the prophet Esaias. Blessed were the eyes of the disciples which saw the Emmanuel, the Messiah, the object of the hopes and desires of so many prophets and righteous men. All this marks judgment, and a called and spared remnant.[34]

[34] Compare Mark 4: 33, 34. It was adapted to all if they had ears to hear, but was darkness to the wilful.

The character of the classes to whom the Word comes

I would now make a few remarks on the character of the persons of whom the Lord speaks in the parable.

When the Word is sown in a heart that does not understand it, when it produces no relation of intelligence, of feeling, or of conscience between the heart and God, the enemy takes it away: it does not remain in the heart. He who heard it is not the less guilty: that which was sown in his heart was adapted to every need, to the nature and to the condition of man.

The immediate reception of the Word with joy, in the next case, tends rather to prove that the heart will not retain it; for it is scarcely probable in such a case that the conscience was reached. A conscience touched by the Word makes a man serious; he sees himself in the presence of God, which is always a serious thing, whatever may be the attraction of His grace, or the hope inspired by His goodness. If the conscience has not been reached, there is no root. The Word was received for the joy it imparted; when it brings tribulation, it is given up. When the conscience has been already exercised, the gospel brings at once joy; but when not, it awakens the conscience where there is a real work. In the first case it is the answer to and meets the wants already there. In the second it creates those wants.

Every day's history is, alas, the sad and best explanation of the third class. There is no ill-will, there is barrenness.

The Word understood: the true knowledge of God is eternal life

That the Word was understood is only affirmed of those who bear fruit. The true understanding of the Word brings a soul into connection with God, because the Word reveals God—expresses what He is. If I understand it,

I know Him; and the true knowledge of God (that is, of the Father and of His Son Jesus Christ) is eternal life. Now, whatever may be the degree of light, it is always God thus revealed who is made known by the Word that Jesus sows. Thus, being begotten of the Word, we shall produce, in diverse measures, the fruits of the life of God in this world. For the subject here is the effect, in this world, of the reception of the truth brought by Jesus (not heaven, nor that which God does in the heart to make the seed bear fruit).

The parable of the Sower as the great principle of Christ's service

This parable does not speak, as a similitude, of the kingdom, though the Word sown was the Word of the kingdom, but of the great elementary principle of the service of Christ in the universality of its application, and as it was realized in His own Person and service while on the earth, and after He was gone, though fuller subjects of grace might then be brought out.

Similitudes of the kingdom characterized by the King's absence: their two divisions

In the six following parables we find similitudes of the kingdom. We must remember that it is the kingdom established during the rejection of the King,[35] and which consequently has a peculiar character. That is to say, it is characterized by the absence of the King, adding to this, in the explanation of the first parable, the effect of His return.

The first three of these six parables present the kingdom in its outward forms in the world. They are ad-

---

[35] Remark here, that chapter 12 having brought before us the judgment of the Jewish people, we have now the kingdom as it is in the absence of the King, chapter 13; the assembly as built by Christ, chapter 16; and the kingdom in glory, chapter 17.

dressed to the multitude. The last three present the kingdom according to the estimate of the Holy Ghost, according to the reality of its character as seen by God—the mind and counsel of God in it. They are addressed consequently to the disciples alone. The public establishment of the kingdom in the righteousness and power of God is also announced to the latter, in the explanation of the parable of the tares.

The outward form of the kingdom

Let us consider first the exterior of the kingdom publicly announced to the multitude—the outward form which the kingdom would assume.

We must remember that the King, that is, the Lord Jesus, was rejected on earth; that the Jews, in rejecting Him, had condemned themselves; that, the Word of God being used to accomplish the work of Him whom the Father had sent, the Lord thus made it known that He established the kingdom, not by His power exercised in righteousness and in judgment, but by bearing testimony to the hearts of men; and that the kingdom now assumed a character connected with man's responsibility, and with the result of the Word of light being sown in the earth, addressed to the hearts of men, and left as a system of truth to the faithfulness and the care of men (God, however, still holding good His sovereign right for the preservation of His children and of the truth itself). This latter part is not the subject of these parables. I have introduced it here because it might otherwise have been supposed that everything depended absolutely on man. Had it been so, alas, all would have been lost.

The parable of the tares: the kingdom here on earth in men's hands

The parable of the tares is the first. It gives us a general idea of the effect of these sowings as to the kingdom;

or rather, the result of having for the moment committed the kingdom here below to the hands of men.

The result was that the kingdom here below no longer presented as a whole the appearance of the Lord's own work. *He* sows not tares. Through the carelessness and the infirmity of men, the enemy found means to sow these tares. Observe that this does not apply to the heathen or to the Jews, but to the evil done among Christians by Satan through bad doctrines, bad teachers and their adherents. The Lord Jesus sowed. Satan, while men slept, sowed also. There were judaizers, philosophers, heretics who held with both the former on the one hand, or on the other opposed the truth of the Old Testament.

Nevertheless Christ had only sown good seed. Must the tares then be rooted out? Clearly the condition of the kingdom during the absence of Christ depends on the answer to this question; and it throws light also upon that condition. But there was still less power to bring in a remedy than there had been to prevent the evil. All must remain unremedied until the King's interposition at the time of harvest. The kingdom of heaven *on earth,* such as it is in the hands of men, must remain a mingled system. Heretics, false brethren, will be there, as well as the fruit of the Lord's Word, testifying, in this last dealing of God with him, man's inability to maintain that which is good and pure in its pristine state. So it has ever been.[36]

Execution of judgment on what is not of God

At the time of harvest (a phrase that designates a certain space of time during which the events connected with the harvest will take place)—"at the time of harvest" the Lord will deal first, in His providence, with the tares.   I

---

[36] It is a solemn thought that the first act of man has been to spoil what God has set up good. So with Adam, so with Noah, so with the law, so with the priesthood of Aaron, so with the son of David, so even Nebuchadnezzar, so the Church. In Paul's days all sought their own, not the things of Jesus Christ. All is made good, better, and stable in the Messiah.

say, "in His providence," because He employs the angels. The tares shall be bound in bundles ready to be burnt.

We must observe that outward things in the world are the subject here—acts which root out corruption—corruption that has grown up in the midst of Christianity.

The servants are not capable of doing this. The intermingling (caused by their weakness and carelessness) is such, that in gathering out the tares they would root up the wheat also. Not only discernment, but the practical power of separation would be wanting to carry out their purpose. When once the tares are there, the servants have nothing to do with them as to their presence in this world, in Christendom. Their service is with the good. The work of purging Christendom from them was not in their province. It is a work of *judgment* on that which is not of God, belonging to Him who can execute it according to the perfection of a knowledge that embraces everything, and a power that nothing escapes; which, if two men are in one bed, knows how to take the one and leave the other. The execution of judgment on the wicked in this world does not belong to the servants of Christ.[37] He will accomplish it by the angels of His power, to whom He commits the execution of this work.

Gathering the wheat

After the binding of the tares He gathers the wheat into His garner. There is no binding the wheat in bundles; He takes it all to Himself. Such is the end of that which concerns the outward appearance of the kingdom here below. This is not all that the parable can teach us, but it ends the subject of which this part of the chapter speaks. During the absence of Jesus the result of His sowing will be marred, as a whole down here, by the work of the enemy. At the close He will bind all the enemy's

---

[37] I speak here of those who will have been His servants on earth during His absence. For angels are also His servants, as well as the saints of the age to come.

work in bundles; that is, He will prepare them in this world for judgment. He will then take away the Church. It is evident that this terminates the scene below which goes on during His absence. The judgment is not yet executed. Before speaking of it the Lord gives other pictures of the forms which the kingdom will assume during His absence.

The grain of mustard-seed: the form of a great power

That which had been sown as a grain of mustard-seed becomes a great tree; a symbol that represents a great power in the earth. The Assyrian, Pharaoh, Nebuchadnezzar, are set before us in the Word as great trees. Such would be the form of the kingdom, which began in littleness through the Word sown by the Lord, and afterwards by His disciples. That which this seed produced would gradually assume the form of a great power, making itself prominent on the earth, so that others would shelter themselves under it, as birds under the branches of a tree. This has, indeed, been the case.

The leaven: corruption in the doctrine

We next find that it would not only be a great tree in the earth, but that the kingdom would be characterized as a system of doctrine, which would diffuse itself—a profession, which would enclose all it reached within its sphere of influence. The whole of the three measures would be leavened. I need not dwell here on the fact that the word "leaven" is always used in a bad sense by the sacred writers; but the Holy Ghost gives us to understand that it is not the regenerative power of the word in the heart of an individual, bringing him back to God; neither is it simply a power acting by outward strength, such as Pharaoh, Nebuchadnezzar, and the other great trees of Scripture. But it is a system of doctrine that should characterize the mass, pervading it throughout. It is not faith properly so called, nor is it life. It is a religion; it is Christendom. A profession of doctrine, in hearts which will bear neither the truth nor God, connects itself always with corruption in the doctrine itself.

This parable of the leaven concludes His instructions to the multitude. All was now addressed to them in parables, for they did not receive *Him* their King, and He spoke of things that supposed His rejection, and an aspect of the kingdom unknown to the revelations of the Old Testament, which have in view either the kingdom in power, or a little remnant receiving, amid sufferings, the word of the Prophet-King who had been rejected.

With His disciples, in the house, in secluded intimacy

After this parable Jesus no longer remains by the seaside with the multitude—a place suited to the position in which He stood towards the people after the testimony borne at the end of chapter 12, and whither He had repaired on quitting the house. He now re-enters the house with His disciples; and there, in secluded intimacy with them, He reveals the true character—the object—of the kingdom of heaven, the result of that which was done in it, and the means which should be taken to cleanse everything on earth, when the outward history of the kingdom during His absence should have terminated. That is to say, we find here that which characterizes the kingdom to the spiritual man, that which he understands as the true mind of God with regard to the kingdom, and the judgment which should purge out from it all that was contrary to Him—the exercise of power which should render it outwardly in accordance with the heart of God.

The explanation of the parable of the tares to His own disciples

We have seen its outward history ending with this, the wheat hidden in the garner, and the tares left in bundles

on the earth ready to be burnt. The explanation of this
parable resumes the history of the kingdom at that period;
only it gives us to understand and distinguish the different parts of the intermixture, ascribing each part to its
true author. The field is the world,[38] there the Word was
sown for the establishment, in this manner, of the kingdom. The good seed were the children of the kingdom;
they belonged to it really according to God; they are its
heirs. The Jews were no longer so, and it was no longer
the privilege of natural birth. The children of the kingdom were born of the Word. But among these, in order
to spoil the Lord's work, the enemy introduced all sorts
of people, the fruit of the doctrines which he had sown
among those who were born of the truth. This is the work of
Satan in the place where the doctrine of Christ had been
planted. The harvest is the end of the age.[39] The reapers
are the angels. It will be remarked here that the Lord
does not explain historically that which took place, but
the terms used to bring in the issue when the harvest is
come. The fulfilment of that which is historical in the
parable is supposed; and He passes on to give the great
result outside that which was the kingdom during His
absence on high. The wheat (that is, the Church) is in
the barn, and the tares in bundles on the earth. But He
takes all that constitutes these bundles, all that as evil
offends God in the kingdom, and casts it into the furnace
of fire, where there is wailing and gnashing of teeth.
After this judgment the righteous shall shine forth like
Himself, the true Sun of that day of glory—of the age
to come, in the kingdom of their Father. Christ will have
received the kingdom from the Father whose children they

[38] Manifestly it was not in the Church that the Lord began to sow: it
did not then exist. But He distinguishes Israel here from the world,
and speaks of the latter. He looked for fruit in Israel; He sows in the
world, because Israel after all His culture brought forth no fruit.

[39] Not merely the instant that terminates it, but the acts that accomplish the purpose of God in terminating it—*synteleia*.

were; and they shall shine forth in it with Him according to that character.

Thus we find for the multitude, the results on earth of the divine sowing, and the machinations of the enemy—the kingdom presented under this form; afterwards the confederacies of the wicked among themselves apart from their natural order as growing in the field; and the taking away of the Church. For His own disciples, the Lord explains all that was necessary to make them fully understand the language of the parable. We then find the judgment executed by the Son of Man upon the wicked, who are cast into the fire; and the *manifestation* of the righteous in glory (these last events taking place after the Lord had risen up and put an end to the outward form of the kingdom of heaven upon earth, the wicked being gathered in companies, and the saints taken up to heaven).[40]

The treasure hidden in the field

And now, having explained the public history and its results in judgment and in glory for the full instruction of His disciples, the Lord communicates to them the thoughts of God with respect to what was going on upon earth, while the outward and earthly events of the kingdom were being developed—that which the spiritual man should discern in them. To him, to one who understood the purpose of God, the kingdom of heaven was like a treasure hidden in a field. A man finds the treasure, and buys the field in order to possess it. The field was not his object, but the treasure that was in it. Thus Christ has purchased the world. He possesses it by right. His object is the treasure hidden in it, His own people, all the glory of the redemption connected with it; in a word, the Church looked at, not in its moral and in a certain sense divine

---

[40] Remark too here that the kingdom of heaven is parcelled out into two parts, the kingdom of the Son of Man, and the kingdom of our Father: the objects of judgment in what is subjected to Christ, and a place like His before the Father for sons.

beauty, but as the special object of the desires and of the sacrifice of the Lord—that which His heart had found in this world according to the counsels and the mind of God.

In this parable it is the powerful attraction of this "new thing," which induces the one who has found it to purchase the whole place, that he may obtain possession of it.

The Jews were nothing new; the world had no attraction; but this new treasure induced the One who had discovered it to sell all He had that He might gain it. In fact Christ forsook everything. He not only emptied Himself to redeem us, but He renounced all that belonged to Him as Man, as the Messiah on earth, the promises, His royal rights, His life, to take possession of the world which contained in it this treasure, the people whom He loved.

The pearl of great price

In the parable of the pearl of great price we have again the same idea, but it is modified by others. A man was *seeking* goodly pearls. He knew what he was about. He had taste, discernment, knowledge, as to that which he sought. It was the well-known beauty of the thing that caused his research. He knows when he has found one corresponding to his ideas, that it is worth while to sell all that he may acquire it. It is worth this in the eyes of one who can estimate its value. And he buys nothing else along with it. Thus Christ has found in the Church by itself a beauty and (because of this beauty) a value, which made Him give up all to obtain it. It is just so with regard to the kingdom. Considering the state of man, of the Jews even, the glory of God required that all should be given up in order to have this new thing; for there was nothing in man that He could take to Himself. Not only He was content to give up all for the possession of this new thing, but that which His heart seeks for, that which He finds nowhere else, He finds in that which God has given Him in the kingdom. He bought no other pearls. Until He found this pearl, He had no inducement to sell all that He had. As soon as He sees it, His mind is made up; He forsakes all for it. Its value decides Him, for He knows how to judge, and He seeks with discernment.

I do not say that the children of the kingdom are not actuated by the same principle. When we have learnt what it is to be a child of the kingdom, we forsake all that we may enjoy it, that we may be of the pearl of great price. But we do not buy that which is not the treasure, in order to obtain it; and we are very far from seeking goodly pearls before we have found the one of great price. In their full force these parables only apply to Christ. The intention in these parables is to bring out that which was then doing, in contrast with all that had taken place before—with the Lord's relations to the Jews.

The net cast into the sea: the good fish

There remains yet one of the seven—that of the net cast into the sea. In this parable there is no change in the persons employed, that is to say, in the parable itself. The same persons who cast the net draw it to shore, and make the separation by gathering the good fish into vessels, taking no further notice of the bad. Securing the good fish is the work of those who draw the net to shore. It is only when landed that this is done. The sorting is their work, doubtless; but they have only to do with the good fish. They know them. This is their business, the object of their fishing. Others indeed come, and are found in the net together with the good; but these are not good. No other judgment is needed. The fishermen know the good. These are not such. They leave them. This forms a part of the history of the kingdom of heaven. The judgment of the wicked is not found here. The bad are left on the shore, when the fishermen gather the good into vessels. The final destiny of either good or bad is not given here. It does not take place on the shore with respect to the good; nor as to the bad by simply leaving them there. It is subsequent to the action of the parable; and, with respect to the bad, it does not take place merely by their separation from the good with whom they had been intermingled, but by their destruction. Neither in this parable, nor in that of the tares and wheat, does the execution of judgment form part of the parable itself. There the tares are bound and left on the field; here they are cast away out of the netful.

Thus the gospel net has been cast into the sea of the nations, and has enclosed of all kinds. After this general gathering, which has filled the net, the agents of the Lord, having to do with the good, gather them together, separating them from the bad. Remark here that this is a similitude of the kingdom. It is the character which the kingdom assumes when the gospel has assembled together a mass of good and bad. At the end, when the net has been drawn so that all kinds are enclosed in it, the good are set apart because they are precious, the others are left. The good are gathered into divers vessels. The saints are gathered, not by the angels, but by the work of those who have labored in the name of the Lord. The distinction is not made by judgment, but by the servants occupied with the good.

The public execution of judgment

The execution of the judgment is another matter. The laborers have nothing to do with that. At the end of the age, the angels shall come forth and sever the wicked from among the just, not the just from among the rest as the fishermen did, and shall cast them into the furnace of fire, where there shall be wailing and gnashing of teeth. Here nothing is said of their being occupied about the just. Gathering them into vessels was not the angels' work, but that of the fishermen. The angels are in both parables occupied with the wicked. The public result had been given, whether during the period of the kingdom of heaven, or afterwards, in the parable of the tares. It is not repeated here. The work to be done with regard to the righteous when the net is full is added here. The destiny of the wicked is repeated to distinguish the work done with respect to them from that wrought by means of the fishermen, who gather the good into divers vessels. Still it is presented under another aspect; and the just are left where they were. In the parable of the tares the judgment of the wicked is declared as in this. They are cast out into weeping and gnashing of teeth, but there the general state of the kingdom is revealed, and we have the righteous shining forth as the sun—the higher part of the kingdom. Here it is only what the intelligent understand, what the spiritual mind sees; the just are put into vessels. There is a separation by spiritual power before judgment, which there was not in the general public state of the kingdom, but only what providence did publicly in the field, and the good grain received above. Here the separation is by dealings with the good. This was the main point for spiritual intelligence. Public display is not the point; only judgment will be executed on the wicked, in fact; then the just will be left there.[41]

The explanation of the parable of the fish

In the explanation of the second parable, it is absolute judgment in the case of the tares, destroying and consuming that which remains on the field, already collected together and separated providentially from the wheat. The angels are sent at the end, not to separate the tares from the wheat (that was done), but to cast the tares into the

[41] In all symbolical prophecies and parables, the explanation goes beyond the parable and adds facts; because the judgment executed publicly testifies of that which in the time of the parable can only be discerned spiritually. This latter may be spiritually understood. The result is, judgment will publicly declare it, so that we are always to go beyond the parable in the explanation. Judgment explains publicly what is only understood spiritually before, and brings in a new order of things. (Compare Dan. 7.)

fire, thus cleansing the kingdom. In the explanation of
the parable of the fish (ver. 49) the sorting itself takes
place. There will be just ones on the earth, and the wicked
will be separated from among them. The practical instruction of this parable is the separation of the good
from the wicked, and the gathering together in companies
of many of the former; this is done more than once, many
others of the same being gathered elsewhere into one also.
The servants of the Lord are the instruments employed in
what takes place in the parable itself.

"Things new and old"

These parables contain things new and old. The doctrine of the kingdom, for instance, was a well-known doctrine. That the kingdom should take the forms described
by the Lord, that it should embrace the whole world without distinction, the people of God drawing their existence
not from Abraham but from the Word—all this was quite
new. All was of God. The scribe had knowledge of the
kingdom, but was entirely ignorant of the character it
would assume, as the kingdom of heaven planted in this
world by means of the word, on which all here depends.

Work resumed among the Jews: Christ rejected as Prophet as well as King

The Lord resumes His work among the Jews.[42] To
them He was only "the carpenter's son." They knew His
family after the flesh. The kingdom of heaven was noth-

[42] The chapters which follow are striking in their character. Christ's
Person as the Jehovah of Psalm 132 is brought out, but Israel sent away,
the disciples left alone, while He prays on high. He returns, rejoins
the disciples, and the Gadarene world owns Him. Then we have in
chapter 15 the full moral description of the ground on which Israel
stood actually, and ought to stand, but carried much farther out into
what man's heart is; and then what God is, revealed in grace to faith,
even if in a Gentile. Historically He still owns Israel, but in divine perfection, and now in human administrative power; and then (chap. 16)
the Church is brought in prophetically; and in chapter 17 the kingdom
of glory in vision. In chapter 16 they are forbidden to say He is the
Christ. This is over.

ing in their eyes. The revelation of this kingdom was carried on elsewhere, and there the knowledge of divine things were communicated. The former saw nothing beyond those things which the natural heart could perceive. The blessing of the Lord was arrested by their unbelief: He was rejected as prophet, as well as king, by Israel.

Chapter 14

The death of John the Baptist

OUR Gospel resumes the historical course of these revelations, but in such a manner as to exhibit the spirit by which the people were animated. Herod (loving his earthly power and his own glory more than submission to the testimony of God, and more bound by a false human idea than by his conscience, although in many things he appears to have owned the power of the truth) had cut off the head of the forerunner of the Messiah, John the Baptist; whom he had already imprisoned, in order to remove out of the sight of his wife the faithful reprover of the sin in which she lived.

Jesus as Jehovah, the Supplier of all His people's wants

Jesus is sensible of the import of this, which is reported to Him. Accomplishing in lowly service (however personally exalted above him), together with John, the testimony of God in the congregation, He felt Himself united in heart and in His work to him; for faithfulness in the midst of all evil binds hearts very closely together; and Jesus had condescended to take a place in which faithfulness was concerned. (See Psalm 40: 9, 10.) On hearing therefore of John's death He retires into a desert place. But while departing from the multitude who thus began to act openly in the rejection of the testimony of God, He does not cease to be the supplier of all their wants, and to testify thus that He who could divinely minister to all their need was amongst them. For the multitude, who felt these wants and who, if they had not faith, yet admired the power of Jesus, follow Him into the desert place; and Jesus, moved with compassion, heals all their sick. In the evening His disciples beg Him to send the multitude away that they may procure food. He refuses and bears a remarkable testimony to the presence, in His own Person, of Him who was to satisfy the poor of His people with bread. (Psalm 132.) Jehovah, the Lord, who established the throne of David, was there in the Person of Him who should inherit that throne. I doubt not the twelve baskets of fragments refer to the number which, in Scripture, always designates the perfection of administrative power in man.

The disciples as ministers of the blessing and power of the kingdom

Remark also here, that the Lord expects to find His twelve disciples capable of being the instruments of His acts of blessing and power, administering according to His own power the blessings of the kingdom. "Give *ye* them," said He, "to eat." This applies to the blessing of the Lord's kingdom, and to the disciples of Jesus, the twelve, as being its ministers; but it is likewise an all-important principle with regard to the effect of faith in every intervention of God in grace. Faith should be able to use the power that acts in such intervention, to produce the works which are proper to that power, according to the order of the dispensation and the intelligence it has repecting it. We shall find this principle again elsewhere more fully developed.

The disciples wished to send the multitude away, not knowing how to use the power of Christ. They should have been able to avail themselves of it in Israel's behalf, according to the glory of Him who was among them.

The disciples in the midst of the sea: Jesus in the storm and in the calm

If now the Lord demonstrated with perfect patience by His actions that He who could thus bless Israel was in the midst of His people, He does not the less bear testimony to His separation from that people in consequence of their unbelief. He makes His disciples get into a ship to cross the sea alone; and, dismissing the multitude Himself, He goes up into a mountain apart to pray; while the ship that contained the disciples was tossing on the waves of the sea with a contrary wind: a living picture of that which has taken place. God has indeed sent forth His people to cross the stormy sea of the world alone, meeting with an opposition against which it is hard to strive. Meanwhile Jesus prays alone on high. He has sent away the Jewish people, who had surrounded Him during the period of His presence here below. The departure of the disciples, besides its general character, sets before us peculiarly the Jewish remnant. Peter individually, in coming out of the ship, goes in figure beyond the position of this remnant. He represents that faith which, forsaking the earthly accommodation of the ship, goes out to meet Jesus who has revealed Himself to it, and walks upon the sea—a bold undertaking, but based on the word of Jesus, "Come." Yet remark here that this walk has no other foundation than, "If it be Thou," that is to say, Jesus Himself. There is no support, no possibility of walking, if Christ be lost sight of. All depends on Him. There is a known means in the ship; there is nothing but faith, which looks to Jesus, for walking on the water. Man, as mere man, sinks by the very fact of being there. Nothing can sustain itself except that faith which draws from Jesus the strength that is in Him, and which therefore imitates

Him. But it is sweet to imitate Him; and one is then nearer to Him, more like Him. This is the true position of the Church, in contrast with the remnant in their ordinary character. Jesus walks on the water as on the solid ground. He who created the elements as they are could well dispose of their qualities at His pleasure. He permits storms to arise for the trial of our faith. He walks on the stormy wave as well as on the calm. Moreover the storm makes no difference. He who sinks in the waters does so in the calm as well as in the storm, and he who can walk upon them will do so in the storm as well as in the calm—that is to say, unless circumstances are looked to and so faith fail, and the Lord is forgotten. For often circumstances make us forget Him where faith ought to enable us to overcome circumstances through our walking by faith in Him who is above them all. Nevertheless —blessed be God!—He who walks in His own power upon the water is there to sustain the faith and the wavering steps of the poor disciple; and at any rate that faith had brought Peter so near to Jesus that His outstretched hand could sustain him. Peter's fault was that he looked at the waves, at the storm (which, after all, had nothing to do with it), instead of looking at Jesus, who was unchanged, and who was walking on those very waves, as his faith should have observed. Still the cry of his distress brought the power of Jesus into action, as his faith ought to have done; only it was now to his shame, instead of being in the enjoyment of communion and walking like the Lord.

In the ship and with the remnant: in Gennesaret and in future in the world

Jesus having entered the ship, the wind ceases. Even so it will be when Jesus returns to the remnant of His people in this world. Then also will He be worshipped as the Son of God by all that are in the ship, with the remnant of Israel. In Gennesaret Jesus again exercises the power which shall hereafter drive out from the earth all the evil that Satan has brought in. For when He returns, the world will recognize Him. It is a fine picture of the result of Christ's rejection, which this Gospel has already made known to us as taking place in the midst of the Jewish nation.

Chapter 15

God's rejection of the Jewish system

CHAPTER 15 displays man and God, the moral contrast between the doctrine of Christ and that of the Jews; and thus the Jewish system is rejected morally by God. When I speak of the system, I speak of their whole moral condition, systematized by the hypocrisy that sought to conceal iniquity, while increasing it in the sight of God, before whom they presented themselves. They made use of His name in order to sink lower, under the pretence of piety, than the laws of natural conscience. It is thus that a religious system becomes the great instrument of the power of the enemy, and more especially when that, of which it still bears the name, was instituted by God. But then man is judged, for Judaism was man with God's law and God's culture.

The Lord's exposure and judgment of the leaders' hypocrisy, selfishness and avarice

The judgment which the Lord pronounces on this system of hypocrisy, while manifesting the consequent rejection of Israel, gives rise to instruction that goes thus much farther; and which, searching the heart of man, and judging man according to that which proceeds from it, proves the heart to be a spring of all iniquity; and thus makes it evident that all true morality has its basis in the convic-

tion and confession of sin. For, without this, the heart
is always false and flatters itself in vain. Thus also Jesus
goes to the root of everything, and comes out of the
special and temporary relations of the Jewish nation, to
enter on the true morality which belongs to all ages. The
disciples did not observe the traditions of the elders; about
these the Lord did not concern Himself. He avails Himself of the accusation, to lay it upon the conscience of
their accusers, that the judgment occasioned by the rejection of the Son of God was authorized also on the
ground of those relationships that already existed between
God and Israel. They made the commandment of God
of none effect through their traditions; and that in a
most important point, and one even on which all earthly
blessings depended for the children of Israel. By their
own ordinances also Jesus exposes the consummate hypocrisy, the selfishness and avarice, of those who pretended
to guide the people, and to form their heart to morality
and to the worship of Jehovah. Isaiah had already pronounced their judgment.

Man shown in his real colors before God

Afterwards He shows the multitude that it was a question of what man was, of what proceeded from his heart,
from within him; and points out the sad streams that
flow from that corrupt spring. But it was the simple
truth with respect to the heart of man, as known by God,
which scandalized the self-righteous men of the world,
which was unintelligible even to the disciples. Nothing so
simple as the truth when it is known; nothing so difficult,
so obscure, when a judgment is to be formed respecting
it by the heart of man, who does not possess the truth;
for he judges after his own thoughts, and the truth is not
in them. In short, Israel, and specially religious Israel,
and true morality are set in contrast: man is set in his
proper responsibility, and in his real colors before God.

Outside forms or inward purity

Jesus searches the heart; but, acting in grace, He acts according to the heart of God, and manifests it by coming out, both for the one and for the other, of the conventional terms of God's relationship with Israel. A divine Person, God, may walk in the covenant He has given, but cannot be confined to it. And the unfaithfulness of His people to it is the occasion of the revelation of Him passing out beyond that place. And note, here, the effect of traditional religion in blinding moral judgment. What clearer or plainer than that what came out of the mouth and heart defiled a man, not what he ate? But the disciples through the vile influence of Pharisaic teaching, putting outside forms for inward purity, could not understand it.

The Canaanite's request: the Lord's seeming harshness

Christ now leaves the borders of Israel, and His disputes with the learned men of Jerusalem, to visit those places which were farthest off from Jewish privileges. He departs into the coast of Tyre and Sidon, the cities which He had Himself used as examples of that which was farthest from repentance; see chapter 11, where He classes them with Sodom and Gomorrha as more hardened than they. A woman comes out of these countries. She was one of the accursed race, according to the principles that distinguished Israel. She was a Canaanite. She comes to beg the interposition of Jesus on behalf of her daughter, who was possessed by a devil.

In begging this favor, she addresses Jesus by the title, which faith knew to be His connection with the Jews—"Son of David." This gives rise to a full development of the Lord's position, and, at the same time, of the conditions under which man might hope to share the effect of His goodness, yea, to the revelation of God Himself.

As the *Son of David,* He has nothing to do with a *Canaanite.* He makes her no answer. The disciples desired to get rid of her by granting her request, in order to have done with her importunity. The Lord answers them, that He was not sent but to the lost sheep of the house of Israel. This was indeed the truth. Whatever may have been the counsels of God manifested on occasion of His rejection (see Isaiah 49), He was the minister of the circumcision for the truth of God, to fulfil His promises made to the fathers.

Taking her real place the Canaanite tastes God's sovereign divine goodness to Gentiles

The woman, in more simple and direct language, the more natural expression of her feelings, begs for the merciful interposition of Him in whose power she trusted. The Lord answers her, that it is not meet to take the children's bread and give it to dogs. We see here His true position, as come to Israel; the promises were for the children of the kingdom. The Son of David was the minister of these promises. Could He as such blot out the distinction of the people of God?

But that faith which derives strength from necessity, and which finds no resource but in the Lord Himself, accepts the humiliation of its position, and deems that with Him there is bread for the hunger of those who have no right to it. It perseveres, too, because there is a felt want, and faith in the power of Him who is come in grace.

What had the Lord done by His apparent harshness? He had brought the poor woman to the expression, to the sense, of her real place before God, that is to say, to the truth as to herself. But, then, was it the truth to say that God was less good than she believed, less rich in mercy towards the destitute, whose only hope and trust was in that mercy? This would have been to deny the character and the nature of God, of which He was the expression, the truth, and the witness, on earth; it would have been to deny Himself, and the object of His mission. He could not say, "God has not a crumb for such." He answers, in fulness of heart, "O woman, great is thy faith; be it unto thee even as thou wilt." God comes out of the narrow limits of His covenant with the Jews, to act in His sovereign goodness according to His own nature. He comes out to be God in goodness, and not merely Jehovah in Israel.

The sense of need and the Source of blessing

But this goodness is exercised towards one who is brought, in the presence of that goodness, to know that she has no right to it. To this point the seeming harshness of the Lord had been leading her. She received all from grace, while in herself unworthy of all. It is thus, and thus only, that every soul obtains blessing. It is not merely the sense of need—the woman had that from the beginning, it was that which brought her there. It is not sufficient merely to own that the Lord Jesus can meet that need—the woman came with that acknowledgment; we must be in the presence of the only source of blessing, and be brought to feel that, although we are there, we have no right to avail ourselves of it. And this is a terrible position. When it comes to this, all is grace. God can then act according to His own goodness, and He answers every desire which the heart can form for its happiness.

The heart of man and the heart of God: God's wisdom, faithfulness and grace

Thus we see Christ here as a minister of the circumcision for the truth of God, to fulfil the promises made to the fathers, and that the Gentiles also might glorify God for His mercy, as it is written. At the same time this last truth makes manifest the real condition of man, and the full and perfect grace of God. On this He acts, while still faithful to His promises; and the wisdom of God is displayed in a manner that calls forth our admiration.

We see how much the introduction, in this place, of the story of the Syro-Phenician woman develops and illustrates this part of our Gospel. The beginning of the chapter shows forth the moral condition of the Jews, the falseness of Pharisaic and sacerdotal religiousness; brings out the real state of man as man, what the heart of man was the source of; and then reveals the heart of God as manifested in Jesus. His dealings with this woman display the faithfulness of God to His promises; and the blessing finally granted exhibits the full grace of God, in connection with the manifestation of the real condition of man, acknowledged by conscience—grace rising above the curse which lay upon the object of this grace—rising above everything to make itself a way to the need which faith presented to it.

In Galilee: renewed evidences of Jehovah's compassions and tender mercies

The Lord now departs thence and goes into Galilee, the place where He was in connection with the despised remnant of the Jews. It was neither Zion, nor the temple, nor Jerusalem, but the poor of the flock, where the people were sitting in gross darkness. (Isa. 8, 9.) Thither His compassions follow this poor remnant, and are again exercised in their behalf. He renews the evidences, not only of His tender mercies, but of His presence who satisfied the poor of His people with bread. Here however it is not in the administrative power which He could bestow on His disciples, but according to His own perfection and acting from Himself. He provides for the remnant of His people. Accordingly it is the fulness of *seven* baskets of fragments that is gathered up. He departs also without anything else taking place.

We have seen eternal morality, and truth in the inward parts, substituted for the hypocrisy of forms, man's use of legal religion and man's heart shown to be a source of evil and nought else, God's heart fully revealed that rises above all dispensation to show full grace in Christ. Thus dispensations are set aside though fully owned, and man and God fully shown out in doing so. It is a wonderful chapter as to what is everlasting in truth as to God, and as to what the revelation of God shows man to be. And this, note, gives occasion to the revelation of the assembly in the next chapter, which is not a dispensation but founded on what Christ is, Son of the living God. In chapter 12 Christ was dispensationally rejected, and the kingdom of heaven substituted in chapter 13. Here man is set aside and what he had made of law, and God acts in His own grace above all dispensations. Then come the assembly and the kingdom in glory.

Chapter 16

The Lord's answer to unbelief in heart and will

CHAPTER 16 goes farther than the revelation of the simple grace of God. Jesus reveals what was about to be formed in the counsels of that grace, where He was owned, showing the rejection of the proud among His people, that He abhors them as they abhor Him. (Zech. 11.) Shutting their eyes (through perversity of will) to the marvellous and beneficent signs of His power, which He constantly bestowed on the poor who sought Him, the Pharisees and Sadducees—struck with these manifestations, yet unbelieving in heart and will—demand a sign from heaven. He rebukes them for their unbelief, showing them that they knew how to discern the signs of the

weather; yet the signs of the times were far more striking.
They were the adulterous and wicked 'géneration, and *He
leaves them*: significant expressions of what was now
passing in Israel.

The forgetful disciples warned and reminded in patient grace

He warns His forgetful disciples against the devices of
these subtle adversaries to the truth, and to Him whom
God had sent to reveal it. Israel is abandoned, as a nation, in the persons of their leaders. At the same time in
patient grace He recalls His disciples to the remembrance
of what explained His words to them.

The Father's revelation of the Person of Christ to Peter

Afterwards He questions His disciples as to what men
in general said of Him. It was all matter of opinion, not
of faith; that is, the uncertainty that belongs to moral indifference, to the absence of that conscious need of soul
which can rest only in the truth, in the Saviour one has
found. He then inquires what they themselves said of
Him. Peter, to whom the Father had deigned to reveal
Him, declares his faith, saying, "Thou art the Christ, the
Son of the *living* God." No uncertainty, no mere opinion
is here, but the powerful effect of the revelation, made by
the Father Himself, of the Person of Christ, to the disciple whom He had elected for this privilege.

Three classes displayed

Here the condition of the people displays itself in a
remarkable manner, not, as in the preceding chapter, with
respect to the law, but with respect to Christ, who had
been presented to them. We see it in contrast with the

revelation of His glory to those who followed Him. We have thus three classes: first, haughty unbelieving Pharisees; next, persons conscious and owning there was divine power and authority in Christ, but indifferent; lastly, the revelation of God and divinely given faith.

Grace contrasted with disobedience to, and perversion of, the law

In the fifteenth chapter, grace towards one who had no hope but in it, is put in contrast with disobedience to and hypocritical perversion of the law, by which the scribes and Pharisees sought to cover their disobedience with the pretence of piety.

The revelation of Christ's Person as the foundation of the assembly and administration of the kingdom

The sixteenth chapter, judging the unbelief of the Pharisees respecting the Person of Christ, and setting aside these perverse men, brings in the revelation of His Person as the foundation of the assembly, which was to take the place of the Jews as the witness for God in the earth; and announces the counsels of God with respect to its establishment. It shows us, in adjunction to this, the administration of the kingdom, as it was now being established on the earth.

Christ the Messiah, the Son of God

Let us consider, first, the revelation of His Person.

Peter confesses Him to be the Christ, the fulfilment of the promises made by God, and of the prophecies that announced their realization. He was the One who should come, the Messiah whom God had promised.

Moreover, He was the Son of God. The second Psalm

had declared that, in spite of the schemings of the leaders
of the people, and the haughty animosity of the kings of
the earth, God's King should be anointed on the hill of
Zion. He was the Son, begotten of God. The kings and
judges of the earth[43] are called to submit themselves to
Him, lest they should be smitten with the rod of His
power, when He takes the heathen for His inheritance.
Thus the true believer waited for the Son of God born in
due time upon this earth. Peter confessed Jesus to be the
Son of God. So had Nathanael also: "Thou art the Son
of God, Thou art the King of Israel." And, still later,
Martha did the same.

The Son of the living God, the rock foundation of the unchangeable power of life

Peter however, especially taught of the Father, adds to
his confession a word simple, yet full of power: "Thou
art the Son of the *living* God." Not only He who fulfils
the promises, and answers to the prophecies; it is of the
living God that He is the Son, of Him in whom *is* life and
life-giving power.

He inherits that power of life in God which nothing can
overcome or destroy. Who can vanquish the power of
Him—of this Son—who came forth from "Him that
liveth"? Satan has the power of death; it is he who holds
man under the dominion of this dreadful consequence of
sin; and that, by the just judgment of God which constitutes its power. The expression "The gates of hades,"
of the invisible world, refers to this kingdom of Satan. It
is then on this power, which' leaves the stronghold of the
enemy without strength, that the assembly is built. The
life of God shall not be destroyed. The Son of the living

---

[43] The study of the Psalms will have made us understand that this
is the connection with the establishment of the Jewish remnant in
blessing in the last days.

God shall not be overcome. That, then, which God founds upon this rock of the unchangeable power of life in His Son shall not be overthrown by the kingdom of death. If man has been overcome and has fallen under the power ·of this kingdom, God, the living God, will not be overcome by it. It is on this that Christ builds His assembly. It is the work of Christ based on Him as Son of the living God, not of the first Adam nor based on him—His work accomplished according to the power which this truth reveals. The Person of Jesus, the Son of the living God, is its strength. It is the resurrection that proved it. There He is declared to be the Son of God with power. Accordingly it is not during His life, but when raised from the dead, that He begins this work. Life was in Himself; but it is after the Father had burst the gates of hades—nay, He Himself in His divine power had done so and was risen—that He begins to build by the Holy Ghost as ascended on high, that which the power of death or of him who wielded it—already overcome—can never destroy. It is His Person that is here contemplated, and it is on His Person that all is founded. The resurrection is the proof that He is the Son of the living God, and that the gates of hades can do nothing against Him; their power is destroyed by it. Hence we see how the assembly (though formed on earth) is much more than a dispensation, the kingdom is not.

The work of the cross was needed; but it is not the question here of that which the righteous judgment of God required, or of the justification of an individual, but of that which nullified the power of the enemy. It was the Person of Him whom Peter was given to acknowledge, who lived according to the power of the life of God. It was a peculiar and direct revelation from heaven by the Father. Doubtless Christ had given proofs enough of who He was; but proofs had proved nothing to man's heart. The Father's revelation was the way of knowing

who He was, and this went far beyond the hopes of a
Messiah.

The name given to Peter

Here, then, the Father had directly revealed the truth
of Christ's own Person, a revelation which went beyond
all question of relationship with the Jews. On this foundation Christ would build His assembly. Peter, already
so named by the Lord, receives a confirmation of that
title on this occasion. The Father had revealed to Simon,
the son of Jonas, the mystery of the Person of Jesus; and
secondly, Jesus also betokens, by the name He gives
him,[44] the steadfastness, the firmness, the durability, the
practical strength, of His servant favored by grace. The
right of bestowing a name belongs to a superior, who can
assign to the one who bears it his place and his name, in
the family or the situation he is in. The right, where real,
supposes discernment, intelligence, in that which is going
on. Adam names the animals. Nebuchadnezzar gives new
names to the captive Jews; the king of Egypt to Eliakim,
whom he had placed on the throne. Jesus therefore takes
this place when He says, *The Father* hath revealed this
unto thee; and I *also* give you a place and a name connected with this grace. It is on that which the Father
hath revealed unto thee that I am going to build My
assembly,[45] against which (founded on the life that comes
from God) the gates of the kingdom of death shall never

---

[44] The passage (chap. 16: 18) should be read, "And I also say unto
thee."

[45] It is important here to distinguish the Church which Christ builds,
not yet finished, but which He Himself builds, and that which is, as a
manifested whole in the world, built up in responsibility by man. In
Ephesians 2: 20, 21 and 1 Peter 2: 4, 5 we have this divine building
growing and built up. No mention of man's work is found in either
passage; it is a divine one. In 1 Corinthians 3 Paul is a wise master
builder; others may build in wood, hay and stubble. The confusion of
these has been the basis of Popery and other corruptions found in what
is called the Church. His Church, looked at in its reality, is a divine
work which Christ accomplishes and which abides.

prevail; and I who build, and build on this immovable foundation—I give you the place of a *stone* (*Peter*) in connection with this living temple. Through the gift of God thou belongest already by nature to the building—a living stone, having the knowledge of that truth which is the foundation, and which makes of every stone a part of the edifice. Peter was pre-eminently such by this confession; he was so in anticipation by the election of God. This revelation was made by the Father in sovereignty. The Lord assigns him, withal, his place, as possessing the right of administration and authority in the kingdom He was going to establish.

Thus far with respect to the assembly, now mentioned for the first time, the Jews having been rejected because of their unbelief, and man a convicted sinner.

The kingdom of God on earth governed from heaven: its keys

Another subject presents itself in connection with this of the assembly that the Lord was going to build; namely, the kingdom which was going to be established. It was to have the form of the kingdom of heaven; it was so in the counsels of God; but it was now to be set up in a peculiar manner, the King having been rejected on earth.

But, rejected as He was, the keys of the kingdom were in the Lord's hand; its authority belonged to Him. He would bestow them on Peter, who, when He was gone, should open its doors to the Jews first, and then to the Gentiles. He should also exercise authority from the Lord within the kingdom; so that whatsoever he bound on earth in the name of Christ (the true King, although gone up to heaven) should be bound in heaven; and if he loosed anything on earth, his deed should be ratified in heaven. In a word, he had the power of command in the kingdom of God on earth, this kingdom having now the character of kingdom of heaven, because its King was in heaven,[46] and heaven would stamp his acts with its authority. But it is heaven sanctioning his earthly acts, not his binding or loosing for heaven. The assembly connected with the character of Son of the living God and built by Christ, though formed on earth, belongs to heaven; the kingdom, though governed from heaven, belongs to earth—has its place and ministration there.

God's future purposes in the assembly and kingdom connected with Peter

These four things then are declared by the Lord in this passage—1st, the revelation made by the Father to Simon; 2nd, the name given to this Simon by Jesus, who was going to build His assembly on the foundation revealed in that which the Father had made known to Simon; 3rd, the assembly built by Christ Himself, not yet complete, on the foundation of the Person of Jesus

[46] Remark here what I have spoken of elsewhere—there are no keys of or to the church or assembly. Peter had the keys of administration in the kingdom. But the idea of keys in connection with the Church, or the power of the keys in the Church, is a pure fallacy. There are none such at all. The Church is built; men do not build with keys, and it is Christ (not Peter) who builds it. Further, the acts thus sanctioned were acts of administration down here. Heaven put its sanction on them, but they did not relate to heaven, but to earthly administration of the kingdom.

Further, it is to be remarked that what is conferred here is individual and personal. It was a name and authority conferred on Simon, son of Jonas.

Some further remarks here may help us to understand more fully the bearing of these chapters. In the parable of the sower (chap. 13) the Person of the Lord is not brought forward, only that it is sowing, not reaping. In the first similitude of the kingdom He is Son of Man, and the field is the world. He is quite out of Judaism. In chapter 14 we have the state of things from John's rejection, to the time the Lord is owned on His return where He had been rejected. In chapter 15 is the moral controversy, and God in grace in Himself as above evil. On this I dwell no further. But in chapter 16 we have the Person of the Son of God, the living God, and hereon the assembly, and Christ the builder; in chapter 17 the kingdom with the Son of Man coming in glory. The keys (however heaven sanctioned Simon's use of them) were, as we have seen, of the kingdom of heaven (not of the assembly); and that, the parable of the tares shows, was to be corrupted and spoiled, and this irremediably. Christ builds the Church, not Peter. Compare 1 Peter 2: 4, 5.

acknowledged as Son of the living God; 4th, the keys of
the kingdom that should be given to Peter, that is to say,
authority in the kingdom as administering it on the part
of Christ, ordering in it that which was His will, and
which should be ratified in heaven. All this is connected
with *Simon* personally, in virtue of the Father's election
(who, in His wisdom, had chosen him to receive this
revelation), and of Christ's authority (who had bestowed
on him the name that distinguished him as personally enjoying this privilege).

The Lord's death announced: the transition from the Messianic system to the establishment of the assembly

The Lord having thus made known the purposes of
God with regard to the future—purposes to be accomplished in the assembly and in the kingdom—there was no
longer room for His presentation to the Jews as Messiah.
Not that He gave up the testimony, full of grace and
patience towards the people, which He had borne throughout His ministry. No; that indeed continued, but His
disciples were to understand that it was no longer their
work to proclaim Him to the people as the Christ. From
this time also He began to teach His disciples that He
must suffer and be killed and be raised again.

Peter doing the adversary's work: the only path is the cross

But, blessed and honored as Peter was by the revelation
which the Father had made to him, his heart still clung
in a carnal manner to the human glory of his Master (in
truth, to his own), and was still far from rising to the
height of the thoughts of God. Alas, he is not the only
instance of this. To be convinced of the most exalted
truths, and even to enjoy them sincerely as truths, is a
different thing from having the heart formed to the sentiments, and to the walk here below, which are in accord-

ance with those truths. It is not sincerity in the enjoyment of the truth that is wanting. What is wanting is to have the flesh, self, mortified—to be dead to the world. We may sincerely enjoy the truth as taught of God, and yet not have the flesh mortified or the heart in a state which is according to that truth in what it involves down here. Peter (so lately honored by the revelation of the glory of Jesus, and made in a very special manner the depositary of administration in the kingdom given to the Son—having a distinguished place in that which was to follow the Lord's rejection by the Jews) is now doing the adversary's work with respect to the perfect submission of Jesus to the suffering and ignominy that were to introduce this glory and characterize the kingdom. Alas, the case was plain; he savored the things of men, and not the things of God. But the Lord, in faithfulness, rejects Peter in this matter, and teaches His disciples that the only path, the appointed and necessary path, is the cross; if any one would follow Him, *that* is the path *He* took. Moreover what would it profit a man to save his life and lose all—to gain the world and lose his soul? For this was the question,[47] and not now the outward glory of the kingdom.

Unbelief among the Jews and in the disciples' hearts

Having examined this chapter, as the expression of the transition from the Messianic system to the establishment of the assembly founded on the revelation of the Person of Christ, I desire also to call attention to the characters of unbelief which are developed in it, both among the Jews and in the hearts of the disciples. It will be profitable to observe the forms of this unbelief.

First of all, it takes the grosser form of asking a sign

[47] In the Epistle of Peter we continually find these same thoughts—the words, "living hope," "living stone"—applied to Christ, and afterwards to Christians. And again, in accordance with our present subject, salvation through life in Christ, the Son of the living God, we find "receiving the end of our faith, even the salvation of [our] souls." We may read all the verses by which the apostle introduces his instructions.

from heaven. The Pharisees and Sadducees unite to show their insensibility to all that the Lord had done. They require proof to their natural senses, that is, to their unbelief. They will not believe God, either in hearkening to His words or in beholding His works. God must satisfy their wilfulness, which would be neither faith nor the work of God. They had understanding for human things that were much less clearly manifested, but none for the things of God. A Saviour lost to them, as Jews on earth, should be the only sign granted them. They would have to submit, willing or not, to the judgment of the unbelief they displayed. The kingdom should be taken from them; the Lord leaves them. The sign of Jonah is connected with the subject of the whole chapter.

We next see this same inattention to the power manifested in the works of Jesus; but it is no longer the opposition of the unbelieving will; occupation of heart with present things withdraws such from the influence of the signs already given. This is weakness, not ill-will. Nevertheless they are guilty; but Jesus calls them "men of little faith," not "hypocrites," and "a wicked and adulterous generation."

We then see unbelief manifesting itself in the form of indolent opinion, which proves that the heart and conscience are not interested in a subject that ought to command them—a subject that if the heart would really face its true importance, it would have no rest until it had arrived at certainty with respect to it. The soul here has no sense of need; consequently there is no discernment. When the soul feels this need, there is but one thing that can meet it; there can be no rest till it is found. The revelation of God that created this need does not leave the soul in peace until it is assured of possessing that which awakened it. Those who are not sensible of this need can rest in probabilities, each according to his natural character, his education, his circumstances. There is enough to awaken curiosity—the mind is occupied about it, and

judges.   Faith has wants, and, in principle, intelligence
as to the object which meets those wants; the soul is exercised till it finds that which it needs. The fact is that God
is there.

Peter's living faith as a living stone in the temple

This is Peter's case. The Father reveals His Son to
him. Though weak, living faith was found in him, we see
the condition of his soul when he says, "Lord, to whom
shall we go? Thou hast the words of eternal life; and we
believe and are sure that Thou art the Christ, the Son of
the living God." Happy the man to whom God reveals
such truths as these, in whom He awakens these wants!
There may be conflict, much to learn, much to mortify;
but the counsel of God is there, and the life connected
with it. We have seen its effect in the case of Peter. Every
Christian has his own place in the temple of which Simon
was so eminent a stone. Does it then follow that the heart
is, practically, at the height of the revelation made to it?
No; there may be, after all, the flesh not yet mortified on
that side where the revelation touches our earthly position.

The revelation given to Peter implying Christ's rejection on earth and the cross as the entrance into the kingdom

In fact the revelation made to Peter implied the rejection of Christ on earth—necessarily led to His humiliation and death. That was the point. To substitute the
revelation of the Son of God, the assembly and the heavenly kingdom, for the manifestation of the Messiah on
earth—what could it mean, except that Jesus was to be
delivered up to the Gentiles to be crucified, and after that
to rise again? But morally Peter had not attained to this.
On the contrary, his carnal heart availed itself of the
revelation made to him, and of that which Jesus had said
to him, for self-exaltation. He saw, therefore, the personal
glory without apprehending the practical moral conse-

quences. He begins to rebuke the Lord Himself, and seeks to turn Him aside from the path of obedience and submission. The Lord, ever faithful, treats him as an adversary. Alas! how often have we enjoyed some truth, and that sincerely, and yet have failed in the practical consequences that it led to on earth! A heavenly glorified Saviour, who builds the assembly, implies the cross on earth. The flesh does not understand this. It will raise its Messiah to heaven, if you will; but to take its share of the humiliation that necessarily follows is not its idea of a glorified Messiah. The flesh must be mortified to take this place. We must have the strength of Christ by the Holy Ghost. A Christian who is not dead to the world is but a stumbling-stone to every one who seeks to follow Christ.

These are the forms of unbelief that precede a true confession of Christ, and that are found, alas, in those who have sincerely confessed and known Him (the flesh not being so mortified that the soul can walk in the height of that which it has learnt of God, and the spiritual understanding being obscured by thinking of consequences which the flesh rejects).

The glorious title of "the Son of Man" replacing that of the Messiah

But if the cross were the entrance into the kingdom, the revelation of the glory would not be delayed. The Messiah being rejected by the Jews, a title more glorious and of far deeper import is unfolded: the Son of Man should come in the glory of the Father (for He was the Son of God), and reward every man according to his works. There were even some standing there who should not taste of death (for of this they were speaking) till they had *seen* the manifestation of the glory of the kingdom that belonged to the Son of Man.

We may remark here the title of "Son of God" established as the foundation; that of Messiah given up so far

as concerned the testimony rendered in that day, and re-
placed by that of "Son of Man," which He takes at the
same time as that of the Son of God, and which had a
glory that belonged to Him in His own right. He was to
come in the glory of His Father as Son of God, and in
His own kingdom as Son of Man.

Christ as the Son of Man in the Psalms

It is interesting to remember here the instruction given
us in the beginning of the Book of Psalms. The righteous
man, distinguished from the congregation of the wicked,
had been presented in the first Psalm. Then, in the second, we have the rebellion of the kings of the earth and
the rulers against the Lord and against His Anointed
(that is, His Christ). Now upon this the decree of Jehovah is declared. Adonai, the Lord, shall mock at them
from heaven. Further, Jehovah's King shall be established
on Mount Zion. This is the decree: "Jehovah hath said
unto Me, Thou art my Son; this day[48] have I begotten
Thee." The kings of the earth and the judges are commanded to kiss the Son.

Now in the Psalms that follow, all this glory is darkened. The distress of the remnant, in which Christ has a
part, is related. Then, in Psalm 8, He is addressed as Son
of Man, Heir of all the rights conferred in sovereignty
upon man by the counsels of God. The name of Jehovah
becomes excellent in all the earth. These Psalms do not
go beyond the earthly part of these truths, excepting where
it is written, "He that sitteth in the heavens shall laugh
at them;" while in Matthew 16 the connection of the Son
of God with this, His coming with His angels (to say
nothing of the assembly), are set before us. That is to

---

[48] We have seen that Peter went beyond this. Christ is here seen as the
Son born on the earth in time, not as the Son from eternity in the
bosom of the Father. Peter, without the full revelation of this last
truth, sees Him to be the Son according to the power of divine life in His
own Person, upon which *the assembly* consequently could be built. But
here we are to consider that which belongs to the kingdom.

say, we see that the Son of Man will come in the glory of heaven. Not that His dwelling there is the truth declared; but that He is invested with the highest glory of heaven when He comes to set up His kingdom on earth. He comes in His kingdom. The kingdom is established on the earth; but He comes to take it with the glory of heaven. This is displayed in the following chapter, according to the promise here in verse 28.

A sample of the coming glory given to confirm the disciples' faith

In each Gospel that speaks of it, the transfiguration immediately follows the promise of not tasting death before seeing the kingdom of the Son of Man. And not only so, but Peter (in his second Epistle, 1: 16), when speaking of this scene, declares that it was a manifestation of the power and coming of our Lord Jesus Christ. He says that the word of prophecy was confirmed to them by the view of His majesty; so that they knew that whereof they spoke, in making known to them the power and the coming of Christ, having beheld His majesty. In fact it is precisely in this sense that the Lord speaks of it here, as we have seen. It was a sample of the glory in which He would hereafter come, given to confirm the faith of His disciples in the prospect of His death which He had just announced to them.

Chapter 17

The Transfiguration

IN chapter 17 Jesus leads them up into a high mountain, and there is transfigured before them: "His face did shine as the sun, and His raiment was white as the light." Moses and Elias appeared also, talking with Him.

I leave the subject of their discourse, which is deeply interesting, till we come to the Gospel of Luke, who adds a few other circumstances, which, in some respects, give another aspect to this scene.

Here the Lord appears in glory, and Moses and Elias with Him: the one the legislator of the Jews; the other (almost equally distinguished) the prophet who sought to bring back the ten apostate tribes to the worship of Jehovah, and who, despairing of the people, went back to Horeb, whence the law was given, and afterwards was taken up to heaven without passing through death.

Peter's error: the Object of the Father's delight to be ours

These two persons, pre-eminently illustrious in the dealings of God with Israel, as the founder and the restorer of the people in connection with the law, appear in company with Jesus. Peter (struck with this apparition, rejoicing to see his Master associated with these pillars of the Jewish system, with such eminent servants of God, ignorant of the glory of the Son of Man, and forgetting the revelation of the glory of His Person as the Son of God) desires to make three tabernacles, and to place the three on the same level as oracles. But the glory of God manifests itself; that is to say, the sign known in Israel as the abode (*shechinah*) of that glory,[49] and the voice of the Father is heard. Grace may put Moses and Elias in the same glory as that of the Son of God, and associate them with Him; but if the folly of man, in his ignorance, would place them together as having in themselves equal authority over the heart of the believer, the Father must at once vindicate the rights of His Son. Not a moment elapses before the Father's voice proclaims the glory of the Person of His Son, His relation to Himself, that He is the object of His entire affection, in whom is all His

[49] Peter, taught of the Holy Ghost, calls it "the excellent glory."

delight. It is *He* whom the disciples are to hear. Moses and Elias have disappeared. Christ is there alone, as the One to be glorified, the One to teach those who hear the Father's voice. The Father Himself distinguishes Him, presents Him to the notice of the disciples, not as being worthy of *their* love, but as the object of His own delight. In Jesus He was Himself well pleased. Thus the Father's affections are presented as ruling ours—setting before us one common object. What a position for poor creatures like us! What grace![50]

Jesus the sole dispenser of the knowledge and mind of God

At the same time the law, and all idea of the restoration of the law under the old covenant, were passed away; and Jesus, glorified as Son of Man, and Son of the living God, remains the sole dispenser of the knowledge and the mind of God. The disciples fall on their faces, sore afraid, on hearing the voice of God. Jesus, to whom this glory and this voice were natural, encourages them, as He always did when on earth, saying, "Be not afraid." Being with Him who was the object of the Father's love, why should they fear? Their best Friend was the manifestation of God on the earth; the glory belonged to Him. Moses and Elias had disappeared, and the glory also, which the disciples

[50] It was not in connection with the divine validity of their testimony, that Moses and Elias disappear. There could not be a stronger confirmation of it, as indeed Peter says, than this scene. But not only they were not the subjects of God's testimony as Christ was, but their testimony did not refer nor their exhortations reach to the heavenly things which were now to be revealed in association with the Son from heaven. Even John the Baptist makes this difference (John 3: 31-34). Hence, as there set forth, the Son of Man must be lifted up. So here, the Lord charges the disciples not to say He was the Messiah, for the Son of Man must suffer. It was the turning-point of the Lord's life and ministry, and the coming glory of the kingdom shown to the disciples, but then He must suffer. (See John 12: 27.) The Jewish history was closed in chapter 12, indeed in chapter 11, and the ground of the change laid. John and He both rejected, perfect submission, then all things delivered unto Him of His Father, and He revealing the Father. Compare John 13, 14. But Matthew 13—apart from Judaism, He begins with what He brought, not looking for fruit in man.

were not yet able to bear; Jesus—who had been thus
manifested to them in the glory given Him, and in the
rights of His glorious Person, in His relations with the
Father—Jesus remains the same to them as they had ever
known Him. But this glory was not to be the subject of
their testimony until He, the Son of Man, was risen from
the dead—the suffering Son of Man. The great proof
should then be given, that He was the Son of God with
power. Testimony thereunto should be rendered, and He
would ascend personally into that glory which had just
shone forth before their eyes.

The coming and rejection of Elias and of the Son of Man

But a difficulty arises in the minds of the disciples
caused by the doctrine of the scribes with regard to Elias.
These had said that Elias must come before the manifestation of the Messiah; and in fact the prophecy of Malachi authorized this expectation. Why then, ask they, say
the scribes that Elias must first come? (that is to say,
before the manifestation of the Messiah); whereas we
have now seen that Thou art He, without the coming of
Elias. Jesus confirms the words of the prophecy, adding,
that Elias should restore all things. "But," continues the
Lord, "I say unto you, that he is come already, and they
have done unto him whatsoever they listed; likewise shall
also the Son of Man suffer of them." Then understood
they that He spoke of John the Baptist, who came in the
spirit and power of Elias, as the Holy Ghost had declared
by Zacharias his father.

Let us say a few words on this passage. First of all,
when the Lord says, "Elias truly cometh first, and shall
restore all things," He does but confirm that which the
scribes had spoken, according to Malachi's prophecy, as
though He had said, "They are in the right." He then
declares the effect of the coming of Elias: "He shall re-

store all things." But the Son of Man was yet to come. Jesus had said to His disciples, "Ye shall not have gone over the cities of Israel till the Son of Man be come." Nevertheless He had come, and was even now speaking with them. But this coming of the Son of Man of which He spoke, is His coming in glory, when He shall be manifested as the Son of Man in judgment according to Daniel 7. It was thus that all which had been said to the Jews should be accomplished; and in Matthew's Gospel He speaks to them in connection with this expectation. Nevertheless it was needful that Jesus should be presented to the nation and should suffer. It was needful that the nation should be tested by the presentation of the Messiah according to the promise. This was done, and as God had also foretold by the prophets, "He was rejected of men." Thus also John went before Him, according to Isaiah 40, as the voice in the wilderness, even in the spirit and power of Elias; he was rejected as the Son of Man should also be.[51]

The rejection of the Son of Man; temporary setting aside of the nation and restoration of all things

The Lord then, by these words, declares to His disciples, in connection with the scene they had just left, and with all this part of our Gospel, that the Son of Man, as now presented to the Jews, was to be rejected. This same Son of Man was to be manifested in glory, as they had seen for a moment on the Mount. Elias indeed was to come, as the scribes had said; but that John the Baptist had fulfilled that office in power for this presentation of the Son of Man; which (the Jews being left, as was fitting, to their own responsibility) would only end in His rejection, and in the setting aside of the nation until the days in

---

[51] Hence also John Baptist rejects the application of Malachi 4: 5, 6, to himself; while Isaiah 40 and Malachi 3: 1 are applied to him in Luke 1: 76; 7: 27.

which God would begin again to connect Himself with His people, still dear to Him, whatever their condition might be. He would then restore all things (a glorious work, which He would accomplish by bringing again His Firstborn into the world). The expression "restore all things" refers *here* to the Jews, and is used morally. In Acts 3 it refers to the effect of the Son of Man's own presence.

The last step in the testing of the Jews: pure grace

The temporary presence of the Son of Man was the moment in which a work was accomplished on which eternal glory depends, in which God has been fully glorified, above and beyond all dispensation and in which God and so man has been revealed, a work of which even the outward glory of the Son of Man is but the fruit, so far as that depends on His work, and not on His divine Person; a work in which morally He was perfectly glorified in perfectly glorifying God. Still, with respect to the promises made to the Jews, it was but the last step in the testing to which they were subjected by grace. God well knew that they would reject His Son; but He would not hold them as definitively guilty until they had really done it. Thus in His divine wisdom (while afterwards fulfilling His unchangeable promises) He presents Jesus to them—His Son, their Messiah. He gives them every necessary proof. He sends them John the Baptist in the spirit and power of Elias, as His forerunner. The Son of David is born at Bethlehem with all the signs that should have convinced them; but they were blinded by their pride and self-righteousness, and rejected it all. Nevertheless it became Jesus in grace to adapt Himself, as to His position, to the wretched condition of His people. Thus also, the Antitype of the David rejected in his day, He shared the affliction of His people. If the Gentiles oppressed them, their King must be associated with their distress, while giving every proof of what He was and seeking them in love. He rejected, all becomes pure grace. They have no longer a right to anything according to the promises, and are reduced to receive all from that grace, even as a poor Gentile would do. God will not fail in grace. Thus God has put them on the true footing of sinners, and will nevertheless fulfil His promises. This is the subject of Romans 11.

John the Baptist and Elias

Now the Son of Man who shall return will be this same Jesus who went away. The heavens will receive Him until the times of the restitution of all things of which the prophets have spoken. But he who was to be His forerunner in this temporary presence here could not be the same Elias. Accordingly John was conformed to the then manifestation of the Son of Man, saving the difference that necessarily flowed from the Person of the Son of Man, who could be but one, while that could not be the case with John the Baptist and Elias. But even as Jesus manifested all the power of the Messiah, all His rights to everything that belonged to that Messiah, without assuming as yet the outward glory, His time not being come (John 7), so John fulfilled morally and in power the mission of Elias to prepare the way of the Lord before Him (according to the true character of His coming, as then accomplished), and answered literally to Isaiah 40, and even to Malachi 3, the only passages applied to him. This is the reason that John said he was not Elias, and that the Lord said, "*If ye can receive* it, this is Elias which was for to come." Therefore also John never applied Malachi 4: 5, 6 to himself; but he announces himself as fulfilling Isaiah 40: 3-5, and this in each of the Gospels, whatever may be its particular character.[52]

[52] See previous note.

The believer's unbelief: felt want and its remedy

But let us go on with our chapter. If the Lord takes up into the glory, He comes down into this world, even now in Spirit and in sympathy, and meets the crowd and Satan's power with which we have to do. While the Lord was on the Mount, a poor father had brought to the disciples his son who was a lunatic and possessed by a devil. Here is developed another character of man's unbelief, that even of the believer—inability to make use of the power which is, so to say, at his disposal in the Lord. Christ, Son of God, Messiah, Son of Man, had overcome the enemy, had bound the strong man and had a right to cast him out. As man, the obedient One in spite of Satan's temptations, He had overcome him in the wilderness, and had thus a right as man to dispossess him of his dominion over a man as to this world; and this He did. In casting out devils and healing the sick, He delivered man from the power of the enemy. "God," said Peter, "anointed Jesus of Nazareth with the Holy Ghost and with power, and he went about doing good and healing all those that were oppressed by the devil." Now this power should have been used by the disciples, who ought to have known how to avail themselves by faith of that which Jesus had thus manifested on earth; but they were not able to do it. Yet what availed it to bring this power down here, if the disciples had not faith to use it? The power was there: man might profit by it for complete deliverance from all the oppression of the enemy; but he had not faith to do so— even believers had not. The presence of Christ on earth was useless, when even His own disciples knew not how to profit by it. There was more faith in the man that brought his child than in them, for felt want brought him to its remedy. All therefore come under the Lord's sentence, "O faithless and perverse generation!" He must leave them; and that which the glory had revealed above, unbelief shall realize below.

Individual faith met with blessing

Observe here, that it is not evil in the world which puts an end to a particular intervention of God; on the contrary, it occasions the intervention in grace. It was on account of Satan's dominion over men that Christ came. He departs, because those who had received Him are incapable of using the power that He brought with Him, or that He bestows for their deliverance; they cannot profit by the very advantages then enjoyed. Faith was wanting. Nevertheless observe also this important and touching truth that, as long as such dispensation from God continues, Jesus does not fail to meet individual faith with blessing, even when *His disciples* cannot glorify Him by the exercise of faith. The same sentence that judges the unbelief of the disciples calls the distressed father to the enjoyment of the blessing. After all, to be able to avail ourselves of His power, we must be in communion with Him by the practical energy of faith.

He blesses then the poor father according to his need; and, full of patience, He resumes the course of instruction He was giving His disciples on the subject of His rejection and His resurrection as the Son of Man. Loving the Lord, and unable to carry their ideas beyond the circumstances of the moment, they are troubled; and yet this was redemption, salvation, the glory of Christ.

The Master's instruction: association with Himself

Before however going farther, and teaching them that which became the disciples of a Master thus rejected and the position they were to occupy, He sets before them His divine glory, and their association with Him who had it, in the most touching manner, if they could but have understood it; and at the same time with perfect condescension and tenderness He places Himself with them, or rather He places them in the same place with Himself, as Son of the great King of the temple and of all the earth.

The tribute money: divine condescension

Those who collected the tribute-money for the service of the temple come and ask Peter if his Master does not pay it. Ever ready to put himself forward, forgetful of the glory he had seen, and the revelation made to him by the Father, Peter, coming down to the ordinary level of his own thoughts, anxious that his Master should be esteemed a good Jew and without consulting Him, replies that He does. The Lord anticipates Peter on his coming in, and shows him His divine knowledge of that which took place at a distance from Himself. At the same time, He speaks of Peter and Himself as both children of the King of the temple (Son of God still keeping in patient goodness His lowly place as a Jew), and both therefore free from the tribute. But they should not offend. He then commands creation, (for He can *do* all things, as He *knows* all things,) and causes a fish to bring precisely the sum required, coupling anew the name of Peter with His own. He had said, "Lest *we* offend them;" and now, "Give unto them for Me and thee." Marvellous and divine condescension! He who is the searcher of hearts, and who disposes at will of the whole creation, the Son of the sovereign Lord of the temple, puts His poor disciples into this same relationship with His heavenly Father, with the God who was worshipped in that temple. He submits to the demands that would have been rightly made on strangers, but He places His disciples in all His own privileges as Son. We see very plainly the connection between this touching expression of divine grace and the subject of these chapters. It demonstrates all the significance of the change that was taking place.

Peter's Epistles in connection with Chaps. 16, 17

It is interesting to remark that the first epistle of Peter is founded on Matthew 16, and the second on chapter 17, which we have just been considering.[53] In chapter 16 Peter taught of the Father, confessed the Lord to be the Son of the living God; and the Lord said that on this rock He would build His church, and that he who had the power of death should not prevail against it.   Thus also Peter, in his first epistle, declares that they were born again unto a living hope by the resurrection of Jesus Christ from the dead. Now it is by this resurrection that the power of the life of the living God was manifested. Afterwards he calls Christ the living stone, in coming unto whom we, as living stones, are built up a holy temple to the Lord.

In his second epistle he recalls, in a peculiar manner, the glory of the transfiguration, as a proof of the coming and the kingdom of the Son of Man. Accordingly he speaks in that epistle of the judgment of the Lord.

Chapter 18

God's ways in the new order of things: the character of the true testimony to be rendered

IN chapter 18 the great principles proper to the new order of things are made known to the disciples.   Let us search a little into these sweet and precious instructions of the Lord.

They may be looked at in two ways. They reveal the ways of God with regard to that which was to take the place of the Lord upon earth, as a testimony to grace and truth. Besides this, they depict the character which is in itself the true testimony to be rendered.

[53] Both these epistles, after stating redemption by the precious blood of Christ and being born of the incorruptible seed of the Word, treat of the government of God; the first, its application to His own, preserving them, the second, to the wicked and the world, going on thus to the elements melting with fervent heat, and the new heavens and the new earth.

This chapter supposes Christ rejected and absent, the glory of chapter 17 not yet come. It passes over chapter 17 to connect itself with chapter 16 (except so far as the last verses of chapter 17 give a practical testimony to His abdication of His true rights until God should vindicate them). The Lord speaks of the two subjects contained in chapter 16, the kingdom and the church.

"As little children"—the spirit becoming the followers of a rejected Lord

That which would be proper for the kingdom was the meekness of a little child, which is unable to assert its own rights in the face of a world that passes it by—the spirit of dependence and humility. They must *become* as little children. In the absence of their rejected Lord this was the spirit that became His followers. He who received a little child in the name of Jesus received Himself. On the other hand, he who put a stumbling-block in the way of one of those little ones who believed in Jesus[54] should be visited with the most terrible judgment. Alas! the world do this; but woe unto the world on that account. As to the disciples, if that which they most valued became a snare to them, they must pluck it out and cut it off— must exercise the utmost carefulness in grace not to be a snare to a little one believing in Christ, and the most unrelenting severity as to themselves, in whatever might be a snare to them. Loss of what was most precious here was nothing, compared with their eternal condition in another world; for that was in question now, and sin could have no place in God's house. Care for others, even the weakest, severity with self was the rule of the kingdom that no snare or evil might be. As to offence, full grace in forgiveness. They were not to despise these little

---

[54] The Lord here distinguishes a believing little one. In the other verses, He speaks of a little child, making its character, as such, a model of that of the Christian in this world.

ones; for if unable to force their own way in this world, they were the objects of the Father's special favor, as those who, in earthly courts, had the peculiar privilege of seeing the king's face. Not that there was no sin in them, but that the Father did not despise those that were far from Him. The Son of Man was come to save the lost.[55] And it was not the Father's will that one of these little ones should perish. He spoke, I doubt not, of little children like those whom He took in His arms; but He inculcates on His disciples the spirit of humility and dependence on the one hand, and on the other, the spirit of the Father, which they were to imitate in order to be truly the children of the kingdom; and not to walk in the spirit of man, who seeks to maintain his place and his own importance, but to humble themselves and submit to contumely; and at the same time (and this is true glory) to imitate the Father, who considers the lowly and admits them into His presence. The Son of Man was come on behalf of the worthless. This is the spirit of grace spoken of at the end of chapter 5. It is the spirit of the kingdom.

The assembly to occupy the place of Christ on earth: Christ in the midst

But the assembly more especially was to occupy the place of Christ on earth. With respect to offences against oneself, this spirit of meekness became His disciple; he was to gain his brother. If the latter would hearken, the thing was to be buried in the heart of the one whom he had offended; if not, two or three more were then to be taken with him by the offended person to reach his conscience, or serve as witnesses; but if these appointed means were unavailing, it must be made known to the assembly;

---

[55] As doctrine, the sinful condition of the child, and its need of the sacrifice of Christ, are clearly expressed here. He does not say, "Seek," as to them. The employing the parable of the lost sheep is striking here.

and if this did not produce submission, he who had done
the wrong should be to him as a stranger, as a heathen
and a publican was to Israel. The public discipline of the
assembly is not treated of here, but the spirit in which
Christians were to walk. If the offender bowed when
spoken to, even seventy times seven times a day, he was
to be forgiven. But though Church discipline be not
spoken of, we see that the assembly took the place of
Israel on earth. The *without* and *within* henceforth applied to it. Heaven would ratify that which the assembly
bound on earth, and the Father would grant the prayer
of two or three who should agree together in making their
request; for Christ would be in the midst wherever two
or three should be gathered together in or to His name.[56]
Thus, for decisions, for prayers, they were as Christ on
the earth, for Christ Himself was there with them. Solemn
truth! immense favor, bestowed on two or three when
really gathered together in His name; but which forms a
subject of the deepest grief when this unity is pretended
to, while the reality is not there.[57]

---

[56] It is important to call to mind here, that—while the Holy Ghost
is personally fully recognized in Matthew, as in the birth of the Lord,
and (chapter 10) as acting and speaking in the disciples in their service,
as a divine Person, as it is ever from Him alone we can act rightly—
the coming of the Holy Ghost, in the order of divine dispensation, forms
no part of the teaching of this Gospel, though recognized as a fact in
chapter 10. The view of Christ in Matthew closes with His resurrection,
and the Jewish body are sent out from Galilee as an accepted body to the
world to evangelize the Gentiles, and He declares He will be with them
to the end of the age. So here He is in the midst of two or three
gathered to His name. The Church here is not the Body by the baptism
of the Holy Ghost; it is not the house where the Holy Ghost dwells on
earth; but where the two or three meet to His name, there Christ is.
Now I do not doubt that all good from life on, and the Word of life,
comes from the Spirit, but this is another thing, and the assembly here
is not the Body, nor the house, through the coming down of the Holy
Ghost. This was a subsequent teaching and revelation, and remains
blessedly true; but it is Christ in the midst of those assembled to His
name. Even in chapter 16 it is He builds, but that is another thing.
Of course, it is spiritually He is present.

[57] It is very striking to find here, that the only succession in the office
of binding and loosing which Heaven sanctions is that of two or three
assembled in Christ's name.

The spirit of the kingdom—grace and lowliness

Another element of the chapter proper to the kingdom, which had been manifested in God and in Christ, is pardoning grace. In this also the children of the kingdom are to be imitators of God, and always to forgive. This refers only to wrongs done to oneself, and not to public discipline. We must pardon to the end, or rather, there must be no end; even as God has forgiven us all things. At the same time, I believe that the dispensations of God to the Jews are here described. They had not only broken the law, but they had slain the Son of God. Christ interceded for them, saying, "Father, forgive them, for they know not what they do." In answer to this prayer, a provisional pardon was preached by the Holy Ghost, through the mouth of Peter. But this grace too was rejected. When it was a question of showing grace to the Gentiles, who, no doubt, owed them the hundred pence, they would not hear of it, and they are given up to punishment,[58] until the Lord can say, "They have received double for all their sins."

In a word, the spirit of the kingdom is not outward power, but lowliness; but in this condition there is nearness to the Father, and then it is easy to be meek and humble in this world. One who has tasted the favor of God will not seek greatness on earth; he is imbued with the spirit of grace, he cherishes the lowly, he pardons those who have wronged him, he is near God, and resembles Him in his ways. The same spirit of grace reigns, whether in the assembly or in its members. It alone represents Christ on the earth; and to it relate those regulations which are founded on the acceptance of a people as belonging unto God. Two or three really gathered together in the name of Jesus act with His authority, and

---

[58] This giving up, and the formal opening into the intermediate heavenly place connected with the Son of Man in glory are in Acts 7, where Stephen recites their history from Abraham, the first called as root of promise, to that day.

enjoy His privileges with the Father, for Jesus Himself is there in their midst.

Chapter 19

Principles which govern human nature: the true character of the marriage bond

CHAPTER 19 carries on the subject of the spirit that is suited to the kingdom of heaven, and goes deep into the principles which govern human nature, and of what was now divinely introduced. A question asked by the Pharisees—for the Lord had drawn nigh to Judea—gives rise to the exposition of His doctrine on marriage; and turning away from the law, given on account of the hardness of their hearts, He goes back[59] to God's institution,

[59] The connection is here traced between the new thing and nature, as God had originally formed it, passing over the law as something merely come between. It was a new power, because evil had come in, but it recognized God's creation, while proving the state of the heart, not yielding to its weakness. Sin has corrupted what God created good. The power of the Spirit of God, given to us through redemption, raises man and his path wholly out of the whole condition of flesh, introduces a new divine power by which he walks in this world, after the example of Christ. But with this there is the fullest sanction of what God Himself originally established. It is good, though there may be what is better. The way the law is passed over to go back to God's original institution, where spiritual power did not take the heart wholly out of the whole scene, though walking in it, is very striking. In marriage, the child, the character of the young man, what is of God and lovely in nature is recognized of the Lord. But the state of man's heart is searched out. This does not depend on character but motive, and is fully tested by Christ (there is an entire dispensational change, for riches were promised to a faithful Jew), and a rejected Christ—the path to heaven— everything, and the test of everything, that is of the heart of man.

God made man upright with certain family relationships. Sin has wholly corrupted this old or first creation of man. The coming of the Holy Ghost has brought in a power which lifts, in the second Man, out of the old creation into the new, and gives us heavenly things—only not yet as to the vessel, the body; but it cannot disown or condemn what God created in the beginning. That is impossible. In the beginning God made them. When we come to heavenly condition, all this, though not the fruits of its exercises in grace, disappears. If a man in the power of the Holy Ghost has the gift to do it, and be entirely heavenly, so much the better; but it is entirely evil to condemn or speak against the relationships which God originally created, or diminish or detract from the authority which God has connected with them. If a man can live wholly above and out of them all, to serve Christ, it is all well; but it is rare and exceptional.

according to which one man and one woman were to unite together, and to be one in the sight of God. He establishes, or rather re-establishes, the true character of the indissoluble bond of marriage. I call it indissoluble, for the exception of the case of unfaithfulness is not one; the guilty person had already broken the bond. It was no longer man and woman one flesh. At the same time, 'if God gave spiritual power for it, it was still better to remain unmarried.

Instruction with respect to children

He then renews His instruction with respect to children, while testifying His affection for them: here it appears to me rather in connection with the absence of all that binds to the world, to its distractions and its lusts, and owning what is lovely, confiding, and externally undefiled in nature; whereas, in chapter 18, it was the intrinsic character of the kingdom. After this, He shows (with reference to the introduction of the kingdom in His Person) the nature of entire devotedness and sacrifice of all things, in order to follow Him, if truly they only sought to please God. The spirit of the world was opposed at all points—both carnal passions and riches. No doubt the law of Moses restrained these passions; but it supposes them, and, in some respects, bears with them. According to the glory of the world, a child had no value. What power can it have there? It is of value in the Lord's eyes.

The motives of the heart tested: earthly riches

The law promised life to the man that kept it. The Lord makes it simple and practical in its requirements, or, rather, recalls them in their true simplicity. Riches were not forbidden by the law; that is to say, although moral obligation between man and man was maintained by the law, that which bound the heart to the world was not judged by it. Rather was prosperity, according to the government of God, connected with obedience to it. For it supposed this world, and man alive in it, and tested him there. Christ recognizes this; but the motives of the heart are tested. The law was spiritual, and, the Son of God there; we find again what we found before—man tested and detected, and God revealed. All is intrinsic and eternal in its nature, for God is revealed already. Christ judges everything that has a bad effect on the heart, and acts upon its selfishness, and thus separates it from God. "Sell that thou hast," says He, "and follow Me." Alas, the young man could not renounce his possessions, his ease, himself. "Hardly," says Jesus, "shall a rich man enter into the kingdom." This was manifest: it was the kingdom of God, of heaven; self and the world had no place in it. The disciples, who did not understand that there is no good in man, were astonished that one so favored and well-disposed should be still far from salvation. Who then could succeed? The whole truth then comes out. It is impossible to men. They cannot overcome the desires of the flesh. Morally, and as to his will and his affections, these desires are the man. One cannot make a negro white, or take his spots from the leopard: that which they exhibit is in their nature. But to God— blessed be His name!—all things are possible.

Renunciation for Jesus' sake: its reward

These instructions with regard to riches give rise to Peter's question, What shall be the portion of those who have renounced everything? This brings us back to the glory in chapter 17. There would be a regeneration; the state of things should be entirely renewed under the dominion of the Son of Man. At that time they should sit on twelve thrones, judging the twelve tribes of Israel. They should have the first place in the administration of the earthly kingdom. Every one, however, should have his own place; for whatever any one renounced for Jesus' sake, he should receive a hundredfold and everlasting life. Nevertheless these things would not be decided by appearance here; nor by the place men held in the old system, and before men: some that were first should be last, and the last first. In fact, it was to be feared that the carnal heart of man would take this encouragement, given in the shape of reward for all his labor and all his sacrifices, in a mercenary spirit, and seek to make God his debtor; and, therefore, in the parable by which the Lord continues His discourse (chap. 20), He establishes the principle of grace and of God's sovereignty in that which He gives, and towards those whom He calls, in a very distinct manner, and makes His gifts to those whom He brings into His vineyard depend on His grace and on His call.

Chapter 20

Laborers in God's vineyard: God's call and His grace

WE may remark that, when the Lord answers Peter, it was the consequence of having left all for Christ upon His call. The motive was Christ Himself: therefore He says, "Ye which have followed Me." He speaks also of those who had done it for His name's sake. This was the motive. The reward is an encouragement, when, for His sake, we are already in the way. This is always the case when reward is spoken of in the New Testament.[60] He who was called at the eleventh hour was dependent on this call for his entrance into the work, and if, in his kindness, the master chose to give him as much as the others, they should have rejoiced at it. The first adhered to jus-

---

[60] Indeed, reward is in Scripture always an encouragement to those who are in sorrow and suffering by having from higher motives entered into God's way. So Moses; so even Christ, whose motive in perfect love we know, yet for the joy set before Him endured the cross despising the shame. He was the *archegos kai teleiotes* in the path of faith.

tice; they received that which was agreed upon; the last
enjoyed the grace of his master. And it is to be remarked
that they accept the principle of grace, of confidence in it.
"Whatsoever is right I will give!" The great point in the
parable is that—confidence in the grace of the master of
the vineyard, and grace as the ground of their action. But
who understood it? A Paul might come in late, God having then called him, and be a stronger testimony to grace
than the laborers who had wrought from the dawning of
the gospel day.

Sharing in the Lord's sufferings

The Lord afterwards pursues the subject with His disciples. He goes up to Jerusalem, where the Messiah ought
to have been received and crowned, to be rejected and put
to death, but after that to rise again; and when the sons of
Zebedee come and ask him for the two first places in the
kingdom, He answers that He can lead them indeed to
suffering; but as to the first places in His kingdom, He
could not bestow them, except (according to the Father's
counsels) on those for whom the Father had prepared
them. Wondrous self-renunciation! It is for the Father,
for us, that He works. He disposes of nothing. He can
bestow on those who will follow Him a share in His sufferings: everything else shall be given according to the
counsels of the Father. But what real glory for Christ
and perfection in Him, and what a privilege for us to
have this motive only, and to partake in the Lord's sufferings! and what a purification of our carnal hearts is
here proposed to us, in making us act only for a suffering
Christ, sharing His cross, and committing ourselves to God
for recompense!

The spirit of Christ a spirit of service

The Lord then takes occasion to explain the sentiments
that become His followers, the perfection of which they

had seen in Himself.   In the world, authority was sought for; but the spirit of Christ was a spirit of service, leading to the choice of the lowest place, and to entire devotedness to others. Beautiful and perfect principles, the full bright perfection of which was displayed in Christ. The renunciation of all things, in order to depend confidingly on the grace of Him whom we serve, the consequent readiness to take the lowest place, and thus to be the servant of all— this should be the spirit of those who have part in the kingdom as now established by the rejected Lord. It is this that becomes His followers.[61]

Christ's last presentation to Israel as the Son of David: the beginning of the closing scenes of His life

With the end of verse 28 this portion of the Gospel terminates, and the closing scenes of the blessed Saviour's life begin. At verse 29[62] begins His last presentation to Israel as the Son of David, the Lord, the true King of Israel, the Messiah. He begins His career in this respect at Jericho, the place where Joshua entered the land—the place on which the curse had so long rested. He opens the blind eyes of His people who believe in Him and receive Him as the Messiah, for such He truly was, although

[61] Observe the way in which the sons of Zebedee and their mother come to seek the highest place, at the moment when the Lord was preparing unreservedly to take the very lowest. Alas! we see so much of the same spirit.   The effect was to bring out how absolutely He had stripped Himself of everything. These are the principles of the heavenly kingdom: perfect self-renunciation, to be contented in thorough devotedness; this is the fruit of love that seeketh not her own—the yieldingness that flows from the absence of self-seeking; submission when despised; meekness and lowliness of heart. The spirit of service to others is that which love produces at the same time as the humility which is satisfied with this place. The Lord fulfilled this even unto death, giving His life as a ransom for many.

[62] The case of the blind man at Jericho is, in all the first three Gospels, the commencement of the final circumstances of Christ's life which led on to the cross, the general contents and teachings of each being closed. Hence He is addressed as Son of David, being the last presentation of Himself as such to them, God's testimony being given to Him as such.

rejected. They salute Him as Son of David, and He answers their faith by opening their eyes. They follow Him —a figure of the true remnant of His people, who will wait for Him.

Chapter 21

The Lord's entry into Jerusalem as King and Lord

A FTERWARDS (chap. 21), disposing of all that belonged to His willing people, He makes His entry into Jerusalem as King and Lord, according to the testimony of Zechariah. But although entering as King—the last testimony to the beloved city, which (to their ruin) was going to reject Him—He comes as a meek and lowly King. The power of God influences the heart of the multitudes, and they salute Him as King, as Son of David, making use of the language supplied by Psalm 118,[63] which celebrates the millennial sabbath brought in by the Messiah, then to be acknowledged by the people. The multitude spread their garments to prepare the way for their meek, though glorious King; they cut down branches from the trees to bear Him testimony; and He is conducted in triumph to Jerusalem, while the people cry, "Hosanna [save now] to the Son of David: Blessed is He that cometh in the name of the Lord; Hosanna in the highest!" Happy for them if their hearts had been changed to retain this testimony in the Spirit. But God sovereignly disposed their hearts to bear this testimony; He could not allow His Son to be rejected without receiving it.

The King's review of all as the true Judge

And now the King is going to review everything, still maintaining His position of humility and of testimony.

---

[63] This psalm is peculiarly prophetic of the time of His future reception, and is often cited in connection with it.

Apparently the different classes come to judge Him, or to perplex Him; but in fact they all present themselves before Him to receive at His hands, one after another, the judgment of God respecting them. It is a striking scene that opens before us—the true Judge, the everlasting King, presenting Himself for the last time to His rebellious people with the fullest testimony to His rights and to His power; and they, coming to harass and condemn Him, led by their very malice to pass before Him one after another, laying open their real condition, to receive their judgment from His lips, without His forsaking for a moment (unless in cleansing the temple, before this scene commenced) the position of Faithful and True Witness in all meekness on the earth.

The Lord as Messiah and Jehovah

The difference between the two parts of this history is distinguishable. The first presents the Lord in His character of Messiah and Jehovah. As Lord, He commands the ass to be brought. He enters the city, according to the prophecy, as King. He cleanses the temple with authority. In answer to the priests' objection He quotes Psalm 8, which speaks of the manner in which Jehovah caused Himself to be glorified, and perfected the praises due to Him out of the mouth of babes. In the temple also He heals Israel. He then leaves them, no longer lodging in the city, which He could no longer own, but with the remnant outside. The next day, in a remarkable figure He exhibits the curse about to fall upon the nation. Israel was the fig-tree of Jehovah; but it cumbered the ground. It was covered with leaves, but there was no fruit. The fig-tree, condemned by the Lord, presently withers away. It is a figure of this unhappy nation, of man in the flesh with every advantage, which bore no fruit for the Husbandman.

No fruit for God

Israel in fact possessed all the outward forms of religion, and were zealous for the law and the ordinances, but they bore no fruit unto God. So far as placed under responsibility to bring forth fruit, that is to say, under the old covenant, they will never do so. Their rejection of Jesus put an end to all hope. God will act in grace under the new covenant; but this is not the question here. The fig-tree is Israel as they were, man cultivated by God, but in vain. All was over. That which He said to the disciples of the mountain's removing, while it is a great general principle, refers also, I doubt not, to that which should take place in Israel by means of their ministry. Looked at corporately on the earth as a nation, Israel should disappear, and be lost among the Gentiles. The disciples were those whom God accepted according to their faith.

Details of judgment on the nation's various classes

We see the Lord entering Jerusalem as a king—Jehovah, the King of Israel—and judgment pronounced on the nation. Then follow the details of judgment on the different classes of which it was composed. First come the chief priests and elders, who should have guided the people; they draw near to the Lord and question His authority. Thus addressing Him, they took the place of heads of the nation, and assumed to be judges, capable of pronouncing on the validity of any claims that might be made; if not, why concern themselves with Jesus?

The Lord, in His infinite wisdom, puts a question to them which tests their capability and by their own confession they were incapable. How then judge Him?[64] To tell them the foundation of His authority was useless. It was too late now to tell them. They would have stoned

---

[64] This throwing back on conscience is often the wisest answer, when the will is perverse.

Him, if He had alleged its true source. He replies, "Decide on John the Baptist's mission." If they could not do this, why inquire respecting His? They cannot do it. If they acknowledged John to have been sent of God, it would be acknowledging Christ. To deny it would be to lose their influence with the people. Of conscience there was no question with them. They confess their inability. Jesus then declines their competency as leaders and guardians of the faith of the people. They had judged themselves; and the Lord proceeds to set their conduct, and the Lord's dealings with them, plainly before their eyes, from verse 28 to chapter 22: 14.

Perversity and rebellion: self-condemnation

First, while professing to do the will of God, they did it not; while the openly wicked had repented and done His will. They, seeing this, were still hardened. Again, not only had natural conscience remained untouched, whether by the testimony of John, or by the sight of repentance in others, but, although God had used every means to make them bring forth fruit worthy of His culture, He had found nothing in them but perversity and rebellion. The prophets had been rejected, and His Son would be so likewise. They desired to have His inheritance for themselves. They could not but acknowledge that in such case the consequence must necessarily be the destruction of those wicked men, and the bestowal of the vineyard on others. Jesus applies the parable to themselves, by quoting Psalm 118, which announces that the stone rejected by the builders should become the head-stone of the corner; moreover, that whosoever should fall on this stone—as the nation was at that moment doing—should be broken; but that on whomsoever it should fall—and this would be the lot of the rebellious nation in the last days—it should grind them to powder. The chief priests and the Pharisees understood that He spoke of them, but they dared not lay hands on Him, because the multitude took Him for a prophet. This is the history of Israel, as under responsibility, even till the last days. Jehovah was seeking fruit in His vineyard.

Chapter 22

The marriage feast: grace despised by Israel: its judgment: the bringing in of the Gentiles

IN chapter 22 their conduct with respect to the invitations of grace is presented in its turn. The parable is therefore a similitude of the kingdom of heaven. The purpose of God is to honor His Son by celebrating His marriage. First of all the Jews, already invited, are bidden to the marriage feast. They would not come. This was done during Christ's life-time. Afterwards, all things being ready, He again sends forth messengers to induce them to come. This is the mission of the apostles to the nation, when the work of redemption had been accomplished. They either despise the message or slay the messengers.[65] The result is the destruction of those wicked men and of their city. This is the destruction that fell upon Jerusalem. On their rejection of the invitation, the destitute, the Gentiles, those who were outside, are brought in to the feast, and the wedding is furnished with guests. Another thing is now presented. It is true, that we have seen the judgment of Jerusalem in this parable, but, as it is a similitude of the kingdom, we have the judgment of that which is within the kingdom also. There must be fitness for the occasion. For a wedding feast there must be a wedding garment. If Christ is to be glorified, everything must be according to His glory. There may be an out-

---

[65] Contempt and violence are the two forms of the rejection of the testimony of God, and of the true witness. They hate the one and love the other, or cleave to the one and despise the other.

ward entrance into the kingdom, a profession of Christianity; but he who is not clothed with that which appertains to the feast will be cast out. We must be clothed with Christ Himself. On the other hand, all is prepared —nothing is required. It was not the guest's part to bring anything; the King provided all. But we must be imbued with the spirit of that which is done. If there is any thought of what was suitable to a wedding feast, the need of a wedding garment to appear in would surely be felt: if not, the honor of the King's Son has been forgotten. The heart was a stranger to it; the man himself shall become so by the judgment of the King when He takes cognizance of the guests who have come in.

Thus also grace has been shown to Israel, and they are judged for refusing the invitation of the great King to the marriage of His Son. And then the abuse of this grace by those who appear to accept it is also judged. The bringing in of the Gentiles is declared.

Here concludes the history of the judgment of Israel in general, and of the character which the kingdom would assume.

The Pharisees and Herodians answered

After this (chap. 22: 15, *et seq.*) the different classes of the Jews come forward, each in turn. First, the Pharisees and the Herodians (that is, those who favored the authority of the Romans, and those who were opposed to it) seek to entangle Jesus in His talk. The blessed Lord answers them with that perfect wisdom that ever displayed itself in all He said and all He did. On their part, it was pure wickedness manifesting a total want of conscience. It was their own sin that had brought them under the Roman yoke — a position contrary indeed to that which should have belonged to the people of God on earth. Apparently therefore Christ must either become an object of suspicion to the authorities, or renounce His claim to be the Messiah and consequently the Deliverer. Who had occasioned this dilemma? It was the fruit of their own sins. The Lord shows them that they had themselves accepted the yoke. The money bore the mark of this: let them render it then to those unto whom it belonged, and let them also —which they were not doing—render unto God the things that were God's. He leaves them under the yoke which they were obliged to confess they had accepted. He reminds them of the rights of God, which they had forgotten. Such might moreover have been Israel's state according to the establishment of power in Nebuchadnezzar, as a "spreading vine of low stature."

The unbelief of the Sadducees

The Sadducees come next before Him, and question Him as to the resurrection, thinking to prove its absurdity. Thus, as the condition of the nation had been exhibited in His discourse with the Pharisees, the unbelief of the Sadducees is displayed here. They thought only of the things of this world, seeking to deny the existence of another. But whatever the state of degradation and subjection into which the people had fallen, the God of Abraham, of Isaac, and of Jacob, changed not. The promises made to the fathers remained sure, and the fathers were living to enjoy these promises hereafter. It was the Word and the power of God which were in question. The Lord maintains them with power and evidence. The Sadducees were silenced.

The essence of the perfect law

The lawyers, struck with His reply, ask a question, which gives the Lord occasion to extract from the whole law that which, in the sight of God, is its essence, presenting thus its perfection, and that which—by whatever means it may be reached—forms the happiness of those that walk in it. Grace alone rises higher.

Here their questioning ceases. All is judged, all is brought to light with respect to the position of the people, and the sects of Israel; and the Lord has laid before them the perfect thoughts of God respecting them, whether on the subject of their condition, of His promises, or of the substance of the law.

The Lord's question: its only answer: the true position of Christ

It was now the Lord's turn to propose His question in order to bring out His own position. He asks the Pharisees to reconcile the title of Son of David with that of Lord which David himself gave Him, and that in connection with the ascension of this same Christ to sit at the right hand of God until God had made all His enemies His footstool, and established His throne in Zion. Now this was the whole of Christ's position at that moment. They were unable to answer Him, and no man durst ask Him any more questions. In fact, to understand that psalm would have been to understand all the ways of God with respect to His Son at the time they were going to reject Him. This necessarily closed these discourses by showing the true position of Christ, who, although the Son of David, must ascend on high to receive the kingdom, and, while waiting for it, sit at the right hand of God according to the rights of His glorious Person—David's Lord, as well as David's Son.

The condition, privileges and responsibility of all classes of the Jews

There is another point of interest to be remarked here. In these interviews and these discourses with the different classes of the Jews, the Lord brings out the condition of the Jews on all sides with respect to their relations with God, and then the position which He took Himself. He first shows their national position towards God, as under responsibility to Him, according to natural conscience and the privileges belonging to them. The result would be their cutting off, and the bringing in of others into the Lord's vineyard. This is chapter 21: 28-46. He then exhibits their condition with regard to the grace of the kingdom, and the introduction of Gentile sinners. Here also the result is the cutting off and the destruction of the city.[66] Afterwards the Herodians and the Pharisees, the friends of the Romans and their enemies, the pretended friends of God, bring out the true position of the Jews with respect to the imperial power of the Gentiles and to God. In His interview with the Sadducees, He shows the certainty of the promises made to the fathers, and the relationship in which God stood to them in respect of life and resurrection. After this He puts the real meaning of the law before the scribes; and then the position which He took, Himself the Son of David, according to Psalm 110, which was linked with His rejection by the leaders of the nation who stood around Him.

Chapter 23

The position of the disciples as part of the nation

CHAPTER 23 clearly shows how far the disciples are viewed in connection with the nation, inasmuch as

[66] Observe here, that from chapter 21: 28 to the end, we have the responsibility of the nation looked at as in possession of their original privileges, according to which they ought to have borne fruit. Not having done so, another is put in their place. This is not the cause of the judgment which was, and yet is in a more terrible way to be, executed in Jerusalem, and which even then accomplished the destruction of the city. The death of Jesus, the last of those who had been sent to look for fruit, brings judgment on His murderers (Matt. 21: 33-41). The destruction of Jerusalem is the consequence of the rejection of the testimony to the kingdom sent to call them in grace. In the first case, the judgment was upon the husbandmen—the scribes, and chief priests, and leaders of the people. The judgment executed on account of the rejection of the testimony to the kingdom goes much farther. (See chap. 22: 7.) Some despise the message, others ill-treat the messengers; and, grace being thus rejected, the city is burned up, and its inhabitants cut off. Compare chap. 23: 36, and see the historical prophecy in Luke 21. The distinction is maintained in all three Gospels.

they were Jews, although the Lord judges the leaders, who
beguiled the people and dishonored God by their hypocrisy. He speaks to the multitude and to His disciples,
saying, "The scribes and the Pharisees sit in Moses' seat."
Being thus expositors of the law, they were to be obeyed
in all that they said according to that law, although their
own conduct was but hypocrisy. That which is important
here is the position of the disciples; it is in fact the same
as that of Jesus. They are in connection with all that is
of God in the nation, that is to say, with the nation as the
recognized people of God—consequently, with the law as
possessing authority from God. At the same time the
Lord judges, and the disciples also were practically to
judge, the walk of the nation, as publicly represented by
their leaders. While still forming part of the nation, they
were carefully to avoid the walk of the scribes and Pharisees. After having reproached these pastors of the nation
with their hypocrisy, the Lord points out the way in which
they themselves condemned the deeds of their fathers—
by building the sepulchres of the prophets whom they had
slain. They were, then, the children of those who slew
them, and God would put them to the test by sending
them also prophets and wise men and scribes, and they
would fill up the measure of their iniquity by putting
these to death and persecuting them—condemned thus out
of their own mouths—in order that all the righteous blood
which had been shed, from Abel's to that of the prophet
Zechariah, should come upon this generation. Frightful
amount of guilt, accumulated from the beginning of the
enmity which sinful man, when placed under responsibility, has ever shown to the testimony of God; and which
increased daily, because the conscience became more hardened each time that it resisted this testimony! The truth
was so much the more manifest from its witnesses having
suffered. It was a rock, exposed to view, to be avoided in
the people's path. But they persisted in their evil course,
and every step in advance, every similar act, was the

proof of a still increasing obduracy. The patience of God, while graciously dealing in testimony, had not been un-observant of their ways, and under this patience all had accumulated. All would be heaped up on the head of this reprobate generation.

Remark here the character given to the apostles and Christian prophets. They are scribes, wise men, prophets, sent to the Jews—to the ever-rebellious nation. This very clearly brings out the aspect in which this chapter regards them. Even the apostles are "wise men," "scribes," sent to the Jews as such.

But the nation — Jerusalem, God's beloved city — is guilty and is judged. Christ, as we have seen, since the cure of the blind man near Jericho, presents Himself as Jehovah the King of Israel. How often would He have gathered the children of Jerusalem, but they would not! And now their house should be desolate, until (their hearts being converted) they should use the language of Psalm 118, and, in desire, hail His arrival who came in the name of Jehovah, looking for deliverance at His hands, and praying to Him for it—in a word, until they should cry Hosanna to Him that should come. They would see Jesus no more until, humbled in heart, they should pro-nounce Him blessed whom they were expecting, and whom they now rejected—in short, until they were pre-pared in heart. Peace should follow, desire precede, His appearing.

The position of the Jews before God

The last three verses exhibit clearly enough the posi-tion of the Jews, or of Jerusalem, as the centre of the system before God. Long since, and many times, would Jesus, Jehovah the Saviour, have gathered the children of Jerusalem together, even as a hen gathereth her chick-ens under her wings, but they would not. Their house should remain forsaken and desolate, but not for ever.

After having killed the prophets, and stoned the messengers sent unto them, they had crucified their Messiah, and rejected and slain those whom He had sent to proclaim grace unto them even after His rejection. Therefore should they see Him no more until they had repented, and the desire to see Him was produced in their hearts, so that they should be prepared to bless Him, and would bless Him in their hearts, and confess their readiness to do so. The Messiah, who was about to leave them, should be seen of them no more until repentance had turned their hearts unto Him whom they were now rejecting. Then they should *see* Him. The Messiah, coming in the name of Jehovah, shall be manifested to His people Israel. It is Jehovah *their* Saviour who should appear, and the Israel who had rejected Him should see Him as such. The people should thus return into the enjoyment of their relationship with God.

Such is the moral and prophetic picture of Israel. The disciples, as Jews, were viewed as part of the nation, though as a remnant *spiritually* detached from it, and witnessing in it.

Chapter 24

The Olivet discourse: prophecy and instruction

WE have already seen that the rejection of the testimony to the kingdom in grace, is the cause of the judgment that falls upon Jerusalem and its inhabitants. Now in chapter 24 we have the position of this testimony in the midst of the people; the condition of the Gentiles, and the relation in which they stood to the testimony rendered by the disciples; after this, the condition of Jerusalem, consequent upon her rejection of the Messiah, and her contempt for the testimony; and then the universal overthrow at the end of those days: a state of things which should be ended by the appearance of the Son of Man, and the gathering together of the elect of Israel from the four winds.

We must examine this remarkable passage, at once a prophecy, and instruction to the disciples for their direction in the path they must follow amid the coming events.

Jesus departs from the temple, and that for ever—a solemn act, which, we may say, executed the judgment He had just pronounced. The house was now desolate. The hearts of the disciples were still bound to it by their former prepossessions. They draw His attention to the magnificent buildings that composed it. Jesus announces to them its entire destruction. Seated apart with Him on the Mount of Olives, the disciples inquire when these things were to happen, and what would be the sign of His coming and of the end of the age. They class together the destruction of the temple, the coming of Christ, and the end of the age. We must observe, that here the end of the age is the end of the period during which Israel was subject to the law under the old covenant: a period which was to cease, giving place to the Messiah and to the new covenant. Observe also that God's government of the earth is the subject, and the judgments that should take place at Christ's coming, which would put an end to the existing age. The disciples confounded that which the Lord had said of the destruction of the temple with this period.[67] The Lord treats the subject from His own point of view (that is to say, with regard to the testimony which the disciples were to render in connection with the

---

[67] In fact, this position of Israel, and the testimony connected with it, were interrupted by the destruction of Jerusalem; and this is the reason why that event presents itself to the mind in connection with this prophecy, of which it is certainly not the fulfilment. The Lord is not yet come, neither the great tribulation; but the state of things to which the Lord alludes, to the end of verse 14, was violently and judicially interrupted, by the destruction of Jerusalem, so that in this point of view there is a connection.

Jews during His absence and to the end of the age). He adds nothing as to the destruction of Jerusalem, which He had already announced. The time of His coming was purposely hidden. Moreover the destruction of Jerusalem by Titus put an end, in fact, to the position which the Lord's instructions had in view. There was no longer any cognizable testimony among the Jews. When this position shall be resumed, the applicability of the passage will also recommence. After the destruction of Jerusalem until that time the Church only is in question.

The divisions of the discourse

The Lord's discourse is divided into three parts—

1. The general condition of the disciples and of the world during the time of the testimony, to the end of verse 14;

2. The period marked out by the fact that the abomination of desolation stands in the holy place (ver. 15);

3. The Lord's coming and the gathering together of the elect in Israel (ver. 29).

Testimony among the people and among the Gentiles until the end of the age

The time of the disciples' testimony is characterized by false Christs and false prophets among the Jews; persecution of those who render testimony, betraying them to the Gentiles. But there is yet something more definite with regard to those days. There would be false Christs in Israel. There would be wars, famines, pestilences, earthquakes. They were not to be troubled: the end would not be yet. These things were only a beginning of sorrows. They were principally outward things. There were other events which would bring them into greater trial, and test them more thoroughly—things more from within. The disciples should be delivered up, put to death.

hated of all nations. The consequence of this among those who made profession would be that many would be offended; they would betray one another. False prophets would arise and deceive many, and, because iniquity abounded, the love of many should wax cold—a sorrowful picture. But these things would give occasion for the exercise of a faith that had been put to the proof. He who endured to the end should be saved. This concerns the sphere of testimony in particular. That which the Lord says, is not absolutely limited to the testimony in Canaan; but as it is from thence the testimony goes forth, it is all connected with that land as the centre of God's ways. But, in addition to this, the gospel of the kingdom should be preached in all the world for a witness unto all nations, and then should the end come—the end of this age. Now, although heaven is the source of authority when the kingdom shall be established, Canaan and Jerusalem are its earthly centre. So that the idea of the kingdom, while extending throughout the world, turns our thoughts to the land of Israel. It is "this gospel of the kingdom"[68] which is here spoken of; it is not the proclamation of the union of the Church with Christ, nor redemption in its fulness, as preached and taught by the apostles after the ascension, but the kingdom which was to be established on the earth, as John the Baptist, and as the Lord Himself, had proclaimed. The establishment of the universal authority of the ascended Christ should be preached in all the world to test their obedience, and to furnish those who had ears to hear with the object of faith.

This is the general history of that which would take

---

[68] The gospel of the kingdom was confined to Israel in chapter 10 and here this, though no subject of the teaching, is the subject supposed up to verse 14, but there is no formal distinction made: the mission in chapter 28 is to the Gentiles; but then there is nothing of the kingdom but rather the contrary, though Christ be only risen, but all power given to Him in heaven and earth.

place until the end of the age, without entering on the subject of the proclamation which founded the assembly properly so called. The impending destruction of Jerusalem, and the refusal of the Jews to receive the gospel, caused God to raise up a special testimony by the hands of Paul, without annulling the truth of the coming kingdom. That which follows proves that such a going forth of testimony of the kingdom will take place at the end, and that the testimony will reach all nations before the coming of that judgment which will put an end to the age.

The great tribulation: "the time of the end"

But there will be a moment when, within a certain sphere (that is, in Jerusalem and its vicinity) a special time of suffering shall set in as regards the testimony in Israel. In speaking of the abomination that maketh desolate, the Lord refers us to Daniel, that we may understand whereof He speaks. Now Daniel (chap. 12, where this tribulation is spoken of) brings us definitely to the last days—the time when Michael shall stand up for Daniel's people, that is, the Jews, who are under the dominion of the Gentiles—the days in which there shall be a time of trouble, such as never had been nor ever again should be, and in which the remnant should be delivered. In the latter part of the previous chapter of that prophet, this time is called "the time of the end," and the destruction of the king of the north is prophetically declared. Now the prophet announces that 1335 days before the full blessing (Blessed is he that has part therein!) the daily sacrifice should be taken away, and the abomination that maketh desolate set up; that from this moment there should be 1290 days (that is, one month more than the 1260 days spoken of in the Apocalypse, during which the woman who flees from the serpent is nourished in the wilderness; and also than the three years and a half of

Daniel 7). At the end, as we find here, the judgment comes and the kingdom is given to the saints.

The time and people to whom the prophecy applies

Thus it is proved that this passage refers to the last days and to the position of the Jews at that time. The events of the time past since the Lord uttered it confirm this thought. Neither in 1260 days, nor in 1260 years, after the days of Titus, nor in 30 days or years after, did any event take place which could be the accomplishment of these days in Daniel. The periods are gone by many years ago. Israel has not been delivered, neither has Daniel stood in his lot at the end of those days. It is equally plain that Jerusalem is in question in the passage, and its vicinity, for they that are in Judea are commanded to flee into the mountains. The disciples who shall be there at that time are to pray that their flight may not be on a sabbath day—an additional testimony that it is Jews who are the subject of the prophecy; but a testimony also of the tender care which the Lord takes of those who are His, thinking even in the midst of these unparalleled events, of whether it would be wintry weather at the time of their flight.

The Jewish remnant in question, not the assembly

Besides this, other circumstances prove, if further proof were needed, that it is the Jewish remnant who are in question, and not the assembly. We know that all believers are to be caught up to meet the Lord in the air. They will afterwards return with Him. But here there will be false Christs on the earth, and people will say, "He is here in the wilderness," "He is there in the secret chambers." But the saints who shall be caught up and return with the Lord have nothing at all to do with false Christs on earth, since they will go up to heaven to be with Him there, before He returns to the earth; while it is easy to understand that the Jews, who are expecting earth-ly deliverance, should be liable to such temptations, and that they should be deceived by them unless kept by God Himself.

The coming of the Son of Man

This part then of the prophecy applies to the last days, the last three years and a half before the judgment which will be suddenly poured out at the coming of the Son of Man. The Lord will come suddenly as a flash of lightning, as an eagle to its prey, unto the spot where the object of His judgment is found. Immediately after the tribulation of those last three years and a half, the whole hierarchical system of government shall be shaken and utterly over-thrown. Then shall appear the sign of the Son of Man in *heaven,* and they shall see the Son of Man coming in the clouds of heaven with power and great glory. This verse (30) contains the answer to the second part of the disciples' inquiry in verse 3. The Lord gives His dis-ciples the warnings necessary for their guidance; but the world would see no signs, however plain they might be to those that understand. But this sign should be at the moment of the Lord's appearing. The brightness of His glory whom they had despised would show them who it was that came; and it would be unexpected. What a ter-rible moment, when, instead of a Messiah who should answer to their worldly pride, the Christ whom they had despised shall appear in the heavens!

Afterwards the Son of Man, thus come and manifested, would send to gather all the elect of Israel from the four corners of the earth. It is this which ends the history of the Jews, and even that of Israel, in answer to the dis-ciples' question, and unfolds the dealings of God with respect to the testimony among the people who had re-jected it, announcing the time of their deep distress, and the judgment that shall be poured out in the midst of this

scene when Jesus comes, the subversion of all powers great
and small being complete.

The importance of the capture of Jerusalem: the Jews as a distinct race today

The Lord gives the history of the testimony in Israel,
and that of the people themselves, from the moment of
His departure until His return; but the length of time,
during which there should be neither people nor temple
nor city, is not specified.   It is this which gives importance
to the capture of Jerusalem.   It is not here spoken of in
direct terms—the Lord does not describe it; but it put an
end to that order of things to which His discourse applies,
and this application is not resumed until Jerusalem and
the Jews are again brought forward. The Lord announced
it at the beginning. The disciples thought that His coming would take place at the same time. He answers them
in such a manner that His discourse should be of use to
them until the capture of Jerusalem. But when once the
abomination of desolation is mentioned, we find ourselves
carried on into the last days.

The disciples were to understand the signs He gave
them. I have already said that the destruction of Jerusalem, by the fact itself, interrupted the application of
His discourse. The Jewish nation was set aside; but verse
34 has a much wider sense, and one more really proper to
it. Unbelieving Jews should exist, as such, until all was
accomplished. Compare Deuteronomy 32: 5, 20, where
this judgment on Israel is specially in view. God hides
His face from them until He shall see what their end will
be, for they are a very froward generation, children in
whom is no faith. This has taken place. They are a distinct race of people unto this day. That generation exists
in the same condition—a monument of the abiding certainty of God's dealings, and of the Lord's words.

To conclude, the government of God, exercised with

regard to this people, has been traced to its end. The
Lord comes, and He gathers together the dispersed elect
of Israel.

The judgment of nations on earth according to their treatment of the messengers of the kingdom

The prophetic history continues in chapter 25: 31,
which is connected with chapter 24: 30. And as chapter
24: 31 relates the gathering together of Israel after the
appearance of the Son of Man, chapter 25: 31 announces
His dealings in judgment with the Gentiles. He will appear doubtless as the lightning with regard to the apostasy,
which will be as a dead body in His sight. But when He
shall come solemnly to take His earthly place in glory,
that will not pass away like lightning. He shall sit upon
the throne of His glory, and all nations shall be gathered
before Him on His throne of judgment, and they shall be
judged according to their treatment of the messengers of
the kingdom, who had gone out to preach it unto them.
These messengers are the brethren (ver. 40); those who
had received them are the sheep; those who had neglected
their message are the goats. The account which begins chapter 25: 31, of the separation of sheep and goats
and of its result, pictures the nations who are judged on
earth according to their treatment of these messengers.
It is the judgment of the living, so far at least as regards
the nations—a judgment as final as that of the dead. It
is not Christ's judgment in battle, as in Revelation 19. It
is a session of His supreme tribunal in His right of government over the earth, as in Revelation 20: 4. I speak of
the principle or rather of the character of the judgment.
I do not doubt that these brethren are Jews, such as the
disciples were, that is to say, those who will be in a similar
position as to their testimony. The Gentiles, who had
received this message, should be accepted, as though they
had treated Christ in the same manner. His Father had

prepared for them the enjoyment of the kingdom; and they should enter into it, being still on earth, for Christ was *come down* in the power of eternal life.[69]

Christ's disciples outside the testimony in Israel

I have, for the moment, passed over all between chapter 24: 31 and chapter 25: 31, because the end of this last chapter completes all that concerns the government and the judgment of the earth. But there is a class of persons whose history is given us in its great moral features intermediately between these two verses I have just mentioned.

These are the disciples of Christ, outside the testimony borne in the midst of Israel, to whom He has committed His service, and a position in connection *with Himself,* during His absence. This position and this service are in connection with Christ Himself, and not in connection with Israel, wherever it may be that this service is accomplished.

Discriminating judgment in the last days in the Lord's own household

There are however, before we come to these, some verses of which I have not yet spoken, which apply more particularly to the state of things in Israel, as warning to the disciples who are there, and describe the discriminating judgment which takes place among the Jews in the last days. I speak of them here, because all this part of

[69] There is no possible ground for applying this parable to what is called the general judgment, an expression indeed wholly unscriptural. First, there are three parties, not merely two—goats, sheep, and brethren; then, it is the judgment of the Gentiles only; and, further, the ground of judgment is wholly inapplicable to the great mass even of these last. The ground of judgment is the way these brethren have been received. Now none have been sent at all to the vast majority of the Gentiles in long ages. The time of this ignorance God winked at, and another ground of judgment as to them is given in the beginning of Romans. Christians and Jews have been already treated of in chapters 24 and the previous part of chapter 25. It is just those whom the Lord finds on earth when He comes, and who will be judged according to their treatment of the messengers He has sent.

the discourse—namely, from chapter 24: 31 to chapter
25: 31—is an exhortation, an address from the Lord, on
the subject of their duties during His absence. I refer to
chapter 24: 32-44. They speak of the continual expectation which their ignorance of the moment when the Son of
Man would come imposed on the disciples, and in which
the disciples were intentionally left (and the judgment is
the earthly one); while from verse 45, the Lord addresses
Himself more directly, and at the same time in a more
general manner, to their conduct during His absence, not
in connection with Israel, but with His own—His household. He had committed to them the task of supplying
them with suitable food in due season. This is the responsibility of ministry in the assembly.

Collective responsibility in service

It is important to remark that in the first parable the
state of the assembly is looked at as a whole; the parable
of the virgins and that of the talents give individual responsibility. Hence *the* servant who is unfaithful is cut
off and has his portion with hypocrites. The state of the
responsible assembly depended on their waiting for Christ,
or their heart saying He delays His coming. It would be
on His return that judgment should be pronounced on
their faithfulness during the interval. Faithfulness should
be approved in that day. On the other hand, practical
forgetfulness of His coming would lead to licence and
tyranny. It is not an intellectual system that is meant
here: "The evil servant says *in his heart*, My lord delayeth his coming;" his will was concerned in it. The result was that the fleshly will manifested itself. It was no
longer devoted service to His household, with a heart set
upon the Master's approval at His return; but worldliness
in conduct, and the assumption of arbitrary authority, to
which the service appointed him gave occasion. He eats
and drinks with the drunken, he unites himself to the

world and partakes in its ways; he smites his fellow-servants at his will. Such is the effect of putting off during His absence, deliberately in heart, the Lord's return and holding the assembly to be settled down here; instead of faithful service, worldly-mindedness and tyranny. Is it not too true a picture?

Reward for service in the assembly

What is it that has happened to those who had the place of service in the house of God? The consequences on either hand are these: the faithful servant, who from love and devotion to his Master applied himself to the welfare of His household, should be made ruler on his Master's return over *all His goods;* those who have been faithful in the service of the house shall be set over all things by the Lord, when He takes His place of power and acts as King. All things are given into the hands of Jesus by the Father. Those who in humility have been faithful to His service during His absence shall be made rulers over all that is committed to Him, that is, over all things —they are but the "goods" of Jesus. On the other hand, he who during the Lord's absence had set himself up as master, and followed after the spirit of the flesh and of the world to which he had united himself, should not merely have the world's portion; his Master should come quite unexpectedly, and he should receive the punishment of hypocrites. What a lesson for those who take to themselves a place of service in the assembly! Observe here, that it is not said he is drunken himself, but that he eats and drinks with those that are so. He allies himself with the world and follows its customs. This moreover is the general aspect which the kingdom will assume in that day, although the heart of the evil servant was wicked. The Bridegroom would indeed tarry; and the consequences that might be expected from the heart of man will not fail to be realized. But the effect, we then find, is to make manifest those who had[70] really the grace of Christ and those who had not.

Chapter 25

The Ten Virgins: individual responsibility during Christ's absence

PROFESSORS, during the Lord's absence, are here presented as virgins, who went out to meet the Bridegroom, and light Him to the house. In this passage He is not the Bridegroom of the Church. No others go to meet Him for His marriage with the Church in heaven. The bride does not appear in this parable. Had she been introduced, it would have been Jerusalem on earth. The assembly is not seen in these chapters as such.

It is here individual[71] responsibility during the absence of Christ. That which characterized the faithful at this period was that they came out from the world, from Judaism, from everything, even religion connected with the world, to go and meet the coming Lord. The Jewish remnant, on the contrary, wait for Him in the place where they are. If this expectation were real, the characteristic of one governed by it would be the thought of that which was necessary for the coming One—the light, the oil. Otherwise, to be the companions of professors meanwhile, and to carry lamps with them, would satisfy the heart. Nevertheless they all took a position; they go out, they leave the house to go out and meet the Bridegroom. He

---

[70] How solemn the testimony given here to the effect of the assembly's losing the present expectation of the Lord's return! What causes the professing Church to run into hierarchical oppression and worldliness so as to be cut off in the end as hypocrites, is saying in the heart, My lord delayeth his coming—giving up the present expectation. That has been the source of the ruin. The true Christian position was lost as soon as they began to put off the Lord's coming; and they are treated, note, though in this state, as the responsible servant.

[71] The servant in chapter 24 is collective responsibility.

tarries. This also has taken place. They *all* fall asleep.
The whole professing Church has lost the thought of the
Lord's return—even the faithful who have the Spirit.
They must also have gone in again somewhere to sleep
at ease—a place of rest for the flesh. But at midnight,
unexpectedly, the cry is raised, "Behold, the bridegroom;
go ye out to meet him." Alas, they needed the same call
as at first. They must again *go out* to meet Him. The
virgins rise, and trim their lamps. There is time enough
between the midnight cry and the Bridegroom's arrival
to prove the condition of each. There were some who had
no oil in their vessels. Their lamps were going out.[72]
The wise had oil. It was impossible for them to share it
with the others. Those only who possessed it went in with
the Bridegroom to take part in the marriage. He refused
to acknowledge the others. What business had they there?
The virgins were to give light with their lamps. They had
not done it. Why should they share the feast? They had
failed in that which gave this place. What title had they
to be at the feast? The virgins of the feast were virgins
who accompanied the Bridegroom. These had not done
so. They were not admitted. But even the faithful ones
had forgotten the coming of Christ. They fell asleep. But,
at least, they possessed the essential thing that corre-
sponded to it. The grace of the Bridegroom causes the cry
to be raised which proclaims His arrival. It awakens
them: they have oil in their vessels; and the delay, which
occasions the lamps of the unfaithful to go out, gives the
faithful time to be ready and at their place; and, forgetful
as they may have been, they go in with the Bridegroom
to the wedding feast.[73]

[72] The word rather signifies "torches." With them they had, or
should have, oil in vessels to feed the flame.

[73] And note here, the waking up is by the cry; it wakes up all. There
is enough to rouse all professors to needed activity; but the effect of
this is to put them to the test, and separate them. It was not the time
of getting oil or supplies of grace to those already professors; conversion
is not the subject of the parable. The question of getting oil is only,
I doubt not, to show it was not the time of doing so.

Individual faithfulness to an absent Master: the three servants

We pass now from state of soul to service.

For in truth (ver. 14) it is as a man who had gone away from his home—for the Lord dwelt in Israel—and who commits his goods to his own servants, and then departs. Here, we have the principles that characterize faithful servants, or the contrary. It is not now the personal individual expectation, and the possession of the oil, requisite for a place in the Lord's glorious train; neither is it the public and general position of those who were in the Master's service, characterized as position and as a whole, and therefore represented by a single servant; it is individual faithfulness in the service, as before in the expectation of the Bridegroom. The Master on His return will reckon with each one. Now what was their position? What was the principle that would produce faithfulness? Observe, first of all, that it is not providential gifts, earthly possessions, that are meant. These are not the "goods" that Jesus committed to His servants when He went away. They were gifts which fitted them to labor in His service while He was absent. The Master was sovereign and wise. He gave differently to each, and to each according to his capacity. Each was fitted for the service in which he was employed, and the gifts needed for its fulfilment were bestowed on him. Faithfulness to perform it was the only thing in question. That which distinguished the faithful from the unfaithful was confidence in their Master. They had sufficient confidence in His well-known character, in His goodness, His love, to labor without being authorized in any other manner than by their knowledge of His personal character, and by the intelligence which that confidence and that knowledge produced. Of what use to give them sums of money, except to trade with them? Had He failed in wisdom when He bestowed these gifts? The devotedness that flowed from knowledge of their Master counted upon the love of Him whom they knew. They labored, and they were rewarded. This is the true character, and the spring, of service in the Church. It is this that the third servant lacked. He did not know his Master—he did not trust in Him. He could not even do that which was consistent with his own thoughts. He waited for some authorization which would be a security against the character his heart falsely gave his Master. Those who knew their Master's character entered into His joy.

The difference between this parable and that of Luke 19

There is this difference between the parable here and that in Luke 19, that in the latter each man receives one pound; his responsibility is the only question. And consequently he who gained ten pounds is set over ten cities. Here the sovereignty and the wisdom of God are concerned, and he who labors is guided by the knowledge he has of his Master; and the counsels of God in grace are accomplished. He who has the most receives yet more. At the same time the reward is more general. He who has gained two talents, and he who has gained five, enter alike into the joy of the Lord whom they have served. They have known Him in His true character, they enter into His full joy. The Lord grant it unto us!

The parable of the Ten Virgins limited to the heavenly portion of the kingdom

There is more than this in the second parable—that of the virgins. It refers more directly and more exclusively to the heavenly character of Christians. It is not the assembly, properly so called, as a body; but the faithful have *gone out* to meet the Bridegroom, who was returning to the marriage. At the time of His return to execute judgment, the kingdom of heaven will assume the char-

acter of persons come out from the world, and still more
from Judaism—from all that, in point of religion, belongs
to the flesh—from all established worldly form—to have
to do with the coming Lord alone, and to go out to meet
Him. This was the character of the faithful from the
beginning, as having part in the kingdom of heaven, if
they had understood the position in which they were
placed by the Lord's rejection. The virgins, it is true, had
gone in again; and this falsified their character; but the
midnight cry brought them back into their true place.
Therefore they go in with the Bridegroom, and there is no
question of judging and rewarding, but of being with Him.
In the first parable, and in that of Luke, the subject is His
return to earth, and individual recompense—the results,
in the kingdom, of their conduct during the King's absence.[74] Service and its results are not the subject in the
parable of the virgins. Those who have no oil do not go
in at all. This is enough. The others have blessing in
common; they go in with the Bridegroom to the marriage.
There is no question of particular reward, nor of difference
in conduct between them. It was the heart's expectation,
though grace had to bring them back into it. Whatever
the place of service might have been, the reward was sure.
This parable applies and is limited to the heavenly portion of the kingdom as such. It is a similitude of the kingdom of heaven.

The Master's delay

We may also remark here, that the delay of the Master
is noticed in the third parable likewise—"after a long
time" (ver. 19). Their faithfulness and their constancy
were thus put to the test. May the Lord give unto us to
be found faithful and devoted, now in the end of the

[74] In that of the talents in Matthew, we get indeed the ruling over
many things, the kingdom, but it is more full through the expression,
"Enter thou into the joy of thy Lord"; and the blessing is conferred on
all alike who were faithful in service, great or small.

ages, that He may say unto us, "Good and faithful servants!" It is worthy of remark that in these parables those who are in service, or go out at first, are the same as those found at the end. The Lord would not hold out the supposition of delay beyond "we who are alive and remain."[75]

Weeping and gnashing of teeth are his portion who has not known his Master, who has outraged Him by the thoughts he entertained of His character.

The judgment on earth of the living: the four different parties

In verse 31 the prophetic history is resumed from verse 31 of chapter 24. There we saw the Son of Man appear like a flash of lightning, and afterwards gather together the remnant of Israel from the four corners of the earth. But this is not all. If He thus appears in a manner as sudden as unexpected, He also establishes His throne of judgment and glory on the earth. If He destroys His enemies whom He finds in rebellion against Himself, He also sits upon His throne to judge all nations. This is the judgment on earth of the living. Four different parties are here found together; the Lord, the Son of Man Himself—the brethren—the sheep—and the goats. I believe the brethren here to be Jews, His disciples as Jews, whom He had employed as His messengers, to preach the kingdom during His absence. The gospel of the kingdom was to be preached as a testimony to all nations; and then the end of the age should come. At the time here spoken of, this had been done. The result should be manifested before the throne of the Son of Man on earth.

He calls these messengers therefore His brethren. He had told them they should be ill-treated: they had been so. Still there were some who had received their testimony.

[75] So in the churches in Revelation, He takes existing churches, though I doubt not it is a complete history of the Church.

The King's affection for, and value of, His faithful servants

Now such was His affection for His faithful servants, so highly did He value them, that He judged those to whom the testimony was sent according to the manner in which they had received these messengers, whether well or ill, as though it had been done to Himself. What an encouragement for His witnesses during that time of trouble, tried as their faith should be in service! At the same time it was justice morally to those who were judged; for they had rejected the testimony by whomsoever it was rendered. We have also the result of their conduct, both the one and the other. It is the King—for this is the character Christ has now taken on earth—who pronounces judgment; and He calls the sheep (those who had received the messengers, and had sympathized with them in their afflictions and persecutions) to inherit the kingdom prepared for them from the foundation of the world; for such had been the purpose of God with respect to this earth. He had always the kingdom in view. They were the blessed of His (the King's) Father. It was not children who understood their own relation with their Father; but they were the receivers of blessing from the Father of the King of this world. Moreover they were to enter into everlasting life; for such was the power, through grace, of the word which they had received into their heart. Possessed of everlasting life, they should be blessed in a world that was blessed also.

They who had despised the testimony, and those that bore it, had despised the King who sent them; they should go away into everlasting punishment.

The effect of Christ's return

Thus the whole effect of Christ's coming, with regard to the kingdom and to His messengers during His absence, is unfolded: with respect to the Jews, as far as verse 31 of chapter 24; with respect to His servants during His absence, to the end of verse 30 of chapter 25, including the kingdom of heaven in its present condition, and the heavenly rewards that shall be given; and then, from verse 31 to the end of chapter 25, with respect to the nations who shall be blessed on the earth at His return.

Chapter 26

The Lord's announcement of His betrayal and death: God's counsels and His submission

THE Lord had finished His discourses. He prepares (chap. 26) to suffer, and to make His last and touching adieus to His disciples, at the table of His last passover on earth, at which He instituted the simple and precious memorial which recalls His sufferings and His love with such profound interest. This part of our Gospel requires little explanation—not, assuredly, that it is of less interest, but because it needs to be felt rather than explained.

With what simplicity the Lord announces that which was to happen! (ver. 2). He had already arrived at Bethany, six days before the passover (John 12: 1): there He abode, with the exception of the last supper, until He was taken captive in the garden of Gethsemane, although He visited Jerusalem, and partook of His last meal there.

We have already examined the discourses uttered during those six days, as well as His actions, such as the cleansing of the temple. That which precedes this chapter (26) is either the manifestation of His right as Emmanuel, King of Israel, or that of the judgment of the great King with respect to the people—a judgment expressed in discourses to which the people could make no answer; or, finally, the condition of His disciples during

His absence. We have now His submission to the sufferings appointed Him, to the judgment about to be executed upon Him; but which was, in truth, only the fulfilment of the counsels of God His Father, and of the work of His own love.

Man's iniquitous counsels fulfilling the marvellous ones of God

The picture of man's dreadful sin in the crucifixion of Jesus unfolds before our eyes. But the Lord Himself (chap. 26: 1) announces it beforehand with all the calmness of One who had come for this purpose. Before the consultations of the chief priests had taken place, Jesus speaks of it as a settled thing: "Ye know that after two days is the feast of the passover, and the Son of Man is betrayed to be crucified."

Afterwards (ver. 3) the priests, the scribes, and the elders assemble to concert their plans for obtaining possession of His Person, and ridding themselves of Him.

In a word, *first*, the marvellous counsels of God, and the submission of Jesus, according to His knowledge of those counsels and of the circumstances which should accomplish them; and, *afterwards*, the iniquitous counsels of man, which do but fulfil those of God. Their purposed arrangement of detail not to take Him on the feast day as they dreaded the people (chap. 26: 5) was not God's and fails: He was to suffer at the feast.

Judas in the hand of Satan by divine intention

Judas was but the instrument of their malice in the hand of Satan; who, after all, did but arrange these things according to divine intention. They wished, but in vain, to avoid taking Him at the time of the feast, on account of the multitude, who might favor Jesus, if He appealed to them. They had done so at His entrance into Jerusalem. They supposed Jesus would do so, for wickedness

always reckons on finding its own principles in others.
This is why it so frequently fails in circumventing the
upright—they are artless. Here it was the will of God,
that Jesus should suffer at the feast. But He had prepared a gracious relief to the heart of Jesus—a balm to
His heart more than to His body—a circumstance which
is used by the enemy to drive Judas to extremity and put
him in connection with the chief priests.

At Bethany for the last time: Mary's estimate of the Lord's preciousness accepted

Bethany (linked in memory with the last moments of
peace and tranquillity in the Saviour's life, the place
where dwelt Martha and Mary, and Lazarus the risen
dead)—Bethany[76] receives Jesus for the last time: the
blessed but momentary retreat of a heart which, ever
ready to pour itself out in love, was ever straitened in a
world of sin, that did not and could not respond to it;
yet a heart which has given us, in His relations with this
beloved family, the example of an affection perfect, yet
human, which found sweetness in being responded to and
appreciated. The nearness of the cross, where He would
have to set His face as a flint, did not deprive His heart
of the joy or the sweetness of this communion, while
rendering it solemn and affecting. In doing the work of
God He did not cease to be Man. In everything He condescended to be ours. He could no longer own Jerusalem,
and this sanctuary sheltered Him for a moment from the
rude hand of man. Here He could display what He ever
was as Man. It is with reason, that the act of one who in
a certain sense could appreciate what He felt[77] (whose
affection instinctively entered into the rising enmity

[76] It was not in Martha's house this scene took place, but that of Simon
the leper: Martha served and Lazarus sat at meat. This makes the intelligent act of Mary more entirely personal.

[77] No instance is found of the disciples ever understanding what
Jesus said to them.

against the object she loved and was drawn out by it), and the act that expressed the estimate her heart had of His preciousness and grace should be told in all the world. This is a scene, a testimony, that brings the Lord sensibly near to us, that awakens a feeling in our hearts which sanctifies by binding them to His beloved Person.

The Lord's daily life: His estimate of Mary's devotion

His daily life was one continued tension of soul, in proportion to the strength of His love—a life of devotedness in the midst of sin and misery. For a moment He could, and would own (in presence of the power of evil, now to have its way, and the love that clung to Him thus bowing under it, through true knowledge of Him cultivated in sitting at His feet) that devotedness to Himself, drawn out by that which His soul was in divine perfectness bowing to. He could give an intelligent voice, its true meaning, to that which divinely wrought affection silently acted on.[78]

The reader will do well carefully to study this scene of touching condescension and outpouring of heart. Jesus, Emmanuel, King and Supreme Judge, had just been causing all things to pass in judgment before Him. (From chap. 21 to the end of 25.) He had finished that which He had to say. His task here, in this respect, was accomplished. He now takes the place of Victim; He has only to suffer, and can allow Himself freely to enjoy the touching expressions of affection that flow from a heart devoted to Him. He could but taste the honey and pass on; but He does taste it, and did not reject an affection which His heart could and did appreciate.

[78] Christ meets the heart of the poor woman in the city which was a sinner, and told God's mind out there, and told it to her. He meets Mary's heart here, and justifies and satisfies her affection, and gave the divine estimate of what she did. He met Mary Magdalene's heart at the sepulchre, to whom the world was emptiness if He was not there, and tells God's mind in its highest forms of blessing. Such is the effect of attachment to Christ.

Deep affection for the Lord drawn out by the perfectness of Jesus

Again, observe the effect of deep affection for the Lord. This affection necessarily breathes the atmosphere in which, at that moment, the spirit of the Lord is found. The woman who anointed Him was not informed of the circumstances about to happen, nor was she a prophetess. But the approach of that hour of darkness was felt by one whose heart was fixed on Jesus.[79] The different forms of evil developed themselves before Him, and displayed themselves in their true colors; and, under the influence of one master, even Satan, grouped themselves around the only object against whom it was worth while to array this concentration of malice, and who brought their true character out into open daylight.

But the perfectness of Jesus, which drew out the enmity, drew out the affection in her; and she (so to speak) reflected the perfectness in the affection; and as that perfectness was put in action and drawn to light by the enmity, so was her affection. Thus Christ's heart could not but meet it. Jesus, by reason of this enmity, was still more the object that occupied a heart which, doubtless led of God, instinctively apprehended what was going on. The time of testimony, and even that of the explanation of His relationship to all around Him, was over. His heart was free to enjoy the good and true and spiritual affections of which He was the object; and which, whatever might be their human form, showed so plainly their divine origin, in that they were attached to that object on which, at this solemn moment, all the attention of heaven was centred.

---

[79] The enmity of the chiefs of Israel was known to the disciples— "Master, the Jews of late sought to stone Thee, and goest Thou thither again?" And afterwards by Thomas—a gracious testimony to the love of one who afterwards showed his unbelief as to Jesus' resurrection— "Let us go that we may die with Him." Mary's heart doubtless felt this enmity, and as it grew, her attachment to the Lord grew with it.

The Lord's omniscience

Jesus Himself was conscious of His position. His thoughts were on His departure. During the exercise of His power, He hides—He forgets—Himself. But *now* oppressed, rejected, and like a lamb led to the slaughter, He feels that He is the just object of the thoughts of those who belong to Him, of all who have hearts to appreciate that which God appreciates. His heart is full of the coming events. See verses 2, 10-13, 18, 21.

The tact of devotedness

But yet a few words more on the woman who anointed Him. The effect of having the heart fixed in affection on Jesus is shown in her in a striking manner. Occupied with Him, she is sensible of His situation. She feels what affects Him; and this causes her affection to act in accordance with the special devotedness which that situation inspires. As hatred against Him rose up to murderous intent, the spirit of devotedness to Him grows in answer to it in her. Consequently, with the tact of devotedness, she does precisely that which was suited to His situation. The poor woman was not intelligently aware of this; yet she did the thing that was meet. Her value for the Person of Jesus, so infinitely precious to her, made her quick-sighted with respect to that which was passing in His mind. In her eyes Christ was invested with all the interest of His circumstances; and she lavishes upon Him that which expressed her affection. Fruit of this sentiment, her action met the circumstances; and, although it was but the instinct of her heart, Jesus gives it all the value which His perfect intelligence could attribute to it, embracing at once the sentiments of her heart and the coming events.

The selfish cold-heartedness and treachery of others brought out by Mary's devotedness

But this testimony of affection and devotedness to Christ brings out the selfishness, the want of heart, of the others. They blame the poor woman. Sad proof (to say nothing of Judas[80]) how little the knowledge of that which concerns Jesus necessarily awakens suitable affection in our hearts! After this Judas goes out, and agrees with the unhappy priests to betray Jesus to them for the price of a slave.

The Lord pursues His career of love; and as He had accepted the poor woman's testimony of affection, so He now bestows on His disciples one of infinite value to our souls. Verse 16 concludes the subject of which we have been speaking: Christ's knowledge, according to God, of that which awaited Him; the conspiracy of the priests; the affection of the poor woman, accepted by the Lord; the selfish cold-heartedness of the disciples; the treachery of Judas.

The memorial of the true passover: a slain Saviour: an entirely new order of things

The Lord now institutes the memorial of the true passover. He sends the disciples to make arrangements for the celebration of the feast at Jerusalem. He points out Judas as the one who would deliver Him up to the Jews. It will be noticed, that it was not merely His knowledge of the one who should betray Him which the Lord here expresses—He knew that when He called him; but He says "One *of you* shall betray Me." It was *that* which touched His heart: He wished it to touch theirs likewise.

He then points out that it is a Saviour slain who is to be remembered. It is no longer a question of the living

---

[80] Judas's heart was the spring of this evil, but the other disciples, not occupied with Christ, fall into the snare.

Messiah: all that was over. It was no longer the remembrance of Israel's deliverance from the slavery of Egypt. Christ, and Christ slain, began an entirely new order of things. Of Him they were now to think—of Him slain on earth. He then draws their attention to the blood of the new covenant, adding that which extends it to others besides the Jews without naming them—"It is shed for many." Moreover, this blood is not, as at Sinai, only to confirm the covenant, for fidelity to which they were responsible; it was shed for the remission of sins. So that the Lord's supper presents the remembrance of Jesus slain, who, by dying, has broken with the past; has laid the foundation of the new covenant; obtained the remission of sins; and opened the door to the Gentiles. It is only in His death that the supper presents Him to us. His blood is apart from His body; He is dead. It is neither Christ living on the earth, nor Christ glorified in heaven. He is separate from His people, as to their joys on earth; but they are to expect Him as the companion of the happiness He has secured for them—for He condescends to be so—in better days: "I will not drink henceforth of this fruit of the vine, until that day when I drink it new [81] with you in My Father's kingdom." But, these links broken, who, save Jesus, could sustain the conflict? All would forsake Him. The testimonies of the Word should be accomplished. It was written, "I will smite the Shepherd, and the sheep shall be scattered abroad."

The promise of a risen Saviour in Galilee

Nevertheless He would go, to renew His relationship, as a risen Saviour, with these poor of the flock, to the same place where He had already identified Himself with them during His life. He would go before them into Galilee. This promise is very remarkable, because the Lord resumes, under a new form, His Jewish relationship

---

[81] "New" is not anew (*neon*), but in a new way (*kainon*).

with them and with the kingdom. We may here remark that, as He had judged all classes (to the end of chap. 25), He now exhibits the character of His relationship with all those among whom He maintained any. Whether it is the woman, or Judas, or the disciples, each one takes his place in connection with the Lord. This is all we find here. If Peter had natural energy enough to go a little farther, it would only be for a deeper fall in the place where the Lord alone could stand.

At Gethsemane in supplication with His Father: the anticipation of the cup of suffering

And now He isolates Himself to present, in supplication to His Father, the sufferings that awaited Him.

But while isolating Himself for prayer, He takes three of His disciples with Him, that in this solemn moment they may watch with Him. They were the same three who were with Him during the transfiguration. They were to see His glory in the kingdom, and His sufferings. He goes a little way beyond them. As for them, they fall asleep, as they did on the mount of transfiguration. The scene here is described in Hebrews 5: 7. Jesus was not yet drinking the cup, but it was before His eyes. On the cross He drank it, made sin for us, His soul feeling itself forsaken of Him. Here it is the power of Satan, using death as a terror with which to overwhelm Him. But the consideration of this subject will be more in place when we come to Luke's Gospel.

Complete submission

We here see His soul under the load of death—by anticipation—as He alone could know it, nor had it as yet lost its sting. We know who has the power of death, and death as yet had the full character of the wages of sin, and the curse, of God's judgment. But He watches and He prays. As Man, subjected by His love to this assault in the presence of the most powerful temptation to which He could be exposed, on the one hand He watches; on the other, He presents His anguish to His Father. His communion was not interrupted here, however great His distress. This distress only cast Him the more, in all submission and in all reliance, upon His Father. But if we were to be saved, if God was to be glorified in Him who had undertaken our cause, the cup must not pass away from Him. And His submission is complete.

Peter reminded of false confidence

He tenderly reminds Peter of his false confidence,[82] making him sensible of his weakness; but Peter was too full of himself to profit by it; he awakes from his sleep, but his self-confidence is not shaken. A sadder experience was needed for its cure.

The cup taken from the Father's hand

The Lord therefore takes the cup, but He takes it from His Father's hand. It was *His* will that He should drink it. Committing Himself thus entirely to His Father, it is neither from the hand of His enemies, nor from that of Satan (though they were the instruments), that He takes it. According to the perfection with which He had subjected Himself to the will of God in this matter, committing all to Him, it is from His hand alone that He receives it. It is the Father's will. It is thus that we escape from second causes, and from the temptations of the enemy, by seeking only the will of God who directs

[82] It is wonderful to see the Lord in the full agony of the anticipated cup, only as yet presenting it to His Father, not drinking the cup; yet turning to the disciples and speaking to them in calm grace as if in Galilee, and turning back to the dreadful conflict of spirit Himself exactly for what was before His soul. In Matthew He is victim, I add, and every aggravation, with no alleviating circumstance, is here what His soul meets.

all things. It is from Him we receive affliction and
trial, if they come.

The betrayal: submission to man's malice, the power of darkness and God's judgment of sin: in the hands of the Jews

The disciples need no longer watch: the hour is come.[83]
He was to be betrayed into the hands of men. This was
saying enough. Judas designates Him by a kiss. Jesus
goes to meet the multitude, rebuking Peter for seeking to
resist with carnal weapons. Had Christ wished to escape,
He could have asked for twelve legions of angels and
had them; but all things must be fulfilled.[84] It was the
hour of His submission to the effect of the malice of man
and the power of darkness, and God's judgment against
sin. He is the Lamb for the slaughter. Then all the disciples forsake Him. He surrenders Himself, setting before the crowd that came what they were doing. If no one
can prove Him guilty, He will not deny the truth. He
confesses the glory of His Person as Son of God, and
declares that henceforth they should see the Son of Man,
no longer in the meekness of One who would not break
the bruised reed, but coming in the clouds of heaven, and
sitting on the right hand of power. Having borne this
testimony, He is condemned on account of that which He
said of Himself—for the confession of the truth. The
false witnesses did not succeed. The priests and the heads
of Israel were guilty of His death, by virtue of their own
rejection of the testimony He rendered to the truth. He
was the Truth; they were under the power of the father
of lies. They rejected the Messiah, the Saviour of His

[83] I purpose speaking on the Lord's sufferings when studying the Gospel
of Luke, where they are described more in detail; because it is as *Son of
Man* that He is there especially presented.

[84] Remark here in so solemn and crucial a moment, the place that the
Lord gives to the Scriptures: that thus it must be, for it was there (ver.
54). They are the Word of God.

people.   He would come to them no more, except as
Judge.

Jesus as the Victim

They insult and outrage Him.   Each one, alas, takes,
as we have seen, his own place—Jesus, that of Victim;
the others, the place of betrayal, rejection, abandonment,
denial of the Lord.   What a picture!   What a solemn
moment!   Who could stand in it?   Christ alone could
steadily pass through it.   And He passed through it as a
victim.   As such, He must be stripped of all, and that in
the presence of God.   Everything else disappeared, except the sin which led to it; and, according to grace, that
also before the powerful efficacy of this act.   Peter, self-
confident, hesitating, detected, answering with untruth,
swearing, denies his Master; and, painfully convinced of
man's powerlessness against the enemy of his soul and
against sin, he goes out and weeps bitterly: tears, which
cannot efface his guilt, but which, while proving the
existence, through grace, of uprightness of heart, bear
witness to that powerlessness which uprightness of heart
cannot remedy.[85]

Chapter 27

Delivered up to the Gentiles: the evil of Satan and
man displayed

AFTER this (chap. 27), the unhappy priests and heads
of the people deliver up their Messiah to the Gentiles, as He had told His disciples.   Judas, in despair

[85] I think it will be found, on comparing the Gospels, that the Lord
was examined at Caiaphas's over night, when Peter denies Him, and that
they met formally again in the morning, and, asking the blessed Lord, received from Himself the confession on which they led Him to Pilate.   Over
night it was only the active leaders.   In the morning there was a formal
assembling of the Sanhedrim.

under Satan's power, hangs himself, having cast the reward of his iniquity at the feet of the chief priests and elders. Satan was forced to bear witness, even by a conscience that he had betrayed, to the Lord's innocence. What a scene! Then the priests who had made no conscience of buying His blood from Judas, scruple to put the money into the treasury of the temple, because it was the price of blood. In the presence of that which was going on man was obliged to show himself as he is and the power of Satan over him. Having taken counsel, they buy a burying-ground for strangers. These were profane enough in their eyes for that, provided they themselves were not defiled with such money. Yet it was the time of God's grace to the stranger, and judgment on Israel. Moreover they established thereby a perpetual memorial of their own sin and of the blood which has been shed. Aceldama is all that remains in this world of the circumstances of this great sacrifice. The world is a field of blood, but it speaks better things than that of Abel.

This prophecy, we know, is in the book of Zechariah. The name "Jeremiah" may have crept into the text when there was nothing more than "by the prophet;" or it might be because Jeremiah stood first in the order prescribed by the Talmudists for the books of prophecy; for which reason, very likely, also, they said, "Jeremiah, or one of the prophets," as in chapter 16: 14. But this is not the place for discussion on the subject.

The King of the Jews before Pilate: Pilate's condemnation

Their own part in the Jewish scene closes. The Lord stands before Pilate. Here the question is not whether He is the Son of God, but whether He is the King of the Jews. Although He was this, yet it was only in the character of Son of God that He would allow the Jews to receive Him. Had they received Him as the Son of God, He would have been their King. But that might not be: He must accomplish the work of atonement. Having rejected Him as Son of God, the Jews now deny Him as their King. But the Gentiles also become guilty in the person of their head in Palestine, the government of which had been committed to them. The Gentile head should have reigned in righteousness. His representative in Judea acknowledges the malice of Christ's enemies; his conscience, alarmed by his wife's dream, seeks to evade the guilt of condemning Jesus. But the true prince of this world, as regards present exercise of dominion, was Satan. Pilate, washing his hands (futile attempt to exonerate himself) delivers up the guiltless to the will of His enemies, saying, at the same time, that he finds no fault in Him. And he releases to the Jews a man guilty of sedition and murder, instead of the Prince of life. But it was again on His own confession, and that only, that He was condemned, confessing the same thing in the Gentile court as He had done in the Jewish, in each the truth, witnessing a good confession of what concerned the truth as to those before whom He was.

The Jews' choice of Barabbas: a rejected Saviour the universal touchstone

Barabbas,[86] the expression of the spirit of Satan who was a murderer from the beginning, and of rebellion against the authority which Pilate was there to maintain —Barabbas was loved by the Jews; and with him, the wrongful carelessness of the governor, who was powerless against evil, endeavored to satisfy the will of the people whom he ought to have governed. "All the people" make themselves guilty of the blood of Jesus in the solemn word, which remains fulfilled to this day, till sovereign grace,

[86] Strange to say, this means "son of Abba," as if Satan was mocking them with the name.

according to God's purpose, takes it off—solemn but terrible word, "His blood be upon us and upon our children." Sad and frightful ignorance which self-will has brought upon a people who rejected the light!   Alas, how each one, I again say, takes his own place in the presence of this touchstone—a rejected Saviour.   The company of the Gentiles, the soldiers, do that in derision, with the brutality habitual to them as heathen and as executioners, which the Gentiles shall do with joyful worship, when He whom they now mocked shall be truly the King of the Jews in glory.   Jesus endures it all.   It was the hour of His submission to the full power of evil: patience must have its perfect work, in order that His obedience may be complete on every side.   He bore it all without relief, rather than fail in obedience to His Father.   What a difference between this and the conduct of the first Adam surrounded with blessings!

The crucifixion: the abyss of His sufferings

Every one must be the servant of sin, or of the tyranny of wickedness, at this solemn hour, in which all is put to the proof.   They compel one Simon (known afterwards, it appears, among the disciples) to bear the cross of Jesus; and the Lord is led away to the place of His crucifixion.   There He refuses that which might have stupefied Him.   He will not shun the cup He had to drink, nor deprive Himself of His faculties in order to be insensible to that which it was the will of God He should suffer.   The prophecies of the Psalms are fulfilled in His Person, by means of those who little thought what they were doing.   At the same time, the Jews succeeded in becoming to the last degree contemptible.   Their *King* was hung.   They must bear the shame in spite of themselves.   Whose fault was it?   But, hardened and senseless, they share with a malefactor the miserable satisfaction of insulting the Son of God, their King, the Mes-

siah, to their own ruin, and quote, so blinding is unbelief, from their own Scriptures, as the expression of
their own mind, that which in them is put into the mouth
of the unbelieving enemies of Jehovah. Jesus felt it all;
but the anguish of His trial, where after all He was a
calm and faithful witness, the abyss of His sufferings,
contained something far more terrible than all this malice
or abandonment of man. The floods doubtless lifted up
their voices.[87] One after another the waves of wickedness dashed against Him; but the depths beneath that
awaited Him, who could fathom? *His* heart, *His* soul—
the vessel of a divine love—could alone go deeper than
the bottom of that abyss which sin had opened for man,
to bring up those who lay there, after He had endured its
pains in His own soul. A heart that had been ever
faithful was forsaken of God. Where sin had brought
man, love brought the Lord, but with a nature and an
apprehension in which there was no distance, no separation, so that it should be felt in all its fulness. No one
but He who was in that place could fathom or feel it.

Forsaken of God: glorifying God

It is too a wonderful spectacle to see the one righteous
Man in the world declare at the end of His life He was
forsaken of God. But thus it was He glorified Him as
none else could have done it, and where none but He
could have done it—made sin, in the presence of God as
such, with no veil to hide, no mercy to cover or bear it
with.

The fathers, full of faith, had in their distress experienced the faithfulness of God, who answered the expectation of their hearts. But Jesus (as to the condition of
His soul at that moment) cried in vain. "A worm and
no man" before the eyes of men, He had to bear the
forsaking of the God in whom He trusted.

[87] We find in Matthew, specially collected, the dishonor done to the Lord
and the insults offered Him, and with Mark the forsaking of God.

Their thoughts far from His, they that surround Him did not even understand His words, but they accomplished the prophecies by their ignorance. Jesus, bearing testimony by the loudness of His voice that it was not the weight of death that oppressed Him, gives up the ghost.

The efficacy of Christ's death: the rent veil

The efficacy of His death is presented to us in this Gospel in a double aspect. First, the veil of the temple was rent in twain from the top to the bottom. God, who had been always hidden behind the veil, discovered Himself completely by means of the death of Jesus. The entrance into the holy place is made manifest—a new and living way which God has consecrated for us through the veil. The entire Jewish system, the relations of man with God under its sway, its priesthood, all fell with the rending of the veil. Every one found himself in the presence of God without a veil between. The priests were to be always in His presence. But, by this same act, the sin, which would have made it impossible for us to stand there, was for the believer entirely put away from before God. The holy God, and the believer, cleansed from his sins, are brought together by the death of Christ. What love was that which accomplished this!

Resurrection: sinners without fear before God

Secondly, besides this, such was the efficacy of His death, that when His resurrection had burst the bonds that held them, many of the dead appeared in the city— witnesses of His power who, having suffered death, had risen above it, and overcome it, and destroyed its power, or taken it into His own hands. Blessing was now in resurrection.

The presence therefore of God without a veil, and sinners without sin before Him, proves the efficacy of Christ's sufferings.

The resurrection of the dead, over which the king of terrors had no more right, displayed the efficacy of the death of Christ for sinners, and the power of His resurrection. Judaism is over for those that have faith, and the power of death also. The veil is rent. The grave gives up its prey; He is Lord of the dead and of the living.[88]

The first testimony of faith among the Gentiles to the Person of Christ

There is yet another especial testimony to the mighty power of His death, to the import of that word, "If I be lifted up from the earth, I will draw all men unto Me." The centurion who was on guard at the crucifixion of the Lord, seeing the earthquake and those things that were done, trembling, confesses the glory of His Person; and, stranger as he is to Israel, renders the first testimony of faith among Gentiles: "Truly this was the Son of God."

The instinct of affection: at the foot of the cross

But the narrative goes on. Some poor women—to whom devotedness often gives, on God's part, more courage than to men in their more responsible and busy position—were standing near the cross, beholding what was done to Him they loved.[89]

---

[88] The glory of Christ in ascension, and as Lord of all, does not come within the scope of Matthew historically.

[89] The part that women take in all this history is very instructive, especially to them. The activity of public service, that which may be called "work," belongs naturally to men (all that appertains to what is generally termed ministry), although women share a very precious activity in private. But there is another side of Christian life which is particularly theirs; and that is personal and loving devotedness to Christ. It is a woman, who anointed the Lord while the disciples murmured; women. who were at the cross, when all except John had forsaken Him; women, who came to the sepulchre, and who were sent to announce the truth to the apostles who had gone after all to their *own home;* women, who ministered to the Lord's need. And indeed this goes farther. Devotedness in service is perhaps the part of man; but the instinct of affection,

But they were not the only ones who filled the place of the terrified disciples. Others—and this often happens —whom the world had held back, when once the depth of their affection is stirred by the question of His sufferings whom they really loved, when the moment is so painful that others are terrified, then (emboldened by the rejection of Christ) they feel that the time is arrived for decision and become fearless confessors of the Lord. Hitherto associated with those that have crucified Him, they must now either accept that act, or declare themselves. Through grace they do the latter.

"With the rich in His death"

God had prepared all beforehand. His Son was to have His tomb with the rich. Joseph comes boldly to Pilate and asks for the body of Jesus. He wraps the body, which Pilate grants him, in a clean linen cloth, and lays it in his own sepulchre, which had never served to hide the corruption of man. Mary Magdalene and the other Mary,[90] for they were known—sat near the sepulchre, bound by all that remained to their faith of Him whom they had loved and followed with adoration during His life.

that which enters more intimately into Christ's position, and is thus more immediately in connection with His sentiments, in closer communion with the sufferings of His heart—this is the part of woman: assuredly a happy part. The activity of service for Christ puts man a little out of this position, at least if the Christian is not watchful. Everything has however its place. I speak of that which is characteristic; for there are women who have served much, and men who have felt much. Note also here, what I believe I have remarked, that this clinging of heart to Jesus is the position where the communications of true knowledge are received. The first full gospel is announced to the poor woman that was a sinner who washed His feet, the embalming for His death to Mary, our highest position to Mary Magdalene, the communion Peter desired to John who was in His bosom. And here the women have a large share.

[90] That is, Mary, the wife of Cleophas, and mother of James and Joses, constantly spoken of as "the other Mary." In John 19: 25, Mary the wife of Cleophas has been taken as in apposition with His mother's sister. But this is simply a mistake. It is another person. There were four—three Marys and His mother's sister.

The involuntary witness of unbelief

But unbelief has no faith in itself, and, fearing lest that which it denies be true, it mistrusts everything. The chief priests request Pilate to guard the sepulchre, in order to frustrate any attempt the disciples might make to found the doctrine of the resurrection on the absence of the body of Jesus from the tomb in which it had been laid. Pilate bids them secure the sepulchre themselves; so that all they did was to make themselves involuntary witnesses to the fact, and assure us of the accomplishment of the thing they dreaded. Thus *Israel* was guilty of this effort of futile resistance to the testimony which Jesus had rendered to His own resurrection. They were a testimony against themselves to its truth. The precautions which Pilate would not perhaps have taken they carried to the extreme, so that all mistake as to the fact of His resurrection was impossible.

Jesus' ministry and service still with the poor of the flock

The Lord's resurrection is briefly related in Matthew. The object is again, after the resurrection, to connect the ministry and service of Jesus—now transferred to His disciples—with the poor of the flock, the remnant of Israel. He again assembled them in Galilee, where He had constantly instructed them, and where the despised, among the people dwelt afar from the pride of the Jews. This connected their work with His, in that which especially characterized it with reference to the remnant of Israel.

Chapter 28

Faith's full assurance of the fact of the Lord's resurrection

I SHALL examine the details of the resurrection elsewhere. Here I only consider its bearing in this Gospel.

The sabbath ended (Saturday evening with us—chap. 28), the two Marys come to see the sepulchre. At this moment that was all they did. Verses 1, 2 are not consecutive, 2-4 go together. When the earthquake and its attendant circumstances took place, no one was there except the soldiers. At night all was secure. The disciples knew nothing of it in the morning. When the women arrived at dawn, the angel who sat at the door of the sepulchre re-assured them with the tidings of the Lord's resurrection. The angel of the Lord had come down and opened the door of the tomb, which man had closed with every possible precaution.[91] They had in truth only guaranteed by unexceptionable witnesses the truth of the apostles' preaching, by placing the soldiers there. The women, by their visit the evening before, and in the morning when the angel spoke to them, received a full assurance to faith of the fact of His resurrection. All that is presented here is the facts. The women had been there in the evening. The intervention of the angel certified to the soldiers the true character of His coming forth from the tomb; and the visit of the women in the morning established the fact of His resurrection as an object of faith to themselves. They go and announce it to the disciples, who—so far from having done that which the Jews imputed to them—did not even believe the assertions of the women. Jesus Himself appears to the women who were returning from the sepulchre, having believed the words of the angel.

The disciples' commission

As I have already said, Jesus connects Himself with His former work among the poor of the flock, afar from the seat of Jewish tradition, and from the temple, and from all that linked the people with God according to the old covenant. He appoints His disciples to meet Him

[91] But I apprehend the Lord Jesus had left the tomb before the stone was rolled away; that was for mortal eyes.

there, and there they find Him and recognize Him; and it is there, in this former scene of the labors of Christ, according to Isaiah 8, 9, that they receive their commission from Him.   Hence we have not the ascension of Christ at all in this Gospel, but all power is given unto Him in heaven and in earth, and accordingly the commission given to His disciples extends to all nations (Gentiles).   To them they were to proclaim His rights, and make disciples of them.

A risen, mighty Saviour: the revelation and confession of the Father, Son and Holy Ghost as the holy name for all nations

It was not however the name of the Lord only, nor in connection with His throne at Jerusalem.   Lord of heaven and earth, His disciples were to proclaim Him throughout all nations, founding their doctrine on the confession of the Father, of the Son, and of the Holy Ghost.   They were to teach, not the law, but the precepts of Jesus.   He would be with them, with the disciples who thus confessed Him, unto the end of the age. It is this which connects all that will be accomplished until Christ sits upon the great white throne, with the testimony that He Himself rendered on the earth in the midst of Israel.   It is the testimony of the kingdom, and of its Head, once rejected by a people that knew Him not.   It links the testimony to the nations with a remnant in Israel owning Jesus as Messiah but now risen from the dead, as He had said, but not to a Christ known as ascended on high.   Nor does it present Jesus alone, nor Jehovah, as any longer the subject of testimony, but the revelation of Father, Son, and Holy Ghost as the holy name by which the nations were connected with God.

MARK

The special character of Mark's Gospel: its subject

THE Gospel according to Mark has a character that differs in certain respects from all the others. Each Gospel, as we have seen, has its own character; each is occupied with the Person of the Lord in a different point of view: as a divine Person, the Son of God; as the Son of Man; as the Son of David, the Messiah presented to the Jews, Emmanuel. But Mark is occupied with none of these titles. It is *the Servant* we find here—and in particular His service as bearing the Word—the active service of Christ in the gospel. The glory of His divine Person shows itself, it is true, in a remarkable manner through His service, and, as it were, in spite of Himself, so that He avoids its consequences. But still service is the subject of the book. Doubtless we shall find the character of His teaching developing itself (and truth consequently shaking off the Jewish forms under which it had been held), as well as the account of His death, on which all depended for the establishment of faith. But that which distinguishes this Gospel is the character of service and of Servant that is attached to the life of Jesus—the work that He came to accomplish personally as living on the earth. On this account the history of His birth is not found in Mark. It opens with the announcement of the beginning of the gospel. John the Baptist is the herald, the forerunner, of Him who brought this good news to man.

Chapter I

The mission of John the Baptist

THE message is new—at least in the absolute and complete character it assumes, and in the direct and immediate application. It was not the Jewish privileges which should be obtained by repenting and returning to the Lord. The Lord was coming according to His promise. To prepare His way before Him, John was preaching repentance for the remission of sins. It was this they needed: remission of sins for the repentant was the great thing, the formal object of John's mission.

Repentance and remission of sins: governmental and justifying forgiveness

Repentance and remission of sins refer clearly to the responsibility of man, here of Israel, in his natural standing with God; and clearing that as to man's state relatively to God, morally and responsibly qualify him for the reception of purposed blessing—morally in that he judges the sins in principle as God does, and responsibly by God's forgiving them all. Hence also remission is necessarily a present actual thing. There is a governmental forgiveness as well as a justifying one, but the principle is the same, and the latter is the basis of the former. Only where it is governmental it may be accompanied by various accompanying dealings of God, only the sin is no longer imputed as to present relationship with God; as in justifying, this is eternally true. In justifying forgiveness—as in Romans 4, showing by its use of Psalm 32 the common character of non-imputation—it is founded on the work of Christ, and hence is absolute and unchangeable. Sin is not imputed and never can be, because the work is done and finished which puts it away out of God's sight: that—eternal, absolute, and immutable in

itself—is the basis of all God's dealings with man in
grace. Grace reigns through righteousness. Hebrews 9,
10 unfold this, where the conscience and coming to God,
and that in the holiest, are concerned. So Romans 3 to 5,
where the question is judicial, a matter of judgment,
wrath, and justifying. It is the basis of blessings, not the
end, great as it is in itself—peace with God and reconciliation. Here it was the ground of all the blessings
Israel will have by the new covenant (founded on Christ's
death), but being rejected, those who believed entered
into better and heavenly blessings. In Exodus 32: 14, 34,
we get governmental forgiveness, not justifying. In the
case of David's great sin, it was pardoned when owned,
the iniquity of it put away, but severe chastisement connected with it because he had given occasion to the
enemies of the Lord to blaspheme. God's glory in righteousness had to be maintained before the world. (2 Sam.
12: 13, 14.)

Here it was a proposal of present forgiveness to Israel,
which will be accomplished in the last days; and then, as
their long rejection will have closed in governmental forgiveness, they will also through the death and blood-
shedding of Christ, at least the remnant, be forgiven and
justified for the enjoyment of the promises under the
new covenant. (Compare Acts 3.)

The people's conscience stirred: confession of sins

The prophets had indeed announced pardon if the people returned to the Lord; but here it was the present
object of the address. The people go out in a body to
avail themselves of it. Conscience at least was stirred;
and whatever might be the pride of their leaders, the
sense of Israel's condition was felt by the people, as soon
as anything outside the routine of religion acted on the
heart and conscience—that is to say, when God spoke.
They confess their sins. With some perhaps it was only

natural conscience, that is, not a really quickening work; but at any rate it was wrought upon by the testimony of God.

John's proclamation

But John, rigidly separate from the people, and living apart from human society, proclaims another, mightier than he, whose shoe-latchet he was not worthy to unloose: *He* would not merely preach repentance accepted by the baptism of water; He would bestow the Holy Ghost, power, on those who received His testimony. Here our Gospel passes on rapidly to the service of Him whom John thus declared. It only sets forth summarily that which introduces Him into this service.

The Lord's position in service on earth

The Lord takes His place among the repentant of His people, and, submitting to John's baptism, He sees heaven open to Him, and the Holy Ghost descending upon Him like a dove. The father acknowledges Him as His Son on earth, in whom He is well pleased. He is then led by the Holy Ghost into the wilderness, where He undergoes the temptation of Satan for forty days; He is with the wild beasts, and angels exercise their ministry towards Him. Here we see His whole position—the character which the Lord takes on earth—all its features and relations with that which surrounded Him, gathered into these two or three verses. It has been treated of in its details in Matthew.

The Lord's path of ever-ready service: His Word of power

After this John disappears from the scene, giving place to the public ministry of Christ, of whom he was only the herald; and Christ Himself appears in the place of testimony, declaring that the time was fulfilled; that it was now no question of prophecies or of days to come; that God was going to set up His kingdom, and that they ought to repent and receive the good news which at that very moment was proclaimed to them.

Our Evangelist passes [1] rapidly on to every branch of the service of Christ. Having presented the Lord as undertaking the public ministry which called on men to receive the good news as a present thing (the time of the fulfilment of the ways of God being come), he exhibits Him as calling others to accomplish this same work in His name by following Him. His Word does not fail in its effect: those whom He calls forsake all and follow Him.[2] He goes into the city to teach on the sabbath-day. His Word does not consist of arguments which evidence the uncertainty of man, but comes with the authority of One who knows the truth which He proclaims—authority which in fact was that of God, who can communicate truth. He speaks also as One who possesses it; and He gives proof that He does. The Word, which thus presents itself to men, has power over demons. A man possessed by an evil spirit was there. The evil spirit bore testimony, in spite of himself, to Him who spake, and whose presence was insupportable to him; but the Word that aroused him had power to cast him out. Jesus rebukes him—commands him to hold his peace and to come out of the man; and the evil spirit, after manifesting the reality of his presence and his malice, submits, and departs from the man. Such was the power of the Word of Christ. It is not surprising that the fame of this act should spread through all the country; but the Lord continues His path of service wherever work presented itself.

---

[1] This rapidity characterizes Mark, as does the word "immediately" (*eutheos*).

[2] It is the fact in itself which is given here, as also in Matthew. Luke's account will give occasion to enter more into detail as to the call of the disciples. From John the Baptist's days they had been more or less associated with the Lord—at least these had.

He goes into the house of Peter, whose wife's mother lay sick of a fever. He heals her immediately; and when the sabbath was ended, they bring Him all the sick. He, ever ready to serve, (precious Lord!) heals them all.

The character of His service in dependence on His God and Father

But it was not to surround Himself with a crowd that the Lord labored; and in the morning, long before day, He departs into the wilderness to pray. Such was the character of His service—wrought in communion with His God and Father, and in dependence upon Him. He goes alone into a solitary place. The disciples find Him, and tell Him that all are seeking Him; but His heart is in His work. The general desire does not bring Him back. He goes on His way to fulfil the work which was given Him to do—preaching the truth among the people; for this was the service to which He devoted Himself.

The healing of the leper: service in the might of love

But, however devoted to this service, His heart was not made rigid by pre-occupation; He was always Himself with God. A poor leper comes to Him, acknowledging His power, but uncertain as to His will, as to the love that wielded that power. Now this dreadful disease not only shut the man himself out, but defiled every one who even touched the sufferer. But nothing stops Jesus in the service to which His love calls Him. The leper was wretched, an outcast from his fellow-creatures and from society, and excluded from Jehovah's house. But the power of God was present. The leper must be re-assured as to the good-will on which his dejected heart could not reckon. Who would care for such a wretch as he? He had faith as to the power that was in Christ; but his thoughts of himself concealed from him the ex-

tent of the love that had visited him. Jesus puts forth
His hand and touches him.

The lowliest of men approaches sin, and that which
was the token of sin, and dispels it; the Man, who in
the might of His love touched the leper without being
defiled, was the God who alone could remove the leprosy
which made one afflicted with it miserable and outcast.

The Lord's authority declaring His love and divinity

The Lord speaks with an authority that declares at
once His love and His divinity: "I will; be thou clean."
I will—here was the love of which the leper doubted, the
authority of God who alone has the right to say I WILL.
The effect followed the expression of His will. This is
the case when God speaks. And who healed leprosy except Jehovah only? Was He the One who had come
down low enough to *touch* this defiled being that defiled
every other that had to do with him? Yes, the only One;
but it was God who had come down, love which had
reached so low, and which, in thus doing, showed itself
mighty for every one that trusted in it. It was undefilable
purity in power, and which could therefore minister in
love to the vilest and delights to do so. He came to
defiled man, not to be defiled by the contact, but to remove the defilement. He touched the leper in grace, but
the leprosy was gone.

He hides Himself from human acclamations, and bids
the man who had been healed to go and show himself
to the priests according to the law of Moses. But this
submission to the law bore testimony in fact to His
being Jehovah, for Jehovah alone, under the law, sovereignly cleansed the leper. The priest was but the witness
that it had been done. This miracle being noised abroad,
by attracting the multitude, sends Jesus away into the
wilderness.

Chapter 2

Divine rights of pardon in exercise

AFTERWARDS (chap. 2) He goes again into the city, and immediately the multitude gather together. What a living picture of the Lord's life of service! He preaches to them. This was His object and His service. (See chap. 1: 38.) But again, in devoting Himself to the humble accomplishment of it as committed to Him, His service itself, His love—for who serves like God when He deigns to do it?—bring out His divine rights. He knew the real source of all these evils, and He could bring in its remedy. "Thy sins," said He to the poor paralytic man, who was brought to Him with a faith that overcame difficulties, persevering in spite of them—that perseverance of faith which is fed by the sense of want, and certainty that power is to be found in Him who is sought—"Thy sins are forgiven thee." To the reasoning of the scribes He gives an answer that silenced every gainsayer. He exercises the power that authorized Him to pronounce the pardon of the poor sufferer.[3] The murmuring of the scribes brought out doctrinally *who* was there; as the verdict of the priests, who pronounce the leper clean, put the seal of their authority upon the truth that Jehovah, the healer of Israel, was there. That which Jesus carries on is His work, His testimony. The effect is to make it manifest that Jehovah is there, and has visited His people. It is Psalm 103 which is fulfilled, with respect to the rights and the revelation of the Person of Him who wrought.

---

[3] We must distinguish between governmental forgiveness and absolute pardon of sins. Only, such as man is, there could not have been the former without the latter. But till Christ was rejected and had died, this was not fully brought out.

The call of Levi, of sinners, a new development of the Lord's ministry

Jesus leaves the city; the people flock around Him; and again He teaches them. The call of Levi gives occasion for a new development of His ministry. He was come to call sinners, and not the righteous. After this He tells them that He could not put the new divine energy, unfolded in Himself, into the old forms of Pharisaism. And there was another reason for it—the presence of the Bridegroom. How could the children of the bride-chamber fast while the Bridegroom was with them? He should be taken from them, and then would be the time to fast. He proceeds to insist on the incompatibility between the old Jewish vessels and the power of the gospel. The latter would but subvert Judaism, to which they sought to attach it. That which took place when the disciples went through the cornfields confirms this doctrine.

The new things of grace and power: old things passed away

Ordinances lost their authority in the presence of the King ordained of God, rejected and a pilgrim on the earth. Moreover the sabbath—a sign of the covenant between God and the Jews—was made for man, and not man for the sabbath; therefore He, the Son of Man, was Lord of the sabbath. As Son of David rejected, the ordinances lost their force, and were subordinate to Him. As Son of Man possessor (in the sight of God) of all the rights which God had bestowed on man, He was Lord of the sabbath, which was made for man. In principle the old things were passed away. But this was not all. It was in fact the new things of grace and power, which did not admit of the old order of things. But the question was, whether God could act in grace, and bestow blessing, in sovereignty, on His people—whether He must submit to

the authority of men availing themselves of His ordinances against His goodness, or do good according to His
own power and love as being above all. Was man to
limit the operation of God's goodness? And this, in
truth, was the new wine which the Lord brought to man.

Chapter 3

The withered hand healed: the Lord's service to God's goodness and rights

SUCH was the question raised in the synagogue (chap.
3) on the occasion of the man with the withered
hand. The Lord sets it publicly before their conscience;
but neither heart nor conscience answered Him; and He
acts in His service according to the goodness and rights of
God, and heals the man.[4] The Pharisees and their enemies, the Herodians—for all were against God and
united in this—consult together how they might destroy
Christ. Jesus departs to the sea-coast.[5] There the multitude follow Him, because of all that He had done; so that
He is obliged to have a boat, that He may be outside the
crowd. Spirits are subject to Him, compelled to own that
He is the Son of God; but He forbids them to make Him
known.

Self-effacing service not circumscribed by Judaism

Service in preaching, and in seeking souls, in devoting
Himself to all, showing Himself by His acts to be the
possessor of divine power, hiding Himself from the

---

[4] One cannot but see how the old system, based on what man ought to be
for God, is being set aside for what God is for man. But, the former
having been established by God, nothing but the words and works of Jesus
would have justified the Jews in giving it up. As it was, it was clearly
opposition and hatred to the full revelation of Him who had ordained the
other. Compare John 15: 22, 24.

[5] That is, the Sea of Tiberias.

notice of men, in order to fulfil, apart from their applause, the service He had undertaken—such was His human life on earth. Love and divine power were disclosed in the service which that love impelled Him to accomplish, and in the accomplishment of which that power was exercised. But this could not be circumscribed by Judaism, however subject the Lord was to the ordinances of God given to the Jews.

Man's carnal opposition: wilful deliberate unbelief brings hopeless condemnation

But, God being thus manifested, the carnal opposition of man soon shows itself.[6] Here, then, the description of Christ's service ends, and its effect is manifested. This effect is developed in that which soon follows, with respect both to the iniquity of man and to the counsels of God. Meanwhile the Lord appoints twelve of His disciples to accompany Him, and to go forth preaching in His name. He could not merely work miracles but communicate to others the power to work them, and that by way of authority. He goes back into the house, and the multitude re-assemble. And here the thoughts of man display themselves at the same time as those of God. His friends search for Him as one who was beside Himself. The scribes, possessing influence as learned men, attribute to Satan a power which they could not deny. The Lord answers them by showing that in general all sin could be pardoned; but that to acknowledge the power, and attribute it to the enemy, rather than own Him who wielded it, was taking the place not of ignorant unbelief but of adversaries, thus blaspheming against the Holy

[6] This is the secret of all the history of Jesus, Son of David. All the promises being in Him for the Jews, the servant of every want too and every sorrow, yet being God and God manifested in Him, man could not bear it. The mind of the flesh is enmity against God.

Ghost—was a sin that could never be pardoned. The "strong man" was there; but Jesus was stronger than he, for He cast out the devils. Would Satan endeavor to overthrow his own house? The fact that the power of Jesus manifested itself in this manner left them without excuse. *God's* "strong man" was then come: Israel rejected Him; and, as regards their leaders, by blaspheming against the Holy Ghost, they brought themselves under hopeless condemnation. The Lord therefore immediately distinguishes the remnant who received His word from all natural connection He had with Israel. His mother or His "brethren" are the disciples who stand around Him, and those who do the will of God. This really sets aside Israel at that time.

Chapter 4

Then present and future character and result of the Lord's service

THIS introduces the true character and result of His own service, and all the history of the service that should be accomplished unto a far distant future; as well as the responsibility of His disciples, with regard to the share they would have in it, and the quietness of one who trusted in God while thus laboring; the storms also that should occur, that should exercise faith while Jesus apparently took no notice of them; and the just confidence of faith, as well as the power that sustained it.

The whole character of the work at that moment, and until the Lord's return, is described in this fourth chapter.

The Sower and the seed

The Lord resumes in it His habitual work of instruction, but in connection with the development that had just taken place of His relationship with the Jews. He sows. Fruit He no longer sought in His vineyard. In verse 11 we see that the distinction between the Jews and His disciples is marked. To the latter it was given to know the mystery of the kingdom, but to *those that were without* all these things were done in parables. I do not repeat the remarks I made in speaking of the contents of this parable in Matthew. But that which follows in verse 21 belongs essentially to the Gospel by Mark. We have seen that the Lord was occupied in preaching the gospel of the kingdom, and He committed the preaching of this gospel to others also. He was a sower, and He sowed the Word. That was His service, and it was theirs likewise. But is a candle lit to be hidden? Moreover nothing should be hidden. If man did not manifest the truth he had received, God would manifest all things. Let every one take heed to it.

The object of the service committed to the disciples

In verse 24 He applies this principle to His disciples. They must take heed to what they heard, for God would act towards them according to their fidelity in the administration of the Word committed to them. The love of God sent the Word of grace and of the kingdom unto men. That it should reach their conscience was the object of the service committed to the disciples. Christ communicated it to them; they were to make it known to others in all its fulness. According to the measure with which they gave free course to this testimony of love (conformably to the gift they had received), so should it be measured unto them in the government of God. If they hearkened unto that which He communicated to them, they should receive more; for, as a general principle, he who made that which reached him his own should have yet more, and from him who did not truly make it his own it should be taken away.

The absence of the King: His return at harvest time

The Lord then shows them how it should be with regard
to Himself. He had sown, and, even as the seed springs
up and grows without any act on the sower's part, so
would Christ allow the gospel to spread in the world
without interposing in any apparent way, it being the
peculiar character of the kingdom that the King was not
there. But, when harvest time comes, the sower has again
to do with it. So should it be with Jesus: He would
return to look after the harvest. He was personally engaged in the sowing and in the harvest. In the interval,
all went on apparently as if left to itself, really without
the interference of the Lord in Person.

The mustard-seed: the formation of a great earthly power as the result of the truth preached

The Lord makes use of another similitude to describe
the character of the kingdom. The small seed that He
sowed should become a great system, highly exalted in
the earth, capable of affording temporal protection to those
that took shelter in it. Thus we have the work of preaching the Word; the responsibility of the laborers to whom
the Lord would entrust it during His absence; His own
action at the beginning and at the end, at seed-time and
at harvest, Himself remaining at a distance during the interval; and the formation of a great earthly power as the
result of the truth which He preached, and which created
a little nucleus around Himself.

The storm: the Creator's presence: the disciples' unbelief

One part of the history of His followers was yet to be
shown. They should find most serious difficulties in their
way. The enemy would raise up a storm against them.

Apparently Christ took no notice of their situation. They call upon Him, and awake Him by cries, which He answers in grace. He speaks to the wind and the sea, and there is a great calm. At the same time He rebukes their unbelief. They should have counted on Him and on His divine power, and not have thought that He was going to be swallowed up by the waves. They should have remembered their own connection with Him—that, by grace, they were associated with Him. What tranquillity was His! The storm does not disturb Him. Devoted to His work, He took His rest at the moment when service did not require His activity. He rested during the passage. His service only afforded Him those moments snatched by circumstances from labor. His divine tranquillity, which knew no distrust, allowed Him to sleep during the storm. It was not so with the disciples; and, forgetful of His power, unaware of the glory of Him who was with them, they think only of themselves, as though Jesus had forgotten them. One word on His part displays in Him the Lord of creation. This is the real state of the disciples when Israel is set aside. The storm arises. Jesus appears to take no heed. Now faith would have recognized that they were in the same ship with Him. That is to say, if Jesus leaves the seed He has sown to grow until the harvest, He is, none the less, in the same vessel; He shares, not the less truly, the lot of His followers, or rather they share His. The dangers are the danger He and His work are in. That is, there is really none. And how great is the foolishness of unbelief. Think of their supposing, when the Son of God is come into the world to accomplish redemption and the settled purposes of God, that by, to man's eye, an accidental storm, He and all His work should be unexpectedly sunk in the lake! We are, blessed be His name, in the same boat with Him. If the Son of God does not sink, neither shall we.

Chapter 5

The demoniac delivered from Satan's power called to serve in Jesus' absence

BUT, in another sense, they are not with Him. They are called to serve, when He quits the scene of His labor. We learn this from the demoniac Legion (chap. 5), delivered from his miserable condition. Man—and Israel in particular—was completely under the power of the enemy. Christ, as to the work of His power, completely delivered the one in whose behalf this power was exercised. He is clothed—not naked—in his right mind, and sitting at the feet of Jesus to hear His words. But the people of the place are afraid, and send Jesus away— what the world has done with Christ; and in the history of the herd of swine we have the picture of Israel after the remnant has been healed. They are unclean, and Satan drives them to destruction. Now, when Jesus departs, he who had personally experienced the mighty effects of His love would have liked to be with Him; but he was to go home and bear testimony to those around him of all that Jesus had done. He was to serve in the absence of Jesus. In all these narratives we see the work and the devotedness of the servant, but at the same time the divine power of Jesus manifested in this service.

Healing of incurable disease and life given to the dead

In the circumstances that follow the cure of the demoniac, we find the true position of Jesus portrayed in His work. He is called upon to heal the daughter of Jairus— even as He came to heal the Jews, had that been possible. As He went toward the house of Jairus to perform this work, a poor incurable woman touches the hem of His garment with faith, and is instantly healed. This was the case with Jesus during His passage among the Jews. In the multitude that surrounded Him, some souls through grace touched Him by faith. In truth, their disease was in itself incurable; but Jesus had life in Himself according to the power of God, and faith drew out its virtue by touching Him. Such are brought to acknowledge their condition, but they are healed. Outwardly He was in the midst of all Israel—faith reaped the benefit in the sense of its own need and of the glory of His Person. Now, with respect to the one who was the object of His journey, remedy was unavailing. Jesus finds her dead, but does not miss the object of His journey. He raises her again, for He can give life. Thus too with respect to Israel. On the way, those who had faith in Jesus were healed, incurable as they were in themselves; but in fact, as to Israel, the nation was dead in trespasses and sins. Apparently this put a stop to the work of Jesus. But grace will restore life to Israel in the end. We see the perfect grace of Jesus intercepting the effect of the bad tidings brought from the ruler's house. He says to Jairus, as soon as the messenger has told him of his daughter's death, and the inutility of troubling the Master any farther, "Be not afraid, only believe." In effect, although the Lord restores life to a dead Israel in the end of the ages, nevertheless it is by faith that it takes place. The case of the poor woman, although in its direct application it does not go beyond the Jews, yet applies in principle to the healing of every Gentile who, through grace, is brought to touch Jesus by faith.

This history then gives the character of His service, the manner in which—on account of man's condition—it had to be accomplished.

Chapter 6

Patient service accompanied by the testimony of judgment for rejection of His mission

IN that which follows, the history (properly so called) of His service is resumed. Only we see Him already rejected by a blinded people, in spite of the power which He had manifested, and which bore testimony to the glory of His Person. Nevertheless He pursues His service, and sends forth His disciples in order that no effort might be wanting; but with the testimony of the judgment that awaited those who should be guilty of the rejection of His mission—a rejection that was already taking place. The Lord however continues to give proof in mercy and in goodness that Jehovah, who had compassion on His people, was there; until at length He had to prepare His disciples for the certain result of His work, namely, His death by the hand of the Gentiles, to whom the chief priests would deliver Him.

The Lord's service, limited by Israel's unbelief, widened elsewhere

To the Jews He was the carpenter, the son of Mary. Their unbelief stopped the beneficent hand of God with regard to themselves. Jesus carries on His work elsewhere, and sends forth His disciples—an act which implied the possession of divine power. It was still to Israel that the mission they received from Him directed them, and they were to pronounce judgment upon the land of Emmanuel, the land of Israel, as a polluted land, wherever their testimony should be rejected. They were to go forth resting on the mighty protection of Him who sent them, and they should lack nothing. He was sovereign Lord: all things were at His disposal. Christ can not only communicate blessings as the channel of blessing Himself, but can also

confer on His disciples the power of casting out devils.
The disciples fulfil their task. This passage shows forth
in a remarkable manner the position and glory of Christ.
He is the Servant—for men, the carpenter's son. In His
new service, He takes no place but the filling up of that
which God had given Him to do. He *could do no* mighty
works there, because of their unbelief—ever ready to
serve, but shut up, straitened in the exercise of His love,
where no door opened to receive its influence; and nature
judging according to sight never does. Only where a need
was, His love never tired, works—must work. The few
sick folk profit by a love that despises none, because it
never seeks itself.

Divine power and love shown in the dependent
Servant

But, in the following verse, He who could not work
mighty works (because His service was dependent on
divine conditions, on which God could found and carry
on His intercourse with men, in order to reveal Himself)
now gives power to others over all unclean spirits, a
power which is divine. Any can work miracles, if God
gives the power; but God alone can give it. They are to
lack nothing, for Emmanuel was there; and to announce
judgment if their message was rejected. Divine love had
made Him entirely a dependent Servant; but the dependent Servant was God present in grace and righteousness.

The murderous opposition of the authorities in Israel:
the death of John the Baptist

But the effect of all these manifestations of power is,
that the conscience of the king who then reigned in Israel
is awakened; and the Evangelist opens to us the history
of the murderous opposition of the authorities in Israel

to the witnesses for the truth. Herod had put John to death, in order to gratify the iniquity of a woman who pleased him—iniquity that he shared with her. A dance was worth the life of the prophet of God. Such was the ruler of Israel.

Jesus' compassion and power: satisfying the poor with bread

The apostles return. Jesus withdraws them from the inquisitive and needy crowd, by going into a desert place; but the multitude follow Him. Jesus, rejected as He is by the land He loved, has compassion on the poor of the flock, and manifests in their behalf the power of Jehovah to bless them according to Psalm 132. He satisfies the poor with bread. Having sent the people away, He crosses the sea on foot; and, rejoining His disciples, the wind ceases—a figure, of which we have spoken when meditating on Matthew. Their work was finished. As to themselves, in spite of all His miracles, their hearts at that time were still hard, and forgot the miracles, one after the other. The Lord pursues His work of blessing. It was but to touch Him and be healed.

Chapter 7

The heart of man and the heart of God

The ruling power in exercise among the Jews had shown itself hostile to the testimony of God, and had put to death the one whom He had sent in the way of righteousness. The scribes, and those who pretended to follow righteousness, had corrupted the people by their teaching, and had broken the law of God.

They washed cups and pots, but not their hearts; and, provided that the priests—religion—gained by it, set

aside the duties of children to their parents. But God
looked at the heart, and from the heart of man proceeded
every kind of impurity, iniquity, and violence. It was
that which defiled the man, not having his hands un-
washed. Such is the judgment on religiousness without
conscience and without fear of God, and the true discernment of what the heart of man is in the sight of God,
who is of purer eyes than to behold iniquity.

But God must also show His own heart; and if Jesus
judged that of man with the eye of God—if He manifested
His ways and His faithfulness to Israel; He displayed
nevertheless through it all, what God was to those who
felt their need of Him and came to Him in faith, owning
and resting upon His pure goodness. From the land of
Tyre and Sidon comes a woman of the condemned race,
a Gentile and a Syrophenician. The Lord replies to her,
on her request that He would heal her daughter, that
the children (the Jews) must first be filled; that it was
not right to take the children's bread and cast it to the
dogs: an overwhelming answer, if the sense she had of
her need and of the goodness of God had not gone beyond,
and set aside, every other thought. These two things made
her humble of heart, and ready to own the sovereign
favor of God towards the people of His choice in this
world. Had He not a right to choose a people? And
she was not one of them. But that did not destroy His
goodness and His love. She was but a Gentile dog, yet
such was the goodness of God that He had bread even
for dogs. Christ, the perfect expression of God, the manifestation of God Himself in the flesh, could not deny His
goodness and His grace, could not say that faith had higher
thoughts of God than were true, for He was Himself that
love. The sovereignty of God was acknowledged—no pretension made to any right whatsoever. The poor woman
rested only upon grace. Her faith, with an intelligence
given of God, laid hold of the grace which went beyond the
promises made to Israel. She penetrates into the heart of

the God of love, as He is revealed in Jesus, even as He penetrates into ours, and she enjoys the fruit of it. For this was brought in now: God Himself directly in presence of and connection with man, and man as he was before God— not a rule or system for man to prepare himself for God.

Hearing and speech bestowed in grace apart from the multitude

In the next miracle, we see the Lord, by the same grace, bestowing hearing and speech upon a man who was deaf and unable even to express his thoughts. He could have received no fruit from the Word, from God, and could give no praise to Him. The Lord is returned into the place where He arose as light on Israel; and here He deals with the remnant alone. He takes the man apart from the multitude. It is the same grace that takes the place of all pretensions to righteousness in man, and that manifests itself to the destitute. Its form, though exercised now in favor of the remnant of Israel, is suited to the condition of Jew or Gentile—it is grace. But as to these too it is the same: He takes the man apart from the crowd, that the work of God may be wrought: the crowd of this world had no real part therein. We see Jesus here, His heart moved at the condition of man, and more especially at the state of His ever-loved Israel, of which this poor sufferer was a striking picture. He causes the deaf to hear and the dumb to speak. So was it individually, and so will it be with the whole remnant of Israel in the latter days. He acts Himself, and He does all things well. The power of the enemy is des- troyed, the man's deafness, his inability to use his tongue as God gave it him, are taken away by His love who acts with the power of God.

The miracle of the loaves bore witness to the presence of the God of Israel, according to His promises; this, to the grace that went beyond the limits of these promises, on the part of God, who judged the condition of those who asserted a claim to them according to righteousness, and that of man, evil in himself; and who delivered man and blessed him in love, withdrawing him from the power of Satan, and enabling him to hear the voice of God, and to praise Him.

Hidden from the Jews, in rejection: need met in grace and power by the One who alone can supply it

There are yet some remarkable features in this part of the history of Christ, which I desire to point out. They manifest the spirit in which Jesus labored at this moment. He departs from the Jews, having shown the emptiness and hypocrisy of their worship, and the iniquity of every human heart as a source of corruption and sin.

The Lord—at this solemn moment, which displayed the rejection of Israel—goes far away from the people to a place where there was no opportunity for service among them, to the borders of the stranger and Canaanite cities of Tyre and Sidon (chap. 7: 24), and (His heart oppressed) would have no one know where He was. But God had been too plainly manifested in His goodness and His power, to allow Him to be hidden whenever there was need. The report of what He was had gone abroad, and the quick eye of faith discovered that which alone could meet its need. It is this that finds Jesus (when all, that had outwardly a right to the promises, are deceived by this pretension itself and by their privileges). Faith it is that knows its need, and knows that only, and that Jesus alone can meet it. That which God is to faith is manifested to the one that needs it, according to the grace and power that are in Jesus. Hidden from the Jews, He is grace to the sinner. Thus, also (chap. 7: 33), when He heals the deaf man of his deafness and of the impediment in his speech, He takes him aside from the multitude, and looks up to heaven and sighs. Oppressed in His heart by the unbelief of the people, He takes the object of the exercise of His power aside, looks up to the sovereign Source of all goodness, of all help for man, and grieves at the thought of the condition in which man is found. This case then exemplifies more particularly the remnant according to the election of grace from among the Jews, who are separated by divine grace from the mass of the nation, faith, in these few, being in exercise. The heart of Christ is far from repulsing His (earthly) people. His soul is overwhelmed by the sense of the unbelief that separates them from Him and from deliverance; nevertheless He takes away from some the deaf heart, and looses their tongue, in order that the God of Israel may be glorified.

Thus also on the death of Lazarus, Christ grieves at the sorrow which death brings upon the heart of man. There, however, it was a public testimony.

Faith not forsaken, but power not exercised where there is manifest unbelief

We shall find in chapter 8 another example of that which we have been noticing. Jesus leads the blind man out of the town. He does not forsake Israel wherever there is faith; but He separates the one who possesses it from the mass, and brings him into connection with the power, the grace, the heaven, whence blessing flowed—blessing consequently which extended to the Gentiles. Power was not exercised in the midst of manifest unbelief. This clearly marks out the position of Christ with regard to the people. He pursues His service, but He retires to God because of Israel's unbelief: but it is to the God of all grace. There His heart found refuge till the great hour of atonement.

Chapter 8

God's unwearied intervention in power in spite of rejection

IT is on this account, as it appears to me, that we have (chap. 8) the second miracle of the multiplication of the loaves. The Lord acts again in favor of Israel, no longer as administering Messianic power in the midst of the people (which was implied, as we have seen, in the number twelve), but in spite of His rejection by Israel, continuing to exercise His power in a divine manner and apart from man. The number seven [7] has always the force of superhuman perfection—that which is complete: this however applied to what is complete in the power of evil as well as good, when it is not human and subordinate to God. Here it is divine. It is that intervention of God which is unwearied, and which is according to His own power, which it is the principal object of the repetition of the miracle to display.

The condition of the heads of Israel and of the remnant displayed

Afterwards the condition both of the heads of Israel and of the remnant is displayed. The Pharisees require a sign; but no sign should be given to that generation. It was simply unbelief when abundant proofs of who He was were before them; they were the very things which had led to the demand. The Lord departs from them. But the blind and unintelligent condition of the remnant is also manifested. The Lord warns them to beware of the spirit and the teaching of the Pharisees, the false pretenders to a holy zeal for God; and of the Herodians, the

[7] It may be remarked that seven is the highest prime, that is indivisible, number; twelve, the most divisible there is.

servile votaries of the spirit of the world, who, to please
the emperor, set God entirely aside.

In using the word "leaven," the Lord gives the disciples occasion to show their deficiency in spiritual intelligence. If the Jews learnt nothing from the Lord's
miracles, but still asked for signs, even the disciples did
not realize the divine power manifested in them. I do
not doubt that this condition is set forth in the blind man
of Bethsaida.

The blind man of Bethsaida: the disciples' condition: the announcement of the Lord's death and resurrection

Jesus takes him by the hand and leads him out of the
town, away from the multitude, and uses that which was
of Himself, that which possessed the efficacy of His own
Person, to perform the cure.[8] The first effect well depicts
the condition of the disciples. They saw, doubtless, but in
a confused manner, "men, as trees, walking." But the
Lord's love is not wearied by their unbelieving dulness of
intelligence; He acts according to the power of His own
intention towards them, and causes them to see clearly.
Afterwards—away from Israel—the uncertainty of unbelief is seen in juxtaposition with the *certainty* of faith
(however obscure its *intelligence* may be), and Jesus, for-
bidding the disciples to speak of that which they certainly believed (the time was gone by for convincing Israel
of Christ' rights as Messiah), announces to them that
which should happen to Himself, for the accomplishment
of God's purposes in grace as Son of Man, after His
rejection by Israel.[9] So that everything is now, as we

[8] Spittle, in connection with the sanctity of the Rabbins, was highly esteemed by the Jews in this respect; but here its efficacy is connected with
the Person of Him who used it.

[9] We have nothing here of the Church, nor of the keys of the kingdom.
These depend on what is not introduced here as a part of Peter's confession—the Son of the living God. We have the glory of the kingdom coming in power, in contrast with the rejected Christ the prophet-servant in
Israel.

may say, in its place. Israel does not recognize the Messiah in Jesus; consequently He no longer addresses the people in that character. His disciples believe Him to be the Messiah, and He tells them of His death and resurrection.

Peter's opposition as the instrument of Satan

Now there may be (and it is a most important practical truth) true faith, without the heart being formed according to the full revelation of Christ, and without the flesh being practically crucified in proportion to the measure of knowledge one has of the object of faith. Peter acknowledged indeed, by the teaching of God, that Jesus was the Christ; but he was far from having his heart pure according to the mind of God in Christ. And when the Lord announces His rejection, humiliation and death, and that before all the world, the flesh of Peter—wounded by the idea of a Master thus despised and rejected—shows its energy by daring to rebuke the Lord Himself. This attempt of Satan's to discourage the disciples by the dishonor of the cross stirs up the Lord's heart. All His affection for His disciples, and the sight of those poor sheep before whom the enemy was putting a stumblingblock, bring a vehement censure upon Peter, as being the instrument of Satan and speaking on his part. Alas for us! The reason was plain—he savored the things *of men*, and not those of God; for the cross comprises in itself all the glory of God. Man prefers the glory of man, and thus Satan governs him. The Lord calls the people and His disciples, and explains distinctly to them that if they would follow Him, they must take part with Him, and bear their cross. For thus, in losing their life, they would save it, and the soul was worth all beside. Moreover, if any one was ashamed of Jesus and of His words, the Son of Man would be ashamed of him, when He should come in the glory of His Father with the holy angels. For glory belonged to Him, whatever might be His humiliation. He then sets this before His chief disciples, in order to strengthen their faith.

Chapter 9

The transfiguration: the coming of the kingdom in power and glory on earth

IN Matthew we saw the transfiguration announced in terms that related to the subject of that Gospel—the rejected Christ taking His glorious position as Son of Man. In each of the Gospels it is in connection with the moment when this transition is clearly set forth; but in each case with a particular character. In Mark we have seen the humble and devoted service of Christ in proclaiming the kingdom, whatever might be the divine glory that shone through His humiliation. Accordingly the manifestation of the transition to glory is here announced as the coming of the kingdom in power. There is nothing that very particularly distinguishes the recital here from that in Matthew, excepting that the isolation of Jesus and the three disciples at this moment is more strongly marked in verse 2, and that the facts are related without addition. The Lord afterwards charges them to tell no one what they had seen, until after His resurrection from among the dead.

We may remark here, that it is indeed the kingdom in power that is manifested. It is not the power of the Holy Ghost bringing the sinner as a holy member of the body into connection with Christ the Head, revealing to it the heavenly glory of Christ as He is at the right hand of the Father. Christ is on earth. He is there in connection with the great witnesses of the Jewish economy (the law and prophecy), but witnesses who give place entirely

to Him, while participating with Him in the glory of
the kingdom.   But Christ is manifested in glory on the
earth—the Man in glory is recognized as Son of God, as
He is known in the cloud.   It was the glory as it shall
be manifested on the earth, the glory of the kingdom,
and God is still in the cloud, though revealing His glory
in it.   This is not *our* position as yet without a veil; only
that the veil as to our relationship with God is rent from
top to bottom, and we have boldness to enter into the
holiest by the blood of Christ.   But this is spiritual privilege, not public display—our veil as to that, our body,
is not rent; but Christ's, as the title of entrance, is.[10]

A new order of things established in resurrection

But the position of glory could not be taken by the
Lord, nor the glorious reign be established, excepting in
a new order of things.   Christ must rise from the dead
to establish it.   It did not accord with His presentation
as Messiah, as He then was. Therefore He commands His
disciples not to make it known till after His resurrection.
It would then be a powerful confirmation of the doctrine
of the kingdom in glory.   This manifestation of the glory
confirmed the faith of the disciples at that time (as
Gethsemane taught them the reality of His sufferings, and
of His conflicts with the prince of darkness); and would
afterwards form a subject of their testimony, and its
confirmation, when Christ should have taken His new
position.

We may see the character of this manifestation, and its
relation to the earthly kingdom of glory of which the
prophets had spoken, in 2 Peter 1: 19. Read there, "We
have the word of prophecy confirmed."

---

[10] The entrance into the cloud does not form part of the revelation here.
We find it in Luke.   The cloud for Israel was the place where God dwelt;
it was (Matt. 17) a bright cloud.

The Son of Man as the Resurrection and the Life

The disciples had stopped at the threshold. In fact, although their eyes were opened, they saw "men as trees, walking." What, they questioned between themselves, could this "rising from among the dead" mean? Resurrection was known to them; all the sect of the Pharisees believed in it. But this power, which delivered from the condition in which man and even the saints were found, implying too that others were still left in it when that power was exercised, of this they were totally ignorant. That there was a resurrection in which God would raise up all the dead at the last day, they had no doubt. But that the Son of Man was the resurrection and the life— the absolute triumph over death of the last Adam, the Son of God having life in Himself, manifested by His resurrection *from among* the dead (a deliverance that shall be accomplished in the saints also in due time), of this they understood nothing. Doubtless they received the Lord's words as true, as having authority; but His meaning was incomprehensible to them.

The difficulties of unbelief

Now unbelief never fails to find out difficulties that justify it in its own eyes which refuse to perceive the divine proofs of the truth—difficulties great enough in appearance, and which may trouble the minds of those who, through grace, are inclined to believe, or who have believed, but are still weak in the faith.

The prophets had said that Elias must first come. The scribes insisted on this. Struck with the glory that undeniably confirmed the pretensions of Christ, the disciples speak to Him of this difficulty. The conviction which the sight of the glory brought to their mind, made them confess the difficulty with regard to which they had previously been silent, not daring to bring it forward.

But now the proof is strong enough to embolden them to face the difficulty.

Sufferings before glory

In fact, the Word spoke of it, and Jesus accepts it as the truth; Elias was to come and restore all things. And he shall indeed come before the manifestation of the glory of the Son of Man; but first of all the Son of Man must suffer and be rejected. This also was written, as well as the mission of Elias. Moreover, before this manifestation of Christ, which tested the Jews as to their responsibility, God had not failed to supply them with a testimony according to the spirit and power of Elias; and they had ill-treated him as they listed. It was written that the Son of Man should suffer before His glory, as truly as that Elias should come. However, as we have said, in point of testimony to the Jews, he who took morally the place of Elias had come. They had treated him as they were going to treat the Lord. Thus also John had said that he was not Elias, and he quotes Isaiah 40, which speaks of the testimony; but he never quotes Malachi 4, which relates to Elias personally. The Lord (Matt. 11: 10) applies Malachi 3: 1; but John, Isaiah.

Great need: weak and wavering faith: almighty power to heal

Come down from the mountain, the people rush towards Him, astonished apparently at this mysterious absence from His disciples, and salute Him with the reverence with which His whole life had inspired them. But that which had taken place in His absence only confirmed the solemn truth that He must depart, which had just been demonstrated by a more glorious testimony. The remnant even, they who believed, knew not how to profit by the power which was now on earth. The faith of those even who believed did not realize the presence of

the Messiah—the power of Jehovah, the Healer of Israel:
wherefore then still remain among the people and the disciples?   The poor father expresses his affliction in a
touching manner in words that show a heart brought by
the sense of its need to a right condition, but very weak
in faith.   The miserable state of his child is related, and
his heart presents a true picture of the condition of the
remnant—faith that required support on account of the
unbelief under which it was buried.   Israel was in no
better condition than the poor child.   But power was
present, capable of all things.   That was not the difficulty.
Is there faith to profit by it? was the question.   "If Thou
canst," said the afflicted father to Jesus.   "*If thou canst*"
(replied the Lord) applies to thy faith; "if thou canst
believe, all things are possible."   The poor father, true of
heart, confesses his own state with grief, and seeks, in
the goodness of Christ, help for his failure.   Thus the
position of Israel was plainly shown forth.   Almighty
power was present to heal them, to deliver them from
the power of Satan.   It was to be done through faith, for
the soul was to return to God.   And there was faith in
those who, touched by the testimony of His power, and
moved by the grace of God, sought in Jesus the remedy
for their woes and the foundation for their hopes.   Their
faith was weak and wavering; but wherever it existed,
Jesus acted with the sovereign power of His own grace,
and of the goodness of God that finds its measure in itself.   However far unbelief may have gone in those who
should profit by the grace of a dispensation, wherever
there is a need to meet, Jesus answers to it when He is
looked to.   And this is a great mercy and encouragement
for us.

Nevertheless, for this power to be exercised by man
himself (to which God called him), it was needful that
he should draw very near to God—that he to whom it
was committed should accustom himself to communion
with God, by withdrawing from all that connected him
with the world and the flesh.

Unbelief brought to Jesus: the enemy cast out

Let us here recapitulate the principles of this narrative with respect to their general application. The Lord, who was going away, to be seen no more of the world until He came in glory, finds, on coming down from the mount of transfiguration, a case of the power of Satan over man, over the Jewish people. It had continued from almost the commencement of the child's existence. The faith that recognizes the intervention of God in Christ, and takes shelter in it from present evil, is weak and wavering, pre-occupied with the evil, the sight of which conceals in great measure the power that masters and takes it away. Still the sense of need is deep enough to make it have recourse to that power.

It is the unbelief which knows not how to count on the power that is present, which puts an end to the relations of Christ with man. It is not man's misery that does so —it was this that brought Him down to earth. But the almighty power is present—it only needs faith to profit by it. But if the heart, on account of the enemy's power, turns to Jesus, it can (thank God) bring its unbelief to Him as well as all the rest. There are love and power in Him for every kind of weakness. The people crowd around, attracted by the sight of the enemy's power. Can the Lord heal him? But can he allow the testimony of Satan's power to invade their hearts? This is the curiosity of men whose imagination is filled with the effect of the enemy's presence. But, whatever might be the unbelief of man, Christ was present, the testimony of a power that, in love to men, destroyed the effects of the power of the enemy. The people gather round—Jesus sees it, and with a word casts out the enemy. He acts according to the necessity of His power, and the purposes of the love of God. Thus the effort of the enemy occasioned the intervention of Jesus, which the weakness of the father's faith tended to arrest. Nevertheless, if we lay all our infirmity, as well as our misery, before Christ, He answers according to the fulness of His power.

Intelligence in the ways of God hindered by the flesh

On the other hand, if the flesh meddles with the thoughts of faith, it hinders intelligence in the ways of God. While journeying, Christ explained His death and His new condition in resurrection. Why blame the lack of intelligence which hid all this from them, and filled their minds with ideas of earthly and Messianic glory? The secret of their want of intelligence lay here. He had told them plainly; but on the way they disputed among themselves which should have the first place in the kingdom. The thoughts of the flesh filled their heart, in regard to Jesus, with exactly the opposite of that which engaged the mind of God respecting Him. Infirmity, presented to Jesus, finds an answer in power and in sovereign grace; the flesh and its desires hide from us, even when thinking of Him, all the import of the thoughts of God. It was their own glory they were seeking in the kingdom; the cross—the true path to glory—was unintelligible to them.

The disciples instructed as to their Lord's rejection

After this the Lord resumes with His disciples the great subject before Him at this moment; and which was, in every way, that which now must be decided. He was to be rejected; and He separates Himself from the multitude, with His disciples, to instruct them on this point. Preoccupied with His glory, with His rights as Messiah, they do not understand it. Their faith even, such as it was, blinds them to all beyond that; because, while rightly attaching itself to the Person of Christ, it connected—or rather, their own hearts, in which the faith existed, connected—with Christ the accomplishment of that which their flesh desired and sought in Him for themselves. How

subtle is the heart! This betrays itself in their dispute
for pre-eminence. Their faith is too weak to bear elucida-
tions that contradicted their ideas (ver. 32). These ideas
are manifested without disguise among themselves. Jesus
reproves them, and gives them a little child for an example, as He had so often done before. He that would
follow Christ must have a spirit quite opposite to that
of the world—a spirit belonging to that which was weak
and despised by the pride of the world. In receiving such
a one, they would receive Christ; in receiving Christ, they
would receive the Father. It was eternal things that
were in question, and the spirit of a man must then be
the spirit of a child.

Instruction for the Christian life as set apart for God and sharing the Lord's rejection

The world was so contrary to Christ, that he who was
not against Him was for Him.[11] The Son of Man was
to be rejected. Faith in His Person was the thing, not
now individual service to Him. Alas, the disciples were
still thinking of themselves: "He followeth not *us*." They
must share His rejection; and if any one gave them a cup
of cold water, God would remember it. Whatever would
cause them to stumble in their walk, were it even their
own right eye or hand, they would do well to cut off;
for it was not the things of an earthly Messiah that were
in question, but the things of eternity. And all should be
tested by the perfect holiness of God, and that in judgment by one means or another. Every one should be
salted with fire—the good and the bad. Where there was

[11] Some have difficulty in reconciling this with: "Forbid him not; he
that is not with Me is against Me." But they coalesce when the main
point is seen; Christ was a divine criterion of man's state, and brought
things to an issue. The world was wholly, absolutely, against Him. If
a man was not, there was no middle state, he was for Him. But things
being brought to an issue, if a man was not for Him, he was of the
world, and so against Him.

life, the fire would only consume the flesh; for when we
are judged, we are chastened of the Lord, that we should
not be condemned with the world. If the judgment
reaches the wicked (and assuredly it shall reach them),
it is condemnation—a fire that is not quenched. But, for
the good, there was also something else: they should be
salted with salt. Those who were consecrated to God,
whose life was an offering to Him, should not lack the
power of holy grace, which binds the soul to God and in-
wardly preserves it from evil. Salt is not the gentleness
that pleases (which grace produces without doubt), but
that energy of God within us which connects everything
in us with God, and dedicates the heart to Him, binding
it to Him in the sense of obligation and of desire, rejecting all in oneself that is contrary to Him (obligation that
flows from grace, but which acts all the more powerfully
on that account). Thus, practically, it was distinctive
grace, the energy of holiness, which separates from all
evil; but by setting apart for God. Salt was good: here
the effect produced in the soul, the condition of the soul,
is so called, as well as the grace that produces this condition. Thus they who offered themselves to God were
set apart for Him; they were the salt of the earth. But
if the salt lose its savor, wherewith can it be salted? It
is used for seasoning other things; but if the salt needs
it for itself, there is nothing left that can salt *it*. So would
it be with Christians; if they who were of Christ did not
render this testimony, where should anything be found,
apart from Christians, to render it to them and produce it
in them? Now this sense of obligation to God which
separates from evil, this judgment of all evil in the heart,
must be in oneself. It is not a question of judging others,
but of placing oneself before God, thus becoming the salt,
having it in oneself. With regard to others, one must seek
peace; and real separation from all evil is that which
enables us to walk in peace together.

In a word, Christians were to keep themselves separate

from evil and near to God in themselves; and to walk with God in peace among one another.

No instruction could be more plain, more important, more valuable. It judges, it directs, the whole Christian life in a few words.

The relations of God with man: the Lord's obedience as Man

But the end of the Lord's service drew near. Having described in these principles the exigencies of eternity and the character of Christian life, He brings back all the relations of God with man to their original elements, setting aside the world and its glory, and Jewish glory also, as to its immediate accomplishment, and pointing out the path of eternal life in the cross, and in the saving power of God. Nevertheless He takes the place of obedience Himself, and of service—the true place of man—in the midst of all this: God Himself being introduced on the other hand, in His proper character as God, in His nature and in His divine rights; the special glory that belongs to dispensations, and the relationships proper to them, being left out.

Chapter 10

The relationships of nature re-established

IT is a striking principle which meets us here—the relationships of nature (as God has Himself created them at the beginning) re-established in their original authority, while the heart is judged, and the cross the sole means of drawing nigh to the God who was their creative source. On earth Christ could offer nothing but the cross to those who followed Him. The glory to which the cross would lead has been shown to some of them; but as to

Himself He took the place of servant. It was the knowledge of God by Him that should form them for this glory and lead them to it; for in fact *that* was life eternal. All other intermediate ways had, in the hands of men, become hostile to the God who had granted them, and therefore to His manifestation in the Person of Christ.

The family: the law and the heart of man: natural uprightness and man's true condition

We find then (vers. 1-12) the original relationship of man and wife as formed by the creative hand of God; in verses 13-16 the interest which Jesus took in young children, their place in the compassionate eye of God, the moral value of that which they represented before men. In verse 17 we come to the law, to the world, and to the heart of man in presence of the two. But at the same time we see that Jesus takes pleasure in that which is amiable in the creature as a creature—a principle of deep interest unfolded in this chapter—while still applying the touchstone morally to his heart. With respect to the law, as the natural heart can see it (that is, the outward action it requires), the young man had kept it; and with a natural sincerity, an uprightness, that Jesus could appreciate as a creature-quality, and which we ought always to recognize where it exists. It is important to remember, that He who as man was perfectly separated unto God— and that, because He had the thoughts of God—could recognize the unchangeable obligations of the relationships established by God Himself; and also, whatever there was amiable and attractive in the creature of God as such. Having the thoughts of God—being God manifest in the flesh, how could He but recognize that which was of God in His creature? And while doing this, He must establish the obligations of the relationships in which He has placed him, and exhibit the tenderness He felt for the infant representatives of the spirit which He

prized. He must love the natural uprightness that may
be developed in the creature. But He must judge the
true condition of man fully brought out, and the affections
that rested on objects raised up by Satan, and the will
that rejected and turned away from the manifestation of
God that called him to forsake these vanities and follow
Him, thus putting his heart morally to the proof.

The law used for self-righteousness

Jesus exhibits the absolute perfection of God in yet
another manner. The young man saw the exterior of
Christ's perfection, and, trusting to the power of man
to perform that which is good, and seeing its practical
fulfilment in Jesus, applies to Him—and, humanly speaking, with sincerity—to learn, from One in whom he saw
so much perfection, though viewing Him merely as a
Rabbi, the rule of eternal life. This thought is expressed
in his sincere and cordial salutation. He runs, he kneels,
to the Teacher who, morally, stood so high in his estima-
tion, saying, "Good Master." The human limit of his
ideas of this goodness, and his confidence in the powers
of man, are manifested by the words, "What shall I do
that I may inherit eternal life?" The Lord, taking up
the whole import of his word, replies, "Why callest thou
Me good? There is none good but One, that is God."
What God has created he who knows God will respect,
when it presents itself as such in its true place. But God
alone is good. Man, if intelligent, will not make himself
out good before God, nor dream of human goodness. This
young man had at least the hope of becoming good by
the law,[12] and he believed that Jesus was so as a Man.
But the greatest advantages which the flesh could recognize, and which answered to its nature, did but the more
effectually shut the door of life and heaven to man. The

---

[12] He does not ask, note, What must I do to be saved? He assumed
that by the law he was to get life.

flesh used the law for self-righteousness, man being not good but a sinner. And, in fact, if we have to seek for righteousness, it is because we have it not (that is to say, because we are sinners and cannot attain this righteousness in ourselves). Moreover worldly advantages, which appeared to render man more capable of doing good, bound his heart to perishing things, and strengthened selfishness, and made him attach little value to the image of God.

Peter's difficulty: man in the presence of God

But the instructions of this chapter carry on still farther the subject of man's condition before God. The ideas of the flesh accompany and give their form to the heart's affections, in one who is already quickened by the Spirit of grace acting through the attraction of Christ, until the Holy Ghost Himself communicates to those affections the strength of His presence, by giving them the glory of Christ in heaven for their object; and at the same time causing the light of that glory to shine (for the believer's heart) upon the cross, investing it with all the value of the redemption it accomplished, and of the divine grace that was its source, and producing conformity to Christ in every one that bears it with Him. Peter did not understand how any one could be saved, if such advantages as the Jews possessed in their relationship to God (and which were specially present in the case of this young man) only barred up the way to the kingdom of God. The Lord meets him upon this very ground; for man in the presence of God was now the question. As far as man was concerned, it was *impossible*—a second profound truth—with respect to his condition. Not only was there none good excepting God, but no one could be saved, according to what man was. Whatever advantages he might have as means, they would avail him nothing in his state of sin. But the Lord introduces an-

other source of hope—"With God all things are possible."
The whole of this, indeed all this part of the Gospel,
while it sets aside the Jewish system, does so, because,
while that was founded on testing the possibility by the
possession of divinely given ordinances of acquiring
righteousness, and a standing before God as yet unrevealed,
this revealed God and brought man and man's heart face
to face, as a present thing, with Him; in grace, but still
face to face as he was. The disciples, not having yet received the Holy Ghost, are still under the influence of the
old system, and only see men as trees walking; and this is
fully developed in this chapter. The kingdom indeed they
could think of, but still with fleshly thoughts.

Following the Lord and its reward

But the flesh, the carnal mind, enters yet farther into
the career of the life of grace. Peter reminds the Lord
that the disciples had forsaken all to follow Him. The
Lord replies, that every one [13] who had done so should
have everything that would make him happy in his social
affections, as God had formed him, and all this world
could give as to the real enjoyment of it and a hundredfold, together with the opposition that He Himself met
with in this world; but in the world to come (Peter was
not thinking of that) not some private individual advantage, but everlasting life. He went beyond the sphere of
promise connected with the Messiah on earth, to enter,
and to make others enter, into that which was eternal.
As to individual reward, that could not be judged of
according to appearances.

The cross: the place of service, humiliation and obedience

But further, they followed indeed Jesus, and thought
of the reward, but thought little of the cross which led

[13] This went beyond even the disciples' connection with the Jews, and
in principle admitted the Gentiles.

to it; they were amazed therefore at seeing Jesus deliberately going up to Jerusalem, where people sought to kill Him, and they were afraid. Although following Him, they were far from the height of realizing all that the path implied. Jesus sedulously explains it to them—His rejection, and His entrance into the new world by resurrection. John and James, little affected by the Lord's communications, use their faith in the royalty of Christ to present the carnal desires of their heart, namely, to be on His right and left hand in the glory. Again the Lord assures them that they should participate in the cross with Him, and takes the place Himself of the accomplishment of His service and of bringing others into fellowship with His sufferings. As for the glory of the kingdom, it would be theirs for whom the Father had prepared it: the disposal of it was not in His hands save to them. This is the place of service, of humiliation, and of obedience, in which this Gospel always presents Him. Such should be the place of His disciples.

We have seen what the flesh was in an upright young man whom Jesus loved, and in His disciples who knew not how to take the true position of Christ. The contrast of this with the full triumph of the Holy Ghost is remarkable, as we find it in the comparison of this chapter with Philippians 3.

Human righteousness made worthless to Paul: the righteousness of God by faith bright with Christ's glory

We have in Saul a man outwardly blameless, according to the law, like the young man in the Gospel; but he has seen Christ in glory, and, by the teaching of the Holy Ghost, the righteousness according to which Christ entered into the glory in which He revealed Himself to Saul. All that had been gain to him was loss for Christ. Would he have a carnal righteousness, a human righteousness, even if he could have accomplished it, when he had seen a righteousness bright with the glory of Christ? He possessed the righteousness which was *of God* by faith. What was that righteousness worth for which he had labored, now that he possessed the all-perfect righteousness which God gave by faith? Not sins alone were put away: human righteousness was made worthless by it. But his eyes had been opened to this by the Holy Ghost, and by seeing Christ. The things that engaged the heart of the young man and retained him in the world which Christ forsook, and which in Him had rejected God—could these things retain one who had seen Christ in the other world? They were but as dung to him. He had forsaken everything in order to possess this Christ. He considered them as utterly worthless. The Holy Ghost, in revealing Christ, had completely delivered him.

The disciples' amazement and fear contrasted with Paul's desire

But this manifestation to the heart of Christ glorified goes yet farther. He who thus breaks with the world must follow the One whose glory he would reach; and this is to put himself under the cross. The disciples had forsaken all to follow Him. Grace had attached them to Christ that they might follow Him. The Holy Ghost had not yet linked them with His glory. He goes up to Jerusalem. They are amazed at it; and, in following Him (although He goes before them, and they have His guidance and His presence), they are afraid. Paul *seeks* to know the power of His resurrection: he *desires* to have fellowship with His sufferings, and to be conformed unto His death. Instead of amazement and fear, there are full spiritual intelligence and the desire of conformity to that death which the disciples feared; because he found Christ morally in it, and it was the pathway to the glory he had seen.

Christ Himself desired, not a good place near Him

Moreover this sight of Christ purifies the desires of
the heart with respect even to the glory. John and James
desire for themselves the best place in the kingdom—a
desire that availed itself (with a carnal and selfish object)
of the intelligence of faith—a half-sighted intelligence that
sought the kingdom at once, and not the glory and the
world to come. Paul had seen Christ: his only desire
in the glory was to possess Him—"That I may win
Christ," and a new state conformed to it; not a good
place near Him in the kingdom, but Himself. This is
deliverance—the effect of the presence of the Holy Ghost
revealing a glorified Christ.

The cross as faith's only path to God: Christ the leader in it

We may remark, that in every case the Lord brings in
the cross. It was the only passage from this world of
nature, to the world of glory and of eternal life.[14] To the
young man He exhibits the cross; to the disciples that
follow Him He exhibits the cross; to John and James,
who sought a good place in the kingdom, He exhibits the
cup they would have to drink in following Him. Eternal
life, although received now, was, in possession and enjoyment according to God's purpose, on the other side of the
cross.

Observe also, that the Lord was so perfectly, divinely,
above the sin in which nature lay, that He could recognize
all that was of God in nature, and show at the same time
the impossibility of any relation between God and man
on the ground of what man is. Advantages were but hin-

---

[14] From the transfiguration until His rights as Son of David are in
question, it is the cross that is presented. Prophet and preacher until
then, that ministry ended with the transfiguration, in which His future
glory shone in this world upon the cross that was to close His service here
below.   But before He reached the cross, He presented Himself as King.
Matthew begins with the King, but Mark is essentially the Prophet.

drances. That which is death to the flesh must be gone
through: we must have divine righteousness, and enter
in spirit (hereafter in fact) into another world, in order
to follow Him and to be with Him—to "win Christ."
Solemn lesson!

In result, God alone is good, and—sin having come
in—it is *impossible,* if He be manifested, that man can
be in relationship with God; but with Him all is possible.
The cross is the only path to God. Christ leads to it, and
we must follow Him in this path, which is that of eternal
life. A child-like spirit enters into it by grace; the spirit
of service and of self-renunciation walks in it. Christ
walked in it, giving His life a ransom for many. This
part of the Lord's instruction ends here. Lowliness of
service is the place into which Christ brings us; in such
He had walked. This chapter is worthy of all the attention which the Christian through grace can devote to it.
It speaks of the ground man can stand upon, how far
God owns what is natural, and the disciples' path down
here.

Christ's last dealings with the Jews: the need and faith of the blind man at Jericho met in power

At verse 46 another subject begins. The Lord enters on
the path of His final relationship with Israel, presenting
Himself as King, Emmanuel, rather than as the prophet
who was to be sent. As the Prophet, His ministry had
been accomplished. He had been sent (He told His disciples) to preach. This had led Him to the cross, as we
have seen. He must needs announce it as the result to
those that followed Him. He now resumes His connection with Israel, but as the Son of David. He draws near
to Jerusalem, from which He had departed and where
He was to be rejected, and the power of God manifests
itself in Him. By the way of Jericho, the city of the
curse, enters the One who brings blessing at the price of

the gift of Himself. The poor blind man [15] (and such indeed was the nation of itself) acknowledges Jesus of Nazareth to be the Son of David. The grace of Jesus replies in power to the need of His people, that expressed itself by faith, and that persevered in, in spite of the obstacles put in its way by the multitude who did not feel this need, and who followed Jesus, attracted by the manifestation of His power, without being attached to Him by the faith of the heart. *That* faith has the sense of need. Jesus stands still and calls him, and before all the people manifests the divine power which responded in the midst of Israel to the faith that recognized in Jesus of Nazareth the true Son of David, the Messiah. The poor man's faith had healed him, and he followed Jesus in the way without dissimulation or fear. For the faith which then confessed Jesus to be the Christ was divine faith, although it might perhaps know nothing of the cross which He had just announced to His disciples as the result of His faithfulness and service, and in which faith must follow when genuine.

Chapter 11

Christ presenting Himself at Jerusalem as King

IN that which follows (chap. 11) Jesus presents Himself to Jerusalem as King. His reception shows the extent to which the testimony He had rendered had acted on the hearts of the simple. God ordained therefore that it should take place. There is little difference between the narrative here and in Matthew. Only the kingdom is more simply presented as such: "The kingdom of our father David."

---

[15] I have already noticed that the blind man of Jericho is, in all the first three Gospels, the point where the history of the last dealings of Christ with the Jews and His final sufferings begin, His general ministry and service being closed.

The Judge of all things: man's wisdom in the presence of God

With what dignity, as the Judge of all things, Jesus now takes knowledge of all that was being done in the temple, and goes out without saying anything! The Lord had visited His temple, as also He had entered the city as riding on the ass's colt, whereon never man sat. Israel is judged in the condemned fig-tree.[16] The glory of the Lord, of the house of Jehovah, is vindicated with authority—an authority which He claims, and which He exercises in His own Person. The scribes and chief priests draw back before the ascendency that His Word had given Him over the people, and He goes out of the city without being molested, notwithstanding their malice. The next day He assures His disciples, who were astonished at seeing the fig-tree withered away, that whatsoever they asked in faith should be accomplished; but that they must act in grace, if they would enjoy this privilege. The scribes and priests and elders are confounded, and demand His authority. He addresses their conscience, but in such a manner as to demonstrate their incompetency to ask Him such a question, exposing at the same time their insincerity. They could not decide with respect to the baptism of John: by what right then could they subject Him to their questions respecting His own claims? They could not decide when the case was before them. On the other hand, they must either sanction His work by their reply, or lose their authority with the people by denying the baptism of John who had borne testimony to Christ. It was no longer a question of winning these men; but what an empty thing is the wisdom of man in the presence of God and His wisdom!

---

[16] That is man under the old covenant, flesh under divine requirement, and no fruit to grow on it for ever.

Different characteristics of the Gospels of Matthew and Mark as to the change of dispensation

The change of dispensation has a more definite place in Matthew, and the sin which rejected the King. In Mark it is more the service of Christ as the Prophet. Afterwards, as we have seen, He presents Himself as King. And, in both Gospels, we see that it is Jehovah who fills the office which He has deigned to undertake.

Consequently we find in Matthew more personal accusations, as in the parable of the two sons (chap. 21: 28-32), and the detail of the change of dispensation in the parable of the marriage feast (chap. 22: 1-14); neither of which is in Mark. In our Gospel, the unchangeable dignity of His Person, and the simple fact that the Prophet and King were rejected (rejection that led to Israel's judgment) are set before us by the Spirit of God. Otherwise it is the same general testimony we have reviewed in Matthew.

Chapter 12

The law as the principle of blessing: the touchstone of the heart in Christ's rejection

THE Lord afterwards gives the substance of the whole law, as the principle of blessing between the creature and God, and that which formed the touchstone for the heart in the rejection of Christ. I say for the heart, because the trial was really there, although it was in the understanding that it appeared. Even when there were really orthodox principles (Christ being rejected), the heart that was not attached to His Person could not follow Him in the path to which His rejection led. The system of God's counsels which depended on that rejection was a difficulty. Those who were attached to His Person followed Him, and found themselves in it, with-

out having well understood it beforehand. Thus the
Lord gives the pith of the law—the whole law as essentially divine instruction—and the point at which the
counsels of God are transplanted into the new scene,
where they will be fulfilled apart from the wickedness or
ill-will of man. So that in these few verses (chap. 12:
28-37) the law and the Son of David are presented, and
the latter taking His place as Son of Man—the Lord—
at the right hand of God. This was the secret of all that
was going on. The union of His Body, the assembly,
with Himself was all that remained behind. Only in
Mark the Prophet recognizes the moral condition, under
the law, that tends towards entrance into the kingdom
(ver. 34). This scribe had the spirit of understanding.

True and false devotion

The picture of the condition that would bring in judgment, which we find in Matthew 23, is not given here.
It was not His subject. (See *ante*, p. 166.) Jesus, still
as the Prophet, warns His disciples morally; but the judgment of Israel, for rejecting the Son of David, is not
here before His eyes in the same manner (that is to say,
it is not the subject of which the Holy Ghost is here
speaking). The real character of the scribes' devoutness
is pointed out, and the disciples are warned against them.
The Lord makes them feel also what it is that, in the
eyes of God, gives true value to the offerings that were
brought to the temple.

Chapter 13

The disciples' service in Israel and in testimony, continuing the Lord's preaching

IN chapter 13 the Lord takes up much more the service
of the apostles in the circumstances that would surround them, than the development of the dispensations

and the ways of God with respect to the kingdom—a point of view more presented in Matthew, who treats of this subject.

It will be observed, that the disciples' question takes only a general view of the subject which pre-occupied them. They ask when the judgment upon the temple and all these things shall be fulfilled. And from verses 9-13, although some circumstances found in Matthew 24 are included, the passage relates even more to that which is said in Matthew 10. It speaks of the service which the disciples would accomplish in the midst of Israel, and in testimony against persecuting authorities, the gospel being preached in all nations before the end came. They were, as preachers, to fill the place which Jesus had occupied among the people, only that the testimony was to extend much farther. It would be in the face of all possible suffering and most trying persecutions.

Forewarned of coming days of unparalleled distress

But there would be a moment when this service should end. The well-known sign of the abomination that maketh desolate would point it out. They were then to flee. These would be the days of unparalleled distress, and of signs and wonders, which, if it were possible, would deceive the very elect. But they were forewarned. Everything should be shaken after that time, and the Son of Man should come. Power should take the place of testimony, and the Son of Man should gather together His elect (of Israel) from all parts of the earth.

The judgment on Jerusalem near at hand and that which is still future

It appears to me that in this Gospel, more than in any other, the Lord brings together the judgment on Jerusalem then at hand, and that which is yet to come, carrying the mind on to the latter, because He is here more

occupied with the conduct of His disciples during those
events. Israel, the whole system into which the Lord
had come, was to be set aside provisionally, in order to
bring in the assembly and the kingdom in its heavenly
character, and afterwards the millennium—that is, the
assembly in its glory and the kingdom established in
power—when the legal system and Israel under the first
covenant should be finally set aside. At these two periods
the general position of the disciples would be the same;
but the events of the latter period would be definitive
and important, and the Lord speaks especially of them.
Nevertheless that which was the most imminent, and
which, for the present, set aside Israel and the testimony,
required that a warning should be addressed to the disciples on account of their immediate danger; and they
receive it accordingly.

The effort of the Jews to re-establish their system at
the end, in despite of God, will but lead to open apostasy
and definitive judgment. This will be the time of un-
equalled affliction, of which the Lord speaks. But from
the time of the first destruction of Jerusalem by Titus
until the coming of the Lord, the Jews are considered as
set aside and under this judgment, in what degree soever
it may have been accomplished.

The unknown length of service during the Master's absence

The disciples are commanded to watch, for they know
not the hour. It is the conduct of the disciples in this
respect which is here especially before the eyes of the
Lord. It is of this great day, and the hour of its arrival,
that the angels and even the Son, as Prophet, know not.
For Jesus must sit at the right hand of God *until* His
enemies are made His footstool, and the time of His rising
up is not revealed. The Father has kept it, says Jesus,
in His own power. See Acts 3, where Peter proposes
to the Jews the Lord's return. They rejected his testi-

mony; and now they wait for the full accomplishment of all that has been spoken. Meantime the servants are left to serve during the Master's absence. He commanded the porter in particular to watch. They knew not at what hour the Master would come. This applies to the disciples in their connection with Israel, but at the same time it is a general principle. The Lord addresses it to all.

Chapter 14

Man's purposes and God's arrangements

CHAPTER 14 resumes the thread of the history, but with the solemn circumstances that belong to the close of the Lord's life.

The scribes and Pharisees were already consulting how they might take Him by craft and put Him to death. They feared the influence of the people, who admired the works and goodness and meekness of Jesus. Therefore they wished to avoid taking Him at the time of the feast, when the multitude flocked to Jerusalem: but God had other purposes. Jesus was to be our Paschal Lamb—blessed Lord!—and He offers Himself as the victim of propitiation. Now the counsels of God and the love of Christ being such, Satan was not wanting in suitable agents to perform all that he could do against the Lord. Jesus offering Himself for it, the people would soon be induced to give up, even to the Gentiles, the One who had so much attracted them; and treachery would not be wanting to throw Him without difficulty into the hands of the priests. Still God's own arrangements, which owned Him and displayed Him in His grace, should have the first place; and the supper at Bethany and the supper at Jerusalem should precede—the one, the proposal, and the other, the act of Judas. For, let the wickedness of man be what it may, God always takes the place He chooses, and never allows the enemy power to hide His ways from faith, nor leaves His people without the testimony of His love.

All in God's hands to accomplish His purposes, at the moment, in the manner, and by His chosen instruments

This portion of the history is very remarkable. God brings forward the thoughts and fears of the leaders of the people, in order that we may know them; but everything is absolutely in His own hands; and the malice of man, treachery, and the power of Satan, when working in the most energetic manner (never had they been so active), only accomplish the purposes of God for the glory of Christ. Before the treachery of Judas He has the testimony of Mary's affection. God puts the seal of this affection upon Him who was to be betrayed. And, on the other hand, before being forsaken and delivered up, He can testify all His affection for His own, in the institution of the Lord's supper, and at His own last supper with them. What a beautiful testimony to the interest with which God cares for and comforts His children in the darkest moments of their distress!

Love for Christ to guide suitable conduct

Remark also, in what manner love to Christ finds, amid the darkness that gathers round His path, the light that directs its conduct, and directs it precisely to that which was suitable to the moment. Mary had no prophetic knowledge; but the imminent danger in which the Lord Christ was placed by the hatred of the Jews, stimulates her affection to perform an act which was to be made known wherever the death of Christ and His love for us should be proclaimed in the whole world. This is true intelligence—true guidance in things moral. Her act be-

comes an occasion of darkness to Judas; it is clothed with
the light of divine intelligence by the Lord's own testimony. This love for Christ discerns that which is suitable—apprehends the good and the evil in a just and
seasonable manner. It is a good thing to care for the
poor. But at that moment the whole mind of God was
centred on the sacrifice of Christ. They had always
opportunity to relieve the poor, and it was right to do
so. To put them in comparison with Jesus, at the moment of His sacrifice, was to put them out of their place,
and to forget all that was precious to God. Judas, who
cared only for money, seized the position according to his
own interest. He saw, not the preciousness of Christ,
but the desires of the scribes. His sagacity was of the
enemy, as that of Mary was of God. Things advance:
Judas arranges with them his plan to deliver up Jesus
for money. The thing in fact is settled according to his
thoughts and theirs. Nevertheless it is very remarkable
to see here the way in which—if I may so speak—God
Himself governs the position. Although it is the moment
when the malice of man is at its height, and when the
power of Satan is exerted to the utmost, yet all is accomplished exactly at the moment, in the manner, by the
instruments, chosen of God. Nothing, not the least thing,
escapes Him. Nothing is accomplished but that which
He wills, and as He wills, and when He wills. What consolation for us! and, in the circumstances which we are
considering, what a striking testimony! The Holy Ghost
has therefore reported the desire (easy to be understood)
of the chief priests and scribes to avoid the occasion of
the feast. Useless desire! This sacrifice was to be accomplished at that time; and it is accomplished.

The last Passover during the life of Jesus—Himself the Lamb of God

But the time drew near for the last feast of the Passover that took place during the life of Jesus—the one in

which He was Himself to be the Lamb, and leave no
memorial to faith except that of Himself and of His
work. He therefore sends His disciples to prepare all that
was needed to keep the feast.   In the evening He sits
with His disciples, to converse with them, and to testify
His love for them as their companion, for the last time.
But it is to tell them (for He must suffer everything)
that one of them should betray Him.   The heart at least
of each one of the eleven answered, full of grief at the
thought. [17]   So should one have done who was eating from
the same dish with Him; but woe to that man!   Yet
neither the thought of such iniquity, nor the sorrow of
His own heart, could stop the outflowing of the love of
Christ.   He gives them pledges of this love in the Lord's
supper.   It was Himself, His sacrifice, and not a temporal deliverance, that they were henceforth to remember.
All was now absorbed in Him, and in Him dying on the
cross.   Afterwards, in giving them the cup, He lays the
foundation of the new covenant in His blood (in a figure),
giving it to them as participation in His death—true
draught of life.   When they had all drunk of it, He announces to them that it is the seal of the new covenant—
a thing well known to the Jews, according to Jeremiah;
adding that it was shed for many.   Death was to come
in for the establishment of the new covenant, and for the
ransom of many.   For this, death was necessary, and the
bonds of earthly association between Jesus and His
disciples were dissolved.   He would drink no more of the
fruit of the vine (the token of that connection) until, in
another way, He should renew this association with them

---

[17] There is something very beautiful and touching in this inquiry. Their
hearts were solemnized, and Jesus' words have all the weight of a divine
testimony in their hearts.   They had not a thought of betraying Him,
save Judas; but His word was surely true, their souls owned it, and there
was distrust of themselves in presence of Christ's words.   No boasting
certainty that they would not, but a bowing of heart before the solemn
and terrible words of Jesus.   Judas avoided the question, but afterwards,
not to seem to be but as the rest, asks it, only to be personally marked
out by the Lord, a sure relief to the rest (Matt. 26: 25).

in the kingdom of God. When the kingdom should be established, He would again be with them, and would renew these bonds of association (in another form, and in a more excellent way, no doubt, yet really). But now all was changing. They sing, and go out, repairing to the accustomed place in the Mount of Olives.

Relationship with His disciples to be resumed and established in resurrection

The connection of Jesus with His disciples here below should indeed be broken, but it would not be by His forsaking them. He strengthened, or, at least, He manifested, the sentiments of His heart, and the strength (on His part) of these bonds, in His last supper with them. But they would be offended at His position, and would forsake Him. Nevertheless the hand of God was in all this. *He* would smite the Shepherd. But when once raised from the dead, Jesus would resume His relationship with His disciples—with the poor of the flock. He would go before them to the place where this relationship commenced, to Galilee, afar from the pride of the nation, and where the light had appeared among them according to the Word of God.

The death of Christ as God's judgment on sin ministering its own remedy

Death was before Him. He must pass through it, in order that any relationship whatsoever between God and man might be established. The Shepherd should be smitten by the Lord of hosts. Death was the judgment of God: could man sustain it? There was but One who could. Peter, loving Christ too well to forsake Him in heart, enters so far into the path of death as to draw back again, thus giving a testimony all the more striking to his own inability to traverse the abyss that opened before his eyes in the Person of his disowned Master.

After all, to Peter it was but the outside of what death is. The weakness that his fears occasioned made him unable to look into the abyss which sin has opened before our feet. At the moment when Jesus announces it Peter undertakes to face all that was coming. Sincere in his affection, he knew not what man was, laid bare before God, and in the presence of the power of the enemy who has death for his weapon. He had trembled already; but the sight of Jesus, which inspires affection, does not say that the flesh which prevents our glorifying Him is, in a practical sense, dead. Moreover he knew nothing of this truth. It is the death of Christ which has brought our condition out into full light, while ministering its only remedy—death, and life in resurrection. Like the ark in Jordan, He went down into it alone, that His redeemed people might pass through dryshod. They had not passed this way before.

The perfection and glory brought out by the Lord's trial

Jesus approaches the end of His trial—a trial which only brought out His perfection and His glory, and at the same time glorified God His Father, but a trial which spared Him nothing that would have had power to stop Him, if anything could have done so, and which went on even unto death, and unto the burden of the wrath of God in that death, a burden beyond all our thoughts.

At Gethsemane: the Lord's full knowledge of what lay before Him

He approaches the conflict and the suffering, not with the lightness of Peter who plunged into it because he was ignorant of its nature, but with full knowledge; placing Himself in His Father's presence, where all is weighed, and where the will of Him who laid this task upon

Him is clearly stated in His communion with Him; so that Jesus accomplishes it, even as God Himself looked upon it, according to the extent and the intention of His thoughts and of His nature, and in perfect obedience to His will.

Realizing the whole compass of His sufferings, but in communion with His Father

Jesus goes forward alone to pray. And, morally, He passes through the whole compass of His sufferings, realizing all their bitterness, in communion with His Father. Having them before His own eyes, He brings them before His Father's heart, in order that, if it were possible, this cup might pass from Him. If not, it should at least be from His Father's hand that He received it. This was the piety on account of which He was heard and His prayers ascended upon high. He is there as a Man— glad to have His disciples watch with Him, glad to isolate Himself and pour out His heart into the bosom of His Father, in the dependent condition of a man who prays. What a spectacle!

Peter, who would die for his Master, is not able even to watch with Him. The Lord meekly sets his inconsistency before him, acknowledging that his spirit indeed was full of goodwill, but that the flesh was worthless in conflict with the enemy and in spiritual trial.

The moral character and connection of events in Mark displaying the perfect Man, the faithful Servant

The narrative of Mark, which passes so rapidly from one circumstance (that displays the whole moral condition of the men with whom Jesus was associated) to another, in such a manner as to place all these events in connection with each other, is as touching as the development of the details found in the other Gospels. A moral character is imprinted on every step we take in the history, giving it as a whole an interest that nothing could surpass (excepting that which is above all things, above all thoughts) save that only One, the Person of Him who is here before us. He at least watched with His Father; for after all, dependent as He was by grace, what could man do for Him? Completely Man as He was, He had to lean on One alone, and thus was the perfect Man. Going away again to pray, He returns to find them again sleeping, and again presents the case to His Father, and then awakens His disciples, for the hour was come in which they could do no more for Him. Judas comes with his kiss. Jesus submits. Peter, who slept during the earnest prayer of his Master, awakes to strike when his Master yields Himself as a lamb to the slaughter. He smites one of the assistants, and cuts off his ear. Jesus reasons with those who were come to take Him, reminding them that, when He was constantly exposed, humanly speaking, to their power, they had laid no hands upon Him; but there was a very different reason for its now taking place—the counsels of God and the Word of God must be fulfilled. It was the faithful accomplishment of the service committed to Him. All forsake Him and flee; for who beside Himself could follow this path to the end?

One young man indeed sought to go farther; but as soon as the officers of justice laid hold of him, seizing his linen garment, he fled and left it in their hands. Apart from the power of the Holy Ghost, the farther one ventures into the path in which the power of the world and of death is found, the greater the shame with which one escapes, if God permits escape. He fled from them naked.

The faithful Witness before the high priest: false witnesses: unfaithful Peter

The witnesses fail, not in malice, but in certainty of testimony, even as force could do nothing against Him until the moment God had appointed. The confession of Christ, His faithfulness in declaring the truth in the congregation, is the means of His condemnation. Man can do nothing, although he did everything as regards his will and his guilt. The testimony of His enemies, the affection of His disciples—everything fails: this is man. It is Jesus who bears witness to the truth; it is Jesus who watches with the Father—Jesus who yields Himself to those who were never able to take Him until the hour came that God had appointed. Poor Peter! He went farther than the young man in the garden; and we find him here, the flesh in the place of testimony, in the place where this testimony is to be rendered before the power of its opposer and of his instruments. Alas, he will not escape! The Word of Christ shall be true, if that of Peter be false—His heart faithful and full of love, if that of Peter (alas! like all ours) is unfaithful and cowardly. He confesses the truth, and Peter denies it. Nevertheless the grace of our blessed Lord does not fail him; and, touched by it, he hides his face and weeps.

The rejected King is the Son of the Blessed, the Son of Man

The word of the prophet has now again to be fulfilled. He shall be delivered into the hands of the Gentiles. There He is accused of being a king, the confession of which must assuredly cause His death. But it was the truth.

The confession that Jesus had made before the priests relates, as we have seen in other cases in this Gospel, to His connection with Israel. His service was to preach in the congregation of Israel. He had indeed presented Himself as King, as Emmanuel. He now confesses that He is to Israel the hope of the people, and which here-after He will be. "Art Thou," had the priest said, "the Christ, the Son of the Blessed?" That was the title, the glorious position, of Him who was the hope of Israel, according to Psalm 2. But He adds that which He shall

be (that is to say, the character He would assume, being
rejected by this people, that in which He would present
Himself to the rebellious people); it should be that of
Psalms 8, 110, and also Daniel 7, with its results—that is
to say, the Son of Man at the right hand of God, and
coming in the clouds of heaven. Psalm 8 only presents
Him in a general manner; it is Psalm 110 and Daniel 7
which speak of the Messiah in that particular manner,
according to which Christ here announces Himself. The
blasphemy which the high priest attributed to Him was
only the rejection of His Person. For that which He
said was written in the Word.

Chapter 15

Before Pilate: the Lord's last service: led out to be crucified

BEFORE Pilate, He only witnesses a good confession,
a testimony to the truth where the glory of God
required it, and where this testimony stood opposed to
the power of the adversary. To all the rest He answers
nothing. He lets them go on; and the Evangelist enters
into no details. To render this testimony was the last
service and duty He had to perform. It is rendered. The
Jews make choice of the seditious murderer Barabbas;
and Pilate, hearkening to the voice of the multitude, won
over by the chief priests, delivers Jesus to be crucified.
The Lord submits to the insults of the soldiers, who
mingle the pride and insolence of their class with the
hard-heartedness of the executioner whose function they
performed. Sad specimens of our nature! The Christ
who came to save them was, for the moment, under their
power. He used His own power, not to save Himself,
but to deliver others from that of the enemy. At length
they lead Him away to Golgotha to crucify Him. There

they offer Him a soporific mixture, which He refuses; and
they crucify Him with two thieves, one on His right
hand and the other on His left, thus accomplishing (for
it was all they did or could do) everything that was
written concerning the Lord. It was now the Jews' and
the priests' hour; they had—alas for them!—the desire
of their heart. And they make manifest, without knowing
it, the glory and perfection of Jesus. The temple could
not rise again without being thus cast down; and, as
instruments, they established the fact which He had then
announced. Farther, He saved others and not Himself.
These are the two parts of the perfection of the death of
Christ with reference to man.

God's will accomplished: the Lord's service completed in obedience to the end

But, whatever might be the thoughts of Christ and His
sufferings with regard to men (those dogs, those bulls of
Bashan), the work which He had to accomplish contained
depths far beyond those outward things. Darkness covered the earth—divine and sympathetic testimony of that
which, with far deeper gloom, covered the soul of Jesus,
forsaken of God for sin, but thus displaying incomparably
more than at any other time, His absolute perfection;
while the darkness marked, in an external sign, His entire
separation from outward things, the whole work being
between Him and God alone, according to the perfectness
of both. All passed between Him and His God. Little
understood by others, all is between Himself and God:
and, crying again with a loud voice, He gives up the
ghost. His service was completed. What more had He
to do in a world wherein He only lived to accomplish
the will of God? All was finished, and He necessarily
departs. I do not speak of physical necessity, for He
still retained His strength; but, morally rejected by the
world, there was no longer room in it for His mercy to-

wards it: the will of God was by Himself entirely fulfilled.
He had drunk in His soul the cup of death and of judgment for sin.   There was nothing left Him but the act
of dying; and He expires, obedient to the end, in order
to commence in another world (whether for His soul
separate from the body, or in glory) a life where evil
could never enter, and where the new man will be perfectly happy in the presence of God.

Obedience perfected in death by the Prince of Life

His service was completed. His obedience had its term
in death—His obedience, and therefore His life, as carried
on in the midst of sinners. What would a life have meant
in which there was no more obedience to be fulfilled?
In dying now His obedience was perfected, and He dies.
The way into the holiest is now opened—the veil is rent
from the top to bottom. The Gentile centurion confesses,
in the death of Jesus, the Person of the Son of God.
Until then, the Messiah and Judaism went together. In
His death Judaism rejects Him, and He is the Saviour of
the world. The veil no longer conceals God. In this
respect it was all Judaism could do. The manifestation
of perfect grace is there for the Gentile, who acknowledged—because Jesus gave up His life with a cry that
proved the existence of so much strength—that the Prince
of life, the Son of God, was there. Pilate also is astonished that He is already dead. He only believes it when
certified of its truth by the centurion. As to faith—far
from grace, and even from human justice—he did not
trouble himself at all on that point.

The body of Jesus laid in the tomb

The death of Jesus did not tear Him from the hearts
of those feeble ones who loved Him (who perhaps had
not been in the conflict, but whom grace had now brought
out from their retreat): those pious women who had fol-

lowed Him and had often ministered to His wants, and
Joseph, who, although touched in conscience, had not
followed Him, until now, strengthened at the last by the
testimony of the grace and perfection of Jesus (the in-
tegrity of the counsellor finding in the circumstances, not
an occasion of fear, but that which induced him to declare himself)—these women and Joseph are alike occupied about the body of Jesus. This tabernacle of the
Son of God is not left without those services which were
due from man to Him who had just quitted it. Moreover the providence of God, as well as His operation in
their hearts, had prepared for all this. The body of Jesus
is laid in the tomb, and they all wait for the end of the
sabbath to perform their service to it. The women had
taken knowledge of the place.

Chapter 16

The resurrection: the connection re-established
between Jesus and the remnant

THE last chapter is divided into two parts—a fact
which has even given rise to questions as to the
authenticity of verses 9-20. The first part of the chapter,
verses 1-8, relates the end of the history in connection
with the re-establishment of that which has always been
before us in this Gospel—the relationship of the Prophet
of Israel, and of the kingdom with the people (or at least
with the remnant of the chosen people). The disciples,
and Peter, whom the Lord individually acknowledges in
spite (yea, in grace, because) of his denial of his Master,
were to go and meet Him in Galilee, as He said unto
them. There the connection was re-established between
Jesus in resurrection and the poor of the flock, who waited
for Him (they alone being recognized as the people before
God). The women say nothing to any others. The

testimony of Christ risen was committed only to His disciples, to these despised Galileans. Fear was the means employed by the providence of God to prevent the women speaking of it, as they would naturally have done.

The message sent by Mary Magdalene: the disciples' commission to every creature

Verses 9-20. This is another testimony. The disciples do not appear here as an elect remnant, but in the unbelief natural to man. The message is sent to the whole world. Mary Magdalene, formerly possessed by seven demons—the absolute slave of that dreadful power—is employed to communicate the knowledge of His resurrection to the companions of Jesus. Afterwards Jesus Himself appears to them, and gives them their commission. He tells them to go into all the world, and preach the gospel to *every creature*. It is no longer specifically the gospel of the kingdom. Whosoever throughout the world believed and joined Christ by baptism should be *saved;* he who believed not should be condemned. It was a question of salvation or condemnation—the believer saved, he who refused the message condemned. Moreover, if any one was convinced of the truth but refused to unite with the disciples confessing the Lord, his case would be so much the worse. Therefore it is said, "he who believeth and is baptized." Signs of power should accompany believers, and they should be preserved from that of the enemy.

Signs of power over the enemy's power and the proclamation of grace to all men

The first sign should be their dominion over evil spirits; the second, the proof of that grace which went beyond the narrow limits of Israel, addressing itself to all the world. They should speak divers languages.

Besides this, with respect to the power of the enemy, manifested in doing harm, the venom of serpents and poisons should have no effect upon them, and diseases should yield to their authority.

In a word, it should be the overthrowal of the power of the enemy over man, and the proclamation of grace unto all men.

Christ's ascension to the seat of power: the disciples' sphere of service

Having thus given them their commission, Jesus ascends to heaven, and sits at the right hand of God—the place from which this power shall come forth to bless, and from which He will return to put the poor of the flock in possession of the kingdom. Meanwhile, the disciples occupy His place, extending their sphere of service unto the ends of the earth; and the Lord confirms their word by the signs that follow them.

The accomplishment of the service of the great Servant-Prophet rendered to His Father in view in Mark's Gospel

It may perhaps be thought that I have dwelt little on the sufferings of Christ in that which I have written on Mark. Never will this subject be exhausted; it is as vast as the Person and the work of Christ must be. Blessed be God for it! In Luke we have more details. And I follow the order of thought which the Gospel sets before me; and it appears to me that, with regard to the crucifixion of Christ, it is the accomplishment of His service that the Evangelist has in view. His great subject was the Prophet. He must needs relate His history unto the end; and we possess, in a brief narrative, a very complete picture of the events that mark the end of the Lord's life—of that which He had to fulfil as the Servant of His Father. I have followed this order of the Gospel.

LUKE

The scope of Luke's Gospel: the Mediator, the Son of Man, revealing God in delivering grace

THE Gospel of Luke sets the Lord before us in the character of Son of Man, revealing God in delivering grace among men. Hence the present operation of grace and its effect are more referred to, and even the present time prophetically, not the substitution of other dispensations as in Matthew, but of saving heavenly grace. At first, no doubt (and just because He is to be revealed as man, and in grace to men), we find Him, in a prefatory part in which we have the most exquisite picture of the godly remnant, presented to Israel, to whom He had been promised, and in relationship with whom He came into this world; but afterwards this Gospel presents moral principles which apply to man, whosoever he may be, whilst yet manifesting Christ for the moment in the midst of that people. This power of God in grace is displayed in various ways in its application to the wants of men. After the transfiguration, which is recounted earlier in the narration by Luke[1] than in the other Gospels, we find the judgment of those who rejected the Lord, and the heavenly character of the grace which, because it is grace, addresses itself to the nations, to sinners, without any particular reference to the Jews, overturning the legal principles according to which the latter pretended to be, and as to their external standing were originally

[1] That is, as to the contents of the Gospel. In the ninth chapter His last journey up to Jerusalem begins; and, thence on to the latter part of the eighteenth, where (ver. 31) His going up to that city is noticed, the evangelist gives mainly a series of moral instructions, and the ways of God in grace now coming in. In verse 35 of chapter 18 we have the blind man of Jericho already noticed as the commencement of His last visit to Jerusalem.

called at Sinai to be, in connection with God. Unconditional promises to Abraham, etc., and prophetic confirmation of them, are another thing. They will be accomplished in grace, and were to be laid hold of by faith.
After this, we find that which should happen to the Jews
according to the righteous government of God; and, at the
end, the account of the death and resurrection of the Lord,
accomplishing the work of redemption. We must observe
that Luke (who morally sets aside the Jewish system, and
who introduces the Son of Man as the man before God,
presenting Him as the One who is filled with all the fulness of God dwelling in Him bodily, as the man before
God, according to His own heart, and thus as Mediator
between God and man, and centre of a moral system
much more vast than that of Messiah among the Jews)—
we must observe, I repeat, that Luke, who is occupied with
these new relations (ancient, in fact, as to the counsels
of God), gives us the facts belonging to the Lord's connection with the Jews, owned in the pious remnant of that
people, with much more development than the other
evangelists, as well as the proofs of His mission to that
people, in coming into the world—proofs which ought to
have gained their attention, and fixed it upon the Child
who was born to them.

Christ set forth as a Man on earth

In Luke, I add, that which especially characterizes the
narrative and gives its peculiar interest to this Gospel is,
that it sets before us that which Christ is Himself. It
is not His official glory, a relative position that He assumed; neither is it the revelation of His divine nature,
in itself; nor His mission as the great Prophet. It is Himself, as He was a Man on the earth—the Person whom I
should have met every day had I lived at that time in Judea,
or in Galilee.

Chapter I

The style of Luke and the purpose of his Gospel

I WOULD add a remark as to the style of Luke, which may facilitate the study of this Gospel to the reader. He often brings a mass of facts into one short general statement, and then expatiates at length on some isolated fact, where moral principles and grace are displayed.

Many had undertaken to give an account of that which was historically received among Christians, as related to them by the companions of Jesus; and Luke thought it well—having followed these things from the beginning, and thus obtained exact knowledge respecting them—to write methodically to Theophilus, in order that he might have the certainty of those things in which he had been instructed. It is thus that God has provided for the instruction of the whole Church, in the doctrine contained in the picture of the Lord's life furnished by this man of God; who, personally moved by Christian motives, was directed and inspired by the Holy Ghost for the good of all believers.[2]

The first revelations of stupendous events: Zacharias and Elisabeth

At verse 5 the evangelist begins with the first revelations of the Spirit of God respecting these events, on which the condition of God's people and that of the world entirely depended; and in which God was to glorify Himself to all eternity.

---

[2] The union of motive and inspiration, which infidels have endeavored to set in opposition to each other, is found in every page of the Word. Moreover the two things are only incompatible to the narrow mind of those who are unacquainted with the ways of God. Cannot God impart motives, and through these motives engage a man to undertake some task, and then direct him, perfectly and absolutely, in all that he does? Even if it were a human thought (which I do not at all believe), if God approved of it, could not He watch over its execution so that the results should be entirely according to His will?

But we immediately find ourselves in the atmosphere of Jewish circumstances. The Jewish ordinances of the Old Testament, and the thoughts and expectations connected with them, are the framework in which this great and solemn event is set. Herod, king of Judea, furnishes the date; and it is a priest, righteous and blameless, belonging to one of the twenty-four classes, whom we find on the first step of our way. His wife was of the daughters of Aaron; and these two upright persons walked in all the commandments and ordinances of the Lord (Jehovah) without blame. All was right before God, according to His law in the Jewish sense. But they did not enjoy the blessing that every Jew desired; they had no child. Nevertheless, it was according, we may say, to the ordinary ways of God in the government of His people, to accomplish His blessing while manifesting the weakness of the instrument—a weakness that took away all hope according to human principles. Such had been the history of the Sarahs, the Rebeccas, the Hannahs, and many more, of whom the Word tells us for our instruction in the ways of God.

God's answer to prayer

This blessing was often prayed for by the pious priest; but until now the answer had been delayed. Now, however, when, at the moment of exercising his regular ministry, Zacharias drew near to burn incense, which, according to the law, was to go up as a sweet savor before God (type of the Lord's intercession), and while the people were praying outside the holy place, the angel of the Lord appears to the priest on the right side of the altar of incense. At the sight of this glorious personage Zacharias is troubled, but the angel encourages him by declaring himself to be the bearer of good news; announcing to him that his prayers, so long apparently addressed in vain to God, were granted. Elisabeth should bear a son, and the

name by which he should be called was, "The favor of
the Lord," a source of joy and gladness to Zacharias,
and whose birth should be the occasion of thanksgiving to many. But this was not merely as the son of
Zacharias. The child was the Lord's gift, and should be
great before Him; he should be a Nazarite, and filled
with the Holy Ghost, from his mother's womb: and many
of the children of Israel should he turn to the Lord their
God. He should go before Him in the spirit of Elias,
and with the same power to re-establish moral order in
Israel, even in its sources, and to bring back the diso-
bedient to the wisdom of the just—to make ready a people
prepared for the Lord.

The spirit of Elias

The spirit of Elias was a stedfast and ardent zeal
for the glory of Jehovah, and for the establishment, or
re-establishment by repentance, of the relations between
Israel and Jehovah. His heart clung to this link between
the people and their God, according to the strength and
glory of the link itself, but in the sense of their fallen
condition, and according to the rights of God in connection with these relationships. The spirit of Elias—although indeed the grace of God towards His people had
sent him—was in a certain sense a legal spirit. He asserted the rights of Jehovah in judgment. It was grace
opening the door to repentance, but not the sovereign
grace of salvation, though what prepared the way to it.
It is in the moral force of his call to repentance that
John is here compared to Elias, in bringing back Israel to
Jehovah. And in fact Jesus was Jehovah.

Zacharias' want of faith used of God: Elisabeth's piety

But the faith of Zacharias in God and in His goodness did not come up to the height of his petition (alas,

too common a case!), and when it is granted at a moment that required the intervention of God to accomplish his desire, he is not able to walk in the steps of an Abraham or a Hannah, and he asks how this thing can now take place.

God, in His goodness, turns His servant's want of faith into an instructive chastisement for himself, and into a proof for the people that Zacharias had been visited from on high. He is dumb until the Word of the Lord is fulfilled; and the signs which he makes to the people, who marvel at his staying so long in the sanctuary, explain to them the reason.

But the Word of God is accomplished in blessing towards him; and Elisabeth, recognizing the good hand of God upon her with a tact that belongs to her piety, goes into retirement. The grace which blessed her did not make her insensible to that which was a shame in Israel, and which, although removed, left its traces as to man in the superhuman circumstances through which it was accomplished. There was a rightmindedness in this, which became a holy woman. But that which is rightly concealed from man has all its value before God, and Elisabeth is visited in her retreat by the mother of the Lord. But here the scene changes, to introduce the Lord Himself into this marvellous history which unfolds before our eyes.

The Saviour's birth announced to Mary

God, who had prepared all beforehand, sends now to announce the Saviour's birth to Mary. In the last place that man would have chosen for the purpose of God—a place whose name in the eyes of the world sufficed to condemn those who came from thence—a maiden, unknown to all whom the world recognized, was betrothed to a poor carpenter. Her name was Mary. But everything was in confusion in Israel: the carpenter was of the house of David. The promises of God—who never forgets them, and never overlooks those who are their object—found here the sphere for their accomplishment. Here the power and the affections of God are directed, according to their divine energy. Whether Nazareth was small or great was of no importance, except to show that God does not expect from man, but man from God. Gabriel is sent to Nazareth, to a virgin who was betrothed to a man named Joseph, of the house of David.

The gift of John to Zacharias was an answer to his prayers—God faithful in His goodness towards His people who wait upon Him.

Sovereign grace displayed

But this is a visitation of sovereign grace. Mary, a chosen vessel for this purpose, had found grace in God's sight. She was favored [3] by sovereign grace—blessed among women. She should conceive and bring forth a Son: she should call Him Jesus. He should be great, and should be called the Son of the Highest. God should give Him the throne of His father David. He should reign over the house of Jacob for ever, and His kingdom should have no end.

The birth of the Child presented by the Holy Spirit in a twofold way

It will be observed here, that the subject which the Holy Ghost sets before us is the birth of the Child, as He would be down here in this world, as brought forth by Mary—of Him who should be born.

The instruction given by the Holy Ghost on this point is divided into two parts: first, that which the child to

[3] The expressions, "found favor" (*eures charin*) and "highly favored" (*kecharitomene*) have not at all the same meaning. Personally she had found favor, so that she was not to fear: but God had sovereignly bestowed on her this grace, this immense favor, of being the mother of the Lord. In this she was the object of God's sovereign favor.

be born should be; secondly, the manner of His conception, and the glory which would be its result. It is not
simply the divine nature of Jesus that is presented, the
Word which was God, the Word made flesh; but that
which was born of Mary, and the way in which it should
take place. We know well that it is the same precious
and divine Saviour of whom John speaks that is in
question; but He is here presented to us under another
aspect, which is of infinite interest to us; and we must
consider Him as the Holy Ghost presents Him, as born
of the Virgin Mary in this world of tears.

The Lord Jesus as really and truly Man

To take first the verses 31-33.
It was a child really conceived in Mary's womb, who
brought forth this Child at the time which God had Himself appointed for human nature. The usual time elapsed
before its birth. As yet this tells us nothing of the manner. It is the fact itself, which has an importance that
can neither be measured nor exaggerated. He was really
and truly Man, born of a woman as we are—not as to
the source nor as to the manner of His conception, of
which we are not yet speaking, but as to the reality of
His existence as Man. He was really and truly a human
being. But there were other things connected with the
Person of the One who should be born that are also set
before us. His name should be called Jesus, that is,
Jehovah the Saviour. He should be manifested in this
character and with this power. He was so.

The Child born as Man is "the Son of the Highest"

This is not connected here with the fact, "For He shall
save His people from their sins," as in Matthew, where
it was the manifestation to Israel of the power of Jehovah,
of their God, in fulfilment of the promises made to that
people. Here we see that He has a right to this name; but

this divine title lies hidden under the form of a personal
name; for it is the Son of Man who is presented in this
Gospel, whatever His divine power might be.   Here we
are told, "He"—the One who should be born—"should
be great," and (born into this world) "should be called
the Son of the Highest."   He had been the Son of the
Father before the world was; but this Child, born on
earth, should be called—such as He was down here—the
Son of the Highest: a title to which He would thoroughly
prove His right by His acts, and by all that manifested
what He was.   A precious thought to us and full of glory,
a child born of a woman legitimately bears this name,
"Son of the Highest"—supremely glorious for One who
is in the position of a man, and really was such before
God.

"The Son of David": His endless kingdom and His glory

But other things still were connected with the One
that should be born.   God would give Him the throne of
His father David.   Here again we plainly see that He
is considered as born, as man, in this world.   The throne
of His father David belongs to Him.   God will give it
Him.   By right of birth He is heir to the promises, to the
earthly promises which, as to the kingdom, appertained
to the family of David; but it should be according to the
counsels and the power of God.   He should reign over the
house of Jacob—not only over Judah, and in the weakness of a transitory power and an ephemeral life, but
throughout the ages; and of His kingdom there should
be no end.   As indeed Daniel had predicted, it should
never be taken by another.   It should never be transferred
to another people.   It should be established according to
the counsels of God which are unchangeable, and His
power which never fails.   Until He delivered up the kingdom to God the Father, He should exercise a royalty that

nothing could dispute; which He would deliver up (all things being fulfilled) to God, but the royal glory of which should never be tarnished in His hands.

Such should be the Child born—truly, though miraculously, born as Man. To those who could understand His name it was Jehovah the Saviour.

He should be King over the house of Jacob according to a power that should never decay and never fail, until blended with the eternal power of God as God.

The grand subject of the revelation is, that the Child should be conceived and born; the remainder is the glory that should belong to Him, being born.

Mary's question: her faith

But it is the conception that Mary does not understand. God permits her to ask the angel how this should be. Her question was according to God. I do not think there was any want of faith here. Zacharias had constantly asked for a son—it was only a question of the goodness and the power of God to perform his request—and was brought by the positive declaration of God to a point at which he had only to trust in it. He did not trust to the promise of God. It was only the exercise of the extraordinary power of God in the natural order of things. Mary asks, with holy confidence, since God thus favored her, how the thing should be accomplished, outside the natural order. Of its accomplishment she has no doubt. (See verse 45; "Blessed," said Elisabeth, "is she that believed.") She inquires *how* it shall be accomplished, since it must be done outside the order of nature. The angel proceeds with his commission, making known to her the answer of God to this question also. In the purposes of God, this question gave occasion (by the answer it received) to the revelation of the miraculous conception.

The Son of God as become Man

The birth of Him who has walked upon this earth was the thing in question—His birth of the Virgin Mary. He was God, He became Man; but here it is the manner of His conception in becoming a Man upon the earth. It is not *what* He was that is declared. It is He who was born, such as He was in the world, of whose miraculous conception we here read. The Holy Ghost should come upon her—should act in power upon this earthen vessel, without its own will or the will of any man. God is the source of the life of the Child promised to Mary, as born in this world and by His power. He is born of Mary— of this woman chosen by God. The power of the Highest should overshadow her, and therefore that which *should be born of her* should be called the Son of God. Holy in His birth, conceived by the intervention of the power of God acting upon Mary (a power which was the divine source of His existence on the earth, as man), that which thus received its being from Mary, the fruit of her womb, should even in this sense have the title of Son of God. The Holy Thing which should be born of Mary should be called the Son of God. It is not here the doctrine of the eternal relationship of the Son with the Father. The Gospel of John, the Epistle to the Hebrews, that to the Colossians, establish this precious truth, and demonstrate its importance; but here it is that which was born by virtue of the miraculous conception, which on that ground is called the Son of God.

The angel's announcement to Mary of Elisabeth's blessing

The angel announces to her the blessing bestowed on Elisabeth through the almighty power of God; and Mary bows to the will of her God—the submissive vessel of His purpose, and in her piety acknowledges a height and greatness in these purposes which only left to her, their passive instrument, her place of subjection to the will of God. This was her glory, through the favor of her God.

It was befitting that wonders should accompany, and bear a just testimony to, this marvellous intervention of God. The communication of the angel was not without fruit in the heart of Mary; and by her visit to Elisabeth, she goes to acknowledge the wonderful dealings of God. The piety of the virgin displays itself here in a touching manner. The marvellous intervention of God humbled her, instead of lifting her up. She saw God in that which had taken place, and not herself; on the contrary the greatness of these marvels brought God so near her as to hide her from herself. She yields herself to His holy will: but God has too large a place in her thoughts in this matter to leave any room for self-importance.

Mary's visit to Elisabeth: Elisabeth's recognition of God's grace to the mother of her Lord

The visit of the mother of her Lord to Elisabeth was a natural thing to herself, for the Lord had visited the wife of Zacharias. The angel had made it known to her. She is concerned in these things of God, for God was near her heart by the grace that had visited her. Led by the Holy Ghost in heart and affection, the glory that belonged to Mary, in virtue of the grace of God who had elected her to be the mother of her Lord, is recognized by Elisabeth, speaking by the Holy Ghost. She also acknowledges the pious faith of Mary, and announces to her the fulfilment of the promise she had received (all that took place being a signal testimony given to Him who should be born in Israel and among men).

Mary's thanksgiving, owning God's grace and her own low estate

The heart of Mary is then poured out in thanksgiving. She owns God her Saviour in the grace that has filled her

with joy, and her own low estate—a figure of the condition of the remnant of Israel—and that gave occasion
to the intervention of God's greatness, with a full testimony that all was of Himself. Whatever might be the
piety suitable to the instrument whom He employed, and
which was found indeed in Mary, it was in proportion
as she hid herself that she was great; for then God was
all, and it was through her that He intervened for the
manifestation of His marvellous ways. She lost her place
if she made anything of herself, but in truth she did not.
The grace of God preserved her, in order that His glory
might be fully displayed in this divine event. She recognizes His grace, but she acknowledges that all is grace
towards her.

It will be remarked here that, in the character and the
application of the thoughts that fill her heart, all is Jewish. We may compare the song of Hannah, who prophetically celebrated this same intervention; and see also
verses 54, 55. But, observe, she goes back to the promises
made to the fathers, not to Moses, and she embraces all
Israel. It is the power of God, which works in the midst
of weakness, when there is no resource, and all is contrary to it. Such is the moment that suits God, and, to
the same end, instruments that are null, that God may
be all.

It is remarkable that we are not told that Mary was
full of the Holy Ghost. It appears to me that this is
an honorable distinction for her. The Holy Ghost visited
Elisabeth and Zacharias in an exceptional manner. But,
although we cannot doubt that Mary was under the influence of the Spirit of God, it was a more inward effect,
more connected with her own faith, with her piety, with
the more habitual relations of her heart with God (that
were formed by this faith and by this piety), and which
consequently expressed itself more as her own sentiments.
It is thankfulness for the grace and favor conferred on
her the lowly one, and that in connection with the hopes

and blessing of Israel. In all this there appears to me a very striking harmony in connection with the wondrous favor bestowed upon her. I repeat it, Mary is great inasmuch as she is nothing; but she is favored by God in a way that is unparalleled, and all generations shall call her blessed.

But her piety, and its expression in this song, being more personal, an answer to God rather than a revelation on His part, it is clearly limited to that which was necessarily for her the sphere of this piety—to Israel, to the hopes and promises given to Israel. It goes back, as we have seen, to the farthest point of God's relations with Israel—and they were in grace and promise, not law—but it does not go outside them.

Piety in secret recognized by God

Mary abides three months with the woman whom God had blessed, the mother of him who was to be the voice of God in the wilderness; and she returns to follow humbly her own path, that the purposes of God may be accomplished.

Nothing more beautiful of its kind than this picture of the intercourse between these pious women, unknown to the world, but the instruments of God's grace for the accomplishment of His purpose, glorious and infinite in their results. They hide themselves, moving in a scene into which nothing enters but piety and grace; but God is there, as little known to the world as were these poor women, yet preparing and accomplishing that which the angels desire to fathom in its depths. This takes place in the hill country, where these pious relatives dwelt. They hid themselves; but their hearts, visited by God and touched by His grace, responded by their mutual piety to these wondrous visits from above; and the grace of God was truly reflected in the calmness of a heart that recognized His hand and His greatness, trusting in His goodness and submitting to His will. We are favored in being admitted into a scene, from which the world was excluded by its unbelief and alienation from God, and in which God thus acted.

John, the son of Zacharias and Elisabeth, is born: Zacharias' public announcement of the Coming One and of John's position

But that which piety recognized in secret, through faith in the visitations of God, must at length be made public, and be fulfilled before the eyes of men. The son of Zacharias and Elisabeth is born, and Zacharias (who, obedient to the word of the angel, ceases to be dumb) announces the coming of the Branch of David, the horn of Israel's salvation, in the house of God's elect King, to accomplish all the promises made to the fathers, and all the prophecies by which God had proclaimed the future blessing of His people. The child whom God had given to Zacharias and Elisabeth should go before the face of Jehovah to prepare His ways; for the Son of David was Jehovah, who came according to the promises, and according to the Word by which God had proclaimed the manifestation of His glory.

Israel under present and future blessing from the Christ then at the door—the hope of Israel

The visitation of Israel by Jehovah, celebrated by the mouth of Zacharias, embraces all the blessing of the millennium. This is connected with the presence of Jesus, who brings in His own Person all this blessing. All the promises are Yea and Amen in Him. All the prophecies encircle Him with the glory then to be realized, and make Him the source from which it springs. Abraham rejoiced to see the glorious days of Christ.

The Holy Ghost always does this, when His subject is the fulfilment of the promise in power. He goes on to the full effect which God will accomplish at the end. The difference here is, that it is no longer the announcement of joys in a distant future, when a Christ should be born, when a Child should be brought forth, to bring in their joys in days still obscured by the distance at which they were seen. The Christ is now at the door, and it is the effect of His presence that is celebrated. We know that, having been rejected, and being now absent, the accomplishment of these things is necessarily put off until He returns; but His presence will bring their fulfilment, and it is announced as being connected with that presence.

We may remark here, that this chapter confines itself within the strict limits of the promises made to Israel, that is to say, to the fathers. We have the priests, the Messiah, His forerunner, the promises made to Abraham, the covenant of promise, the oath of God. It is not the law; it is the hope of Israel—founded on the promise, the covenant, the oath of God, and confirmed by the prophets—which has its realization in the birth of Jesus, of the Son of David. It is not, I again say, the law. It is Israel under blessing, not indeed yet accomplished, but Israel in the relationship of faith with God who would accomplish it. It is only God and Israel who are in question, and that which had taken place in grace between Him and His people alone.

Chapter 2

The pagan emperor of the world in Emmanuel's land: imperial glory and authority an instrument in God's hands

IN the next chapter the scene changes. Instead of the relations of God with Israel according to grace, we see first the pagan emperor of the world—the head of Daniel's last empire—exercising his power in Emmanuel's land, and over the people of God, as though God did not know them. Nevertheless we are still in presence of the birth of the Son of David, of Emmanuel Himself; but He is outwardly under the power of the head of the beast, of a pagan empire. What a strange state of things is brought in by sin! Take special notice however that we have grace here: it is the intervention of God which makes all this manifest. Connected with it are some other circumstances which it is well to observe. When the interests and the glory of Jesus are in question, all this power —which governs without the fear of God, which reigns, seeking its own glory, in the place where Christ should reign—all the imperial glory is but an instrument in the hands of God for the fulfilment of His counsels. As to the public fact, we find the Roman emperor exercising despotic and pagan authority in the place where the throne of God should have been, if the sin of the people had not made it impossible.

The world's power set in motion that the Saviour King might be born where God had decreed

The emperor will have all the world registered, and every one goes to his own city. The power of the world is set in motion, and that by an act which proves its supremacy over those who, as the people of God, should have been free from all but the immediate government of their God, which was their glory—an act which proves the complete degradation and servitude of the people. They are slaves, in their bodies and in their possessions, to the heathen, because of their sins.[4] But this act only accomplishes the marvellous purpose of God, causing the Saviour-King to be born in the village where, according to the testimony of God, that event was to take place. And, more than that, the divine Person, who was to ex-

[4] Nehemiah 9: 36, 37.

cite the joy and the praises of heaven, is born among men, Himself a Child in this world.

The state of things in Israel and in the world is the supremacy of the Gentiles and the absence of the throne of God. The Son of Man, the Saviour, God manifested in the flesh, comes to take His place—a place which grace alone could find or take in a world that knew Him not.

This registration is so much the more remarkable, in that, as soon as the purpose of God was accomplished, it was carried no farther; that is to say, not till afterwards, under the government of Cyrenius.[5]

The Son of God born into this world finds no place there

The Son of God is born in this world, but He finds no place there. The world is at home, or at least by its resources it finds a place, in the inn; it becomes a kind of measure of man's place in, and reception by, the world; the Son of God finds none, save in the manger. Is it for nothing that the Holy Ghost records this circumstance? No. There is no room for God, and that which is of God, in this world. So much the more perfect therefore is the love that brought Him down to earth. But He began in a manger and ended on the cross, and along the way had not where to lay His head.

The Son of God—a Child partaking in all the weakness and all the circumstances of human life, thus manifested—appears in the world.[6]

---

[5] I have no doubt that the only right translation of this passage is, "The census itself was first made when Cyrenius was governor of Syria." The Holy Ghost notes this circumstance to show that, when once the purpose of God was accomplished, the decree was not historically carried out till afterwards. A great deal of learning has been spent on what I believe to be simple and clear in the text.

[6] That is to say, as an infant, He did not appear, like the first Adam, coming out, in His perfection, from the hand of God. He is born of a woman, the Son of Man, which Adam was not.

The fulfilment of God's counsels announced by angels: their heavenly chorus of praise

But if God comes into this world, and if a manger receives Him, in the nature He has taken in grace, the angels are occupied with the event on which depends the fate of the whole universe, and the accomplishment of all the counsels of God; for He has chosen weak things to confound things that are mighty. This poor infant is the Object of all the counsels of God, the Upholder and Heir of the whole creation, the Saviour of all who shall inherit glory and eternal life.

Some poor men who were faithfully performing their toilsome labors, afar from the restless activity of an ambitious and sinful world, receive the first tidings of the Lord's presence on earth. The God of Israel did not seek for the great among His people, but had respect to the poor of the flock. Two things here present themselves. The angel who comes to the shepherds of Judea announces to them the fulfilment of the promises of God to Israel. The choir of angels celebrate in their heavenly chorus of praise all the real import of this wondrous event.

"Unto you," says the heavenly messenger who visits the poor shepherds, "is born this day in the city of David a Saviour, which is Christ the Lord." This was proclaiming good tidings to them and to all the people. [7]

The fulness, sovereignty and perfection of God's grace magnified by sin

But in the birth of the Son of Man, God manifest in the flesh, the accomplishment of the incarnation had far deeper importance than this. The fact that this poor infant was there, disallowed and left (humanly speaking) to its fate by the world, was (as understood by the

---

[7] "All the people" (not, as in the Authorized Version, "all people").

heavenly intelligences, the multitude of the heavenly host, whose praises resounded at the angel's message to the shepherds) "Glory to God in the highest, peace on earth, good pleasure [of God] in men." These few words embrace such widely extended thoughts that it is difficult to speak suitably of them in a work like this; but some remarks are necessary. First, it is deeply blessed to see that the thought of Jesus excludes all that could oppress the heart in the scene which surrounded His presence on earth. Sin, alas, was there. It was manifested by the position in which this wondrous infant was found. But if sin had placed Him there, grace had placed Him there. Grace superabounds; and in thinking *of Him*, blessing, grace, the mind of God respecting sin, that which God is, as manifested by the presence of Christ, absorb the mind and possess the heart, and are the heart's true relief in a world like this. We see grace alone; and sin does but magnify the fulness, the sovereignty, the perfection of that grace. God, in His glorious dealings, blots out the sin with respect to which He acts, and which He thus exhibits in all its deformity; but there is that which "much more aboundeth." Jesus, come in grace, fills the heart. It is the same thing in all the details of Christian life. It is the true source of moral power, of sanctification, and of joy.

"Glory to God in the highest" shown in the Child born on the earth

We see next, that there are three things brought out by the presence of Jesus born as a Child on the earth. First, glory to God in the highest. The love of God—His wisdom—His power (not in creating a universe out of nothing, but in rising above the evil, and turning the effect of all the enemy's power into an occasion of showing that this power was only impotence and folly in presence

of that which may be called "the weakness of God")—the
fulfilment of His eternal counsels—the perfection of His
ways where evil had come in—the manifestation of Himself amidst the evil in such a manner as to glorify Himself before the angels: in a word, God had so manifested
Himself by the birth of Jesus, that the hosts of heaven,
long familiar with His power, could raise their chorus,
"Glory to God in the highest!" and every voice unites in
sounding forth these praises. What love like this love?
And "God is love." What a purely divine thought, that
God has become Man! What supremacy of good over
evil! What wisdom in drawing nigh to the heart of man
and the heart of man back to Him! What fitness in
addressing man! What maintenance of the holiness of
God! What nearness to the heart of man, what participation in his wants, what experience of his condition! But
beyond all, God above the evil in grace, and in that grace
visiting this defiled world to make Himself known as He
had never yet been known!

"Peace on earth": Jesus the surety of the eventual fulfilment of the promise

The second effect of the presence of Him who manifested God on the earth is, that peace should be there.
Rejected—His name should be an occasion of strife; but
the heavenly choir are occupied with the fact of His presence, with the result, when fully produced of the consequences, wrapped up in the Person of Him who was
there (looked at in their proper fruits), and they celebrate these consequences. Manifested evil should disappear; His holy rule should banish all enmity and violence. Jesus, mighty in love, should reign, and impart
the character in which He had come to the whole scene
that should surround Him in the world He came into,
that it might be according to His heart who took delight

therein. (Prov. 8: 31.) [8] See, as regards a smaller scale, Psalm 85: 10, 11.

The means of this—redemption, the destruction of Satan's power, the reconciliation of man by faith, and of all things in heaven and earth with God—are not here pointed out. Everything depended on the Person and presence of Him who was born. All was wrapped up in Him. The state of blessing was born in the birth of that Child.

Presented to the responsibility of man, man is unable to profit by it, and all fails. His position thereby becomes only so much the worse.

But, grace and blessing being attached to the Person of Him just born, all their consequences necessarily flow forth. After all it was the intervention of God accomplishing the counsel of His love, the settled purpose of His good pleasure. And, Jesus once there, the consequences could not fail: whatever interruption there might be to their fulfilment, Jesus was their surety. He was come into the world. He contained in His Person, He was the expression of, all these consequences. The presence of the Son of God in the midst of sinners said to all spiritual intelligence, "Peace on the earth."

"The good pleasure of God in men": God's glorious counsels accomplished in Jesus

The third thing was the good pleasure [9]—the affection

---

[8] This quotation leads to a glorious apprehension, both of what was then doing, and of our blessing. The special interest of God is in the sons of men; wisdom (Christ is the wisdom of God) daily Jehovah's delight, rejoicing in the habitable part of His earth, before creation, so that it was counsel, and His delight in the sons of men. His incarnation is the full proof of this. In Matthew we have our Lord, when He takes His place with the remnant as this is, fully revealed, and it is in the Son's taking this place as Man and being anointed of the Holy Ghost, that the whole Trinity is fully revealed. This is a wonderful unfolding of God's ways.

[9] This is the same word as when it is said of Christ, "In whom I am well pleased." It is beautiful to see the unjealous celebration, by these holy beings, of the advancement of another race to this exalted place by the incarnation of the Word. It was God's glory, and that sufficed them. This is very beautiful.

of God—in men. Nothing more simple, since Jesus was
a Man. He had not taken hold of angels.

It was a glorious testimony that the affection, the good
pleasure, of God was centred in this poor race, now far
from Him, but in which He was pleased to accomplish all
His glorious counsels. So John 1, the life was the light
of men.

In a word, it was the power of God present in grace in
the Person of the Son of God taking part in the nature,
and interesting Himself in the lot, of a being who had
departed from Him, and making him the sphere of the
accomplishment of all His counsels, and of the manifestation of His grace and His nature to all His creatures.
What a position for man! For it is indeed in Man that
all this is accomplished. The whole universe was to learn
in man, and in what God therein was for man, that which
God was in Himself, and the fruit of all His glorious
counsels, as well as its complete rest in His presence, according to His nature of love. All this was implied in
the birth of that Child of whom the world took no notice.
Natural and marvellous subject of praise to the holy inhabitants of heaven, unto whom God had made it known!
It was glory to God in the highest.

The faith and joy of the shepherds

Faith was in exercise in those simple Israelites to whom
the angel of the Lord was sent; and they rejoiced in the
blessing fulfilled before their eyes, and which verified the
grace that God had shown in announcing it to them. The
word, "as it was told unto them," adds its testimony of
grace to all that we enjoy by the loving-kindness of God.

The name of the Child: His circumcision under the law; Mary's poverty

The Child receives the name of Jesus on the day of
His circumcision, according to Jewish custom (see chap.

1: 59), but according to the counsels and revelations of God, communicated by the angels of His power. Moreover everything was performed according to the law; for historically we find ourselves still in connection with Israel. He who was born of a woman was born under the law.

The condition of poverty in which Jesus was born is also shown by the sacrifice offered for the purification of His mother.

The Child recognized by the godly remnant

But another point is here made prominent by the Holy Ghost, insignificant as He may apparently be who gave occasion to it.

Jesus is recognized by the godly remnant of Israel, so far as the Holy Ghost acts in them. He becomes a touchstone for every soul in Israel. The condition of the remnant taught by the Holy Ghost (that is, of those who had taken the position of the remnant) was this: They were sensible of the misery and ruin of Israel, but waited upon the God of Israel, trusting to His unchangeable faithfulness for the consolation of His people. They still said: How long? And God was with this remnant. He had made known to those who thus trusted in His mercy the coming of the promised One, who was to be the fulfilment of this mercy to Israel.

Thus, in presence of the oppression of the Gentiles, and of the iniquity of a people who were ripening or rather ripened in evil, the remnant who trust in God do not lose that which, as we saw in the preceding chapter, belonged to Israel. In the midst of Israel's misery they had for their consolation that which promise and prophecy had declared for Israel's glory.

The revelation made to Simeon: the threefold character of his praise

The Holy Spirit had revealed to Simeon that he should not die until he had seen the Lord's Christ. That was the consolation, and it was great. It was contained in the Person of Jesus the Saviour, without going farther into the details of the manner or the time of the accomplishment of Israel's deliverance.

Simeon loved Israel; he could depart in peace, since God had blessed Him according to the desires of faith. The joy of faith ever dwells on the Lord and on His people, but sees, in the relationship that exists between them, all the extent of that which gives rise to this joy. Salvation, the deliverance of God, was come in Christ. It was for the revelation of the Gentiles, till then hidden in the darkness of ignorance without a revelation; and for the glory of Israel, the people of God. This indeed is the fruit of the government of God in Christ, that is to say, the millennium. But if the Spirit revealed to this pious and faithful servant of the God of Israel the future which depended on the presence of the Son of God, He revealed to him that he held the Saviour Himself in his arms; thus giving him present peace, and such a sense of the favor of God that death lost its terrors. It was not a knowledge of the work of Jesus acting on an enlightened and convicted conscience; but it was the fulfilment of the promises to Israel, the possession of the Saviour, and the proof of the favor of God, so that the peace which flowed from thence filled his soul. There were the three things: the prophecy that announced the coming of Christ, the possession of Christ, and the effect of His presence in the whole world. We are here in connection with the remnant of Israel, and consequently find nothing of the Church and of purely heavenly things. The rejection comes afterwards. Here it is all that belongs to the remnant, in the way of blessing, through the presence of Jesus. His *work* is not the present subject.

Simeon's testimony in Israel to the Messiah

What a beautiful picture, and what a testimony rendered to this Child, by the manner in which through the
power of the Holy Ghost He filled the heart of this holy
man at the close of his earthly life!   Observe also what
communications are made to this feeble remnant, unknown
amid the darkness that covered the people.   But the
testimony of this holy man of God, (and how sweet it is
to think how many of these souls, full of grace and of
communion with the Lord, have flourished in the shade,
unknown to men, but well known to and beloved of God;
souls who, when they appear, coming out of their retreat
according to His will in testimony to Christ, bear so
blessed a witness to a work of God which is carried on
in spite of all that man is doing, and behind the painful
and embittered scene that is unfolding on the earth!)
Simeon's testimony here, was more than the expression of
the deeply interesting thoughts which had filled his heart
in communion between himself and God.   This knowledge
of Christ and of the thoughts of God respecting Him,
which is developed in secret between God and the soul,
gives understanding of the effect produced by the manifestation to the world of Him who is its object.   The
Spirit speaks of it by the mouth of Simeon.   In his previous words we received the declaration of the sure fulfilment of God's counsels in the Messiah, the joy of his
own heart.   Now it is the effect of the presentation of
Jesus, as the Messiah to Israel on the earth, which is
described.   Whatever may have been the power of God
in Christ for blessing, He put the heart of man to the
test.   He should thus be, by revealing the thoughts of
many hearts (for He was light), and so much the more
that He was humbled in a world of pride, an occasion of
falling to many, and the means of rising to many from
their low and degraded condition.   Mary herself, although the mother of the Messiah, should have her own

soul pierced through by a sword; for her child should be
rejected, the natural relationship of the Messiah to the
people broken and disallowed.   This contradiction of
sinners against the Lord laid all hearts bare as to their
desires, their hopes, and their ambition, whatever forms
of piety might be assumed.

Such was the testimony rendered in Israel to the
Messiah, according to the action of the Spirit of God
upon the remnant, amid the bondage and misery of that
people: the full accomplishment of the counsels of God
towards Israel, and towards the world through Israel, for
joy of heart to the faithful who had trusted in these
promises, but for a test at that moment to every heart by
means of a Messiah who was a sign spoken against.   The
counsels of God and the heart of man were revealed in
Him.

Malachi's prophecy of God's hidden people: Anna at the throne of God

Malachi had said that those who feared the Lord in the
evil days, when the proud were called happy, should often
speak together.   This time had arrived in Israel.   From
Malachi to the birth of Jesus, there was but the passage
of Israel from misery to pride—a pride moreover that
was dawning even in the days of the prophet.   That
which he said of the remnant was also being accomplished;
they "spake together."   We see that they knew each other,
in this lovely picture of God's hidden people: "She spake
of Him to all them that looked for redemption in Israel."
Anna, a holy widow, who departed not from the temple,
and who deeply felt the misery of Israel, had besieged the
throne of God with a widowed heart, for a people to whom
God was no longer a husband, who were really widowed
like herself; and she now makes known to all who pondered on these things together, that the Lord had visited
his temple.   They had looked for redemption in Jeru-

salem; and now the Redeemer—unknown of men—was there. What a subject of joy to this poor remnant! What an answer to their faith!

The return to Nazareth: the Lord's perfection of obedience as a Child and as a Man

But Jerusalem was not after all the place in which God visited the remnant of His people, but the seat of pride of those who said "the temple of the Lord." And Joseph and Mary, having performed all that which the law required, return with the Child Jesus to take their place together with Him in the despised spot which should give Him its name, and in those regions where the despised remnant, the poor of the flock, had more their place, and where the testimony of God had announced that the light should appear.

There His early days were spent in the physical and mental growth of the true humanity which He had assumed. Simple and precious testimony! But He was not less conscious, when the time was come for speaking to men, of His real relationship to His Father. The two things are united in that which is said at the end of the chapter. In the development of His humanity is manifested the Son of God on earth. Joseph and Mary, who (while marvelling at all that happened to Him) did not thoroughly know by faith His glory, blame the Child according to the position in which He formally stood towards them. But this gives occasion to the manifestation of another character of perfection in Jesus. If He was the Son of God and had the full consciousness of it, He was also the obedient Man, essentially and ever perfect and sinless—an obedient Child, whatever sense He also had of another relationship unconnected in itself with subjection to human parents. Consciousness of the one did not injure His perfection in the other. His being the Son of God secured His perfection as a Man and a Child on the earth.

The Lord's relationship to His Father

But there is another important thing to remark here; it is, that this position had nothing to do with His being anointed with the Holy Ghost. He fulfilled, no doubt, the public ministry which He afterwards entered on according to the power and the perfection of that anointing; but His relationship to His Father belonged to His Person itself. The bond existed between Him and His Father. He was fully conscious of it, whatever might be the means or the form of its public manifestation, and of the power of His ministry. He was all that a child ought to be; but it was the Son of God who was so. His relationship to His Father was as well known to Him, as His obedience to Joseph and to His mother was beautiful, becoming, and perfect.

The unique and incomparable course of the divine Saviour, the Son of Man

Here we close this touching and divine history of the birth and early days of the divine Saviour, the Son of Man. It is impossible to have anything more profoundly interesting. Henceforward it is in His ministry, in His public life, that we shall find Him, rejected of men, but accomplishing the counsels and the work of God; separate from all, in order to do this in the power of the Holy Ghost, given to Him without measure, to fulfil that course with which nothing can be compared, with respect to which it would be lowering the truth to call it interesting. It is the centre and the means, including His death, His offering of Himself without spot to God—and the only possible means—of all relationship between our souls and God; the perfection of the manifestation of His grace, and the foundation of all relationship between any creature and Himself.

Chapter 3

The circumstances surrounding the exercise of the ministry of the Word and the Lord's introduction into the world

IN chapter 3 we find the exercise of the ministry of the Word towards Israel, and that for the introduction of the Lord into this world. It is not the promises to Israel and the privileges secured to them by God, nor the birth of that Child who was Heir to all the promises; the empire, itself a testimony to Israel's captivity, being an instrument for the accomplishment of the Word respecting the Lord. The years are here reckoned according to the reign of the Gentiles. Judea is a province in the hands of the Gentile empire, and the other parts of Canaan are divided under different chiefs, subordinate to the empire.

The Jewish system continues nevertheless; and the high priests were there to note the years of their subjection to the Gentiles by their names and at the same time to preserve the order, the doctrine, and the ceremonies of the Jews, as far as could be done in their circumstances at that period.

Jehovah's message to His people that He Himself would come

Now the Word of God is ever sure, and it is when the relationships of God with His people fail on the side of their faithfulness, that God in sovereignty maintains His relationship by means of communications through a prophet. His sovereign Word maintains it when there are no other means.

But in this case Jehovah's message to His people had a peculiar character; for Israel was already ruined, having forsaken the Lord. The goodness of God had still left the people outwardly in their land; but the throne of the

world was transferred to the Gentiles. Israel was now
called to repent, to be forgiven, and to take a new place
through the coming of the Messiah.

The testimony of God is therefore not in connection
with His ordinances at Jerusalem, although the righteous
submit to them. Nor does the prophet call them back to
faithfulness on the ground on which they were. It is His
voice in the wilderness, making His paths straight, in
order that He may come, as from without, to those who
repented and prepared themselves for His coming. Moreover, since it was the Jehovah Himself who came, His
glory should not be confined within the narrow limits of
Israel. All flesh should see the salvation wrought by God.
The condition of the nation itself was that out of which
God called them to come by repentance, proclaiming the
wrath that was about to fall upon a rebellious people.
Besides, if God came, He would have realities, the true
fruits of righteousness, and not the mere name of a people. And He came in His sovereign power, which was
able to raise up out of nothing that which He would have
before Him. God comes. He would have righteousness
as to man's responsibility, because He is righteous. He
could raise up a seed unto Abraham by His divine power,
and that from the very stones, if He saw fit. It is the
presence, the coming of God Himself, that here characterizes everything.

The conscience of all addressed in warning of judgment at the door

Now, the axe was *already* at the root of the trees, and
each was to be judged according to its fruits. It was in
vain to plead that they were Jews; if they enjoyed that
privilege, where were its fruits? But God did not accept
any according to man's estimate of righteousness and
privilege, nor the proud judgment the self-righteous might
form of others. He addressed Himself to the conscience
of all.

Accordingly the publicans, objects of hatred to the Jews, as instruments of the fiscal oppression of the Gentiles; and the soldiers, who executed the arbitrary mandates of the kings, imposed on the people by the Roman will, or that of heathen governors, were exhorted to act in accordance with that which the true fear of God would produce, in contrast with the iniquity habitually practised in accordance with the will of man; the multitude were exhorted to practical charity, while the people, considered as a people, were treated as a generation of vipers, on whom the wrath of God was coming. Grace dealt with them in warning of judgment, but judgment was at the door.

Summary of verses 3 to 17 of chapter 3

Thus, from verses 3-14, we have these two things: in 3-6 the position of John towards the people as such, in the thought that God Himself would soon appear; in 6-14 his address to the conscience of individuals, verses 7, 8, 9 teaching them that the formal privileges of the people would afford no shelter in the presence of the holy and righteous God, and that to take refuge in national privilege was only to bring wrath upon themselves—for the nation was under judgment and exposed to the wrath of God. In verse 10 he comes to details. In verses 15-17 the question as to the Messiah is solved.

God Himself was coming

The great subject however of this passage—the great truth which the testimony of John displayed before the eyes of the people—was that *God Himself* was coming. Man was to repent. Privileges, granted meanwhile as means of blessing, could not be pleaded against the nature and the righteousness of Him who was coming, nor destroy the power by which He could create a people after His own heart. Nevertheless the door of repentance was open according to His faithfulness towards a people whom He loved.

Messiah's special work

But there was a special work for the Messiah according to the counsels, the wisdom, and the grace of God. He baptized with the Holy Ghost and with fire. That is to say, He brought in the power and the judgment which dispelled evil, whether in holiness and blessing, or in destruction.

He baptizes with the Holy Ghost. This is not merely a renewal of desires, but power, in grace, in the midst of evil.

He baptizes with fire. This is judgment that consumes the evil.

This judgment is thus applied to Israel, His threshing-floor. He would gather His wheat in safety elsewhere; the chaff should be burnt up in judgment.

The end of John's testimony: the beginning of the Lord's identification with His people

But at length John is put in prison by the regal head of the people. Not that this event took place historically at that moment; but the Spirit of God would set forth morally the end of his testimony, in order to commence the life of Jesus, the Son of Man, but born the Son of God in this world.

It is with verse 21 that this history begins, and in a manner both wonderful and full of grace. God, by John the Baptist, had called His people to repentance; and those on whom His word produced its effect came to be baptized by John. It was the first sign of life and of obedience. Jesus, perfect in life and in obedience, come down in grace for the remnant of His people, goes thither, taking His place with them, and is baptized with the baptism of John as they were. Touching and marvellous

testimony! He does not love at a distance, nor merely in
bestowing pardon; He comes by grace into the very place
where the sin of His people had brought them, according
to the sense of that sin which the converting and quickening power of their God had wrought in them. He leads
His people there by grace, but He accompanies them
when they go. He takes His place with them in all the
difficulties of the way, and goes with them to meet all
the obstacles that present themselves; and truly, as identifying Himself with the poor remnant, those excellent of
the earth, in whom was all His delight, calling Jehovah
His Lord; and making Himself of no reputation, not
saying that His goodness extended to God, not taking His
eternal place with God, but the place of humiliation; and,
for that very reason, of perfection in the position to which
He had humbled Himself, but a perfection that recognized
the existence of sin, because in fact there was sin, and it
behooved the remnant to be sensible of it in returning to
God. To be sensible of it was the beginning of good.
Hence He can go with them. But in Christ, however
humble grace might be, His taking that path with them
was grace that wrought in righteousness; for in Him it
was love and obedience, and the path by which He
glorified His Father. He went in by the door.

With the remnant: heaven open on the grace and perfection of Jesus

Jesus therefore, in taking this place of humiliation
which the state of the beloved people required, and to
which grace brought Him, found Himself in the place of
the fulfilment of righteousness, and of all the good pleasure of the Father, of which He thus became the object,
as in this place.

The Father could acknowledge Him, as the One who
satisfied His heart in the place where sin and, at the
same time, the objects of His grace, were found, that He

might give free course to His grace. The cross was the full accomplishment of this. We shall say a word on the difference when speaking of the temptation of the Lord; but it is the same principle as to Christ's loving will and obedience. Christ was here *with* the remnant, instead of being substituted *for* them and put in their place to atone for sin; but the object of the Father's delight had, in grace, taken His place with the people, viewed as confessing their sins [10] before God, and presenting themselves to God as concerned in them, while by this really morally out of them, and renewed in heart to confess them, without which the Lord could not have been with them, except as a witness to preach grace to them prophetically.

Jesus having taken this position, and praying—appearing as the godly Man, dependent on God and lifting up His heart to God, thus also the expression of perfection in that position—heaven opens to Him. By baptism He took His place with the remnant; in praying—being there —He exhibited perfection in His own relationship with God. Dependence, and the heart going up to God, as the first thing and as the expression, so to say, of its existence, is the perfection of man here below; and, in this case, of man in such circumstances as these. Here then heaven can open. And observe, it was not heaven opening to seek some one afar from God, nor grace opening the heart to a certain feeling; but it was the grace and perfection of Jesus which *caused heaven* to open. As it is said, "*Therefore* doth My Father love Me, because I lay down My life." Thus also it is the positive perfection of Jesus [11] that is the reason of heaven's opening. Re-

[10] He took it in and with the godly remnant, in the act which distinguished them from the unrepentant, but was the right place of the people, the first act of spiritual life. The remnant with John is the true Jew taking his true place with God. This Christ goes with them in.

[11] Remark here, Christ has no object in heaven to fix His attention on, as Stephen; He *is* the object of heaven. So He was to Stephen by the Holy Ghost, when heaven was open to the saint. His Person is always clearly evident, even when He puts His people in the same place with Himself or connects Himself with them. See on this Matthew.

mark also here that, when once this principle of reconciliation is brought in, heaven and earth are not so far from
each other. It is true that, till after the death of Christ,
this intimacy must be centred in the Person of Jesus and
realized by Him alone, but that comprised all the rest.
Proximity was established, although the grain of wheat
had to remain alone, until it should "fall into the ground
and die." Nevertheless the angels, as we have seen,
could say, "Peace on earth, the good pleasure [of God]
in men." And we see the angels with the shepherds, and
the heavenly host in the sight and hearing of earth prais-
ing God for that which had taken place; and here, heaven
open upon Man, and the Holy Ghost descending visibly
upon Him.

Let us examine the import of this last case. Christ
has taken His place with the remnant in their weak and
humble condition, but in it fulfilling righteousness. The
entire favor of the Father rests upon Him, and the Holy
Ghost comes down to seal and anoint Him with His
presence and His power. Son of God, Man on earth,
heaven is open to Him, and all the affection of heaven is
centred upon Him, and upon Him associated with His
own.[12] The first step which these humbled souls take in
the path of grace and of life finds Jesus there with them,
and, He being there, the favor and delight of the Father,
and the presence of the Holy Ghost. And let us always
remember that it is upon Him as Man while Son of God.

Jesus as the measure of the position of man accepted before God

Such is the position of man accepted before God. Jesus
is its measure, its expression. It has these two things—

---

[12] I do not speak here of the union of the Church with Christ in
heaven, but His taking His place with the remnant, who come to God
through grace, led by the efficacy of His Word, and by the power of the
Spirit. This is the reason I apprehend that we find all the people
baptized, and then Jesus comes and is associated with them.

the Father's delight, and the power and seal of the Holy
Ghost; and that in this world, and known by him who
enjoys it.　There is now this difference, already noticed,
that we look by the Holy Ghost into heaven where Jesus
is, but we take His place down here.

Let us contemplate man thus in Christ—heaven open—
the power of the Holy Ghost upon Him and in Him—
the testimony of the Father, and the relationship of the
Son with the Father.

Christ's genealogy in Luke: the last Adam

It will be remarked that the genealogy of Christ is here
traced, not to Abraham and David, that He should be
the heir of the promises after the flesh, but to Adam; in
order to exhibit the true Son of God a Man on earth,
where the first Adam lost his title, such as it was.　The
last Adam, the Son of God, was there, accepted of the
Father, and preparing to take upon Himself the difficulties
into which the sin and fall of the first Adam had brought
those of his race who drew nigh to God under the influence of His grace.

The enemy was through sin in possession of the first
Adam; and Jesus must gain the victory over Satan, if He
would deliver those who are under his power.　He must
bind the strong man.　To conquer him practically is the
second part of the Christian life.　Joy in God, conflict
with the enemy, make up the life of the redeemed, sealed
with the Holy Ghost and walking by His power.　In both
these things the believer is with Jesus, and Jesus with him.

Chapter 4

Tested by the enemy

THE unknown Son of God on earth, Jesus is led (chap.
4) into the wilderness by the Holy Ghost, with whom
He had been sealed, to undergo the temptation of the

enemy, beneath which Adam fell. But Jesus endured this temptation in the circumstances in which we stand, not those in which Adam stood; that is to say, He felt it in all the difficulties of the life of faith, tempted in all points like as we are, sin excepted. Take notice here that it is no question of bondage to sin, but of conflict. When it is a question of bondage, it is a question of deliverance, not of conflict. It was in Canaan that Israel fought. They were delivered out of Egypt; they did not fight there.

The moral order of the temptations: simple obedience to the Word of God

In Luke the temptations are arranged according to their moral order: first, that which bodily need required; second, the world; third, spiritual subtlety. In each the Lord maintains the position of obedience and of dependence, giving God and His communications to man— His Word—their true place. Simple principle, which shelters us in every attack, but which, by its very simplicity, is perfection! Nevertheless let us remember that this is the case; for raising ourselves to marvellous heights is not the thing required of us, but the following that which applies to our human condition as the normal rule for its guidance. It is obedience, dependence—doing nothing except as God wills it, and reliance on Him. This walk supposes the Word. But the Word is the expression of the will, the goodness, and the authority of God, applicable to all the circumstances of man as he is. It shows that God interests Himself in all that regards him: why then should man act of himself without looking to God and to His Word? Alas! speaking of men in general, they are self-willed. To submit and be dependent is precisely that which they will not. They have too much enmity to God to trust in Him. It was this, therefore, which distinguished the Lord. The power to work a miracle God could bestow on whom He would. But an obedient man, who had no will to do anything with respect to which the will of God was not expressed, a man who lived by the Word, a man who lived in complete dependence upon God and had a perfect trust, which required no other proof of God's faithfulness than His Word, no other means of certainty that He would intervene than His promise of so doing, and who waited for that intervention in the path of His will—here was something more than power. This was the perfection of man, in the place where man stood (not simply innocence, for innocence has no need of trusting God in the midst of difficulties, and sorrows, and questions raised by sin, and the knowledge of good and evil), and a perfection which sheltered one who possessed it from every attack Satan could make upon him; for what could he do to one who never went beyond the will of God, and to whom that will was the only motive for action? Moreover, the power of the Spirit of God was there. Accordingly we find that simple obedience directed by the Word is the only weapon employed by Jesus. This obedience requires dependence on God, and trust in God, in order to accomplish it.

He lives by the Word: this is dependence. He will not tempt (that is, put God to the test) to see if He is faithful: this is trust.

He acts when God wills, and because He wills, and does that which God wills. All the rest He leaves with God. This is obedience; and, remark, not obedience as submission to God's will where there was an adverse one, but where God's will was the one motive for action. We are sanctified to the obedience of Christ.

Satan overcome

Satan is overcome and powerless before this Last Adam, who acts according to the power of the Spirit, in the place where man is found, by the means which God has given to man, and in the circumstances in which Satan exercises his power. Sin there was none, or it would have been to yield, not to conquer. It was shut out by obedience. But Satan is overcome in the circumstances of temptation in which man is found. Bodily need, which would have become lust if self-will had entered into it, instead of dependence on the will of God; the world and all its glory, which, so far as it is the object of man's covetousness, is in fact the kingdom of Satan (and it was on that ground that Satan tried to bring Jesus, and showed himself to be Satan in so doing); and, lastly, self-exaltation in a religious way through the things which God has given us—these were the points of the enemy's attack. But there was no self-seeking in Jesus.

With the remnant, and alone

We have found, then, in these things which we have been looking at, a Man filled with the Holy Ghost, and born of the Holy Ghost on earth, perfectly well-pleasing to God and the object of His affection, His beloved Son, in the position of dependence; and a Man, the conqueror of Satan amid those temptations by which he usually gains advantage over man—conqueror in the power of the Holy Ghost, and by making use of the Word, as dependent, obedient, and trusting in God in the ordinary circumstances of man. In the first position, Jesus stood with the remnant; in the second, alone—as in Gethsemane and on the cross. Nevertheless, it was for us; and, accepted as Jesus, we have in a certain sense the enemy to overcome. But it is a conquered enemy whom we resist in the strength of the Holy Ghost, who is given unto us in virtue of redemption. If we resist him, he flees; for he has met his conqueror. The flesh does not resist him. He finds Christ in us. Resistance in the flesh does not lead to victory.

The first Adam failure: the Last Adam the Conqueror of Satan

Jesus conquered the strong man and then spoiled his goods; but it was in temptation, obedience, having no will but that of God, dependence, the use of the Word, abiding in subjection to God, that Jesus gained the victory over him. In all this the first Adam failed. After Christ's victory, we also as servants of Christ gain actual victories, or rather the fruits of the victory already gained in the presence of God.

The Lord has now taken His place, so to speak, for the work of the Last Adam—the Man in whom is the Spirit without measure, the Son of God in this world by His birth. He has taken it as the seed of the woman (nevertheless, conceived of the Holy Ghost); He has taken it as the Son of God perfectly well-pleasing to God in His Person as Man here below; and He has taken it as the Conqueror of Satan. Owned to be the Son of God, and sealed with the Holy Ghost by the Father, heaven being open to Him as Man, His genealogy is, however, traced up to Adam; and, the descendant of Adam, without sin, full of the Holy Ghost, He conquers Satan (as the obedient man, having no motive but the will of God), and sets Himself to accomplish the work which God His Father committed to Him in this world, and that as Man, by the power of the Holy Ghost.

The return to Galilee in the Spirit's power

He returns in the power of the Spirit, into Galilee,[13] and His fame spreads through all the region round about.

---

[13] And here note, as anointed with the Holy Ghost and led by Him He goes to be tempted, and returns in the power of it. None was lost, and this power was as much shown in the apparently negative result of overcoming, as in the miraculous manifestation of power afterwards on men.

The announcement of the fulfilment of God's promises in grace and blessing

He presents Himself in this character: "The Spirit of Jehovah is upon Me, because He hath anointed Me to preach the gospel to the poor; He hath sent Me to heal the broken-hearted, . . . to preach the acceptable year of Jehovah." Here He stops. That which follows in the prophet, respecting the deliverance of Israel by the judgment which avenges them of their enemies, is omitted by the Lord.

Now Jesus does not announce promises, but their fulfilment in grace by His own presence. The Spirit is upon this Man, full of grace; and the God of grace in Him manifests His goodness. The time of deliverance is come; the vessel of His favor to Israel is there in their midst.

The examination of the prophecy renders this testimony so much the more remarkable, that the Spirit, having declared the sin of the people and their judgment, in the chapters that precede these words, speaks (when introducing the Christ, the Anointed) only of grace and blessing to Israel: if there is vengeance, it should be executed upon their enemies for the deliverance of Israel.

The perfect manifestation of grace rejected: the result

But here it is grace in His Person, this Man, the Son of God, full of the Holy Ghost, in order to proclaim the mercy of a God who is faithful to His promises, and to comfort and lift up the bruised and the poor in spirit. Blessing was there, presenting itself before them. They could not misunderstand it, but they do not recognize the Son of God. "Is not this Joseph's son?" We have here the whole history of Christ—the perfect manifestation of grace in the midst of Israel, His land, and His people; and they knew Him not. No prophet is accepted in his own country.

But this rejection opened the way to a grace which went beyond the limits that a rebellious people would set to it. The woman of Sarepta, and Naaman, were testimonies of this grace.

Wrath fills the heart of those who reject grace. Unbelieving, and incapable of discerning the blessing that had visited them, they will not have it go elsewhere. The pride which rendered them unable to appreciate grace would not hear of its communication to others.

They seek to destroy Jesus, but He goes on His way. Here is the whole history of Jesus among the people traced beforehand.

The acts and cures characterizing the Lord's ministry of grace

He went His way; and the Spirit preserves to us the acts and the cures which characterize His ministry in the aspect of the efficacy of grace, and of its extension to others besides Israel.

Power was in Him whose grace was rejected. Acknowledged by devils, if not by Israel, He expels them by a word. He heals the sick. All the power of the enemy, all the sad outward effects of sin, disappear before Him. He heals, He withdraws; and when entreated to remain (the effect of His works that procured Him that honor from the people which He did not seek), He goes away to labor elsewhere in the testimony committed to Him. He seeks to accomplish His work, and not to be honored.

He preaches everywhere among the people. He casts out the enemy, He removes sufferings, and proclaims the goodness of God to the poor.

Chapter 5

Others called to be associated with Him in His glorious work

MAN, He was come for men. He will associate others (chap. 5) with Himself in this glorious work. He has a right to do it. If He is in grace a servant, He is so according to the full power of the Holy Ghost. He works a miracle well adapted to strike those whom He would call, and which made them feel that everything was at His disposal, that all depended on Him, that where man could do nothing He could do everything. Peter, stricken in conscience by the presence of the Lord, confesses his unworthiness, but drawn by grace goes to Christ. Grace raises him up, and appoints him to speak of itself to others—to fish for men. Already it was not a preacher of righteousness among the people of God, but one who drew into His net those that were afar off. He attracted to Himself as the manifestation on earth of the power and the character of God. It was grace which was there.

The gracious work of the undefilable all-powerful One

He was there with the will and the power to heal that which was a figure of sin, and incurable but by the intervention of God. But God had intervened; and in grace He can say, and says, to one who acknowledged His power but doubted His will, "I will; be thou clean."[14] Yet He submitted to Jewish ordinances as one obedient to the law. Jesus prayed, as a Man dependent on God. This was His perfection as a Man born under the law. Moreover, He must needs acknowledge the ordinances of God, not yet abrogated by His rejection. But this obedience as Man became a testimony; for the power of

[14] If a man touched a leper, he was unclean. But here grace works, and Jesus undefilable touches the leper (God in grace, undefilable, but a Man touching the defiled thing to cleanse it).

Jehovah alone could heal leprosy, and He had healed it,
and the priests were to acknowledge that which had been
done.

The Son of Man exercising His power and rights as Jehovah to forgive sins

But He brings pardon as well as cleansing. He gives
a *proof* of this by removing all infirmity, and imparting
strength to one who had none. This was not the *doctrine*
that God could pardon. They believed that. But God
had intervened, and pardon was present. They would no
longer have to wait for the last day, nor for a day of
judgment, to know their condition. A Nathan would not
be required to come and proclaim it on the part of a God
who was in heaven while His people were on earth. Pardon
was come, in the Person of the Son of Man come down to
earth. In all this, Jesus gave proofs of the power and the
rights of Jehovah. In this instance it was the fulfilment
of Psalm 103: 3; but, at the same time, He gives these
proofs as accomplished by the power of the Holy Ghost,
without measure in man, in His own Person the true Son
of God. The Son of Man has power on earth to forgive
sins: in fact, Jehovah was come, a Man on earth. The
Son of Man was there before their eyes, in grace, to exercise this power—a proof that God had visited them.

The power of grace displayed in the midst of Israel

In both these instances[15] the Lord, while displaying
a power fitted to extend, and that was to extend, beyond

---

[15] The call of Peter is more general in this respect, that it is connected with the Person of Christ. Nevertheless, although he was a
fisher of men (a word used evidently in contrast with the fishes he was
occupied with), he exercised his ministry more particularly with regard
to Israel. But it was power in the Person of Christ that governed his
heart; so that it was fundamentally, the new thing, but as yet in its
connection with Israel, while extending beyond them. It is at the end
of chapter 7 and in chapter 8 that we enter on ground beyond the narrow limits of Israel.

this sphere, displays it in connection with Israel. The cleansing was a proof of the power of Jehovah in the midst of Israel, and the pardon was in connection with His government in Israel, and therefore proved itself by the perfect cure of the sick man, according to the psalm already quoted.[16] No doubt, these rights were not limited to Israel, but at that moment they were exercised in connection with this nation. He cleansed, in grace, that which Jehovah alone could cleanse. He pardoned that which Jehovah alone could pardon, taking away all the consequence of their sin. It was, in this sense, a governmental pardon; the power of Jehovah present, fully to restore and re-establish Israel—wherever, at least, faith could profit by it. Afterwards, we shall find pardon for peace of soul.

Grace extended beyond Israel

The call of Levi, and that which follows, shows that not only was this power of grace to extend beyond Israel, but that the old vessel was not able to bear it. It must form a vessel for itself.

The perseverance of faith and the power of God

We may also remark here, on the other hand, that faith is characterized by perseverance. In the consciousness of the evil, an evil without remedy, and in the assurance that One able to heal is there, it does not allow itself to be discouraged—does not put off the relief of its need. Now, the power of God *was there* to meet this need.

This terminates that part of the narrative which reveals, in a positive way, divine power, visiting the earth in grace, in the Person of the Son of Man, and exercised in Israel, in the condition in which it found them.

[16] Compare Job 33, 36 and James 5: 14, 15—the first outside dispensations, and James under Christianity. In Israel, it is the Lord Himself in sovereign grace.

The distinct characters of the first part of the Lord's ministry in power and grace

That which follows characterizes its exercise in contrast with Judaism. But that which we have already examined is divided into two parts, having distinct characters which deserve to be noticed. First, from chapter 4: 31-41, it is the power of the Lord manifesting itself on His part, as triumphing (without any particular connection with the mind of the individual) over all the power of the enemy, whether in sickness or in possession. The power of the enemy is there: Jesus casts it out, and heals those who are suffering from it. But, secondly, His occupation is to preach. And the kingdom was not only the manifestation of a power which casts out all that of the enemy, but of a power which brought souls also into connection with God. We see this in chapter 5: 1-26. Here their condition before God, sin, and faith, are in question —in a word, all that belonged to their relationship with God.

Here, consequently, we see the authority of the Word of Christ upon the heart, the manifestation of His glory (He is owned as Lord), conviction of sin, just jealousy for His glory, in the sense of His holiness which should keep itself inviolate; the soul taking God's part against itself, because it loves holiness and respects the glory of God, even while feeling the attraction of His grace; so that, owing to this, everything is forgotten—fish, nets, boat, danger: "one thing" already possesses the soul. The Lord's answer then dispels all fear, and He associates the freed soul with Himself in the grace which He had exercised towards it, and in the work which He wrought in behalf of men. It was already delivered morally from all that was around it; now, in the full enjoyment of grace, it is set free by the power of grace, and wholly given to Jesus. The Lord—perfect manifestation of God in creating new affections by this revelation of God, separates the heart from all that bound it to this world, to the order of the old man, in order to set it apart for Himself—for God. He surrounds Himself with all that is delivered, becoming its centre; and, indeed, delivers by being so.

He then cleanses the leper, which none but Jehovah could do. Still He does not come out of His position under the law; and, however great His fame, He maintains His place of perfect dependence as man before God. The leper, the unclean, may return to God.

He next forgives. The guilty one is no longer so before God; he is pardoned. At the same time he receives strength. Nevertheless it is still the Son of Man who is there. In both cases faith *seeks* the Lord, bringing its need before Him.

The character of grace

The Lord now exhibits the character of this grace in connection with its objects. Being supreme, being of God, it acts in virtue of its rights. Human circumstances do not hinder it. It adapts itself by its very nature to human need, and not to human privileges. It is not subject to ordinances[17] and does not come in through them. The power of God by the Spirit was there, and acted for itself, and produced its own effects, setting aside that which was old—that to which man was attached[18] and to which the power of the Spirit could not be confined.

[17] Christ, born under the law, was subject to them; but that is a different thing. Here it is a divine power acting in grace.

[18] But here also the Lord, in giving the reasons why the disciples did not follow the ordinances, and the institutions, of John and of the Pharisees, connects them with the two principles already pointed out— His position in the midst of Israel, and the power of grace which went beyond its limits. The Messiah, Jehovah Himself, was among them, in this grace (in spite of their failure under the law, in spite of their subjection to the Gentiles) according to which Jehovah named Himself, "I am the Lord that healeth thee." At least, He was there in the supremacy of grace for faith. Those therefore who owned Him as the Messiah, the husband of Israel, could they fast while He was with them? He would leave them: without doubt that would be their time to fast.

Opposition to grace: the old order of things and the new

The scribes and Pharisees would not have the Lord associate with the wicked and disreputable. God seeks those who need Him—sinners—in grace.

When they ask why His disciples do not observe the customs and the ordinances of John and the Pharisees, by which they guided the legal piety of their disciples, it is that the new thing could not be subjected to the forms that belonged to that which was old, and which could not sustain the strength and energy of that which came from God. The old were the forms of man after the flesh; the new, the energy of God, according to the Holy Ghost. Moreover it was not the time for a piety that took the form of self-mortification. What else could man do? But the Bridegroom was there.

Nevertheless, man would prefer that which was old, because it was man, and not the energy of God.

Moreover, secondly, it is always impossible. He could not adapt the new cloth of Christianity to the old garment of Judaism, in its nature incapable of receiving its energy, or adapting itself to grace, worn out withal as a dispensation by sin, and under which Israel was, in judgment, made subject to the Gentiles. Besides, the power of the Spirit of God in grace could not be restricted to the ordinances of the law. It would destroy them by its very strength. The call of Levi violated, and most openly, all the prejudices of the Jews. Their own fellow-countrymen were the instruments of their masters' extortion, and reminded them in the most painful manner of their subjection to the Gentiles. But the Lord was there in grace to seek sinners.

That which the Holy Ghost sets before us is the presence of the Lord, and the rights which are necessarily attached to His Person and to His sovereign grace, which had come into Israel, but necessarily went beyond its limits (setting aside, consequently, the legal system which could not receive the new thing). This is the key to all these narratives. Thus, also, in that which follows respecting the sabbath, the one case shows the supremacy which His glorious Person gave Him over that which was the sign of the covenant itself; and the other, that the goodness of God cannot abdicate its rights and its nature. He would do good even on a sabbath-day.

Chapter 6

The Son of Man manifested as Lord of the Sabbath

THE circumstances related in chapter 6: 1-10 have reference to the same truth, and in an important aspect. The sabbath was the sign of the covenant between Israel and God—rest after finished works. The Pharisees blame the disciples of Christ, because they rub out the ears of corn in their hands. Now a rejected David had overleapt the barrier of the law when his need required it. For when God's Anointed was rejected and cast out, everything became in a manner common. The Son of Man (Son of David, rejected like the son of Jesse, the elect and anointed king) was Lord of the sabbath; God, who established this ordinance, was above the ordinances He had established, and present in grace the obligation of man yielded to the sovereignty of God; and the Son of Man was there with the rights and the power of God. Marvellous fact! Moreover the power of God present in grace did not allow misery to exist, because it was the day of grace. But this was setting aside Judaism. That was the obligation of man to God, Christ was the manifestation of God in grace to men.[19] Availing Him-

---

[19] This is an important point. A part in the rest of God is the distinctive privilege of saints—of God's people. Man had it not at the fall, still God's rest remained the special portion of His people. He did not get it under the law. But every distinct institution under the law is accompanied by an enforcement of the sabbath, the formal expression of the rest of the first Adam, and this Israel will enjoy at the end of this world's history. Till then, as the Lord said so blessedly, "My Father worketh hitherto and I work." For us, the day of rest is not the seventh day, the end of this world's week; but the first day, the day after the sabbath, the beginning of a new week, a new creation, the day of Christ's resurrection, the commencement of a new state for man, for the accomplishment of which all creation round us waits, only we are before God in Spirit as Christ is. Hence the Sabbath, the seventh day, the rest of the first creation on human and legal ground, is always treated with rejection in the New Testament, though not set aside till judgment came, but as an ordinance it died with Christ in the grave, where He passed it—only it was made for man as a mercy. The Lord's day is our day, and precious external earnest of the heavenly rest.

self of the rights that authorized His pretension to assert
those rights, He heals, in full synagogue, the man with
the withered hand.   They are filled with madness at this
manifestation of power, which overflows and carries away
the dykes of their pride and self-righteousness.   We may
observe that all these circumstances are gathered together
with an order and mutual connection that are perfect.[20]

God manifested in a new way: the Sent One sends out His messengers

The Lord had shown that this grace—which had visited Israel according to all that could be expected from
the Lord Almighty, faithful to His promises—could,
nevertheless, not be confined to the narrow limits of that
people, nor be adapted to the ordinances of the law; that
men desired the old things, but that the power of God
acted according to its own nature.   He had shown that
the most sacred, the most obligatory, sign of the old
covenant, must bow to His title superior to all ordinance,
and give place to the rights of His divine love which was
in action.   But the old thing was thus judged, and passing away.   He had shown Himself in everything—in the
calling of Peter especially—to be the new centre, around
which all that sought God and blessing must gather; for
He was the living manifestation of God and of blessing in
men.   Thus God was manifested, the old order of things
was worn out and unable to contain this grace, and the
remnant were separated—around the Lord—from a world
that saw no beauty in Him that they should desire Him.

---

[20] I may remark here that, where chronological order is followed in
Luke, it is the same as in Mark and that of the events, not as in
Matthew put together to bring out the object of the Gospel; only he
occasionally   introduces a circumstance which may have happened at
another time illustrative of the subject historically related.   But in
chapter 9 Luke arrives at the last journey up to Jerusalem (ver. 51),
and, from this on, a series of moral instruction follows to chapter 18: 31,
chiefly, if not all, during the period of this journey, but which for the
most part has little to say to dates.

He now acted on this basis; and if faith sought Him in Israel, this power of grace manifested in a new way. God surrounds Himself with men, as the centre of blessing in Christ as man. But He is love, and in the activity of that love He seeks the lost. None but One, and One who was God and revealed Him, could surround Himself with His followers. No prophet ever did (See John 1). None could send out with the authority and power of a divine message but God. Christ had been sent; He now sends. The name of "apostle" ("sent"), for He so names them, contains this deep and marvellous truth—God is acting in grace. He surrounds Himself with blessed ones. He seeks miserable sinners. If Christ, the true centre of grace and happiness, surrounds Himself with followers, yet He sends also His chosen ones to bear testimony of the love which He came to manifest. God has manifested Himself in Man. In Man He seeks sinners. Man has part in the most immediate display of the divine nature in both ways. He is with Christ as man; and he is sent by Christ. Christ Himself does this as Man. It is man full of the Holy Ghost. Thus we see Him again manifested in dependence on His Father before choosing the apostles; He retires to pray, He passes the night in prayer.

The new Centre: the remnant separated to receive blessing

And now He goes beyond the manifestation of Himself, as personally full of the Holy Ghost to bring in the knowledge of God among men. He becomes the centre, around which all must come who sought God, and a source of mission for the accomplishment of His love—the centre of the manifestation of divine power in grace. And, therefore, He called around Him the remnant who should be saved. His position, in every respect, is summed up in that which is said after He came down from the mountain. He comes down with the apostles from His communion with God. In the plain[21] He is surrounded by the company of His disciples, and then by a great multitude, drawn together by His Word and works. There was the attraction of the Word of God, and He healed the diseases of men, and cast out the power of Satan. This power dwelt in His Person; the virtue that went out of Him gave these outward testimonies to the power of God present in grace. The attention of the people was drawn to Him by these means. Nevertheless we have seen that the old things, to which the multitude were attached, were passing away. He surrounded Himself with hearts faithful to God, the called of His grace. Here therefore He does not, as in Matthew, announce strictly the character of the kingdom, to show that of the dispensation which was at hand, saying, "Blessed are the poor in spirit," &c.; but, distinguishing the remnant, by their attachment to Himself, He declares to the disciples who followed Him that they were these blessed ones. They were poor and despised, but they were blessed. They should have the kingdom. This is important, because it separates the remnant, and puts them in relationship with Himself to receive the blessing. He describes, in a remarkable manner, the character of those who were thus blessed of God.

The divisions and subjects of the Lord's discourse

The Lord's discourse is divided into several branches.

Verses 20-26. The contrast between the remnant, manifested as His disciples, and the multitude who were satisfied with the world, adding a warning to those who stood in the place of disciples, and in that gained the favor of the world. Woe be to such! Remark also here, that it is not a question of persecution for righteousness' sake, as in Matthew, but only for His name's sake. All was marked by attachment to His Person.

Verses 27-36. The character of God their Father in

---

[21] Properly "a level place" on the mountain, *topou pedinou*.

the manifestation of grace in Christ, which they were to imitate. He reveals, note, the Father's name and puts them in the place of children.

Verses 37, 38. This character particularly developed in the position of Christ, as He was on earth at that time, Christ fulfilling His service on earth. This implied government and recompense on God's part, as was the case with regard to Christ Himself.

Verse 39. The condition of the leaders in Israel, and the connection between them and the multitude.

Verse 40. That of the disciples in relation to Christ.

Verses 41, 42. The way to attain it, and to see clearly in the midst of evil, is to put evil away from oneself.

Afterwards, in general, its *own* fruit characterized every tree. Coming around Christ to hear Him was not the question, but that He should be so precious to their hearts that they would put aside every obstacle and practically obey Him.

Summary of Chapters 4, 5 and 6

Let us sum up these things which we have been considering. He acts in a power which dispels evil, because He finds it there, and He is good; and God alone is good. He reaches the conscience, and calls souls to Himself. He acts in connection with the hope of Israel and the power of God to cleanse, pardon and give them strength. But it is a grace which we all need; and the goodness of God, the energy of His love, did not confine itself to that people. Its exercise did not agree with the forms on which the Jews lived (or, rather, could not live); and the new wine must be put into new bottles. The question of the sabbath settled the question of the introduction of this power; the sign of the covenant gave way to it: He who exercised it was Lord of the sabbath. The loving-kindness of the God of the sabbath was not stayed, as if having His hands tied by that which He had established in connection with the covenant. Jesus then assembles the vessels of His

grace and power, according to the will of God, around
Himself. They were the blessed ones, the heirs of the
kingdom. The Lord describes their character. It was
not the indifference and pride that arose from ignorance
of God, justly alienated from Israel, who had sinned
against Him, and despised the glorious manifestation of
His grace in Christ. They share the distress and pain
which such a condition of God's people must cause in
those who had the mind of God. Hated, proscribed, put
to shame for the sake of the Son of Man, who had come
to bear their sorrows, it was their glory. They should
share His glory when the nature of God was glorified in
doing all things according to His own will. They would
not be put to shame in heaven; they should have their
reward there, not in Israel. "In like manner had their
fathers done unto the prophets." Woe unto those that
were at ease in Zion, during the sinful condition of Israel,
and their rejection and ill-treatment of their Messiah! It
is the contrast between the character of the true remnant
and that of the proud among the people.

We then find the conduct that is suitable to the former
—conduct which, to express it in one word, comprises in
its essential elements, the character of God in grace, as
manifested in Jesus on the earth. But Jesus had His own
character of service as the Son of Man; the application
of this to their particular circumstances is added in verses
37, 38. In 39 the leaders of Israel are set before us, and
in verse 40 the portion of the disciples. Rejected like
Himself, they should have His portion; but, assuming
that they followed Him perfectly, they should have it in
blessing, in grace, in character, in position also. What a
favor! [22] Moreover, the judgment of self, and not of one's

[22] This however does not speak of nature intrinsically, for in Christ
was no sin. Nor has the word used for "perfect" that sense. It is one
completely thoroughly instructed, formed completely by the teaching
of his master, *omnibus numeris absolutus*. He will be like him, as his
master, in all in which he was formed by him. Christ was the perfection;
we grow up unto Him in all things unto the measure of the stature of
the fulness of Christ. (See Col. 1: 28.)

brother, was the means of attaining clear moral sight. The tree good, the fruit would be good. Self-judgment applies to the trees. This is always true. In self-judgment, it is not only the fruit that is corrected; it is oneself. And the tree is known by its fruit—not only by good fruit, but by its own. The Christian bears the fruit of the nature of Christ. Also it is the heart itself, and real practical obedience, that are in question.

Here then the great principles of the new life, in its full practical development in Christ, are set before us. It is the new thing morally, the savor and character of the new wine—the remnant made like unto Christ whom they followed, unto Christ the new centre of the movement of the Spirit of God, and of the calling of His grace. Christ has come out of the walled court of Judaism, in the power of a new life and by the authority of the Most High, who had brought blessing into this enclosure, which it was unable to acknowledge. He had come out from it, according to the principles of the life itself which He announced; historically, He was still in it.

Chapter 7

Out of the walled court of Judaism: faith in the heart of a Gentile

HENCE, after this, we find the Spirit acting in the heart of a Gentile (chap. 7). That heart manifested more faith than any among the children of Israel. Humble in heart, and loving the people of God, as such, for the sake of God, whose people they were, and thus raised in his affections above their practical wretched state, he can see in Jesus One who had authority over everything, even as he himself had over his soldiers and servants. He knew nothing of the Messiah, but he recognized in Jesus [23]

[23] We have seen this to be precisely the subject of the Holy Ghost in our Gospel.

the power of God. This was not mere idea; it was faith.
There was no such faith in Israel.

Power exercised to raise the dead: all things new

The Lord then acts with a power which was to be the
source of that which is new for man. *He raises the dead.*
This was indeed going beyond the pale of the ordinances
of the law. He has compassion on the affliction and misery
of man. Death was a burden to him: Jesus delivers him
from it. It was not only cleansing a leprous Israelite, nor
pardoning and healing believers among His people; He
restores life to one who had lost it. Israel, no doubt,
will profit by it; but the power necessary to the accomplishment of this work is that which makes all things
new wherever it may be.

The relative positions of John the Baptist and Christ:
the Lord's testimony to John

The change of which we speak, and which these two
examples so strikingly illustrate, is brought out in treating
of the connection between Christ and John the Baptist,
who sends to learn from the Lord's own mouth who He
is. John had heard of His miracles, and sends his disciples to learn who it was that wrought them. Naturally
the Messiah, in the exercise of His power, would have
delivered him from prison. Was He the Messiah? or was
John to wait for another? He had faith enough to depend
on the answer of One who wrought these miracles; but,
shut up in prison, his mind desired something more positive. This circumstance, brought about by God, gives
rise to an explanation respecting the relative position of
John and Jesus. The Lord does not here receive testimony
from John. John was to receive Christ upon the testimony
He gave of Himself; and that as having taken a position
which would offend those who judged according to Jewish
and carnal ideas—a position which required faith in a

divine testimony, and, consequently, surrounded itself
with those whom a moral change had enabled to appreciate this testimony.   The Lord, in reply to John's messengers, works miracles which prove the power of God
present in grace and service rendered to the poor; and
declares that blessed is he who is not offended at the humble position He had taken in order to accomplish it.   But
He gives testimony to John, if He will receive none from
him.   He had attracted the attention of the people, and
with reason; he was more than a prophet—he had prepared the way of the Lord Himself.   Nevertheless, if he
prepared the way, the immense and complete change to be
made was not itself accomplished.   John's ministry, by its
very nature, put him outside the effect of this change.
He went before it to announce the One who would accomplish it, whose presence would bring in its power on the
earth.   The least therefore *in* the kingdom was greater
than he.

The people's reception of John and the Lord

The people, who had received with humility the word
sent by John the Baptist, bore testimony in their heart to
the ways and the wisdom of God.   Those who trusted in
themselves rejected the counsels of God accomplished in
Christ.   The Lord, on this, declares plainly what their
condition is.   They rejected alike the warnings and the
grace of God.   The children of wisdom (those in whom
the wisdom of God wrought) acknowledged and gave
glory to it in its ways.   This is the history of the reception
both of John and of Jesus. The wisdom of man denounced
the ways of God.   The righteous severity of His testimony
against evil, against the condition of His people, showed
to man's eyes the influence of a devil.   The perfection of
His grace, condescending to poor sinners, and presenting
itself to them where they were, was the wallowing in sin
and the making oneself known by one's associates.   Proud

self-righteousness could bear neither. The wisdom of
God would be owned by those who were taught by it,
and by those alone.

God's ways towards sinners in contrast with the pharisaic spirit

Thereupon these ways of God towards the most wretched sinners, and their effect, in contrast with this pharisaic spirit, are shown, in the history of the woman who
was a sinner in the Pharisee's house; and a pardon is
revealed, not with reference to the government of God in
the earth on behalf of His people (a government with
which the healing of an Israelite under God's discipline
was connected), but an absolute pardon, involving peace
to the soul, is granted to the most miserable of sinners.
It was not here merely the question of a prophet. The
Pharisee's self-righteousness could not discern even that.

The child of wisdom

We have a soul that loves God, and much, because
God is love—a soul that has learnt this with regard to,
and by means of, its own sins, though not yet knowing
forgiveness, in seeing Jesus. This is grace. Nothing
more touching than the way in which the Lord shows the
presence of those qualities which made this woman now
truly excellent—qualities connected with the discernment
of His Person by faith. In her were found divine understanding of the Person of Christ, not reasoned out indeed
in doctrine but felt in its effect in her heart, deep sense
of her own sin, humility, love for that which was good,
devotedness to Him who was good. Everything showed
a heart in which reigned sentiments proper to relationship with God—sentiments that flowed from His presence
revealed in the heart, because He had made Himself
known to it. This, however, is not the place to dwell
upon them; but it is important to remark that which has

great moral value, when what a free pardon really is is to be set forth, that the exercise of grace on God's part creates (when received into the heart) sentiments corresponding to itself, and which nothing else can produce; and that these sentiments are in connection with that grace, and with the sense of sin it produces. It gives a deep consciousness of sin, but it is in connection with the sense of God's goodness; and the two feelings increase in mutual proportion. The new thing, sovereign grace, can alone produce these qualities, which answer to the nature of God Himself, whose true character the heart has apprehended, and with whom it is in communion; and that, while judging sin as it deserves in the presence of such a God.

The hearts of the Pharisee, the sinner and of God manifested in grace

It will be observed, that this is connected with the knowledge of Christ Himself, who is the manifestation of this character; the true source by grace of the feeling of this broken heart; and also that the knowledge of her pardon comes afterward.[24] It is grace—it is Jesus Him-

[24] To explain the expression, "Her sins are forgiven, for she loved much," we must distinguish between grace revealed in the Person of Jesus, and the pardon He announced to those whom the grace had reached. The Lord is able to make this pardon known. He reveals it to the poor woman. But it was that which she had seen in Jesus Himself, which, by grace, melted her heart and produced the love she had to Him—the seeing what He was for sinners like herself. She thinks only of Him: He has taken possession of her heart so as to shut out other influences. Hearing that He is there, she goes into the house of this proud man, without thinking of anything but the fact that Jesus is there. His presence answered, or prevented, every question. She saw what He was for a sinner, and that the most wretched and disgraced found a resource in Him; she felt her sins in the way that this perfect grace, which opens the heart and wins confidence, causes them to be felt; and she loved much. Grace in Christ had produced its effect. She loved because of His love. This is the reason that the Lord says, "Her sins are forgiven, because she loved much." It was not that her love was meritorious for this, but that God revealed the glorious fact that the sins—be they ever so numerous and abominable—of one whose heart was turned to God were fully pardoned. There are many whose hearts are turned to God, and who love Jesus, that do not know this. Jesus pronounces on their case with authority—sends them away in

self—His Person—that attracts this woman and produces
the moral effect. She goes away in peace when she understands the extent of grace in the pardon which He pronounces. And the pardon itself has its force in her mind,
in that Jesus was everything to her. If He forgave, she
was satisfied. Without accounting for it to herself, it
was God revealed to her heart; it was not self-approval,
nor the judgment others might form of the change wrought
in her. Grace had so taken possession of her heart—grace

peace. It is a revelation—an answer—to the wants and affections
produced in the heart made penitent by grace revealed in the Person of
Christ.

If God manifests Himself in this world, and with such love, He must
needs set aside in the heart every other consideration. And thus, without being aware of it, this poor woman was the only one who acted
suitably in those circumstances: for she appreciated the all-importance
of the One who was there. A Saviour-God being present, of what importance was Simon and his house? Jesus caused all else to be forgotten.
Let us remember this.

The beginning of man's fall was loss of confidence in God, by the
seducing suggestion of Satan that God had kept back what would make
man like God. Confidence in God lost, man seeks, in the exercise of his
own will, to make himself happy: lusts, sin, transgression follow. Christ
is God in infinite love, winning back the confidence of man's heart to
God. Removal of guilt, and power to live to God, are another thing,
and found in their own place through Christ, as pardon comes in its
place here. But the poor woman, through grace, had felt that there
was one heart she could trust, if none else; but that was God's.

"God is light" and "God is love." These are the two essential names
of God, and in every true case of conversion both are found. In the
cross they meet; sin is brought fully into the light, but in that by
which love is fully known. So in the heart light reveals sin, that is
God as light does, but the light is there by perfect love. The God who
shows the sins is there in perfect love to do it. Christ was this in this
world. Revealing Himself, He must be both; so Christ was love in the
world, but the light of it. So in the heart. The love through grace
gives confidence, and thus the light is gladly let in, and in the confidence
in the love, and seeing self in the light, the heart has wholly met God's
heart: so with this poor woman. This is where the heart of man and
God always and alone meet. The Pharisee had neither. Pitch-dark,
neither love nor light were there. He had God manifest in the flesh in
his house and saw nothing—only settled that He was not a prophet.
It is a wondrous scene to see these three hearts. Man's as such resting
on false human righteousness, God's, and the poor sinner's—fully meeting it as God did hers. Who was the child of wisdom? for it is a com-
mentary on that expression.

And note, though Christ had said nothing of it, but bowed to the
slight, yet He was not insensible to the neglect which had not met Him
with the common courtesies of life. To Simon He was a poor preacher,
whose pretensions he could judge, certainly not a prophet; for the poor
woman, God in love, and bringing her heart into unison with His as to
her sins and as to herself, for love was trusted in. Note, too, this clinging to Jesus is where true light is found: here the fruitful revelation
of the gospel; to Mary Magdalene, as to the highest privilege of saints.

personified in Jesus—God was so manifested to her, that His approval in grace, His forgiveness, carried everything else with it. If He was satisfied, so was she. She had all in attaching this importance to Christ. Grace delights to bless, and the soul that attaches importance enough to Christ is content with the blessing it bestows. How striking is the firmness with which grace asserts itself, and does not fear to withstand the judgment of man who despises it! It takes unhesitatingly the part of the poor sinner whom it has touched. Man's judgment only proves that he neither knows nor appreciates God in the most perfect manifestation of His nature. To man, with all his wisdom, it is but a poor preacher, who deceives himself in passing for a prophet, and to whom it is not worth while to give a little water for his feet. To the believer it is perfect and divine love, it is perfect peace if he has faith in Christ. Its fruits are not yet before man; they are before God, if Christ is appreciated. And he who appreciates Him thinks neither of himself nor of his fruits (except of the bad), but of the One who was the testimony of grace to his heart when he was nothing but a sinner.

This is the new thing—grace, and even its fruits in their perfection: the heart of God manifested in grace, and the heart of man—a sinner—responding to it by grace, having apprehended, or rather having been apprehended by, the perfect manifestation of that grace in Christ.

Chapter 8

The import and effect of the Lord's ministry in spite of unbelief

IN chapter 8 the Lord explains the import and the effect of His ministry; and especially, I doubt not, its effect among the Jews.

However great the unbelief, Jesus carries on His work
to the end, and the fruits of His work appear. He goes
to preach the good news of the kingdom. His disciples
(the fruit, and the witnesses by grace, in their measure,
in the same manner as Himself, of His mighty Word)
accompany Him; and other fruits of this same Word,
witnesses also by their own deliverance from the power
of the enemy, and by the affection and devotedness flowing from thence by grace—a grace which acted also in
them, according to the love and devotedness that attach
to Jesus. Here women have a good place.[25] The work
was strengthened and consolidated, and characterizes itself
by its effects.

The Sower: the seed sown to produce fruit: the disciples distinguished from the multitude

The Lord explains its true nature. He did not take
possession of the kingdom, He did not seek for fruit; He
sowed the testimony of God in order to *produce* fruit.
This, in a striking way, is the altogether new thing. The
Word was its seed. Moreover it was the disciples only
—who had followed and attached themselves to His Person, by grace and by virtue of the manifestation of the
power and grace of God in His Person—to whom it was
given to understand the mysteries, the thoughts of God,
revealed in Christ, of this kingdom which was not being
openly established by power. Here the remnant is very
clearly distinguished from the nation. To "others" it was
in parables, that they might not understand. For that
the Lord Himself must be received morally. Here this
parable is not accompanied by others. Alone it marks
out the position. The warning, which we considered in

---

[25] It is exceedingly interesting to see the distinct place of the disciples and the women. Nor, as said above, have the women a bad
place. We find them again at the cross and the sepulchre when—at any
rate save John—the disciples had fled, or, even if called by the woman
to the sepulchre, gone home when they saw He was raised!

Mark, is added. Finally the light of God was not manifested in order to be hidden. Moreover everything should be made manifest. Therefore they must take heed how they heard, for, if they possessed that which they heard, they should receive more: otherwise even that should be taken from them.

The place and effect of the Word

The Lord puts a seal upon this testimony, namely, that the thing in question was the Word, which drew to Him and to God those who were to enjoy the blessing; and that the Word was the basis of all relationship with Himself, declaring, when they spoke to Him of His mother and brethren, by whom He was related to Israel after the flesh, that He acknowledged as such none others but those who heard and obeyed the Word of God.

Christ in power in the storm with His disciples

Besides the evident power manifested in His miracles the accounts that follow—to the end of chapter 8—present different aspects of the work of Christ, and of His reception, and of its consequences.

First the Lord—although, apparently, He takes no notice—is associated with His disciples in the difficulties and storms that surround them, because they have embarked in His service. We have seen that He gathered the disciples around Himself: they are devoted to His service. As far as man's power to avert it went, they were in imminent danger. The waves are ready to swallow them up. Jesus, in their eyes, cares nothing about it; but God has permitted this exercise of faith. They are there on account of Christ, and with Him. Christ is with them; and the power of Christ, for whose sake they are in the storm, is there to protect them. They are together with Him in the same vessel. If as to themselves they might perish, they are associated in the counsels of God with Jesus, and His presence is their safeguard. He permits the storm, but He is Himself in the vessel. When He shall awake and manifest Himself, all will be calm.

The demoniac healed as a witness of the Lord's grace and power

In the healing of the demoniac, in the country of the Gadarenes, we have a living picture of what was passing.

As to Israel, the remnant—however great the enemy's power—is delivered. The world beseeches Jesus to depart, desiring their own ease, which is more disturbed by the presence and power of God than by a legion of devils. He goes away. The man who was healed—the remnant—would fain be with Him; but the Lord sends him back (into the world that He quitted Himself) to be a witness of the grace and power of which he had been the subject.

The herd of swine, I doubt not, set before us the career of Israel towards their destruction, after the rejection of the Lord. The world accustoms itself to the power of Satan—painful as it may be to see it in certain cases—never to the power of God.

The effect of faith: healing power in the Person of Christ

The next two histories present the effect of faith, and the real need with which the grace that meets it has to do. The faith of the remnant seeks Jesus to preserve the life of that which is ready to perish. The Lord answers it, and comes Himself to answer it. On the way (it is there He was, and, as to final deliverance, He is still there), in the midst of the crowd that surrounded Him, faith touches Him. The poor woman had a disease which no means at man's disposal could heal. But power is found in the Man, Christ, and comes forth from Him for the healing of man, wherever faith exists, while waiting for the final accomplishment of His mission on earth. She is healed, and confesses before Christ her condition and all that had happened to her: and thus, by means of the effect of faith, testimony is rendered to Christ. The remnant is manifested, faith distinguishes them from the multitude; their condition being the fruit of divine power in Christ.

This principle applies to the healing of every believer, and, consequently, to that of the Gentiles, as the apostle argues. Healing power is in the Person of Christ; faith—by grace and by the attraction of Christ—profits by it. It does not depend on the relationship of the Jew, although, as to his position, he was the first to profit by it. It is a question of what there is in the Person of Christ, and of faith in the individual. If there is faith in the individual, this power acts; he goes away in peace, healed by the power of God Himself.

Jairus' daughter: divine power to raise from the dead exercised in grace

But, in fact, if we consider in full the condition of man, it was not sickness merely which was in question, but death. Christ, before the full manifestation of the state of man, met it, so to speak, on the way; but, as in the case of Lazarus, the manifestation was allowed; and to faith this manifestation took place in the death of Jesus. Thus, here, it is permitted that the daughter of Jairus should die before the arrival of Christ; but grace has come to raise from the dead, with the divine power that alone can accomplish it; and Jesus, in comforting the poor father, bids him not to fear, but only to believe, and his daughter should be made whole. It is faith in His Person, in the divine power in Him, in the grace that comes to exercise it, which obtains joy and deliverance. But Jesus does not seek the multitude here; the manifestation of this power is only for the consolation of those who feel their need of it, and for the faith of those who are really

attached to Him. The multitude know, indeed, that the
maiden is dead; they bewail her, and do not understand
the power of God that can raise her up. Jesus gives back
to her parents the child whose life He had restored. Thus
will it be with the Jews at the end, in the midst of the
unbelief of the many. Meantime by faith we anticipate
this joy, convinced that it is our state by grace; we live:
only that for us it is in connection with Christ in heaven,
the firstfruits of a new creation.

With respect to His ministry, Jesus will have this hidden. He must be received according to the testimony which
He bore to the conscience and to the heart. On the way
this testimony was not entirely finished. We shall see His
last efforts with the unbelieving heart of man in the succeeding chapters.

Chapter 9

Sending forth the twelve disciples: a definite testimony against the people

IN chapter 9 the Lord charges the disciples with the
same mission in Israel as that which He Himself fulfilled. They preach the kingdom, heal the sick, and cast
out devils. But this is added, that their work takes the
character of a final mission. Not that the Lord had
ceased to work, for He also sent forth the seventy; but
final in this sense, that it became a definite testimony
against the people if they rejected it. The twelve were
to shake off the dust from their feet on leaving the cities
that would reject them. This is intelligible at the point
we have reached in the Gospel. It is repeated, with a
yet greater force, in the case of the seventy. We shall
speak of it in the chapter that relates to their being sent
forth. Their mission comes after the manifestation of His

glory to the three disciples. But the Lord as long as He was here continued His exercise of power in mercy, for it was what He personally was here, and sovereign goodness in Him was above all the evil He met with.

The fame of the Lord's marvellous works

To go on with our chapter. That which follows verse 7 shows that the fame of His marvellous works had reached the ears of the king. Israel was without excuse. Whatever little conscience there was felt the effect of His power. The people also followed Him. Gone apart with the disciples, who had returned from their mission, He is soon surrounded by the multitude; again, their servant in grace, however great their unbelief, He preaches to them and heals all who needed it.

The Satisfier of His people with bread: a special proof of the divine power and presence

But He would give them a fresh and very especial proof of the divine power and presence that was among them. It had been said that in the time of Israel's blessing from the Lord, when He should make the horn of David to flourish, He would satisfy the poor with bread. Jesus now does so. But there is more than this here. We have seen throughout this Gospel that He exercises this power, in His humanity, by the unmeasured energy of the Holy Ghost. Hence a marvellous blessing for us, granted according to the sovereign counsels of God, through the perfect wisdom of Jesus in selecting His instruments. He will have the disciples do it. Nevertheless the power that performs it is all His own. The disciples see nothing beyond that which their eyes can estimate. But, if He who feeds them is Jehovah, He ever takes His place Himself in the dependence of the nature He had assumed. He retires with His disciples, and there, afar from the world, He prays. And, as in the two remarkable cases [26] of the descent of the Holy Ghost and the selection of the Twelve, so here also His prayer is the occasion of the manifestation of His glory—glory which was due to Him, but which the Father gave Him as Man, and in connection with the sufferings and the humiliation, which, in His love, He voluntarily underwent.

The suffering Son of Man

The attention of the people was excited, but they did not go beyond the speculations of the human mind with regard to the Saviour. The disciples' faith recognized without hesitation the Christ in Jesus. But He was no longer to be proclaimed as such—the Son of Man was to suffer. Counsels more important, a glory more excellent than that of the Messiah, were to be realized: but it should be through suffering—suffering that, as to human trials, His disciples were to share by following Him. But in losing their life for Him, they would gain it; for in following Jesus, the eternal life of the soul was the question and not merely the kingdom. Moreover He who was now rejected would return in His own glory, namely, as Son of Man (the character He takes in this Gospel), in the glory of the Father, for He was the Son of God, and in that of the angels as Jehovah the Saviour, taking place above them, although (yea, as) Man: He was worthy of this, for He created them. The salvation of the soul, the glory of Jesus acknowledged according to His rights, everything warned them to confess Him while He was despised and disallowed. Now, to strengthen the

[26] Observe also here, that it is not only in the case of acts of power, or in that of testimony to the glory of His Person in answer to His prayer, that these prayers are offered. His conversation with the disciples respecting the change in the dispensations of God (in which He speaks of His sufferings, and forbids them to make Him known as the Christ) is introduced by His prayer when He was in a desert place with them. That His people were to be given up for a time occupied His heart as much as the glory. Moreover, He pours out His heart to God, whatever may be the subject that occupies Him according to the ways of God.

faith of those whom He would make pillars, and through
them the faith of all, He announces that some of them,
before they tasted death (they should neither wait for
death, in which the value of eternal life would be felt,
nor for the return of Christ), should *see* the kingdom
of God.

The transfiguration: the new glory and blessing
dependent on Christ's death

In consequence of this declaration, eight days later He
took the three who afterwards were pillars, and went up
into a mountain to pray. There He is transfigured. He
appears in glory, and the disciples see it. But Moses and
Elias share it with Him. The saints of the Old Testament
have part with Him in the glory of the kingdom founded
upon His death. They speak with Him of His decease.
They had heretofore spoken of other things. They had
seen the law set up, or had sought to bring the people
back to it, for the introduction of blessing; but now that
this new glory is the subject, all depends on the death of
Christ, and on that alone. Everything else disappears.
The heavenly glory of the kingdom and death are in
immediate relationship. Peter sees only the introduction
of Christ into a glory equal to theirs; connecting the latter
in his mind with that which they both were to a Jew,
and associating Jesus with it. It is then that the two
disappear entirely, and Jesus remains alone. It was He
alone whom they were to hear. The connection of Moses
and Elias with Jesus in the glory, depended on the rejection of their testimony by the people to whom they
had addressed it.

The disciples associated on earth with the abode
of glory

But this is not all. The Church, properly so called, is
not seen here. But the sign of the excellent glory, of the

presence of God, shows itself—the cloud in which Jehovah
dwelt in Israel. Jesus brings the disciples to it as witnesses. Moses and Elias disappear, and, Jesus having
brought the disciples close to the glory, the God of Israel
manifests Himself as the Father, and owns Jesus as the
Son in whom He delighted. All is changed in the relationships of God with man. The Son of Man, put to
death on earth, is owned in the excellent glory to be the
Son of the Father. The disciples know Him thus by
the testimony of the Father, are associated with Him, and,
as it were, introduced into connection with the glory in
which the Father Himself thus acknowledged Jesus—in
which the Father and the Son are found. Jehovah makes
Himself known as Father by revealing the Son. And the
disciples find themselves associated on earth with the
abode of glory, from whence, at all times, Jehovah Himself
had protected Israel. Jesus was there with them, and He
was the Son of God. What a position! What a change
for them! It is, in fact, the change from all that was
most excellent in Judaism to connection with the heavenly
glory, which was wrought at that moment, in order to
make all things new.[27]

The heavenly glory: the intimacy of the three
   disciples with the Lord

The personal profit of this passage is great, in that it
reveals to us, in a very striking manner, the heavenly and

[27] It is the display of the kingdom, not of the Church in heavenly
places. I suppose the words "they entered" must refer to Moses and
Elias. But the cloud overshadowed the disciples. Yet it carries us beyond that display. The word "overshadowed" is the same as that used
by the LXX for the cloud coming and filling the tabernacle. We learn
from Matthew it was a bright cloud. It was the Shekinah of glory
which had been with Israel in the wilderness—I may say the Father's
house. His voice came from it. Into this they entered. It is this in
Luke that makes the disciples afraid. God had talked with Moses out
of it; but here they enter into it. Thus, besides the kingdom, there is
the proper dwelling-place of the saints. This is found in Luke only.
We have the kingdom, Moses and Elias in the same glory with the Son,
and others in flesh on the earth, but the heavenly sojourn of the saints
also.

glorious state. The saints are in the same glory as Jesus, they are with Him, they converse familiarly with Him, they converse on that which is nearest to His heart—on His sufferings and death. They speak with the sentiments that flow from circumstances which affect the heart. He was to die in the beloved Jerusalem, instead of their receiving the kingdom. They speak as understanding the counsels of God; for the thing had not yet taken place. Such are the relationships of the saints with Jesus in the kingdom. For, up to this point, it is the manifestation of the glory as the world will see it, with the addition of the intercourse between the glorified and Jesus. The three were standing on the mountain. But the three disciples go beyond this. They are taught of the Father. His own affections for His Son are made known to them. Moses and Elias have borne testimony to Christ, and shall be glorified with Him; but Jesus now remains alone for the Church. This is more than the kingdom, it is fellowship with the Father, and with His Son Jesus (not understood, assuredly, at that time, but now is by the power of the Holy Ghost). It is wonderful, this entrance of the saints into the excellent glory, into the Shekinah, the abode of God; and these revelations on God's part of His own affections for His Son. This is more than the glory. Jesus, however, is always the object that fills the scene for us. Observe also for our position down here, that the Lord speaks as intimately of His death to His disciples on the earth as to Moses and Elias. These are not more intimate with Him than are Peter, James, and John. Sweet and precious thought! And mark how thin a veil there is between us and what is heavenly.[28]

---

[28] Note too that if Jesus takes up the disciples to see the glory of the kingdom, and the entrance of the saints into the excellent glory where the Father was, He came down also and met the crowd of this world and the power of Satan where we have to walk.

The disciples' powerlessness: the grace of Christ unhindered

That which follows is the application of this revelation to the state of things below. The disciples are unable to profit by the power of Jesus, already manifested, to cast out the power of the enemy. And this justifies God in that which was revealed of His counsels on the mount, and leads to the setting aside of the Jewish system, in order to introduce their fulfilment. But this does not hinder the action of the grace of Christ in delivering men while He was yet with them, until man had finally rejected Him. But, without noticing the fruitless astonishment of the people, He insists with His disciples on His rejection and on His crucifixion; carrying this principle on to the renunciation of self, and the humility which would receive that which was least.

Different features of selfishness and of the flesh contrasted with Christ's grace and devotedness

In the remainder of the chapter, from verse 46, the Gospel gives us the different features of selfishness and of the flesh that are in contrast with the grace and devotedness manifested in Christ, and that tend to prevent the believer from walking in His steps. Verses 46-48; 49, 50; 51-56, respectively, present examples [29] of this; and, from 57 to 62, the contrast between the illusive will of man and the efficacious call of grace; the discovery of the repugnance of the flesh, when there is a true call; and the absolute renunciation of all things, in order to obey it, are set before us by the Spirit of God.[30]

---

[29] These three passages point out, each in succession, a more subtle selfishness less easily detected by man: gross personal selfishness, corporate selfishness, and the selfishness that clothes itself with the appearance of zeal for the Lord, but which is not likeness to Him.

[30] Observe that, when the will of man acts, he does not feel the difficulties, but he is not qualified for the work. When there is a true call, the hindrances are felt.

The Lord (in reply to the spirit that sought the aggrandizement of their own company on earth, forgetful of the cross) expresses to the disciples that which He did not conceal from Himself, the truth of God, that all were in such wise against them that, if any one were not so, he was even thereby for them. So thoroughly did the presence of Christ test the heart. The other reason, given elsewhere, is not repeated here. The Spirit, in this connection, confines Himself to the point of view we are considering. Thus rejected, the Lord judges no one. He does not avenge Himself; He was come to save men's lives. That a Samaritan should repulse the Messiah was, to the disciples, worthy of destruction. Christ came to save the lives of men. He submits to the insult, and goes elsewhere. There were some who wished to serve Him here below. He had no home to which He could take them. Meantime, for this very reason, the preaching of the kingdom was the only thing to His unwearying love; the dead (to God) might bury the dead. He who was called, who was alive, must be occupied with one thing, with the kingdom, to bear testimony to it; and that without looking back, the urgency of the matter lifting him above all other thoughts. He who had put his hand to the plough must not look back. The kingdom, in presence of the enmity—the ruin—of man, of all that opposed it, required the soul to be wholly absorbed in its interests by the power of God. The work of God, in the presence of Christ's rejection, demanded entire consecration.

Chapter 10: 1 to 37

The mission of the seventy: its character: testimony rendered in power

THE mission of the seventy follows in chapter 10, a mission important in its character for the development of the ways of God.

This character is, in fact, different in some respects from that of the beginning of chapter 9. The mission is founded on the glory of Christ manifested in chapter 9. This, of necessity, settles the question more decisively of the Lord's relations with the Jews: for His glory came after, and, as to His human position, was the result of His rejection by the nation.

This rejection was not yet accomplished: this glory was only revealed to three of His disciples; so that the Lord still exercised His ministry among the people. But we see these alterations in it. He insists on that which is moral and eternal, the position into which it would bring His disciples, the true effect of His testimony in the world, and the judgment about to fall upon the Jews. Nevertheless the harvest was great. For love, unchilled by sin, saw the need through the outward opposition; but there were few moved by this love. The Lord of the harvest alone could send forth true laborers.

Already the Lord announces that they are as lambs among wolves. What a change from the presentation of the kingdom to the people of God! They were to trust (like the twelve) to the care of the Messiah present on the earth, and who influenced the heart with divine power. They were to go as the Lord's laborers, openly avowing their object, not toiling for their food, but as having claims on His part. Wholly devoted to their work, they were to salute no one. Time pressed. Judgment was coming. There were those in Israel who were not children of peace. The remnant would be distinguished by the effect of their mission on the heart, not yet judicially. But peace should rest on the children of peace. These messengers exercised the power gained by Jesus over the enemy, and which He could thus bestow (and this was much more than a miracle); and they were to declare unto those whom they visited that the kingdom of God had come nigh unto them. Important testimony! When the judgment was not executed, it required faith to recog-

nize it in a testimony. If they were not received, they
were to denounce the city, assuring them that, received
or not, the kingdom of God had come nigh. What a
solemn testimony, now that Jesus was going to be rejected—a rejection that filled up the measure of man's
iniquity! It would be more tolerable for infamous Sodom,
in the day that judgment should be executed, than for
that city.

This clearly points out the the character of the testimony. The Lord denounces [31] the cities in which He
had wrought, and assures His disciples that to reject
them in their mission was the same thing as to reject
Him, and that, in rejecting Him, He who had sent Him
was rejected—the God of Israel—the Father. On their
return they announce the power that had accompanied
their mission; demons were subject to their word. The
Lord replies that in effect these tokens of power had made
present to His mind the full establishment of the kingdom
—Satan cast out entirely from heaven (an establishment
of which these miracles were only a sample); but that
there was something more excellent than this, and in
which they might rejoice—their names were written in
heaven. The power manifested was true, its results sure,
in the establishment of the kingdom; but something else
was beginning to appear—a heavenly people were dawning,
who should have their portion with Him, whom the un-

[31] In verse 25 of this chapter, as well as in chapter 13: 34, we have
examples of the moral order in Luke, of which we have spoken. The
testimonies of the Lord are perfectly in place. They are of infinite
assistance in understanding the whole connection of the passage, and
their position here throws great light on their own meaning. Historical
order is not the question here. The position taken by Israel—by the
disciples—by all, through the rejection of Christ, is the subject of which
the Holy Ghost treats. These passages relate to it, and show very
plainly the condition of the people who had been visited by Jesus, their
true character, the counsels of God in bringing in the heavenly things
through the fall of Israel, and the connection between the rejection of
Christ and the introduction of the heavenly things, and of eternal life,
and of the soul.

Nevertheless the law was not broken. In fact its place was taken
by grace, which, outside the law, did that which could not be done
through the law. We shall see this in going on with our chapter.

belief of the Jews and of the world was driving back to heaven.

The heavenly position of a heavenly people

This very clearly unfolds the position now taken. The testimony of the kingdom rendered in power, leaving Israel without excuse, Jesus passed into another position—into the heavenly one. This was the true subject of joy. The disciples, however, did not yet understand it. But the Person and the power of Him who was to introduce them into the heavenly glory of the kingdom, His right to the glorious kingdom of God, have been revealed to them by the Father. The blinding of human pride, and the Father's grace towards babes, became Him, who fulfilled the counsels of His sovereign grace through the humiliation of Jesus, and were in accordance with His heart who came to fulfil them. Moreover *all things* were given to Jesus. The Son was too glorious to be known, save by the Father, who was Himself only known by the revelation of the Son. To Him must men come. The root of the difficulty in receiving Him lay in the glory of His Person, who was known only to the Father, and this action and glory of the Father, which needed the Son Himself to reveal it. All this was in Jesus there on earth. But He could tell His disciples in private that, having seen in Him the Messiah and His glory, they had seen that which kings and prophets had in vain desired to see. The Father had been proclaimed to them, yet they but little understood it. In the mind of God it was their portion, realized afterwards by the presence of the Holy Ghost, the Spirit of adoption.

The power of the kingdom: the Lord's call to rejoice in a place and name in heaven

We may remark here, the power of the kingdom bestowed on the disciples; their enjoyment at that moment (by the presence of the Messiah Himself, bringing with Him the power of the kingdom which overthrew that of the enemy) of the sight of those things of which the prophets had spoken; at the same time the rejection of their testimony, and the judgment of Israel among whom it was rendered; and, finally, the call of the Lord (while acknowledging in their work all the power that shall establish the kingdom) to rejoice, not in the kingdom thus established on earth, but in that sovereign grace of God who, in His eternal counsels, had granted them a place and a name in heaven, in connection with their rejection on earth. The importance of this chapter is evident in this point of view. Luke constantly brings in the better and unseen part in a heavenly world.

The relationship and glory of the Father and the Son: the lawyer's inquiry as to eternal life

The extent of the dominion of Jesus in connection with this change, and the revelation of the counsels of God that accompanied it, are given us in verse 22, as well as the discovery of the relationships and the glory of the Father and of the Son; at the same time also the grace shown to the humble according to the character and the rights of God the Father Himself. Afterwards we find the development of the change as to moral character. The teacher of the law desires to know the conditions of eternal life. This is not the kingdom, nor heaven, but a part of the Jewish apprehension of the relationship of man with God. The possession of life was proposed to the Jews by the law. It had, by scriptural developments subsequent to the law, been discovered to be eternal life, which they then, at least the Pharisees, attached as such to the observance of that law—a thing possessed by the glorified in heaven, by the blessed on earth during the millennium, which we now possess in earthen vessels; which the law, as interpreted by conclusions drawn from the prophetic books,

proposed as the result of obedience.[32] "The man that
doeth these things shall live by them."

The Lord's answer: the broken law

The lawyer therefore asks *what* it is that he must do.
The answer was plain: the law (with all its ordinances,
its ceremonies, all the conditions of God's government,
which the people had broken, and the violation of which
led to the judgment announced by the prophets—judgment that should be followed by the establishment, on
God's part, of the kingdom in grace)—the law, I say,
contained the kernel of the truth in this respect, and distinctly expressed the conditions of life, if man was to enjoy
it   according   to   human   righteousness—righteousness
wrought by himself, by which he himself should live.
These conditions were summed up in a very few words—to
love God perfectly, and one's neighbor as oneself. The
lawyer giving this summary, the Lord accepts it and repeats the words of the Lawgiver: "This do, and thou shalt
live."   But man has not done it and is conscious that
he has not. As to God he is far away; man easily gets
rid of Him; he will render Him some outward services
and make his boast in them. But man is near; his selfishness makes him alive to the performance of this precept,
which, if observed, would be his happiness—make this
world a kind of paradise. Disobedience to it is repeated
every moment, in the circumstances of each day, which
bring this selfishness into play. All that surrounds him
(his social ties) makes man conscious of these violations
of this precept, even when the soul would not of itself be
troubled about it. Here the lawyer's heart betrays itself.
Who, he asks, is my neighbor?

---

[32] It is to be remarked, that the Lord never used the word *eternal* life
in speaking of the effect of obedience. "The gift of God is eternal life."
If they had been obedient, that life might have been endless; but in
fact and truth, now that sin had entered, obedience was not the way
to have eternal life, and the Lord does not so state it.

Grace manifested and introduced by the Man Christ Jesus: the love of the Good Samaritan

The Lord's answer exhibits the moral change which has taken place through the introduction of grace—through the manifestation of this grace in man, in His own Person. Our relationships with one another are now measured by the divine nature in us, and this nature is love. Man under the law measured himself by the importance he could attach to himself, which is always the opposite of love. The flesh gloried in a nearness to God which was not real, which did not belong to participation in His nature. The priest and the Levite pass by on the other side. The Samaritan, despised as such, did not ask who was his neighbor. The love that was in his heart made him a neighbor to any one who was in need. This is what God Himself did in Christ; but then legal and carnal distinctions disappeared before this principle. The love that acted according to its own impulses found the occasion of its exercise in the need that came before it.

Here ends this part of the Lord's discourses. A new subject begins in verse 38.

Chapters 10: 38 to 11: 13

The two great means of blessing — the Word and prayer

FROM that verse to the end of verse 13 in chapter 11 the Lord makes known to His disciples the two great means of blessing—the Word and prayer. In connection with the Word, we find the energy that attaches itself to the Lord, in order to receive it from Himself, and that leaves everything in order to hear His Word, because the soul is laid hold of by the communications of God in grace. We may remark that these circumstances are connected with the change that had been wrought at that solemn moment. The reception of the Word takes the place of the attentions that were due to the Messiah. These attentions were demanded by the presence of a Messiah on the earth; but, seeing the condition man was in (for he rejected the Saviour), he needed the Word; and Jesus, in His perfect love, will have nothing else. For man, for the glory of God, but one thing was needful; and it is that which Jesus desires. As to Himself, He would go without everything for that. But Martha, though preparing for the Lord, which was right surely, yet shows how much self is inherent in this kind of care; for she did not like to have all the trouble of it.

The prayer taught the disciples

The prayer which He taught His disciples (chap. 11) has respect also to the position into which they came before the gift of the Holy Ghost.[33]   Jesus Himself prayed, as the dependent Man on earth. He had not yet received the promise of the Father, in order to pour it out on His disciples, and could not till His ascension into heaven. These, however, are in relationship with God as their Father. The glory of His name, the coming of His kingdom, were to occupy their first thoughts. They depended on Him for their daily bread. They needed pardon, and to be kept from temptation. The prayer comprised the desire of a heart true to God; the need of the body committed to their Father's care; the grace required for their walk when they had sinned, and in order that their flesh should not manifest itself, that they might be saved from the power of the enemy.

[33] The desire to have a form of prayer given by the Lord has led to a corruption of the text here, recognized by all who have seriously inquired into it (the object being to conform the prayer here to that given in Matthew). It runs thus: "Father, hallowed be Thy name, Thy kingdom come, give us each day our needed bread, and forgive us our sins, for we also forgive every one that is indebted to us, and lead us not into temptation."

Perseverance in prayer to the Father

The Lord then dwells on perseverance, that petitions should not be those of a heart indifferent to the result. He assures them that their prayers should not be in vain; also, that their heavenly Father would give the Holy Spirit to those that asked Him. He puts them into His own relationship on earth with God. Hearkening to God, applying to Him as a Father—it is the whole of practical Christian life.

Chapter 11: 14 to 54

Casting out demons

AFTERWARDS the two great weapons of His testimony are shown forth, namely, casting out demons, and the authority of His Word. He had manifested the power that cast out demons; they attributed it to the prince of the demons. Nevertheless He had bound the strong man; He had spoiled his goods; and this proved that the kingdom of God was indeed come. In such a case as this, God being come to deliver man, everything took its true place; everything was either of the devil, or of the Lord. Moreover, if the unclean spirit had gone out and God was not there, the wicked spirit would come back with others more wicked than himself; and the last state is worse than the first.

The authority of the Word proclaimed: the motives of its hearers

These things were taking place at that time. But miracles were not all. He had proclaimed the Word. A woman, sensible to the joy of having a son like Jesus, declares aloud the value of such a relationship to Him after the flesh; the Lord puts this blessing, as He did

in the case of Mary, on those who heard and kept His
word. The Ninevites had hearkened to Jonah, the queen
of Sheba to Solomon, without even one miracle being
wrought; and a greater than Jonah was now among them.
There were two things there—the testimony plainly set
forth (ver. 33), and the motives which governed those
that heard it. If the true light shone fully into the heart,
there remained no darkness in it. If the perfect truth was
presented according to God's own wisdom, it was the heart
that rejected it. The eye was evil. The notions and
motives of a heart at a distance from God only darkened
it: a heart that had but one object, God and His glory,
would be full of light. Moreover light does not merely
display itself, it enlightens all around it. If God's light
were in the soul, it would be full of it and no part dark.

In the Pharisee's house: judgment consequent on rejection

Verses 37-52. Invited to the Pharisee's house, He
judges the condition of the nation, and the hypocrisy
of its pretended righteousness, putting His finger on the
whited show and inward covetousness and self-seeking,
the making God's law burdensome to others, while neglecting the fulfilment of it themselves, announcing the mission
of the apostles and prophets of the New Testament, the
rejection of whom would fill up the measure of Israel's
iniquity, and bring to a final test those who hypocritically
built the tombs of the prophets their fathers had killed.
And then all the blood, with respect to which God had
exercised His long-suffering, sending testimonies to en-
lighten the people, and which had been shed on account
of those testimonies, should at length be required at the
hand of the rebels. The Lord's words did but stir up the
malice of the Pharisees, who sought to entangle Him
in His talk. In a word we have, on one side, the word
of the testimony set in full relief, in place of the Messiah

fulfilling the promises; and, on the other, the judgment of a nation that had rejected both, and would also reject that which should afterwards be sent to bring them back.

Chapter 12

The disciples encouraged in the place of testimony in the world

CHAPTER 12 puts the disciples into this place of testimony by the power of the Holy Ghost, and with the world opposed to them, after the Lord's departure. It is the Word and the Holy Ghost, instead of the Messiah on the earth. They were neither to fear opposition, nor to trust in themselves, but to fear God and trust to His help; and the Holy Ghost would teach them what to say. All things should be revealed. God reaches the soul: man can only touch the body. Here that which goes beyond present promises, the connection of the soul with God, is put forward. It is coming out from Judaism to be before God. Their calling was to manifest God in the world at all costs—to manifest Him to faith before all things were made manifest. It might cost them dear before men: Jesus would confess them before angels. It is bringing the disciples into the light as God is in it, and the fear of God by the Word and faith when the power of evil was present; all that evil, however secret, would be brought to light.

Nor this only. Blasphemy against the witness given would, in their case, be worse than blaspheming Christ. This might be forgiven (it has been indeed, and will be at the end to the Jews as a nation); but whosoever spoke in blasphemy against the testimony of the disciples blasphemed against the Holy Ghost. It should not be forgiven. But the Lord deals with their heart as well as

with their conscience. He encourages them by three
things: 1st, the protection of Him who counted the hairs
of their head, whatever might be the trials of their faith;
2nd, the fact that, in heaven and before the angels, their
faithfulness to Christ in this painful mission should be
acknowledged by Him; and 3rd, the importance of their
mission, its rejection being more fatally condemning than
the rejection of Christ Himself. God had taken a step,
and a final step, in His grace and in His testimony. The
bringing to light of all things, the care of God, their being
confessed by Christ in heaven, the power of the Holy
Ghost with them—these are the motives and the encour-
agements here given to the disciples for their mission after
the Lord's departure.

The importance of the soul and the future life

That which follows brings out yet more distinctly the
position in which the disciples were placed, according to
the counsels of God, by the rejection of Christ (ver. 13).
The Lord formally refuses to execute justice in Israel.
This was not His place. He deals with *souls,* and directs
their attention to another life which outlasts the present;
and, instead of dividing the inheritance between the
brothers, He warns the multitude to beware of covetousness, instructing them by the parable of the rich man who
was suddenly called hence in the midst of his projects.
What became of his soul?

The great practical principles to guide the disciples'
walk

But, having established this general basis, He turns to
His disciples and teaches them the great practical principles that were to guide their walk. They were not to
think of the morrow, but to trust in God. Moreover they
had no power over it. Let them seek the kingdom of
God, and all that they needed should be added. This

was their position in the world that rejected Him. But besides the Father's heart was interested in them: they were to fear nothing. It was the Father's good pleasure to give them the kingdom. Strangers and pilgrims here, their treasure was to be in heaven; and thus their heart would be there also.[34]   Besides this, they were to wait for the Lord. Three things were to influence their souls: the Father would give them the kingdom, their heart's treasure in heaven, and the expectation of the Lord's return. Until the Lord should come, they were required to watch—to have their lamps burning; their whole position should manifest the effect of the continual expectation of the Lord—should express this expectation. They were to be as men who waited for Him, with their loins girded; and in that case, when all should be according to the Lord's own heart, re-established by His power, and they brought into His Father's house, He would make them sit down, and, in His turn, gird Himself to serve them.

Waiting for Christ Himself the attitude of the heart

It is of all importance to fix the attention of the reader on the point, that what the Lord looks for here is not the holding, however clearly, the Lord's coming at the end of the age, but that the Christian should be *waiting* for Him, in a full profession of Christ, and his heart in spiritual order. Such, the Lord will make to sit down as guests, but such for ever, in His Father's house where He has brought them, and will Himself in love minister the blessing. This love will make the blessings ten thousand-fold more precious, all received from His hand. Love likes to serve, selfishness to be served. But He did not come to be ministered to. This love He will never give up.

[34] Observe here, that the heart follows the treasure. It is not, as men say, Where your heart is, your treasure is—my heart is not in it; but "Where your treasure is, there *will* your heart be also."

Nothing can be more exquisite than the grace expressed in these verses, 35 and 37.[35]

The expectation of the Lord's return with faithfulness in service

On the inquiry of Peter, desirous of knowing to whom Jesus addressed these instructions, the Lord refers him to the responsibility of those to whom He committed duties during His absence. Thus we have the two things that characterize the disciples after the rejection of Christ —the expectation of His return, and service. The expectation, the vigilance that watches with girded loins to receive Him, finds its reward in rest, and in the feast (happiness ministered by Him) at which Jesus girds Himself to serve them; faithfulness in service, by having rule over all that belongs to the Lord of glory. We have seen, besides these special relationships between the walk of the disciples and their position in the world to come, the general truth of the renunciation of the world in which the Saviour had been rejected, and the possession of the kingdom by the gift of the Father.

---

[35] Here we have the heavenly portion of those who wait for the Lord during His absence. It is the character of the true disciple in his heavenly aspect, as service is his place on earth.

Observe also that the Lord was a servant down here. According to John 13 He becomes a servant on ascending to heaven, an Advocate, to wash our feet. In this place He makes Himself a servant for our blessing in heaven. In Exodus 21, if the servant who had fulfilled his service did not wish to go out free, he was brought to the judges, and was fastened to the door by an awl which bored his ear in token of perpetual bondage. Jesus had perfectly accomplished His service to His Father at the end of His life on earth. In Psalm 40 His "ears were digged" (that is, a body prepared, which is the position of obedience: compare Philippians 2). This is the incarnation. Now His service was finished in His life on earth as Man, but He loved us too much— He loved His Father too much in the character of servant—to give it up; and at His death His ear, according to Exodus 21, was bored, and He became a servant for ever—a Man for ever—now to wash our feet; hereafter in heaven, when He shall take us to Himself according to the passage we are considering. What a glorious picture of the love of Christ!

Unfaithful servants and their Master

In that which He says afterwards of the service of those who bear His name during His absence, the Lord also points out those who will be in this position, but unfaithful; thus characterizing those who, while publicly exercising ministry in the Church, should have their portion with the unbelievers. The secret of the evil that characterizes their unbelief would be found in this, that their hearts would put off the return of Jesus, instead of desiring it and hastening it by their aspirations, and serving with humility in the desire of being found faithful. They will say, He is not coming immediately; and, in consequence, they will do their own will, accommodate themselves to the spirit of the world, and assume authority over their fellow-servants. What a picture of that which has taken place! But their Master (for He was so, although they had not truly served Him) would come at a moment when they did not expect Him, as a thief in the night; and, although professing to be His servants, they should have their portion with unbelievers. Nevertheless there would be a difference between the two; for the servant who knew his own Master's will and did not make ready for Him, as the fruit of his expectations, and did not perform his Master's will, should be severely punished; whilst he who had not the knowledge of His will should be punished less severely. I have added "own" to the word "Master," according to the original, which signifies a recognized relationship with the Lord, and its consequent obligation. The other was ignorant of the explicit will of the Lord, but he committed the evil which in any case he ought not to have done. It is the history of true and false servants of Christ, of the professing Church, and of the world in general. But there cannot be a more solemn testimony as to what brought unfaithfulness into the Church, and led to its ruin and approaching judgment, namely, the giving up the present expectation of the Lord's coming.

If it shall be required of persons according to their advantages, who will be so guilty as those that call themselves the ministers of the Lord, if they do not serve Him as in expectation of His return?

The rejected Lord comes to bring conflict and fire on the earth

Nevertheless the Lord, thus rejected, was come to bring conflict and fire on the earth. His presence kindled it even before His rejection, in the baptism of death through which He was to pass, was accomplished. It was not, however, till after this that His love would have full liberty to develop itself in power. Thus His heart, which was love even according to the infinitude of the Godhead, was straitened until the atonement gave free course to it, and to the accomplishment of all the purposes of God, in which His power should be manifested according to that love, and to which this atonement was absolutely necessary as the basis of the reconciliation of all things in heaven and earth.[36]

The evil of the human heart drawn out by the Saviour's presence

Verses 51-53. He shows in detail the divisions that would be the result of His mission. The world would no more endure faith in the Saviour than it did the Saviour Himself, who was its object and whom it confessed. It is well to note how the presence of the Saviour draws out the evil of the human heart. The state described here is in Micah, the description of the most dreadful state of evil conceivable (Micah 7: 1-7).

[36] It is blessed to see here how, let evil in man be what it may, it after all leads to the accomplishment of the counsels of His grace. The unbelief of man drove back divine love into the heart of Christ, unweakened surely, but unable to flow forth and express itself; but its full effect on the cross made it flow forth unhindered, in grace that reigns through righteousness, to the vilest. It is a singularly interesting and blessed passage.

Warning of the existing signs of the times

He then addresses Himself to the people, to warn them of the existing signs of the times in which they lived. He puts this testimony on a twofold ground: the evident signs which God gave; and the moral proofs which, even without the signs, conscience ought to acknowledge, and which thus oblige them to receive the testimony.

Be they ever so blind, they are in the way to the judge. Once delivered up, they should not come out till the chastisement of God was fully executed upon them.[37] (Compare Isaiah 40: 2.)

Chapter 13

The fig-tree in God's vineyard: unfruitfulness followed by just judgment

NOW, at this moment (chap. 13) they reminded Him of a terrible judgment that had fallen upon some among them. He declares to them that neither this case,

---

[37] Let us here, in a note, sum up the contents of these two chapters, that we may better understand the instruction they contain. In the first (12) the Lord speaks, in order to detach the thoughts of all from this world—to the disciples, by directing them to Him who had power over the soul as well as the body, and encouraging them with the knowledge of their Father's faithful care, and His purposes to give them the kingdom; meanwhile they were to be strangers and pilgrims, without anxiety as to all that happened around them—to the multitude, by showing them that the most prosperous man could not secure one day of life. But He adds something positive. His disciples were to expect Him from day to day, constantly. Not only should heaven be their portion, but there they should possess all things. They shall sit at meat, and He will Himself serve them. This is the heavenly portion of the Church at the Lord's return. In service until He comes—service that requires incessant watchfulness: it will then be His turn to serve them. We next have their inheritance, and the judgment of the professing Church and of the world. His teaching produced division, instead of establishing the kingdom in power. But He must die. This leads to another subject—the present judgment of the Jews. They were on the road, with God, towards judgment (chap. 13). The government of God would not manifest itself by distinguishing the wicked in Israel through partial judgments. All should perish, unless they repented. The Lord was cultivating the fig-tree for the final year; if the people of God did not bring forth fruit, it spoilt His garden. To make a pretence of the law in opposition to a God present with them (even He who had given them the law) was hypocrisy. The kingdom was not

nor another which He recalls to their minds, is exceptional: that except they repent, the same thing should
happen to them all. And He adds a parable in order to
make them understand their position. Israel was the
fig-tree in the vineyard of God. For three years He had
been threatening to cut it down; it did but spoil His
vineyard—did but encumber and uselessly cover the
ground. But Jesus was trying for the last time all that
could be done to make it bear fruit; if this did not succeed, grace could but make way for the just judgment of
the Master of the vineyard. Why cultivate that which
only did harm?

to be established by the manifestation on earth of the King's power.
It should grow from a little seed until it became an immense system
of power in the earth, and a doctrine which, as a system, should penetrate the whole mass. On inquiry being made whether the remnant
was numerous, He insists upon entrance by the narrow gate of conversion, and of faith in Himself; for many would seek to enter into the
kingdom and not be able: when once the Master of the house had
risen up and shut the door (that is, Christ being rejected of Israel),
in vain should they say that He had been in their cities. Workers of
iniquity should not enter into the kingdom. The Lord is speaking
here entirely of the Jews. They shall see the patriarchs, the prophets—
Gentiles even from all parts—in the kingdom, and themselves outside.
Nevertheless the accomplishment of the rejection of Christ did not
depend on the will of man, of the false king who sought, by the Pharisees' account, to get rid of Him. The purposes of God, and alas, the
iniquity of man, were fulfilled together. Jerusalem was to fill up the
measure of her iniquity. It could not be that a prophet should perish
except at Jerusalem. But then the putting man to the proof in his
responsibility closes in the rejection of Jesus. He speaks, in touching
and magnificent language, as Jehovah Himself. How many times
this God of goodness would have gathered the children of Zion under
His wings, and they would not! As far as depended on the will of man,
it was complete separation and desolation. And in fact it was so.
All was over now for Israel with Jehovah, but not for Jehovah with
Israel. It was the prophet's part to reckon on the faithfulness of his
God, and—assured that this could not fail, and that, if judgments came,
it would only be for a time—to say, "How long?" (Isaiah 6: 11; Psalm
79: 5.) Distress is complete when there is no faith, no one to say,
"How long?" (Psalm 74: 9.) But here the great Prophet Himself is
rejected. Nevertheless asserting His rights of grace, as Jehovah, He de-
clares to them, unasked, the end of their desolation. "Ye shall not
see Me *until* ye shall say, Blessed is He that cometh in the name of the
Lord." This sudden manifestation of the rights of His divinity, and of
His divinity itself, in grace, when as to their responsibility all was
lost in spite of His gracious culture, is surpassingly beautiful. It is
God Himself who appears at the end of all His dealings. We see from
this recapitulation that chapter 12 gives us the heavenly portion of the
Church, heaven, and the life to come; chapter 13 adding to it (with
verses 54-59 of chapter 12) the government of Israel and of the earth,
with the outward form of that which should replace it here below.

Grace and power displayed to the individual

Nevertheless He acts in grace and in power towards the daughter of Abraham, according to the promises made to that people, and demonstrates that their resistance, pretending to oppose the law to grace, was but hypocrisy.

Outward profession and doctrine in the kingdom of God

However (vers. 18-21) the kingdom of God was to take an unexpected form in consequence of His rejection. Sown by the Word, and not introduced in power, it would grow on the earth until it became a worldly power; and, as an outward profession and doctrine, would penetrate the whole sphere prepared for it in the sovereign counsels of God. Now this was not the kingdom established in power acting in righteousness, but as left to the responsibility of man, although the counsels of God were being accomplished.

The strait gate of the kingdom

At last, the Lord takes up, in a direct manner, the question of the position of the remnant and of the fate of Jerusalem (vers. 22-35).

As He went through the cities and villages, fulfilling the work of grace, in spite of the contempt of the people, some one asked Him whether the remnant, those that would escape the judgment of Israel, should be many. He does not reply as to the number; but addresses Himself to the conscience of the inquirer, urging him to put forth all his energy that he might enter in at the strait gate. Not only would the multitude not enter in, but many, neglecting that gate, would desire to enter into the kingdom and not be able. And moreover, when once the master of the house was risen up, and the door was shut, it would be too late. He would say unto them, "I know

you not, whence ye are." They would plead that He had
been in their city. He would declare that He knew them
not, workers of iniquity: there was "no peace for the
wicked." The gate of the kingdom was moral, real before
God—conversion. The multitude of Israel would not go
in at it; and outside, in tears and anguish, they should
see the Gentiles sitting with the depositaries of the promises; while they, the children of the kingdom, according
to the flesh, were shut out, and so much the more miserable that they had been nigh unto it. And those who
had appeared to be first should be the last, and the last
first.

The last visitation: the fate of Jerusalem foretold

The Pharisees, under pretence of consideration for the
Lord, advise Him to go away. Thereupon He refers
finally to the will of God as to the fulfilment of His work.
It was no question of the power of man over Him. He
should accomplish His work, and then go away; because
Jerusalem had not known the time of her visitation.
Himself, her true Lord, Jehovah, how often would He
have gathered the children of this rebellious city under
His wings, and they would not! Now His last effort in
grace was accomplished, and their house left desolate,
until they should repent, and, returning to the Lord, say
according to Psalm 118, "Blessed is He that cometh in the
name of the Lord." Then He would appear, and they
should see Him.

Nothing can be plainer than the connection and the
force of these conversations. For Israel it was the last
message, the last visitation of God. They rejected it.
They were forsaken of God (though still beloved) until
they should call upon Him whom they had rejected.
Then this same Jesus would appear again, and Israel
should see Him. This would be the day that the Lord
had made.

His rejection—admitting the establishment of the kingdom as a tree and as leaven, during His absence—bore its fruit among the Jews until the end; and the revival amid that nation in the last days, and the return of Jesus on their repentance, will have reference to that great act of sin and rebellion. But this gives rise to further important instructions with regard to the kingdom.

Chapter 14

The rights of grace: hypocrisy judged: the Christian's place in this world

SOME moral details are unfolded in the next chapter (14).[38] The Lord, being invited to eat with a Pharisee, vindicates the rights of grace over that which was the seal of the old covenant, judging the hypocrisy which at any rate broke the sabbath when their own interest was in question. He then shows the spirit of humility and lowliness that became man in the presence of God, and the union of this spirit with love when there was the possession of worldly advantages. By such a walk, which was indeed His own, in opposition to the spirit of the world, one's place there would be lost; the reciprocations of society would not exist: but another hour was beginning to dawn through His rejection, and which in fact was its

[38] Chapters 15 and 16 present the sovereign energy of grace, its fruits, and its consequences, in contrast with all apparent earthly blessing, and God's government on earth in Israel, and the old covenant. The fourteenth, before entering on that full revelation, shows us the place to be taken in such a world as this, in view of the distributive justice of God, of the judgment He will execute when He comes. Self-exaltation in this world leads to humiliation. Self-humiliation—taking the lowest place according to what we are, on the one side, and, on the other, to act in love—leads to exaltation on the part of Him who judges morally. After this we have set before us the responsibility that flows from the presentation of grace; and that which it costs in a world like this. In a word, sin exisiting there, to exalt oneself is ministering to it; it is selfishness, and the love of the world in which it unfolds itself. One sinks morally. It is being far from God morally. When love acts, it is representing God to the men of this world. Nevertheless it is at the cost of all things that we become His disciples.

necessary consequence—the resurrection of the just. Cast out by the world from its bosom, they should have their place apart in that which the power of God should effect. There would be a resurrection of *the just*. Then should they have the reward of all that they had done through love to the Lord and for His name's sake. We see the force with which this allusion applies to the Lord's position at that moment, ready to be put to death in this world.

The great supper of grace: the responsibilities of those entering God's house

And the kingdom, what would then become of it? With reference to it at that moment, the Lord gives its picture in the parable of the great supper of grace (vers. 16-24). Despised by the chief part of the Jews, when God invited them to come in, He then sought out the poor of the flock. But there was room in His house, and He sends out to seek the Gentiles, and bring them in by His call that went forth in efficacious power when they sought Him not. It was the activity of His grace. The Jews, as such, should have no part in it. But those who entered in must count the cost (vers. 25-33). All must be forsaken in this world; every link with this world must be broken. The nearer anything was to the heart, the more dangerous, the more it must be abhorred. Not that the affections are evil things; but, Christ being rejected by this world, everything that binds us to earth must be sacrificed for Him. Cost what it may, He must be followed; and one must know how to hate one's own life, and even to lose it, rather than grow lax in following the Lord. All was lost here in this life of nature. Salvation, the Saviour, eternal life, were in question. To take up one's cross, therefore, and follow Him, was the only way to be His disciple. Without this faith, it were better not to begin building; and, being conscious that the enemy is outwardly much stronger than we are, it must be ascertained whether, come what may, we dare, with settled purpose, go out to meet him by faith in Christ. Everything connected with the flesh as such must be broken with.

Called to witness to God's character as rejected in Christ

Moreover (vers. 34, 35), they were called to bear a peculiar testimony, to witness to the character of God Himself, as He was rejected in Christ, of which the cross was the true measure. If the disciples were not this, they were nothing worth. They were disciples in this world for no other purpose. Has the Church maintained this character? A solemn question for us all!

Chapter 15

The sovereign energy of grace: God's grace contrasted with man's self-righteousness

HAVING thus unfolded the difference in character between the two dispensations, and the circumstances of the transition from the one to the other, the Lord turns (chap. 15) to higher principles—the sources of the one that was brought in by grace.

It is indeed a contrast between the two, as well as the chapters we have been going through. But this contrast rises to its glorious source in God's own grace, contrasted with the miserable self-righteousness of man.

The publicans and sinners draw near to hear Jesus. Grace had its true dignity to those who needed it. Self-righteousness repulsed that which was not as contemptible as itself, and God Himself at the same time in His nature of love. The Pharisees and the scribes murmured against Him who was a witness of this grace in fulfilling it.

I cannot meditate on this chapter, which has been the joy of so many souls, and the subject of so many testimonies to grace, from the time that the Lord pronounced it, without enlarging upon grace, perfect in its application to the heart. Nevertheless I must confine myself here to great principles, leaving their application to those who preach the Word. This is a difficulty that constantly presents itself in this portion of the Word.

God's joy in showing grace

First, the great principle which the Lord exhibits, and on which He founds the justification of God's dealings (Sad state of heart that requires it! Marvellous grace and patience that gives it!)—the great principle, I repeat, is that God finds His own joy in showing grace. What an answer to the horrid spirit of the Pharisees who made it an objection!

It is the Shepherd who rejoices when the sheep is found, the woman when the piece of money is in her hand, the Father when His child is in His arms. What an expression of that which God is! How truly is Jesus the One to make it known! It is on this that all the blessings of man can alone be founded. It is in this that God is glorified in His grace.

The love that seeks: the lost sheep and the lost piece of silver: the work of Christ and that of the Holy Spirit

But there are two distinct parts in this grace—the love that seeks, and the love with which one is received. The first two parables describe the former character of this grace. The shepherd seeks his sheep, the woman her piece of money: the sheep and the piece of silver are passive. The shepherd seeks (and the woman also) until he finds, because he has an interest in the matter. The sheep, wearied with its wanderings, has not to take one

step in returning. The shepherd lays it on his shoulders
and carries it home. He takes the whole charge, happy
to recover his sheep. This is the mind of heaven, whatever the heart of man on earth may be. It is the work of
Christ, the Good Shepherd. The woman sets before us
the pains which God takes in His love; so that it is more
the work of the Spirit, which is represented by that of the
woman. The light is brought—she sweeps the house
until she finds the piece she had lost. Thus God acts in
the world, seeking sinners. The hateful and hating
jealousy of self-righteousness finds no place in the mind
of heaven, where God dwells, and produces, in the happiness that surrounds Him, the reflex of His own perfections.

The love which receives: the prodigal son and the father

But although neither the sheep nor the piece of silver
does anything towards its own recovery, there is a real
work wrought in the heart of one who is brought back;
but this work, necessary as it is for the finding or even
the seeking of peace, is not that on which the peace is
grounded. The return and the reception of the sinner
are therefore described in the third parable. The work
of grace, accomplished solely by the power of God, and
complete in its effects, is presented to us in the first two.
Here the sinner returns, with sentiments which we will
now examine—sentiments produced by grace, but which
never rise to the height of the grace manifested in his
reception until he has returned.

The father's heart: the only measure of the ways of God

First his estrangement from God is depicted. While
as guilty at the moment that he crosses the paternal
threshold, in turning his back upon his father, as when

he eats husks with the swine, man, deceived by sin, is
here presented in the last state of degradation to which
sin conducts him. Having expended all that fell to him
according to nature, the destitution in which he finds
himself (and many a soul feels the famine which it has
brought itself into, the emptiness of all around without a
desire after God or holiness, and often into what is de-
grading in sin) does not incline him towards God, but
leads him to seek a resource in that which Satan's country (where nothing is given) can supply; and he finds
himself among the swine. But grace operates; and the
thought of the happiness of his father's house, and of the
goodness that blessed all around it, awakes in his heart.
Where the Spirit of God works, there are always two
things found, conviction in the conscience and the attraction of the heart. It is really the revelation of God to the
soul, and God is light and He is love; as light, conviction
is produced in the soul, but as love there is the attraction
of goodness, and truthful confession is produced. It is
not merely that we have sinned, but that we have to do
with God and desire to have, but fear because of what He
is, yet are led to go. So the woman in chapter 7.[39] So
Peter in the boat. This produces the conviction that we
are perishing, and a sense, feeble it may be, yet true, of
the goodness of God and the happiness to be found in
His presence, although we may not feel sure of being
received; and we do not remain in the place where we are
perishing. There is the sense of sin, there is humiliation;
the sense that there is goodness in God; but not the sense
of what the grace of God really is. Grace attracts—one
goes towards God, but one would be satisfied to be received as a servant—a proof that, though the heart be
wrought in by grace, it has not yet met God. Progress,
moreover, although real, never gives peace. There is a
certain rest of heart in going; but one does not know what
reception to expect, after having been guilty of forsaking

[39] See page 336.

God. The nearer the prodigal son drew to the house, the more would his heart beat at the thought of meeting his father. But the father anticipates his coming, and acts towards him, not according to his son's deserts, but according to his own heart as a father—the only measure of the ways of God towards us. He is on his son's neck while the latter is still in his rags, before he has had time to say, "Make me as one of thy hired servants." It was no longer time to say it. It belonged to a heart anticipating how it would be received, not to one who had met God. Such an one knows how it has been received. The prodigal arranges to say it (as people speak of an humble hope, and a low place); but though the confession is complete when he arrives, he does not then say, Make me a hired servant. How could he? The father's heart had decided his position by its own sentiments, by its love towards him, by the place his heart had given him towards himself. The father's position decided that of the son. This was between himself and his son; but this was not all. He loved his son, even as he was, but he did not introduce him into the house in that condition. The same love that received him as a son will have him enter the house as a son, and as the son of such a father should be. The servants are ordered to bring the best robe and put it on him. Thus loved, and received by love, in our wretchedness, we are clothed with Christ to enter the house. We do not bring the robe: God supplies us with it. It is an entirely new thing; and we become the righteousness of God in Him. This is heaven's best robe. All the rest have part in the joy, except the self-righteous man, the true Jew. The joy is the joy of the father, but all the house shares it. The elder son is not in the house. He is near it, but he will not come in. He will have nothing to do with the grace that makes the poor prodigal the subject of the joy of love. Nevertheless, grace acts; the father *goes out* and entreats *him* to come in. It is thus that God acted, in the Gospel, towards the Jew. Yet man's righteousness, which is but selfishness and sin, rejects grace. But God will not give up His grace. It becomes Him. God will be God; and God is love.

It is this which takes the place of the pretensions of the Jews, who rejected the Lord, and the accomplishment of the promises in Him.

That which gives peace, and characterizes our position, is not the sentiments wrought in our hearts, although they indeed exist, but those of God Himself.

Chapter 16

The effect of grace on Christian conduct: the unfaithful steward

IN chapter 16, the effect of grace on conduct is presented, and the contrast that exists (the dispensation being changed) between the conduct that Christianity requires with regard to the things of the world, and the position of the Jews in that respect. Now this position was only the expression of that of man made evident by the law. The doctrine thus embodied by the parable is confirmed by the parabolic history of the rich man and Lazarus, lifting up the veil that hides the other world in which the result of men's conduct is manifested.

Man is the steward of God (that is, God has committed His goods to man). Israel stands especially in this position.

But man has been unfaithful; Israel had indeed been so. God has taken away his stewardship; but man is still in possession of the goods to administer them, at least, in fact (as Israel was at that moment). These goods are the things of earth—that which man can possess according to the flesh. Having lost his stewardship by his unfaithfulness, and being still in possession of the goods, he uses them to make friends of his master's debtors by doing them good. This is what Christians should do with earthly possessions, using them for others, having the future in view. The steward might have appropriated the money due to his master; he preferred gaining friends with it (that is, he sacrifices present to future advantage). We may turn the miserable riches of this world into means of fulfilling love. The spirit of grace which fills our hearts (ourselves the objects of grace) exercises itself with regard to temporal things, which we use for others. For us it is in view of the everlasting habitations. "That they may receive you" is equivalent to "that you may be received"—a common form of expression in Luke, to designate the fact without speaking of the individuals that perform it, although using the word *they*.

Earthly and heavenly riches

Observe that earthly riches are not our own things; heavenly riches, in the case of a true Christian, are his own.

These riches are unrighteous, in that they belong to fallen man, and not to the heavenly man, nor had any place when Adam was innocent.

The contrast between the Jewish and Christian dispensations

Now, when the veil is lifted from the other world, the truth is fully brought to light. And the contrast between the Jewish dispensation and the Christian, is clearly unfolded; for Chrisianity reveals that world, and, as to its principle, belongs to heaven.

Judaism, according to God's government on earth, promised temporal blessing to the righteous; but all was in disorder: even the Messiah, the head of the system, was rejected. In a word, Israel, looked at as set under responsibility, and to enjoy earthly blessing on obedience, had entirely failed. Man, in this world, could no longer, on that footing, be the means of bearing testimony to the ways of God in government. There will be a time of earthly judgment, but it was not yet come. Meanwhile, the possession of riches was anything rather than a proof of God's favor. Personal selfishness, and, alas, indifference to a brother in distress at his door, was, instead, the characteristic of its possession among the Jews. Revelation opens the other world to our view. Man, in this world, is fallen, wicked man. If he has received *his* good things here, he has the portion of sinful man; he will be tormented, while the one whom he had despised will find happiness in the other world.

The parabolic history of the rich man and Lazarus: this world and the next

It is not a question here of that which gives title to enter heaven, but of character, and of the contrast between the principles of this world and the invisible world. The Jew made choice of this world; he has lost this and the other also. The poor man whom he had thought contemptible is found in Abraham's bosom. The whole tenor of this parable shows its connection with the question of Israel's hopes, and the idea that riches were a proof of the favor of God (an idea which, false as it may be in every case, is intelligible enough if this world is the scene of blessing under the government of God). The subject of the parable is shown also by that which is found at the end of it. The miserable rich man desires that his brethren might be warned by some one who had risen from the dead. Abraham declares to him the uselessness of this means. It was all over with Israel. God has not again presented His Son to the nation who rejected Him, despising the law and the prophets. The testimony of His resurrection met with the same unbelief that had rejected Him when living, as well as the prophets before Him. There is no consolation in the other world if the testimony of the word to the conscience is rejected in this. The gulf cannot be crossed. A returning Lord would not convince those who had despised the Word. All is in connection with the judgment of the Jews, which would close the dispensation; as the preceding parable shows what the conduct of Christians should be with regard to things temporal. All flows from the grace which, in love on God's part, accomplished the salvation of man, and set aside the legal dispensation and its principles by bringing in the heavenly things.

Chapter 17

Directions for the Christian's walk: the ten lepers

GRACE is the spring of the Christian's walk, and furnishes directions for it. He cannot with impunity (chap. 17) despise the weak. He must not be weary of pardoning his brother. If he have faith but as a grain of mustard seed, the power of God is, so to speak, at his disposal. Nevertheless, when he has done all, he has but done his duty (vers. 5-10). The Lord then shows (vers. 11-37) the deliverance from Judaism, which He still recognized; and, after that, its judgment. He was passing through Samaria and Galilee: ten lepers come towards Him, entreating Him, from a distance, to heal them. He sends them to the priests. This was, in fact, as much as to say, You are clean. It would have been useless to have them pronounced unclean; and they knew it. They take Christ's word, go away with this conviction, and are immediately healed on their way. Nine of them, satisfied with reaping the benefit of His power, pursue their journey to the priests, and remain Jews, not coming out of the old sheepfold. Jesus, indeed, still acknowledged it; but

they only acknowledged Him so far as to profit by His
presence, and remain where they were. They saw nothing
in His Person, nor in the power of God in Him, to attract
them. They remain Jews. But this poor stranger—the
tenth—recognizes the good hand of God. He falls at the
feet of Jesus, giving Him glory. The Lord bids him depart in the liberty of faith—"Go thy way; thy faith hath
saved thee." He has no longer need to go to the priests.
He had found God and the source of blessing in Christ,
and goes away freed from the yoke which was soon to be
judicially broken for all.

The kingdom of God among them with the King in their midst

For the kingdom of God was among them. To those
who could discern it, the King was there in their midst.
The kingdom did not come in such a manner as to attract
the attention of the world. It was there, so that the
disciples would soon desire to see one of those days
which they had enjoyed during the time of the Lord's
presence on earth, but would not see it. He then announces the pretensions of false Christs, the true having
been rejected, so that the people would be left a prey
to the wiles of the enemy. His disciples were not to
follow them. In connection with Jerusalem they would
be exposed to these temptations, but they had the Lord's
directions for guidance through them.

The last days: the return of the Son of Man to earth in discerning, discriminating judgment on earth

Now the Son of Man, in His day, would be like the
lightning: but, before that, He must suffer many things
from the unbelieving Jews. The day would be like that
of Lot, and that of Noe: men would be at ease, following
their carnal occupations, like the world overtaken by the
flood, and Sodom by the fire from heaven. It will be the

revelation of the Son of Man—His public revelation—
sudden and vivid. This referred to Jerusalem. Being
thus warned, their concern was to escape the judgment
of the Son of Man which, at the time of His coming,
would fall upon the city that had rejected Him; for this
Son of Man, whom they had disowned, would come again
in His glory. There must be no looking back; that would
be to have the heart in the place of judgment. Better
lose all, life itself, rather than be associated with that
which was going to be judged. If they should escape
and have their lives spared through unfaithfulness, the
judgment was the judgment of God; He would know how
to reach them in their bed, and to distinguish between
two that were in one bed, and between two women who
ground the corn of the household at the same mill.

This character of the judgment shows that it is not
the destruction of Jerusalem by Titus that is meant. It
was the judgment of God that could discern, take away,
and spare. Neither is it the judgment of the dead, but a
judgment on earth: they are in bed, they are at the mill,
they are on the housetops and in the fields. Warned by
the Lord, they were to forsake all, and to care only for
Him who came to judge. If they asked where this should
be—wherever the dead body lay, there would be the
judgment that would come down like a vulture, which
they could not see, but from which the prey would not
escape.

Chapter 18

Perseverance in prayer the resource of the faithful in the time of judgment

BUT, in the presence of all the power of their enemies
and oppressors (for there would be such, as we have
seen, so that they might even lose their lives), there was

a resource for the afflicted remnant. They were (chap. 18) to persevere in prayer, the resource, moreover, at all times, of the faithful—of man, if he understand it. God would avenge His elect, although, as to the exercise of their faith, He would, indeed, try it. But when He came, would the Son of Man find this faith that waited for His intervention? That was the solemn question, the answer to which is left to the responsibility of man—a question which implies that it could hardly be expected, although it ought to exist. Nevertheless, should there be any faith acceptable to Him who seeks it, it will not be disappointed or confounded.

The twofold presentation of the kingdom in the last days: the day of the judgment of the wicked

It will be observed that the kingdom (and that is the subject) is presented in two ways among the Jews at that time—in the Person of Jesus then present (chap. 17: 21), and in the execution of the judgment, in which the elect ones should be spared, and the vengeance of God be executed in their behalf. On this account, they were only to think of pleasing Him, however oppressive and at ease the world might be. It is the day of the judgment of the wicked, and not that in which the righteous will be caught up to heaven. Enoch and Abraham are more the types of the latter; Noe and Lot, of those who will be spared to live on the earth; only there are oppressors of whom the remnant are to be avenged. Verse 31 shows that they must think only of the judgment and connect themselves with nothing as men. Detached from everything, their only hope would be in God at such a moment.

Characters suitable to the kingdom of God: the spirit of a little child

The Lord then resumes, in verse 9 of chapter 18, the description of those characters which were suitable to the kingdom, to enter it now by following Him. From verse 35 [40] the great transition draws near historically.

Verse 8, then, of chapter 18, ends the prophetic warning with respect to the last days. The Lord afterwards resumes the consideration of the characters which befit the state of things introduced by grace. Self-righteousness is far from being a recommendation for entrance into the kingdom. The most miserable sinner, confessing his sin, is justified before God rather than the self-righteous. He that exalts himself shall be abased, and he that humbles himself shall be exalted. What a pattern and witness of this truth was the Lord Jesus Christ Himself!

The spirit of a little child—simple, believing all that he is told, confiding, of little importance in his own eyes, who must give way to all—this was meet for the kingdom of *God*. What else would He admit?

The rich young ruler and his temporal blessings in contrast with Christ's rejection

Again, the principles of the kingdom, as established by the rejection of Christ, were in full contrast with the temporal blessings attached to obedience to the law, excellent as that law was in its place. Goodness in man there was none: God only is good. The young man who had fulfilled the law in his outward walk is called to leave everything that he may follow the Lord. Jesus knew his circumstances and his heart, and put His finger on the covetousness that ruled him and was fed by the riches he possessed. He was to sell all that he had and follow Jesus; he should have treasure in heaven. The young man went away sorrowful. The riches that, in the eyes of men, appeared to be a sign of God's favor, were but a hindrance when the heart and heaven came in question. The Lord announces at the same time, that

[40] The case of the blind man at Jericho is, as already noted, the beginning (in all the Synoptical Gospels) of the last events of Christ's life.

whosoever should forsake anything that he prized for the sake of the kingdom of heaven should receive much more in this world, and, in the next, life everlasting. We may remark that it is only the principle which is here laid down in reference to the kingdom.

The path to the cross

At last the Lord, on His way to Jerusalem, plainly tells His disciples in private that He was going to be delivered up, to be ill-treated and put to death, and then to rise again. It was the fulfilment of all that the prophets had written. But the disciples understood none of those things.

If the Lord was to make those who followed Him take up the cross, He could not but bear it Himself. He went before His sheep, in this path of self-denial and devotedness, to prepare the way. He went alone. It was a path which His people had not yet trodden, nor indeed could they till after He had done so.

The Lord's last approach to Jerusalem

The history of His last approach to Jerusalem and intercourse with it now commences (ver. 35).

Here then He presents Himself anew as the Son of David, and for the last time; laying on the conscience of the nation His pretensions to that title, while displaying the consequences of His rejection.

Grace near Jericho, the city of the curse, for the blind

Near Jericho,[41] the place of malediction, He gives sight to a blind man who believes in His title of Son of David. So indeed those who possessed that faith did receive their sight to follow Him, and they saw yet greater things than these.

[41] In Luke the coming to Jericho is stated as a general fact, in contrast with His general journey which is in view from chapter 9: 51. In point of fact it was on going out of Jericho He saw the blind man. The general fact is all we have here, to give the whole history, Zacchæus and all, its moral place.

Chapters 19, 20

Grace bringing salvation in Jericho for the lost

IN Jericho He sets forth grace, in spite of the pharisaic spirit. Nevertheless it is as a son of Abraham that He points out Zacchæus, who—in a false position indeed as such—had a tender conscience and a generous heart[42] by grace. His position did not, in the eyes of Jesus, take from him the character of son of Abraham (if it had that effect, who could have been blessed?) and did not bar the way to that salvation which was come to save the lost. It entered with Jesus into the house of this son of Abraham. He brought salvation, whoever might be heir to it.

The Lord's departure predicted: His servant's responsibility in His absence

Nevertheless He does not conceal from them His departure, and the character which the kingdom would assume, owing to His absence. As for them, Jerusalem, and the expectation of the coming kingdom, filled their minds. The Lord therefore explains to them what would take place. *He goes away* to receive a kingdom and to return. Meanwhile He commits some of His goods (the gifts of the Spirit) to His servants to trade with during His absence. The difference between this parable and that in the Gospel by Matthew is this: Matthew presents the sovereignty and the wisdom of the giver, who varies His gifts according to the aptitude of His servants; in Luke it is more particularly the responsibility of the servants, who each receive the same sum, and the one gains by it, in his master's interest, more than the other.

---

[42] I doubt not that Zacchæus sets before Jesus that which he did habitually, before the Lord came to him. Nevertheless salvation came that day to his house.

Accordingly it is not said, as in Matthew, "Enter into the joy of your Lord," the same thing to all, and the more excellent thing; but to the one it is authority over ten cities that is given; to the other, over five (that is to say, a share in the kingdom according to their labor). The servant does not lose that which he has gained, although it was for his master. He enjoys it. Not so with the servant who made no use of his talent; that which had been committed to him is given to the one who had gained ten.

That which we gain spiritually here, in spiritual intelligency and in the knowledge of God in power, is not lost in the other world. On the contrary we receive more, and the glory of the inheritance is given us in proportion to our work. All is grace.

Persistent rejection by the Jews foretold

But there was yet another element in the history of the kingdom. The citizens (the Jews) not only reject the king, but, when he is gone away to receive the kingdom, send a messenger after him to say that they will not have him to reign over them. Thus the Jews, when Peter sets their sin before them, and declares to them that if they repent, Jesus would return, and with Him the times of refreshing, reject the testimony, and, so to say, send Stephen after Jesus to testify that they would have nothing to do with Him. When He returns in glory, the perverse nation is judged before His eyes. The avowed enemies of Christ, they receive the reward of their rebellion.

The Lord's last personal presentation of the kingdom to the people of Jerusalem

He had declared that which the kingdom was—that which it should be. He now comes to present it for the last time in His own Person to the inhabitants of Jerusalem according to the prophecy of Zechariah. This remarkable scene has been considered in its general aspect when studying Matthew and Mark; but some particular circumstances require notice here. All is gathered round His entrance. The disciples and the Pharisees are in contrast. Jerusalem is in the day of her visitation, and she knows it not.

Some remarkable expressions are uttered by His disciples, moved by the Spirit of God, on this occasion. Had they been silent, the stones would have broken out in proclamation of the glory of the rejected One. The kingdom, in their triumphant acclamations, is not simply the kingdom in its earthly aspect. In Matthew it was, "Hosanna to the Son of David," and "Blessed is He that cometh in the name of the Lord; Hosanna in the highest." That was indeed true; but here we have something more. The Son of David disappears. He is indeed the King, who comes in the name of the Lord; but it is no longer the remnant of Israel who seek salvation in the name of the Son of David, acknowledging His title. It is, "Peace in heaven and glory in the highest." The kingdom depends on peace being established in the heavenly places. The Son of Man, exalted on high, and victorious over Satan, has reconciled the heavens. The glory of grace in His Person is established for the everlasting and supreme glory of the God of love. The kingdom on earth is but a consequence of this glory which grace has established. The power that cast out Satan has established peace in heaven. At the beginning, in Luke 2: 14, we have, in the manifested grace, "Glory to God in the highest; peace on earth; the good pleasure [of God] in men." To establish the kingdom, peace is made in heaven; the glory of God is fully established in the highest.

The Lord weeping over Jerusalem: its coming destruction: the vineyard given to others

It will be remarked here that, as He draws nigh to Jerusalem, the Lord weeps over the city. It is not now as in Matthew, where, while discoursing with the Jews, He points it out to them as that which, having rejected and slain the prophets—Emmanuel also, the Lord, who would so often have gathered her children under His wings, having been ignominiously rejected—was now given up to desolation until His return. It is the hour of her visitation, and she has not known it. If only she had, even now, hearkened to the call of the testimony of her God! She is given up into the hands of the Gentiles, her enemies, who will not leave her one stone upon another. That is to say, not having known this visitation of God in grace in the Person of Jesus, she is set aside—the testimony goes no farther—she gives place to a new order of things. Thus the destruction of Jerusalem by Titus is here prominent. It is the moral character of the temple also of which the Lord here speaks. The Spirit does not notice here that it is to be the temple of God for all nations. It is simply (chap. 20: 16) the vineyard is given to others. They fell upon the stone of stumbling then: when it falls on them—when Jesus comes in judgment—it will grind them to powder.

The Sadduces answered: the certainty of the resurrection: future life

In His reply to the Sadducees, three important things are added to that which is said in Matthew. 1st, It is not only the condition of those who are raised, and the certainty of the resurrection; it is an age, which a certain class only, who are accounted worthy of it, shall obtain, a separate resurrection of the just (ver. 35). 2nd, This class is composed of the children of God, as being the children of the resurrection (ver. 36). 3rd, While waiting for this resurrection, their souls survive death; all live unto God, although they may be hidden from the eyes of men (ver. 38).

Characteristics and differences of the accounts of Matthew and Luke of the Lord's prophetic discourse

The parable of the wedding feast is omitted here. In chapter 14 of this Gospel we find it with characteristic elements, a mission to the lanes of the city, to the despised of the nations, which is not in Matthew, who gives us the judgment of Jerusalem instead, before announcing the evangelization of the Gentiles. All this is characteristic. In Luke it is grace, a moral condition of man before God, and the new order of things founded on the rejection of Christ. I will not dwell upon those points which Luke relates in common with Matthew. They naturally meet in the great facts that relate to the Lord's rejection by the Jews, and its consequences.

If we compare Matthew 23 and Luke 20: 45-47, we shall see at once the difference. In Luke the Spirit gives us in three verses that which morally puts the scribes aside. In Matthew their whole position with respect to the dispensation is developed; whether as having a place, so long as Moses continued, or with reference to their guiltiness before God in that place.

Chapter 21

The Character of Luke's Gospel displayed: the present period and its end indicated

THE Lord's discourse in chapter 21 displays the character of the Gospel in a peculiar manner. The spirit

of grace, in contrast with the Judaic spirit, is seen in the
account of the poor widow's offering. But the Lord's
prophecy requires more detailed notice. Verse 6, as we
saw at the end of chapter 19, speaks only of the destruction of Jerusalem as she then stood. This is true also of
the disciples' question. They say nothing of the end of
the age. The Lord afterwards enters upon the duties and
the circumstances of His disciples previous to that hour.
In verse 8 it is said, "The time draweth near," which is
not found in Matthew. He goes much more into detail
with regard to their ministry during that period, encourages them, promises them necessary help. Persecution
should turn to them for a testimony. From the middle of
verse 11 to the end of verse 19 we have details relative
to His disciples, that are not found in the corresponding
passage of Matthew. They present the general state of
things in the same sense, adding the condition of the
Jews, of those especially who, more or less, professedly
received the Word. The whole stream of testimony, as
rendered in connection with Israel, but extending to the
nations, is found in Matthew to the end of verse 14. In
Luke it is the coming service of the disciples, until the
moment when the judgment of God should put an end
to that which was virtually terminated by the rejection
of Christ. Consequently the Lord says nothing in verse
20 of the abomination of desolation spoken of by Daniel,
but gives the fact of the siege of Jerusalem, and its then
approaching desolation—not the end of the age, as in
Matthew. These were the days of vengeance on the Jews,
who had crowned their rebellion by rejecting the Lord.
Therefore Jerusalem should be trodden down by the
Gentiles, until the times of the Gentiles were fulfilled,
that is, the times destined to the sovereignty of the Gentile empires according to the counsel of God revealed in
the prophecies of Daniel. This is the period in which we
now live. There is a break here in the discourse. Its
principal subject is ended; but there are still some events

of the last scene to be revealed, which close the history of this Gentile supremacy.

The end of the age: the coming of the Son of Man

We shall see also that, although it is the commencement of the judgment, from which Jerusalem will not arise until all is accomplished and the song of Isaiah 40 is addressed to her, nevertheless, the great tribulation is not mentioned here. There is great distress, and wrath upon the people, as was indeed the case in the siege of Jerusalem by Titus; and the Jews were also led away captive. Neither is it said, "Immediately after the tribulation of those days." Nevertheless, without designating the epoch, but after having spoken of the times of the Gentiles, the end of the age comes. There are signs in heaven, distress on earth, a mighty movement in the waves of human population. The heart of man, moved by a prophetic alarm, foresees the calamities which, still unknown, are threatening him; for all the influences that govern men are shaken. Then shall they see the Son of Man, once rejected from the earth, coming from heaven with the ensigns of Jehovah, with power and great glory—the Son of Man, of whom this Gospel has always spoken. There the prophecy ends. We have not here the gathering together of the elect Israelites, who had been dispersed, of which Matthew speaks.

Exhortations to watchfulness: the day of distress a token of deliverance to faith

That which follows consists of exhortations, in order that the day of distress may be a token of deliverance to the faith of those who, trusting in the Lord, obey the voice of His servant. The "generation" (a word already explained when considering Matthew) should not pass away till all was fulfilled. The length of the time that has elapsed since then, and that must elapse until the end, is left in darkness. Heavenly things are not measured by dates. Moreover that moment is hidden in the knowledge of the Father. Still heaven and earth should pass away, but not the words of Jesus. He then tells them that, as dwelling on earth, they must be watchful, lest their own hearts should be overcharged with things that would sink them into this world, in the midst of which they were to be witnesses. For that day would come as a snare upon all those who had their dwelling here, who were rooted here. They were to watch and pray, in order to escape all those things, and to stand in the presence of the Son of Man. This is still the great subject of our Gospel. To be with Him, as those who have escaped from the earth, to be among the 144,000 on Mount Zion, will be an accomplishment of this blessing, but the *place* is not named; so that, supposing the faithfulness of those whom He was personally addressing, the hope awakened by His words would be fulfilled in a more excellent manner in His heavenly presence in the day of glory.

Chapter 22

Nearing the end of the Lord's life: the chief priests and Judas: the Passover

IN chapter 22 commence the details of the end of our Lord's life. The chief priests, fearing the people, seek how they may kill Him. Judas, under the influence of Satan, offers himself as an instrument, that they might take Him in the absence of the multitude. The day of Passover comes, and the Lord pursues that which belonged to His work of love in these immediate circumstances. I will notice the points that appertain to the character of this Gospel, the change that took place in immediate and direct connection with the Lord's death.

Thus He desired to eat this last Passover with His disciples, because He would eat thereof no more until it was fulfilled in the kingdom of God, that is, by His death. He drinks wine no more until the kingdom of God shall come. He does not say, until He shall drink it new in the kingdom of His Father, but only that He will not drink it till the kingdom shall come: just as the times of the Gentiles are in view as a present thing, so here Christianity, the kingdom as it is now, not the millennium. Observe also what a touching expression of love we have here: His heart needed this last testimony of affection before leaving them.

The foundation of the new covenant

The new covenant is founded on the blood here drunk in figure. The old was done away. Blood was required to establish the new. At the same time the covenant itself was not established; but everything was done on God's part. The blood was not shed to give force to a covenant of judgment like the first; it was shed for those who received Jesus, while waiting for the time when the covenant itself should be established with Israel in grace.

The disciples' ignorance and innocence

The disciples, believing the words of Christ, do not themselves know, and they ask one another, which of them it could be that should betray Him, a striking expression of faith in all he uttered—for none, save Judas, had a bad conscience—and marked their innocence. And at the same time, thinking of the kingdom in a carnal way, they dispute for the first place in it; and this, in the presence of the cross, at the table where the Lord was giving them the last pledges of His love. Truth of heart there was, but what a heart to have truth in! As for Himself, He had taken the lowest place, and that—as the

most excellent for love—was His alone. They had to
follow Him as closely as they could. His grace recognizes
their having done so, as if He were their debtor for their
care during His time of sorrow on earth. He remembered
it. In the day of His kingdom they should have twelve
thrones, as heads of Israel, among whom they had followed Him.

Sifted by Satan, prayed for by the Saviour

But now it was a question of passing through death;
and, having followed Him thus far, what an opportunity
for the enemy to sift them since they could no longer
follow Him as men living on the earth! All that belonged
to a living Messiah was completely overthrown, and
death was there. Who could pass through it? Satan
would profit by this, and desired to have them that he
might sift them. Jesus does not seek to spare His disciples this sifting. It was not possible, for He must pass
through death, and their hope was in Him. They cannot escape it: the flesh must be put to the test of death.
But He prays for them, that the faith of the one, whom
He especially names, may not fail. Simon, ardent in the
flesh, was exposed more than all to the danger into which
a false confidence in the flesh might lead him, but in
which it could not sustain him. Being however the object
of this grace on the Lord's part, his fall would be the
means of his strength. Knowing what the flesh was,
and also the perfection of grace, he would be able to
strengthen his brethren. Peter asserts that he could do
anything—the very things he should entirely fail in. The
Lord briefly warns him of what he would really do.

The forewarning of change in the absence of the Lord: the enemy's power

Jesus then takes occasion to forewarn them that all
was about to change. During His presence here below,

the true Messiah, Emmanuel, He had sheltered them from all difficulties; when He sent them throughout Israel, they had lacked nothing. But now (for the kingdom was not yet coming in power) they would be, like Himself, exposed to contempt and violence. Humanly speaking, they would have to take care of themselves. Peter, ever forward, taking the words of Christ literally, was permitted to lay bare his thoughts by exhibiting two swords. The Lord stops him by a word that showed him it was of no use to go farther. They were not capable of it at that time. As to Himself, He pursues with perfect tranquillity His daily habits.

Pressed in spirit by that which was coming, He exhorts His disciples to pray, that they enter not into temptation; that is to say, that when the time came that they should be put to the test, walking with God, it should be for them obedience to God, and not a means of departure from Him. There are such moments, if God permits them to come, in which everything is put to the proof by the enemy's power.

At Gethsemane: the perfect, dependent Man

The Lord's dependence as Man is then displayed in the most striking manner. The whole scene of Gethsemane and the cross, in Luke, is the perfect dependent Man. He prays: He submits to His Father's will. An angel strengthens Him: this was their service to the Son of Man.[43] Afterwards, in deep conflict, He prays more

[43] There are elements of the profoundest interest which appear in comparing this Gospel with others in this place; and elements which bring out the character of this Gospel in the most striking way. In Gethsemane we have the Lord's conflict brought out more fully in Luke than anywhere; but on the cross we have His superiority to the sufferings He was in. There is no expression of them: He is above them. It is not, as in John, the divine side of the picture. There in Gethsemane we have no agony, but when He names Himself, they go backward and fall to the ground. On the cross, no "My God, My God, why hast Thou forsaken Me?" but He delivers up His own spirit to God. This is not so in Luke. In Gethsemane we have the Man of sorrows, a Man feeling in all its depths what was before Him, and looking to His Father. "Being in an agony, He prayed more earnestly." On the cross we have One who as Man has bowed to His Father's will, and is in the calmness

earnestly: dependent Man, He is perfect in His dependence. The deepness of the conflict deepens His intercourse with His Father. The disciples were overwhelmed by the shadow only of that which caused Jesus to pray. They take refuge in the forgetfulness of sleep. The Lord, with the patience of grace, repeats His warning, and the multitude arrive. Peter, confident when warned, sleeping at the approach of temptation when the Lord was praying, strikes when Jesus allows Himself to be led as a sheep to the slaughter, and then, alas, denies when Jesus confesses the truth. But, submissive as the Lord was to His Father's will, He plainly shows that His power had not departed from Him. He heals the wound that Peter inflicted on the high priest's servant, and then permits Himself to be led away, with the remark that it was their hour and the power of darkness. Sad and terrible association!

The iniquitous trial: Peter's defection: the Son of Man is the Son of God

In all this scene we behold the complete dependence of the Man, the power of death felt as a trial in all its force; but, apart from that which was going on in His soul and before His Father, in which we see the reality of these two things, there was the most perfect tranquil-

of One who, in whatever sorrow and suffering, is above it all. He tells the weeping women to weep for themselves, not for Him, the green tree, for judgment was coming. He prays for those who were crucifying Him; He speaks peace and heavenly joy to the poor thief who was converted; He was going into Paradise before the kingdom came. The same is seen specially in the fact of His death. It is not, as in John, He gave up His spirit; but, "Father, into Thy hands I commend My spirit." He trusts His spirit in death, as a Man who knows and believes in God His Father, to Him whom He thus knew. In Matthew we have the forsaking of God and His sense of it. This character of the Gospel, revealing Christ distinctively as perfect Man, and the perfect Man, is full of the deepest interest. He passed through His sorrows with God, and then in perfect peacefulness was above them all; His trust in His Father perfect, even in death—a path not trodden by man hitherto, and never to be trodden by the saints. If Jordan overflowed all its banks at the time of harvest, the ark in the depths of it made it a passage dryshod into the inheritance of God's people.

lity, the most gentle calmness towards men [44]—grace that never belies itself. Thus, when Peter denied Him as He had foretold, He looks upon him at the fitting moment. All the parade of His iniquitous trial does not distract His thoughts, and Peter is broken down by that look. When questioned, He has little to say. His hour was come. Subject to His Father's will, He accepted the cup from His hand. His judges did but accomplish that will, and bring Him the cup. He makes no answer to the question whether He is the Christ. It was no longer the time to do so. They would not believe it—would not answer Him if He had put questions to them that would have brought out the truth; neither would they have let Him go. But He bears the plainest testimony to the place which, from that hour, the Son of Man took. This we have repeatedly seen in reading this Gospel. He would sit on the right hand of the power of God. We see also it is the place He takes at present.[45] They immediately draw the right conclusion—"Thou art, then, the Son of God?" He bears testimony to this truth, and all is ended; that is to say, He waives the question, whether He was the Messiah—that was gone by for Israel—He was going to suffer; He is the Son of Man, but thenceforth only as entering into glory; and He is the Son of God. It was all over with Israel as to their responsibility; the heavenly glory of the Son of Man, the personal glory of the Son of God was about to shine forth; and Jesus (chap. 23) is led away to the Gentiles, that all may be accomplished.

[44] It is most striking to see how Christ met, according to divine perfectness, every circumstance He was in. They only drew out the perfectness. He felt them all, was governed by none, but met them—always Himself. This which was always true was wonderfully shown here. He prays with the fullest sense of what was coming upon Him—the cup He had to drink—turns and warns them, and gently rebukes and excuses Peter, as if walking in Galilee, the flesh was weak; and then returns into yet deeper agony with His Father. Grace suited Him with Peter, agony in the presence of God; and He was grace with Peter—in agony at the thought of the cup.

[45] The word "hereafter," in the Authorized Version, should be "henceforth." That is, from this out they would see Him no longer in humiliation, but as the Son of Man in power.

Chapter 23

The guilt of the Gentiles: flagrant injustice

THE Gentiles, however, are not presented in this Gospel as being voluntarily guilty. We see, no doubt, an indifference which is flagrant injustice in a case like this, and an insolence which nothing could excuse; but Pilate does what he can to deliver Christ, and Herod, disappointed, sends Him back unjudged. The will is altogether on the side of the Jews. That is the characteristic of this part of the history in Luke's Gospel. Pilate would rather not have burdened himself with this useless crime, and he despised the Jews; but they were resolved on the crucifixion of Jesus, and require Barabbas to be released—a seditious man and a murderer. (See vers. 20-25.) [46]

The King of the Jews on the cross for the everlasting salvation of souls

Jesus therefore, as He was led to Calvary, announced to the women, who with natural feeling lamented for Him, that it was all over with Jerusalem, that they had to bewail their own fate and not His; for days were coming upon Jerusalem which would make them call those happy who had never been mothers—days in which they would in vain seek refuge from terror and judgment. For if in Him, the true green tree, these things were done, what would become of the dry tree of Judaism without God? Nevertheless, at the moment of His crucifixion, the Lord intercedes for the unhappy people: they knew not what they did—intercession, to which Peter's discourse to the Jews (Acts 3) is the remarkable answer

---

[46] This wilful guilt of the Jews is strongly brought out in John's Gospel also, that is, their national guilt. Pilate treats them with contempt; and there it is they say, "We have no king but Cæsar."

by the Holy Ghost come down from heaven. The rulers among the Jews, completely blinded, as well as the people, taunt Him with being unable to save Himself from the cross—not knowing that it was impossible if He was a Saviour, and that all was taken from them, and that God was establishing another order of things, founded on atonement, in the power of eternal life by the resurrection. Dreadful blindness, of which the poor soldiers were but imitators, according to the malignity of human nature! But the judgment of Israel was in their mouth, and (on God's part) upon the cross. It was the King of the Jews who hung there—abased indeed, for a thief hung by His side could rail on Him—but in the place to which love had brought Him for the everlasting and present salvation of souls. This was manifested at the very moment. The insults that reproached Him for not saving *Himself* from the cross, had His answer in the fate of the converted thief, who rejoined Him the same day in Paradise.

A gross sinner converted by grace on the gibbet: the wickedness of the other thief

This history is a striking demonstration of the change to which this Gospel leads us. The King of the Jews, by their own confession, is not delivered—He is crucified. What an end to the hopes of this people! But at the same time a gross sinner, converted by grace on the very gibbet, goes straight to Paradise. A soul is eternally saved. It is not the kingdom, but a soul—out of the body—in happiness with Christ. And remark here how the presentation of Christ brings out the wickedness of the human heart. No thief would mock at or reproach another thief on the gibbet. But the moment it is Christ who is there, this takes place.

Marks of conversion and remarkable faith: the Lord's reply: the first-fruits of the love that placed them side by side

But I would say a few words on the condition of the other thief, and on the reply of Christ. We see every mark of conversion, and of the most remarkable faith. The fear of God, the beginning of wisdom, is there; conscience upright and vigorous. It is not "and justly" to his fellow, but "*we* indeed justly;" knowledge of the perfect sinless righteousness of Christ as man; the acknowledgment of Him as the Lord, when His own disciples had forsaken and denied Him, and when there was no sign of His glory or of the dignity of His Person. He was accounted by man as one like himself. His kingdom was but a subject of scorn to all. But the poor thief is *taught of God;* and all is plain. He is as sure that Christ will have the kingdom as if He was reigning in glory. All his desire is that Christ should remember him then; and what confidence in Christ is here shown through the knowledge of Him in spite of his acknowledged guilt! It shows how Christ filled his heart, and how his confiding in grace by its brightness shut out human shame, for who would like to be remembered in the shame of a gibbet! Divine teaching is singularly manifested here. Do not we know by divine teaching that Christ was sinless, and to be assured of His kingdom there was a faith above all circumstances? He alone is a comfort to Jesus upon the cross, and makes Him think (in answering his faith) of the Paradise that awaited Him when He should have finished the work that His Father had given Him to do. Observe the state of sanctification this poor man was in by faith. In all the agonies of the cross, and while believing Jesus to be the Lord, he seeks no relief at His hands, but asks that He will remember him in His kingdom. He is filled with one thought—to have his portion with Jesus. He believes that the Lord will re-

turn; he believes in the kingdom, while the King is
rejected and crucified, and when, as to man, there was
no longer any hope. But the reply of Jesus goes farther
in the revelation of that proper to this Gospel, and adds
that which brings in, not the kingdom, but everlasting
life, the happiness of the soul. The thief had asked Jesus
to remember him when He returned in His kingdom. The
Lord replies that he should not wait for that day of
manifested glory which would be visible to the world,
but that this very day he should be with Him in Paradise.
Precious testimony, and perfect grace! Jesus crucified
was more than King—He was Saviour. The poor malefactor was a testimony to it, and the joy and consolation
of the Lord's heart—the first-fruits of the love which
had placed them side by side, where, if the poor thief
bore the fruit of his sins from man, the Lord of glory at
his side was bearing the fruit of them from God, treated
as Himself a malefactor in the same condemnation.
Through a work unknown to man save by faith, the sins
of His companion were for ever put away, they no longer
existed, their remembrance was only that of the grace
which had taken them away, and which had for ever
cleansed his soul from them, making him that moment
as fit to enter Paradise as Christ Himself his companion
there!

Death: the last act of the Lord's life: God reveals Himself

The Lord then, having fulfilled all things, and still full
of strength, commends His spirit to His Father. He commits it to Him, the last act of that which composed His
whole life—the perfect energy of the Holy Ghost acting
in a perfect confidence in His Father, and dependence
upon Him. He commits His spirit to His Father, and
expires. For it was death that He had before Him—but
death in absolute faith which trusted in His Father—

death with God by faith; and not the death that separated from God. Meantime nature veiled itself—acknowledged the departure from this world of Him who had created it. All is darkness. But on the other hand God reveals Himself—the veil of the temple is rent in twain from the top to the bottom. God had hidden Himself in thick darkness—the way into the holiest had not yet been manifested. But now there is no longer a veil; that which has put sin away through perfect love now shines forth, while the holiness of God's presence is joy to the heart, and not torment. What brings us into the presence of perfect holiness without a veil, put away the sin which forbade us to be there. Our communion is with Him through Christ, holy and unblameable before Him in love.

The centurion's confession

The poor centurion, struck with all that had taken place, confesses—such is the power of the cross upon the conscience—that this Jesus whom he has crucified was certainly the righteous Man. I say conscience, because I do not pretend to say that it went any farther than that in the case of the centurion. We see the same effect on the spectators: they went away smiting their breasts. They perceived that something solemn had happened—that they had fatally compromised themselves with God.

The burial of the Lord: everything prepared

But the God of our Lord Jesus Christ, the Father of glory, had prepared everything for the burial of His Son, who had glorified Him by giving Himself up to death. He is with the rich in His death. Joseph, a just man, who had not consented to the sin of his people, lays the Lord's body in a tomb that had never yet been used. It was the preparation before the sabbath; but the sabbath was near. At the time of His death the women—faithful

(though ignorant) to their affection for Him while living
—see where the body is laid, and go to prepare all that
was needed for its embalming. Luke only speaks in general terms of these women: we shall therefore enter on
the details elsewhere, following our Gospel as it presents
itself.

Chapter 24

The resurrection and its many proofs

THE women come, find the stone rolled away, and the
sepulchre no longer containing the body of Him
whom they had loved. While perplexed at this, they see
two angels near them, who ask why they came to seek the
living among the dead, and remind them of the plain
words which Jesus had spoken to them in Galilee. They
go and tell these things to all the disciples, who cannot
believe their account; but Peter runs to the sepulchre,
sees everything in order, and departs, wondering at that
which had come to pass. In all this there was no faith
in the words of Jesus, nor in that which the Scriptures
had spoken. In the journey to Emmaus the Lord connects the Scriptures with all that happened to Himself,
showing to their minds still lingering round the thought
of an earthly kingdom, that according to these Scriptures,
God's revealed counsels, the Christ ought to suffer and
enter into His glory, a rejected and heavenly Christ.
He awakens that ardent attention which the heart feels
whenever it is touched. He then reveals Himself in
breaking bread—the sign of His death: not that this was
the Eucharist, but this particular act was linked with
that event. Then their eyes were opened, and He disappears. It was the true Jesus; but in resurrection. Here
He Himself explained all that the Scriptures had spoken,

and presented Himself in life with the symbol of His death. The two disciples return to Jerusalem.

The Lord had already shown Himself to Simon—an appearance, of which we have no details. Paul also mentions it as the first with reference to the apostles. While the two disciples related that which had happened to them, Jesus Himself stood in their midst. But their minds were not yet formed to this truth, and His presence alarms them. They cannot realize the idea of the resurrection of the body. The Lord uses their confession (very natural, humanly speaking) for our blessing, by giving them the most sensible proofs that it was Himself risen; but Himself, body and soul, the same as before His death. He bids them touch Him, and He eats before their eyes.[47] It was indeed Himself.

The basis of true faith

An important thing remained—the basis of true faith: the words of Christ, and the testimony of Scripture. This He sets before them. But two things were yet required. First, they needed capacity to understand the word. He opens their understanding therefore, that they might understand the Scriptures, and establishes them as witnesses that were not only able to say, "Thus it is, for we have seen it;" but "Thus it must needs have been, for so hath God said in His Word;" and the testimony of Christ Himself was fulfilled in His resurrection.

Grace to be preached among all nations

But now grace was to be preached—Jesus rejected by the Jews, slain and risen again for the salvation of souls, having made peace, and bestowing life according to the

---

[47] Nothing can be more touching than the way in which He cultivates their confidence as that One they had known, the Man, still a true man (though with a spiritual body) as He had been before! "Handle Me and see that it is I Myself." Blessed be God, for ever a Man, the same who has been known in living love in the midst of our weakness.

power of resurrection, the work which cleansed from sin being accomplished, and pardon already granted in thus bestowing it. Grace was to be preached among all nations, that is to say, repentance and pardon to sinners; beginning at that place, with which indeed the patient grace of God still owned a link, through the intercession of Jesus, but which could only be reached by sovereign grace, and in which sin the most aggravated rendered pardon the most necessary, by a testimony which, coming from heaven, must deal with Jerusalem as it dealt with all. They were to preach repentance and remission of sins to all nations, beginning at Jerusalem. The Jew, a child of wrath, even as others, must come in on the same ground. The testimony had a higher source, although it was said "to the Jew first."

The disciples to be endued with power for their mission

But, secondly, something more therefore was needed for the accomplishment of this mission, that is, power. They were to tarry at Jerusalem until they were endued with power from on high. Jesus would send the Holy Ghost whom He had promised, of whom the prophets also had spoken.

The Lord's ascension to heaven characterized by blessing and great joy

While blessing His disciples, heaven and heavenly grace characterizing His relationship with them, Jesus was parted from them, and carried up into heaven; and they returned to Jerusalem with joy.

The great foundation principles of the doctrines and proofs of the resurrection

It will have been remarked that the narrative of Luke is very general here, and contains the great principles on which the doctrines and proofs of the resurrection are founded; the unbelief of the natural heart so graphically painted in the most simple and touching accounts; the disciples' attachment to their own hopes of the kingdom, and the difficulty with which the doctrine of the Word took possession of their hearts, although, in proportion to their realization, their hearts opened to it with joy; the Person of Jesus risen, still a Man, the gracious One they knew; the doctrine of the Word; the understanding of the Word bestowed; the power of the Holy Ghost given—all that belonged to the truth and to the eternal order of things made manifest.

Bethany as the point of contact and connection between Jesus and the disciples

Nevertheless, Jerusalem was still recognized as the first object of grace on earth according to God's dispensations towards her; yet she was not, even as a place, the point of contact and connection between Jesus and His disciples. He does not bless them from Jerusalem, although, in the dealings of God with the earth, they were to tarry there for the gift of the Holy Ghost; for themselves and their relationship with Him He leads them out to Bethany. From thence He had set out to present Himself as King to Jerusalem. It was there that the resurrection of Lazarus took place; there that the family, which present the character of the remnant—attached to His Person, now rejected, with better hopes—in the most striking manner received Jesus. It was thither He retired when His testimony to the Jews was ended, that His heart might rest for a few moments among those whom He loved, who, through grace, loved Him. It was there that He established the link (as to circumstances) between the remnant attached to His Person and heaven. From thence He ascends.

Jerusalem is but the public starting-point of their ministry, as it had been the last scene of His witness. For themselves it was Bethany and heaven which were connected in the Person of Jesus. From thence was the testimony to come for Jerusalem herself. This is the more striking when we compare it with Matthew. There He goes to Galilee, the place of association with the Jewish remnant, and there is no ascension, and the mission is exclusively to the nations. It is a carrying out to them, what was then confined to the Jews and forbidden to be carried further.

NOTE.—In the text I have strictly followed the passage; I add some developments here, connecting this Gospel with the others.

The two distinct parts in the sufferings of Christ

There are two distinct parts in the sufferings of Christ: 1st, that which He suffered from the efforts of Satan—as Man in conflict with the power of the enemy who has dominion over death, but with the sense of what it was from God in view—and this in communion with His Father, presenting His requests to Him; and 2ndly, that which He suffered to accomplish expiation for sin, when actually bearing our sins, made sin for us, drinking the cup which the will of His Father had given Him to drink.

The Lord's temptations in the wilderness and His sufferings at Gethsemane and on the cross

When speaking on the Gospel of John, I shall enter more on the character of the temptations; but I would notice here, that at the commencement of His public life the tempter endeavored to turn Jesus aside by setting before Him the attractiveness of all that which, as privilege, belonged to Him, all that might be agreeable to Christ as Man, as to which His own will might work. He was defeated by the perfect obedience of Christ. He would have Christ, being Son, go out of the place He had taken as servant. Blessed be God he failed. Christ by simple obedience bound the strong man as to this life, and then returning in the power of the Spirit into Galilee spoiled his goods. Putting away sin and bearing our sins was another matter. Satan then departed from Him for a season. In Gethsemane he returns, using the fear of death to throw anguish into the heart of the Lord. And He must needs go through death; and death was not only Satan's power but God's judgment on man, if man was to be delivered from it, for it was man's portion; and He alone, by going down into it, could break its chains. He had become Man, that man might be delivered and even glorified. The distress of His soul was complete. "My soul is exceeding sorrowful, even unto death." Thus His soul was that which the soul of a man ought to be in the presence of death, when Satan puts forth all his power in it, with the cup of God's judgment as yet unemptied in it: only He was perfect in it; it was a part of His perfection put to the test in all that was possible to man. But with tears and supplications He makes His request to Him who had power to save Him from death. For the moment, His agony increases: presenting it to God makes it more acute. This is the case in our own little conflicts. But thus the thing is settled according to perfection before God. His soul enters into it with God; He prays more fervently. It is now evident that this cup—which He puts before His Father's eyes when Satan presents it to Him as the power of death in His soul—must be drunk. As obedience to His Father, He takes it in peace. To drink it is but perfect obedience, instead of being the power of Satan. But it must be drunk in reality; and upon the cross Jesus, the Saviour of our souls, enters into the second phase of His sufferings. He goes under death as the judgment of God, the separation of the soul from the light of His countenance. All that a soul which enjoyed nothing except communion with God could suffer in being deprived of it, the Lord suffered according to the perfect measure of the communion which was interrupted. Yet He gave glory to God—"But Thou art holy, O Thou that inhabitest the praises of Israel." The cup—for I pass over the outrages and insults of men: we may spare them—the cup was drunk. Who can tell the horrors of that suffering? The true pains of death, understood as God understands it, felt—according to the value of His presence—divinely, as by a Man who depended on that presence as man. But all is accomplished; and that which God required in respect to sin is done—exhausted, and He is glorified as to it: so that He has only to bless whosoever comes to Him through a Christ who is alive and was dead, and who lives for ever a Man, for ever before God.

Christ made sin: forsaken of God

The sufferings of Christ in His body (real as they were), the insults and upbraidings of men, were but the preface of His affliction, which, by depriving Him as Man of all consolation, left Him wholly in the place of judgment as made sin, to His sufferings [48] in connection with the judgment of sin, when the God who would have been His full comfort was, as forsaking Him, the source of sorrow which left all the rest as unfelt and forgotten.

---

[48] Psalm 22 is His appeal to God from the violence and wickedness of man, to find Himself there forsaken and only sin in His sight, but perfect there. Christ suffered all from man—hostility, unrighteousness, desertion, denial, betrayal, and then, as trusting in God, forsaking. But what a spectacle, the one righteous Man who did put His trust in Him to have to declare, at the end of His life, openly to all, He was forsaken of God!

JOHN

The peculiar character of John's Gospel

THE Gospel of John has a peculiar character, as every Christian perceives. It does not present the birth of Christ in this world, looked at as the Son of David. It does not trace His genealogy back to Adam, in order to bring out His title of Son of Man. It does not exhibit the Prophet who, by His testimony, accomplished the service of His Father in this respect here below. It is neither His birth, nor the commencement of His Gospel, but His existence before the beginning of everything that had a beginning. "In the beginning *was the Word*." In short it is the glory of the Person of Jesus, the Son of God, above all dispensation—a glory developed in many ways in grace, but which is always itself. It is that which He is; but making us share in all the blessings that flow from it, when He is so manifested as to impart them.

Chapter I

The eternal existence, divine nature and distinct personality of the Word

THE first chapter asserts what He was before all things, and the different characters in which He is a blessing to man, being made flesh. He is, and He is the expression of, the whole mind that subsists in God, the *Logos*. In the beginning He was. If we go back as far as is possible

410

to the mind of man, how far soever beyond all that has had a beginning, He is. This is the most perfect idea we can form historically, if I may use such an expression, of the existence of God or of eternity. "In the beginning *was* the Word." Was there nothing beside Him? Impossible! Of what would He have been the Word? "The Word was *with* God." That is to say, a personal existence is ascribed to Him. But, lest it may be thought that He was something which eternity implies but which the Holy Ghost comes to reveal, it is said that He "was God." In His existence eternal—in His nature divine—in His Person distinct, He might have been spoken of as an emanation in time, as though His personality were of time, although eternal in His nature: the Spirit therefore adds, "In the beginning He was with God." It is the revelation of the eternal *Logos* before all creation. This Gospel therefore really begins before Genesis. The Book of Genesis gives us the history of the world in time: John gives us that of the Word, who existed in eternity before the world was; who—when man can speak of beginning—*was;* and, consequently, did not begin to exist. The language of the Gospel is as plain as possible, and, like the sword of paradise, turns every way, in opposition to the thoughts and reasonings of man, to defend the divinity and personality of the Son of God.

The Creator of all things

By Him also were all things created. There are things which had a beginning; they all had their origin from Him: "All things were made by Him, and without Him was not any thing made that was made." Precise, positive, and absolute distinction between all that has been made and Jesus. If anything has been made, it is not the Word; for all that has been made was made by that Word.

"In Him was light . . . the life of men": shining in darkness

But there is another thing, besides the supreme act of creating all things (an act that characterizes the Word)—there is that which was in Him. All creation was made by Him; but it does not exist in Him. But in Him was life. In this He was in relation with an especial part of creation—a part which was the object of the thoughts and intentions of God. This "life was the light of men," revealed itself as a testimony to the divine nature, in immediate connection with them, as it did not with respect to any others at all.[1] But, in fact, this light shone in the midst of that which was in its own nature [2] contrary to it, and evil beyond any natural image, for where light comes, darkness is no longer: but here the light came, and the darkness had no perception of it—remained darkness, which therefore neither comprehended nor received it. These are the relations of the Word with creation and with man, seen abstractedly in His nature. The Spirit pursues this subject, giving us details, historically, of the latter part.

The manifestation of the Word made flesh: the true Light and its reception

We may remark here—and the point is of importance—how the Spirit passes from the divine and eternal nature

[1] The form of expression in Greek is very strong, as identifying completely the life with the light of men, as co-extensive propositions.

[2] It is not here my object to develop the manner in which the Word meets the errors of the human mind; but, in fact, as it reveals truth on God's part, it also replies, in a remarkable way, to all the mistaken thoughts of man. With respect to the Lord's Person, the first verses of the chapter bear witness to it. Here the error, which made of the principle of darkness a second god in equal conflict with the good Creator, is refuted by the simple testimony that the life was the light, and the darkness a moral condition, without power, and negative, in the midst of which this life was manifested in light. If we have the truth itself, we have no need to be acquainted with error. The voice of the Good Shepherd known, we are sure that none other is of Him. But, in fact, the possession of the truth, as revealed in the Scripture, is an answer to all the errors into which man has fallen, innumerable as they are.

of the Word who was before all things, to the manifestation, in this world, of the Word made flesh in the Person of Jesus. All the ways of God, the dispensations, His government of the world, are passed over in silence. In beholding Jesus on the earth we are in immediate connection with Him as existing before the world was. Only He is introduced by John, and that which is found in the world is recognized as created. John is come to bear witness of the Light. The true Light was that which, coming into the world, shone for all men, and not for the Jews only. He is come into the world; and the world, in darkness and blind, has not known Him. He is come unto His own, and His own (the Jews) have not received Him. But there were some who received Him. Of them two things are said: they have received authority to become the children [3] of God, to take their place as such; and, secondly, they are, in fact, born of God. Natural descent, and the will of man, went for nothing here.

What the Word became on earth

Thus we have seen the Word, in His nature, abstractedly (vers. 1-3); and, as life, the manifestation of divine light in man, with the consequences of that manifestation (vers. 4, 5); and how He was received where it was so (vers. 10-13). This general part, in regard to His nature, ends here. The Spirit carries on the history of

[3] Sons in Paul's writings is the place Christians have in connection with God into which Christ has brought them by redemption, that is, His own relative place with God according to His counsels. Children is that they are of the Father's family. (Both are found in Romans 8: 14-16, and the force of both may there be seen. We cry, "Father," so are children, but by the Spirit we take up the place of grown-up sons with Christ before God.) Up to the end of verse 13, we have abstractedly what Christ intrinsically was and from eternity, and what man was—darkness. This first to the end of verse 5. Then God's dealings, John's place and service; then the Light came, came into the world He had made, and it did not know Him, to His own, the Jews, and they would not have Him. But there were those, born of God, who had authority to take the place of children, a new race.

what the Lord is, manifested as Man on earth. So that, as it were, we begin again here (ver. 14) with Jesus on the earth—what the Word became, not what He was. As light in the world, there was the unanswered claim of what He was on man. Not knowing Him, or rejecting Him where He was dispensationally in relationship was the only difference. Grace in life-giving power then comes in to lead men to receive Him. The world did not know its Creator come into it as light, His own rejected their Lord. Those who were born not of man's will but of God received Him. Thus we have not what the Word was (*en*), but what He became (*egeneto*).

The Word made flesh: the glory of an only Son with the Father

The Word was made flesh, and dwelt among us in the fulness of grace and truth. This is the great fact, the source of all blessing to us,[4] that which is the full expression of God, adapted, by taking man's own nature, to all that is in man, to meet every human need, and all the capacity of the new nature in man to enjoy the expression of all in which God is suited to him. It is more than light, which is pure and shows all things; it is the expression of what God is, and God in grace, and as a source of blessing. And note, God could not be to angels what He is to man—grace, patience, mercy, love, as shown to sinners. And all this He is, as well as the blessedness of God, to the new man. The glory in which Christ was seen, thus manifested (by those who had eyes to see), was that of an only Son with His Father, the one concentrating object of His delight as Father.

These are the two parts of this great truth. The Word, who was with God and who was God, was made flesh;

---

[4] It is indeed the source of all blessing; but the condition of man was such, that without His death no one would have had any part in the blessing. Unless the corn of wheat fall into the ground and die, it abideth alone; but if it die, it bringeth forth much fruit.

and He who was beheld on the earth had the glory of an only Son with the Father.

Grace and truth come in Jesus Christ: God revealed by the Only Son

Two things are the result. Grace (what greater grace? It is love itself that is revealed, and towards sinners) and truth, that are not declared, but *come*, in Jesus Christ. The true relation of all things with God is shown, and their departure from it. This is the groundwork of truth. Everything takes its true place, its true character, in every respect; and the centre to which all refers is God. What God is, what perfect man, what sinful man, what the world, what its prince, Christ's presence brings all out. Grace then and truth are come. The second thing is, that the only Son in the bosom of the Father reveals God, and reveals Him consequently as known by Himself in that position. And this is largely connected with the character and revelation of grace in John: first, fulness, with which we are in communication, and from which we have all received; then relationship.

The fulness of grace and truth received

But there are yet other important instructions in these verses. The Person of Jesus, the Word made flesh, dwelling among us, was full of grace and truth. Of this fulness we have all received: not truth upon truth (truth is simple, and puts everything exactly in its place, morally and in its nature); but we have received that which we needed—grace upon grace, the favor of God abundantly, divine blessings (the fruit of His love) heaped one upon another. Truth shines—everything is perfectly manifested; grace is given.

The witness of John the Baptist to the character and position of the Word made flesh

The connection of this manifestation of the grace of God in the Word made flesh (in which perfect truth also displays itself) with other testimonies of God is then taught us. John bore witness to Him; the service of Moses had quite another character. John preceded Him in his service on earth; but Jesus must be preferred before him; for (humble as He might be) God above all, blessed for ever, He was before John, although coming after him. Moses gave the law, perfect in its place—requiring from man, on God's part, that which man ought to be. Then God was hidden, and God sent out a law showing what man ought to be; but now God has revealed Himself by Christ, and the truth (as to everything) and grace are come. The law was neither the truth, full and entire,[5] in every respect, as in Jesus, nor grace; it was no transcript of God, but a perfect rule for man. Grace and truth came by Jesus Christ, not by Moses. Nothing can be more essentially important than this statement. Law requires from man what he ought to be before God, and, if he fulfils it, it is his righteousness. Truth in Christ shows what man is (not ought to be), and what God is, and, as inseparable from grace, does not require but brings to man what he needs. "If thou knewest the gift of God," says the Saviour to the Samaritan woman. So at the end of the wilderness journey Balaam has to say: "According to this time it shall be said of Jacob and of Israel, What hath God wrought?" The verb "came" is in the singular after grace and truth. Christ is both at once; indeed, if grace were not there He would not be the truth as to God. To require from man what he ought to be was righteous requirement. But to give grace and glory, to *give* His Son was another thing in every respect; only sanctioning the law as perfect in its place.

[5] Indeed it told what man ought to be, not what man or anything actually was, and this is properly truth.

We have thus the character and the position of the
Word made flesh—that which Jesus was here below, the
Word made flesh; His glory *as seen* by faith, that of an
only Son with His Father.   He was full of grace and
truth.   He revealed God as He knew Him, as the only-
begotten Son in the bosom of the Father.   It was not
only the character of His glory here below; it is what
He was (what He had been, what He ever is) in the
Father's own bosom in the Godhead: and it is thus that
He declared Him.   He was before John the Baptist,
although coming after Him; and He brought, in His own
Person, that which was in its nature entirely different
from the law given by Moses.

Here then is the Lord manifested on earth.   His relations with men follow, the positions He took, the characters He assumed, according to the purposes of God, and
the testimony of His word among men.   First of all,
John the Baptist gives place to Him.   It will be remarked
that he bears testimony in each of the parts [6] into which
this chapter is divided—verse 6,[7] in the effect of the
abstract revelation of the nature of the Word; as light,
verse 15, with regard to His manifestation in the flesh;

[6] It will be observed that the chapter is thus divided: 1-18 (this part
is subdivided into 1-5, 6-13, 14-18), 19-28, 29-34 (subdivided into 29-31,
32-34), 35 to the end.   These last verses are subdivided into 35-42,
and 42 to the end.   That is, first, what Christ is abstractedly and intrinsically—John's testimony to Him as light; when come, what He is
personally in the world—John, only forerunner of Jehovah, witness of
Christ's excellency; the work of Christ (Lamb of God, who takes away
the sin of the world, He baptizes with the Holy Ghost, and is Son of God) ;
John gathers to Him; He gathers to Himself.   This goes on till the upright remnant of Israel own Him Son of God, King of Israel; then He
takes the larger character of Son of man.

All the personal characters of Christ, so to speak, are found here and
His work, but not His relative characters, not Christ, not Priest, not
Head of the assembly His body; but Word, Son of God, Lamb of God,
Baptizer with the Holy Ghost; and, according to Psalm 2, Son of God,
King of Israel; and Son of man, according to Psalm 8, whom the angels
serve; God withal, life, and the light of men.

[7] The strictly abstract statement ends in verse 5, and goes by itself.
The reception of Christ as *come into the world* as light introduces John.
We are no longer in what is strictly abstract; though not developing the
object—what the Word became—it is historical as to the reception of the
light, and thus shows what man was, and what he is by grace as born
of God, in respect of the object.

verse 19, the glory of His Person, although coming after John; verse 29, respecting His work and the result; and verse 36, the testimony for the time being, in order that He might be followed, as having come to seek the Jewish remnant.

John's formal testimony to his own office

After the abstract revelation of the nature of the Word, and that of His manifestation in the flesh, the testimony actually borne in the world is given. Verses 19-28 form a kind of introduction, in which, on the inquiry of the scribes and Pharisees, John gives account of himself, and takes occasion to speak of the difference between himself and the Lord. So that, whatever the characters may be that Christ takes in connection with His work, the glory of His Person is ever first in view. The witness is occupied naturally, so to speak, with this, before bearing his formal testimony to the office which he fulfilled. John is neither Elias nor that prophet (that is, the one of whom Moses spoke) nor the Christ. He is the voice mentioned by Isaiah, who was to prepare the way of the Lord before Him. It is not precisely before the Messiah, although He was that; neither is it Elias before the day of Jehovah, but the voice in the wilderness before the Lord (Jehovah) Himself. Jehovah was coming. It is this consequently of which he speaks. John baptized indeed unto repentance; but there was already One, unknown, among them, who, coming after him, was yet his superior, whose shoe's latchet he was not worthy to unloose.

The glorious work of Christ and its result

We have next the direct testimony of John, when he sees Jesus coming to him. He points Him out, not as the Messiah, but according to the whole extent of His work as enjoyed by us in the everlasting salvation He has accomplished, and the full result of the glorious work by which it was accomplished. He is the Lamb of God, one whom God alone could furnish, and was for God, and according to His mind, who takes away the sin (not the sins) of the world. That is to say, He restores (not all the wicked, but) the foundations of the world's relations with God. Since the fall, it is indeed sin—whatever may be His dealings [8]—that God had to consider in His relations with the world. The result of Christ's work shall be, that this will no longer be the case; His work shall be the eternal basis of these relations in the new heavens and the new earth, sin being entirely put aside as such. We know this by faith before the public result in the world.

Although a Lamb for the sacrifice, He is preferred before John the Baptist, for He was before him. The Lamb to be slain was Jehovah Himself.

The place and subject of the testimony

In the administration of the ways of God, this testimony was to be borne in *Israel*, although its subject was the Lamb whose sacrifice reached to the sin of the *world*, and the Lord, Jehovah. John had not known Him personally, but He was the one and only object of his mission.

Jesus sealed by the Holy Spirit, recognized and proclaimed as the Son of God

But this was not all. He had made Himself Man, and as Man had received the fulness of the Holy Ghost, who had descended upon Him and abode upon Him; and the

---

[8] As the flood, law, grace. There was a paradise of innocence, then a world of sin, by-and-by a kingdom of righteousness, finally a world (new heavens and new earth) wherein dwelleth righteousness. But it is everlasting righteousness, and founded on that work of the Lamb of God which can never lose its value. It is an immutable state of things. The Church or assembly is something above and apart from all this, though revealed in it.

Man thus pointed out, and sealed on the part of the Father, was Himself to baptize with the Holy Ghost. At the same time He was pointed out by the descent of the Holy Ghost in another character, to which John therefore bears testimony. Thus subsisting and seen and sealed on the earth, He was the Son of God. John recognizes Him and proclaims Him as such.

The effect of John's testimony to attach the remnant to Jesus, the one centre of gathering

Then comes what may be called the direct exercise and effect of his ministry at that time. But it is always the Lamb of whom he speaks; for that was the object, the design of God, and it is that which we have in this Gospel, although Israel is recognized in its place; for the nation held that place from God.

The naming of Simon, an act of authority

Upon this the disciples of John [9] follow Christ to His abode. The effect of John's testimony is to attach the remnant to Jesus, the centre of their gathering. Jesus does not refuse it, and they accompany Him. Nevertheless this remnant—how far soever the testimony of John might extend—do not, in fact, go beyond the recognition of Jesus as the Messiah. This was the case, historically; [10] but Jesus knew them thoroughly, and declares the character of Simon as soon as he comes to Him, and gives him his appropriate name. This was an act of authority which proclaimed Him the head and centre of the whole system. God can bestow names; He knows all things. He gave this right to Adam, who exercised it according to

[9] Note, it is not on his public testimony, but on the expression of his heart addressed to no one, which they heard.

[10] A principle of the deepest interest to us, as the effect of grace. In receiving Jesus we receive all that He is; notwithstanding that at the moment we may only perceive in Him that which is the least exalted part of His glory.

God with regard to all that was put under him as well as in the case of his wife. Great kings, who claim this power, have done the same. Eve sought to do it, but she was mistaken; although God can give an understanding heart which, under His influence, speaks aright in this respect. Now Christ does so here, with authority and with all knowledge, the moment the case presents itself.

Nathanael, a figure of the remnant, at first rejecting then confessing the Lord as Son of God and King of Israel: the Lord's declaration of Himself as Son of Man

Verse 43.[11] We have next the immediate testimony of Christ Himself and of His followers. In the first place, on repairing to the scene of His earthly pilgrimage, according to the prophets, He calls others to follow Him. Nathanael, who begins by rejecting one who came from Nazareth, sets before us, I doubt not, the remnant of the last days (the testimony to which the gospel of grace belongs came first, verses 29-34). We see him at first rejecting the despised of the people, and under the fig-tree, which represents the nation of Israel; as the fig-tree which was to bear no more fruit, represents Israel under the old covenant. But Nathanael is the figure of a remnant, seen and known by the Lord, in connection with Israel. The Lord who thus manifested Himself to his heart and conscience is confessed as Son of God and King of Israel. This is formally the faith of the spared rem-

---

[11] These verses 38 and 43 take in the two characters in which we have to do with Christ. He receives them and they abide with Him, and He calls upon them to follow Him. We have no world where we can abide, no centre in it which gathers round itself those rightly disposed by grace. No prophet, no servant of God could. Christ is the one centre of gathering in the world. Then following supposes that we are not in God's rest. In Eden no following was called for. In heaven there will be none. It is perfect joy and rest where we are. In Christ we have a divine object, giving us a clear path through a world in which we cannot rest with God, for sin is there.

nant of Israel in the last days according to Psalm 2. But those who thus received Jesus when He was on earth should see yet greater things than those which had convinced them. Moreover thenceforth [12] they should see the angels of God ascending and descending upon the Son of Man. He who by His birth had taken His place among the children of men would, by that title, be the object of service to the most excellent of God's creatures. The expression is emphatic. The angels of God Himself should be in the service of the Son of Man. So that the remnant of Israel without guile acknowledges Him to be the Son of God and King of Israel; and the Lord declares Himself also to be the Son of Man—in humiliation indeed, but the object of service to the angels of God. Thus we have the Person and the titles of Jesus, from His eternal and divine existence as the Word, to His millennial place as King of Israel and Son of Man;[13] which He already was as born into this world, but which will be realized when He returns in His glory.

Review of Chapter I

Before going farther, let us review some points in this chapter. The Lord is revealed as the Word—as God and with God—as light—as life: secondly, as the Word made flesh, having the glory of an only Son with His Father— as such He is full of grace and truth come by Him, of His fulness we have all received, and He has declared the Father (compare chap. 14)—the Lamb of God—the One on whom the Holy Ghost could descend, and who bap-

---

[12] Not "hereafter." Many authorities leave the word out.

[13] Except what concerns the assembly and Israel. Here, He is not High Priest, He is not Head of the Body, He is not revealed as the Christ. John does not give what shows man in heaven, but God in man on earth —not what is heavenly as gone up, but what is divine here. Israel is looked on all through as rejected. The disciples own Him as the Christ, but He is not so proclaimed.

tized with the Holy Ghost—the Son of God:[14] thirdly, His work what He does, Lamb of God taking away sin, and Son of God and King of Israel. This closes the revelation of His Person and work. Then verses 35-42 John's ministry, but where Jesus, as He alone could, becomes the gathering centre. Verse 43, Christ's ministry, in which He calls to follow Him, which, with verses 38, 39, give His double character as the one attractive point in the world; with this His entire humiliation, but owned through a divine testimony reaching the remnant as according to Psalm 2, but the taking His title of Son of Man according to Psalm 8—the Son of Man: we may say, all His personal titles. His relationship to the assembly is not here, nor His function as Priest: but that which belongs to His Person, and the connection of man with God in this world. Thus, besides His divine nature, it is all that He was and will be in this world: His heavenly place and its consequences to faith are taught elsewhere, and barely alluded to, when necessary, in this Gospel.

The character and effect of heart-testimony to Christ

Observe that, in preaching Christ, in a way to a certain degree complete, the heart of the hearer may truly believe and attach itself to Him, though investing Him with a character which the condition of soul cannot yet go beyond, and while ignorant of the fulness in which He has been revealed. Indeed where it is real, the testimony, however exalted in character, meets the heart where it is. John says, "Behold the Lamb of God!" "We have found the Messiah," say the disciples who followed Jesus on John's testimony.

---

[14] Here He is seen as the Son of God in this world; in verse 14, He is in the glory of an only Son with His Father; and verse 18, He is so in the bosom of His Father.

Note also, that the expression of what was in John's heart had greater effect than a more formal, more doctrinal testimony. He beheld Jesus, and exclaims, "Behold the Lamb of God!" The disciples heard him, and followed Jesus. It was, no doubt, his proper testimony on God's part, Jesus being there; but it was not a doctrinal explanation like that of the preceding verses.

Chapter 2

The third testimony to Christ at the marriage feast: millennial blessing

THE two testimonies to Christ that were to be borne in this world, both gathering to Him as centre, had been borne; that of John, and that of Jesus taking His place in Galilee with the remnant—the two days of God's dealings with Israel here below.[15] The third day we find in chapter 2. A marriage takes place in Galilee. Jesus is there; and the water of purification is changed into the wine of joy for the marriage-feast. Afterwards at Jerusalem He cleanses the temple of God with authority, executing judgment on all those who profaned it. In principle these are the two things that characterize His millennial position. Doubtless these things took place historically; but, as introduced here and in this manner, they have evidently a wider meaning. Besides, why the third day? After what? Two days of testimony had taken place—that of John, and that of Jesus; and now

[15] Remark here, that Jesus accepts the place of that centre round which souls are to be gathered—a very important principle. None else could hold this place. It was a divine one. The world was all wrong, without God, and a new gathering out of it was to be made round Him. Next, He furnishes the path in which man was to walk—"Follow Me." Adam in paradise needed no path. Christ gives a divinely-ordered one, in a world where of itself there could not be a right one, for its whole condition was the fruit of sin. Thirdly, He reveals man in His Person as the glorious Head over all, whom the highest creatures serve.

blessing and judgment are accomplished. In Galilee the remnant had their place; and it is the scene of blessing, according to Isaiah 9—Jerusalem is that of judgment. At the feast He would not know His mother: this was the link of His natural relation with Israel, which, looking at Him as born under the law, was His mother. He separates Himself from her to accomplish blessing. It is only in testimony therefore in Galilee, for the moment. It is when He returns that the good wine will be for Israel—true blessing and joy at the end. Nevertheless He still abides with His mother, whom, as to His work, He did not acknowledge. And this also was the case with regard to His connection with Israel.

The Son of God in His Father's house

Afterwards, in judging the Jews and judicially cleansing the temple, He presents Himself as the Son of God. It is His Father's house. The proof of this which He gives is His resurrection, when the Jews should have rejected and crucified Him. Moreover He was not only the Son: it was God who was there—not in the temple. It was empty—that house built by Herod. The body of Jesus was now the true temple. Sealed by His resurrection, the Scriptures and the Word of Jesus were of divine authority to the disciples, as speaking of Him according to the intention of the Spirit of God.

The earthly revelation of Christ closed: heavenly things opened

This subdivision of the book ends here. It closes the earthly revelation of Christ including His death; but even so it is the sin of the world. Chapter 2 gives the millennium; chapter 3 is the work in and for us which qualifies for the kingdom on earth or heaven; and the work for us, closing Messiah's connection with the Jews, opens the

heavenly things by the lifting up of the Son of Man—
divine love and eternal life.

Man's natural state as lost manifested

The miracles that He wrought convinced many as to
their natural understanding. No doubt it was sincerely;
but a just human conclusion. But another truth now
opens. Man, in his natural state,[16] was really incapable
of receiving the things of God; not that the testimony
was insufficient to convince him, nor that he was never
convinced: many were so at this time; but Jesus did not
commit Himself to them. He knew what man was. When
convinced, his will, his nature, was not altered. Let the
time of trial come, and he would show himself as he
was, alienated from God, and even His enemy. Sad but

[16] Observe, that the state of man is here manifested fully and thoroughly. Supposing him to be outwardly righteous according to the
law, and to believe in Jesus according to sincere natural convictions, he
clothes himself with this, in order to hide from himself what he really is.
He does not know himself at all. What he is remains untouched. And
he is a sinner. But this leads us to another observation. There are
two great principles from Paradise itself—responsibility and life. Man
can never disentangle them, till he learns that he is lost, and that no
good exists in him. Then he is glad to know that there is a source of
life and pardon outside himself. It is this which is shown us here.
There must be a new life; Jesus does not instruct a nature which is
only sin. These two principles run through Scripture in a remarkable
way: first, as stated, in Paradise, responsibility and life in power. Man
took of one tree, failing in responsibility, and forfeited life. The law
gave the measure of responsibility when good and evil were known, and
promised life on the ground of doing what it required, satisfying responsibility. Christ comes, meets the need of man's failure in responsibility, and is, and gives, eternal life. Thus, and thus only, can the
question be met, and the two principles reconciled.

Moreover two things are presented in Him to reveal God. He knows
man, and all men. What a knowledge in this world! A prophet knows
that which is revealed to him; he has, in that case, divine knowledge.
But Jesus knows all men in an absolute way. He is God. But when
once He has introduced life in grace, He speaks of another thing; He
speaks that which He knows, and testifies that which He has seen. Now
He knows God His Father in heaven. He is the Son of Man who is in
heaven. He knows man divinely; but He knows God and all His glory
divinely also.

What a magnificent picture, or, rather should I say, revelation, of
that which He is for us! For it is here as Man that He tells us this;
and also, in order that we may enter into it and enjoy it, He becomes
the sacrifice for sin according to the eternal love of God His Father.

too true testimony! The life, the death, of Jesus proves it. He knew it when He began His work. This did not make His love grow cold; for the strength of that love was in itself.

Chapter 3

Nicodemus' sense of need: the necessity of new birth

BUT there was a man—and that a Pharisee—who was not satisfied with this inoperative conviction. His conscience was reached. Seeing Jesus, and hearing His testimony, had produced a sense of need in his heart. It is not the knowledge of grace, but it is with respect to man's condition a total change. He knows nothing of the truth, but he has seen that it is in Jesus, and he desires it. He has also at once an instinctive sense that the world will be against him; and he comes by night. The heart fears the world as soon as it has to do with God; for the world is opposed to Him. The friendship of the world is enmity against God. This sense of need made the difference in the case of Nicodemus. He had been convinced like the others. Accordingly he says, "*We* know that Thou art a teacher come from God." And the source of this conviction was the miracles. But Jesus stops him short; and that on account of the true need felt in the heart of Nicodemus. The work of blessing was not to be wrought by teaching the *old* man. Man needed to be renewed in the source of his nature, without which he could not see the kingdom.[17] The things of God are spiritually discerned; and man is carnal, he has not the Spirit. The Lord does not go beyond the kingdom—which, moreover, was not the law—for Nicodemus ought to have known

---

[17] That is, as it was then come. They saw the carpenter's Son. In glory, of course, every eye on earth shall see it.

something about the kingdom. But He does not begin to
teach the Jews as a prophet under the law. He presents
the kingdom itself; but to see it, according to His testimony, a man must be born again. But the kingdom as
thus come in the carpenter's Son could not be seen without a wholly new nature, it struck no chord of man's
comprehension or Jews' expectation, though testimony
to it was amply given in word and work: as to entering
and having a part in it there is more development as to
the how. Nicodemus sees no farther than the flesh.

The communication of new life through the Word of God and the Spirit

The Lord explains Himself. Two things were necessary
—to be born of water, and of the Spirit. Water cleanses.
And, spiritually, in his affections, heart, conscience,
thoughts, actions, &c., man lives, and in practice is
morally purified, through the application, by the power
of the Spirit, of the Word of God, which judges all
things, and works in us livingly new thoughts and affections. This is the water; it is withal the death of the
flesh. The true water which cleanses in a Christian way
came forth from the side of a dead Christ. He came by
water and blood, in the power of cleansing and of expiation. He sanctifies the assembly by cleansing it through
the washing of water by the Word. "Ye are clean through
the Word which I have spoken unto you." It is therefore the mighty Word of God which, since man must be
born again in the principle and source of his moral being,
judges, as being death, all that is of the flesh.[18]   But

---

[18] Observe here that baptism, instead of being the sign of the gift of
life, is the sign of death. We are baptized to His death. In coming
up out of the water, we begin a new life in resurrection (all that belonged to the natural man being reckoned to be dead in Christ, and
passed away for ever). "Ye are dead;" and "he that is dead is freed
[justified] from sin." But we live also and have a good conscience by
the resurrection of Jesus Christ. Thus Peter compares baptism to the
deluge, through which Noah was saved (*diesothe*), but which destroyed
the old world, that had, as it were, a new life when it emerged from the
flood.

there is in fact the communication of a new life; that which is born of the Spirit is spirit, is not flesh, has its nature from the Spirit. It is not the Spirit—*that* would be an incarnation; but this new life is spirit. It partakes of the nature of its origin. Without this, man cannot enter into the kingdom. But this is not all. If it was a necessity for the Jew, who already was nominally a child of the kingdom, for here we deal with what is essential and true, it was also a sovereign act of God, and consequently it is accomplished wherever the Spirit acts in this power. "So is every one that is born of the Spirit." This in principle opens the door to the Gentiles.

Heavenly things revealed by the Son of Man

Nevertheless Nicodemus, as a master of Israel, ought to have understood this. The prophets had declared that Israel was to undergo this change, in order to enjoy the fulfilment of the promises (see Ezek. 36), which God had given them with regard to their blessing in the holy land. But Jesus spoke of these things in an immediate way, and in connection with the nature and the glory of God Himself. A master in Israel ought to have known that which the sure Word of prophecy contained. The Son of God declared that which He knew, and that which He had seen with His Father. The defiled nature of man could not be in relationship with Him who revealed Himself in heaven whence Jesus came. The glory (from the fulness of which He came, and which formed therefore the subject of His testimony as having seen it, and from which the kingdom had its origin) could have nothing in it that was defiled. They must be born again to possess it. He bore testimony therefore, as having come from above and knowing that which was suitable to God His Father. Man did not receive His testimony. Convinced outwardly by miracles he might be; but to receive that which was befitting the presence of God was another thing. And if Nicodemus could not receive the truth in its connection with the earthly part of the kingdom, of which even the prophets had spoken, what would he and the other Jews do if Jesus spoke of heavenly things? Nevertheless no one could learn anything about them by any other means. No one had gone up there and come down again to bring back word. Jesus only, in virtue of what He was, could reveal them—the Son of Man on earth, existing at the same time in heaven, the manifestation to men of that which was heavenly, of God Himself in man—as God being in heaven and everywhere—as the Son of Man being before the eyes of Nicodemus and of all. Nevertheless He was to be crucified, and thus lifted up from the world to which He had come as the manifestation of the love of God in all His ways and of God Himself, and so only could the door be opened for sinful men into heaven, so only a link formed for man with it.

The necessity of the death of the Son of Man as atonement for sin

For this brought out another fundamental truth. If heaven was in question, something more was needed than being born again. Sin existed. It must be put away for those who should have eternal life. And if Jesus, coming down from heaven, was come to impart this eternal life to others, He must, in undertaking this work, put sin away—be thus made sin—in order that the dishonor done to God should be washed away, and the truth of His character (without which there is nothing sure or good, or righteous) maintained. The Son of Man must be lifted up, even as the serpent was lifted up in the wilderness, that the curse, under which the people were dying, might be removed. His divine testimony rejected, man, as he was down here, showed himself to be incapable of receiving blessing from above. He must be redeemed, his sin expiated and put away; he must be treated according to the reality of his condition, and according to the character of God who cannot deny Himself. Jesus in grace undertook to do this. *It was necessary* that the Son of Man should be lifted up, rejected from the earth by man, accomplishing the atonement before the God of righteousness. In a word, Christ comes with the knowledge of what heaven is and divine glory. In order that man might share it, the Son of Man must die—must take the place of expiation—outside the earth.[19] Observe here the deep and glorious character of that which Jesus brought with Him, of the revelation He made.

The gift of God's Son and the gift of eternal life to all believers

The cross, and the absolute separation between man on earth and God—this is the meeting-place of faith and God; for there is at once the truth of man's condition, and the love that meets it. Thus, in approaching the holy place from the camp, the first thing they met on going through the gate to the court was the altar. It presented itself to every one that quitted the world without, and entered in. Christ, lifted up from the earth, draws all men to Him. But if (owing to man's state of alienation and guilt) it *needed* that the Son of Man should be lifted up from the earth, in order that whosoever believes in Him should have everlasting life, there was another aspect of this same glorious fact; God had so loved the world that He had given His only-begotten Son, that whosoever believes in Him should have everlasting life. On the cross we see the necessity morally of the death of the Son of Man; we see the ineffable gift

---

[19] On the cross, Christ is not on the earth, but lifted up from it, rejected ignominiously by man, but withal through this presented as a victim on the altar to God.

of the Son of God. These two truths unite in the common object of the gift of eternal life to all believers. And if it was to *all* believers, it was a question of man, of God, and of heaven, and went outside the promises made to the Jews, and the limits of God's dealings with that people. For God sent His Son *into the world*, not to condemn it, but to save it. But salvation is by faith; and he who believes in the coming of the Son, putting all things now to the test, is not condemned (his state is decided thereby); he who believes not is condemned already, he has not believed in the only-begotten Son of God, he has manifested his condition.

God's just condemnation: the love of darkness, proof of evil works

And this is the thing that God lays to their charge. Light is come into the world, and they have *loved* darkness because their works were evil. Could there be a more just subject of condemnation? It was no question of their not finding pardon, but of their preferring darkness to light that they might continue in sin.

The contrast between John the Baptist and Christ

The rest of the chapter presents the contrast between the positions of John and of Christ. They are both before the eye. The one is the faithful friend of the Bridegroom, living only for Him; the other is the Bridegroom, to whom all belongs: the one, in himself, an earthly man, great as might be the gift he had received from heaven; the other from heaven Himself, and above all. The bride was His. The friend of the Bridegroom, hearing His voice, was full of joy. Nothing more beautiful than this expression of John the Baptist's heart, inspired by the Lord's presence, near enough to Jesus to be glad and rejoice that Jesus was all. Thus it ever is.

John's testimony and that of the One from heaven

With respect to the testimony, John bore witness in connection with earthly things. For that end he was sent. He who Himself came from heaven was above all, and bore witness of heavenly things, of that which He had seen and heard. No one received His testimony. Man was not of heaven. Without grace one believes according to one's own thoughts. But in speaking as a Man on the earth, Jesus spoke the words of God; and he who received His testimony set to his seal that God was true. For the Spirit is not given by measure. As a witness, the testimony of Jesus was the testimony of God Himself; His words, the words of God. Precious truth! Moreover, He was the Son,[20] and the Father loved Him, and had given all things into His hand. This is another glorious title of Christ, another aspect of His glory. But the consequences of this for man were eternal. It was not almighty help to pilgrims, nor faithfulness to promises, so that His people could trust in Him in spite of all. It was the quickening, life-giving Son of the Father. All was comprised in it. "He who believeth in the Son hath everlasting life; he who believeth not shall not see life." He remains in his guilt. The wrath of God *abides* on him.

Summary of Chapter 3

All this is a kind of introduction. The ministry of the Lord, properly so called, comes after. John (ver. 24) was not yet cast into prison. It was not till after that event that the Lord began His public testimony. The chapter we have been considering explains what His ministry was, the character in which He came, His position, the glory of His Person, the character of the

---

[20] The question presents itself naturally, where John's testimony closes and the evangelist's begins. The last two verses, I apprehend, are the evangelist's.

testimony He bore, the position of man in connection
with the things of which He spake, beginning with the
Jews, and going on, by the new birth, the cross, and the
love of God, to His rights as come into the world, and
the supreme dignity of His own Person, to His properly
divine testimony, to His relationship with the Father, the
object of whose love He was, and who had given all
things into His hand. He was the faithful witness, and
that of heavenly things (see chap. 3: 13), but He was
also the Son Himself come from the Father. Everything
for man rested on faith in Him. The Lord comes out
from Judaism, while presenting the testimony of the
prophets, and brings from heaven the direct testimony of
God and of glory, showing the only ground on which we
can have a part in it. Jew or Gentile must be born again;
and heavenly things could only be entered by the cross,
the wondrous proof of God's love to the world. John
gives place to Him, bringing out—not in public testimony
to Israel but to his disciples—the true glory of His Person
and of His work [21] in this world. The thought of the
bride and Bridegroom is, I believe, general. John says
indeed that he is not the Christ, and that the earthly
bride belongs to Jesus; but He has never taken her; and
John speaks of His rights, which for us are realized in a
better land and another clime than this world. It is, I
repeat, the general idea. But we have now entered on the
new ground of a new nature, the cross, and the world
and God's love to it.

[21] Observe here, that the Lord—while not concealing (vers. 11-13) the
character of His testimony, as indeed He could not—speaks of the
necessity of His death, and of the love of God. John speaks of the
glory of His Person. Jesus magnifies His Father by submitting to the
necessity which the condition of men imposed on Him, if He would bring
them into a new relationship with God. "God," said He, "hath so
loved." John magnifies Jesus. All is perfect and in place. There are
four points in that which is said with regard to Jesus: His supremacy;
His testimony—this is the Baptist's testimony to Him. What follows
(vers. 35, 36)—His having all things given to Him by the Father who
loved Him, life everlasting in contrast with the wrath that is the portion
of the unbeliever from God—is rather the new revelation; the purpose
of God giving all things to Him, and His being Himself eternal life come
down from heaven, is that of John the Evangelist.

Chapter 4

Driven outside Judea, divine grace in Samaria

AND now Jesus, being driven away by the jealousy of the Jews, begins His ministry outside that people, while still acknowledging their true position in the dealings of God. He goes away into Galilee; but His road led Him by Samaria, in which dwelt a mingled race of strangers and of Israel—a race who had forsaken the idolatry of the strangers, but who, while following the law of Moses and calling themselves by the name of Jacob, had set up a worship of their own at Gerizim. Jesus does not enter the town. Being weary He sits down outside the town on the brink of the well—for He must needs go that way; but this necessity was an occasion for the acting of that divine grace which was in the fulness of His Person, and which overflowed the narrow limits of Judaism.

Baptism by Jesus' disciples

There are some preliminary details to remark before entering on the subject of this chapter. Jesus did not Himself baptize, for He knew the whole extent of the counsels of God in grace, the true object of His coming. He could not bind souls by baptism to a living Christ. The disciples were right in so doing. They had so to receive Christ. It was faith on their part.

At Jacob's well in Samaria

When rejected by the Jews, the Lord does not contend. He leaves them; and, coming to Sychar, He found Himself in the most interesting associations as regards the history of Israel, but in Samaria: sad testimony of Israel's ruin. Jacob's well was in the hands of people who called themselves of Israel, but the greater part of whom were not so, and who worshipped they knew not what, although pretending to be of the stock of Israel. Those who were really Jews had driven away the Messiah by their jealousy. He—a man despised by the people—had gone away from among them. We see Him sharing the sufferings of humanity, and, weary with His journey, finding only the side of a well on which to rest at noon. He contents Himself with it. He seeks nothing but the will of His God: it brought Him thither. The disciples were away; and God brought thither at that unusual hour a woman by herself. It was not the hour at which women went out to draw water; but, in the ordering of God, a poor sinful woman and the Judge of quick and dead thus met together.

The heart of the Saviour: the gift of living water

The Lord, weary and thirsty, had no means even to quench His thirst. He is dependent as man, on this poor woman to have a little water for His thirst. He asks it of her. The woman, seeing that He is a Jew, is surprised; and now the divine scene unfolds itself, in which the heart of the Saviour, rejected by men and oppressed by the unbelief of His people, opens to let that fulness of grace flow out which finds its occasion in the necessities and not in the righteousness of men. Now this grace did not limit itself to the rights of Israel, nor lend itself to national jealousy. It was a question of the gift of God, of God Himself who was there in grace, and of God come down so low, that, being born among His people, He was dependent, as to His human position, on a Samaritan woman for a drop of water to quench His thirst. "If thou knewest the gift of God, and [not, who I am, but] who it is that saith unto thee, Give Me to drink;" that is to say, If thou hadst known that God gives freely, and the glory of His Person who was there, and how deeply He had humbled Himself, His love would have been revealed to thy heart, and would have filled it with perfect confidence, in regard even to the wants which a grace like this would have awakened in thy heart. "Thou wouldest have asked," said the divine Saviour, "and He would have given thee" the living water that springeth up into everlasting life. Such is the heavenly fruit of the mission of Christ, wherever He is received.[22] His heart lays it open (it was revealing Himself), pours it out into the heart of one who was its object; consoling itself for the unbelief of the Jews (rejecting the end of promise) by presenting the true consolation of grace to the misery that needed it. This is the true comfort of love, which is pained when unable to act. The floodgates of grace are lifted up by the misery which that grace waters. He makes manifest that which God is in grace; and the God of grace was there. Alas, the heart of man, withered up and selfish, and preoccupied with its own miseries (the fruits of sin), cannot at all understand this. The woman sees something extraordinary in Jesus; she is curious to know what it means —is struck with His manner, so that she has a measure of faith in His words; but her desires are limited to the relief of the toils of her sorrowful life, in which an ardent heart found no answer to the misery it had acquired for its portion through sin.

The stream of grace and its channel

A few words on the character of this woman. I believe the Lord would show that there is need, that the fields were ready for the harvest; and that if the wretched self-righteousness of the Jews rejected Him, the stream of grace would find its channel elsewhere, God having prepared hearts to hail it with joy and thanksgiving, because it answered their misery and need — not the righteous.

[22] Note, too, here, that it is not as with Israel in the wilderness that there was water from the smitten rock to drink. Here the promise is of a well of water springing up unto everlasting life in ourselves.

The channel of grace was dug by the need and the misery which the grace itself caused to be felt.

Isolated by sin: alone with the Lord

The life of this woman was shameful; but she was ashamed of it: at the least her position had isolated her, by separating her from the crowd that forgets itself in the tumult of social life. And there is no inward grief like an isolated heart; but Christ and grace more than meets it. Its isolation more than ceases. He was more isolated than she. She came alone to the well; she was not with the other women. Alone, she met with the Lord, by the wonderful guidance of God who brought her there. The disciples even must go away to make room for her. They knew nothing of this grace. They baptized indeed in the name of a Messiah in whom they believed. It was well. But God was there in grace—He who would judge the quick and the dead—and with Him a sinner in her sins. What a meeting! And God who had stooped so low as to be dependent on her for a little water to quench His thirst!

The woman's sense of need: conscience awakened by the Searcher of hearts

She had an ardent nature. She had sought for happiness; she had found misery. She lived in sin, and was weary of life. She was indeed in the lowest depths of misery. The ardor of her nature found sin no obstacle. She went on, alas, to the uttermost. The will, engaged in evil, feeds on sinful desires, and wastes itself without fruit. Nevertheless her soul was not without a sense of need. She thought of Jerusalem, she thought of Gerizim. She waited for the Messiah, who would tell them all things. Did this change her life? In no wise. Her life was shocking. When the Lord speaks of spiritual things, in language well suited to awaken the heart, directing her attention to heavenly things in a way that one would have thought it impossible to misunderstand, she cannot comprehend it. The natural man cannot understand the things of the Spirit: they are spiritually discerned.

The novelty of the Lord's address excited her attention, but did not lead her thoughts beyond her water-pot, the symbol of her daily toil; although she saw that Jesus took the place of one greater than Jacob. What was to be done? God wrought—He wrought in grace, and in this poor woman. Whatever the occasion might be as regards herself, it was He who had brought her thither. But she was unable to comprehend spiritual things though expressed in the plainest manner; for the Lord spoke of the water that springs up in the soul unto everlasting life. But as the human heart is ever revolving in its own circumstances and cares, her religious need was limited practically to the traditions by which her life, as regarded its religious thoughts and habits, was formed, leaving still a void that nothing could fill. What then was to be done? In what way can this grace act, when the heart does not understand the spiritual grace which the Lord brings? This is the second part of the marvellous instruction here. The Lord deals with her conscience. A word spoken by Him who searches the heart, searches her conscience: she is in the presence of a Man who tells her all that ever she did. For, her conscience awakened by the Word, and finding itself laid open to the eye of God, her whole life is before her.

In the presence of God

And who is He that thus searches the heart? She feels that His word is the Word of God. "Thou art a prophet." Intelligence in divine things comes by the conscience, not by the intellect. The soul and God are together, if we may so speak, whatever instrument is employed. She has everything to learn, no doubt; but she is in the presence of Him who teaches everything. What a step! What a change! What a new position! This soul, which saw no farther than her water-pot and felt her toil more than her sin, is there alone with the Judge of quick and dead—with God Himself. And in what manner? She knows not. She only felt that it was Himself in the power of His own word. But at least He did not despise her, as others did. Although she was alone, she was alone with Him. He had spoken to her of life—of the gift of God; He had told her that she had only to ask and have. She had understood nothing of His meaning; but it was not condemnation, it was grace—grace that stooped to her, that knew her sin and was not repelled by it, that asked her for water, that was above Jewish prejudice with regard to her, as well as the contempt of the humanly righteous —grace which did not conceal her sin from her, which made her feel that God knew it: nevertheless He who knew it was there without alarming her. Her sin was before God, but not in judgment.

Confidence inspired by the grace of God

Marvellous meeting of a soul with God, which the grace of God accomplishes by Christ! Not that she reasoned about all these things; but she was under the effect of their truth without accounting for it to herself; for the Word of God had reached her conscience, and she was in the presence of Him who had accomplished it, and He was meek and lowly, and glad to receive a little water at her hands. Her defilement did not defile Him. She could, in fact, trust in Him, without knowing why. It is thus that God acts. Grace inspires confidence—brings back the soul to God in peace, before it has any intelligent knowledge, or can explain it to itself. In this way, full of trust, she begins (it was the natural consequence) with the questions that filled her own heart; thus giving the Lord an opportunity of fully explaining the ways of

God in grace. God had so ordered it; for the question was far from the sentiments which grace afterwards led her to. The Lord replies according to her condition: salvation was of the Jews. They were the people of God. Truth was with them, and not with the Samaritans who worshipped they knew not what. But God put all that aside. It was now neither at Gerizim nor at Jerusalem, that they should worship the Father who manifested Himself in the Son. God was a spirit, and must be worshipped in spirit and in truth. Moreover the Father sought such worshippers. That is to say, the worship of their hearts must answer to the nature of God, to the grace of the Father who had sought them.[23]　Thus true worshippers should worship the Father in spirit and in truth. Jerusalem and Samaria disappear entirely—have no place before such a revelation of the Father in grace. God no longer hid Himself; He was revealed perfectly in light. The perfect grace of the Father wrought, in order to make Him known, by the grace that brought souls to Him.

The Lord received: its effect—the heart filled with Christ Himself

Now the woman was not yet brought to Him; but, as we have seen in the case of the disciples and of John the Baptist, a glorious revelation of Christ acts upon the soul where it is, and brings the Person of Jesus into connection with the need already felt. "The woman saith unto Him, I know that Messias cometh; and when He is come, He will tell us all things." Small as her intelligence might be, and unable as she was to understand what Jesus had told her, His love meets her where she can receive blessing and life; and He replies, "I, that speak unto thee, am He." The work was done: the Lord

---

[23] It will be found in John's writings that, when responsibility is spoken of, "God" is the word used; when grace to us "the Father" and "the Son." When indeed it is goodness (God's character in Christ) towards the world, then "God" is spoken of.

was received. A poor Samaritan sinner receives the
Messiah of Israel, whom the priests and the Pharisees
had rejected from among the people. The moral effect
upon the woman is evident. She forgets her water-pot,
her toil, her circumstances. She is engrossed by this new
object that is revealed to her soul—by Christ; so engrossed
that, without thinking, she becomes a preacher; that is,
she proclaims the Lord in the fulness of her heart and
with perfect simplicity. He had told her all that she
had ever done. She does not think at that moment of
what it was. *Jesus* had told it her; and the thought of
Jesus takes away the bitterness of the sin. The sense of
His goodness removes the guile of heart that seeks to
conceal its sin. In a word, her heart is entirely filled with
Christ Himself. Many believed in Him through her
declaration—"He has told me all that ever I did;" many
more, when they had heard Him. His own word carried
with it a stronger conviction, as more immediately connected with His Person.

The harvest-fields: the laborers, their wages and the fruit

Meanwhile the disciples come, and—naturally—marvel
at His talking with the woman. Their Master, the Messiah—they understood this; but the grace of God manifested in the flesh was still beyond their thoughts. The
work of this grace was the meat of Jesus, and that in
the lowliness of obedience as sent of God. He was taken
up with it, and, in the perfect humility of obedience, it
was His joy and His food to do His Father's will, and to
finish His work. And the case of this poor woman had a
voice that filled His heart with deep joy, wounded as it
was in this world, because He was love. If the Jews
rejected Him, still the fields in which grace sought its
fruits for the everlasting granary were white already to
harvest. He, therefore, who labored should not fail of

his wages, nor of the joy of having such fruit unto life eternal. Nevertheless, even the apostles were but reapers where others had sown. The poor woman was a proof of this. Christ, present and revealed, met the need which the testimony of the prophet had awakened. Thus (while exhibiting a grace which revealed the love of the Father, of God the Saviour, and coming out, consequently, from the pale of the Jewish system) He fully recognized the faithful service of His laborers in former days, the prophets who, by the Spirit of Christ from the beginning of the world, had spoken of the Redeemer, of the sufferings of Christ and the glories that should follow. The sowers and the reapers should rejoice together in the fruit of their labors.

The divine picture presented in the grace flowing at Sychar's well

But what a picture is all this of the purpose of grace, and of its mighty and living fulness in the Person of Christ, of the free gift of God, and of the incapability of the spirit of man to apprehend it, pre-occupied and blinded as he is by present things, seeing nothing beyond the life of nature, although suffering from the consequences of his sin! At the same time, we see that it is in the humiliation, the deep abasement, of the Messiah, of Jesus, that God Himself is manifested in this grace. It is this that breaks down the barriers, and gives free course to the torrent of grace from on high. We see, also, that conscience is the doorway of understanding in the things of God. We are brought truly into relationship with God when He searches the heart. This is always the case. We are then in the truth. Moreover God thus manifests Himself, and the grace and love of the Father. He seeks worshippers, and that, according to this double revelation of Himself, however great His patience may be with those who do not see farther than the first step of the promises of God. If Jesus is received, there is a thorough change; the work of conversion is wrought; there is faith. At the same time what a divine picture of our Jesus—humbled, indeed, but even thereby the manifestation of God in love, the Son of the Father, He who knows the Father, and accomplishes His work! What a glorious and boundless scene opens before the soul that is admitted to see and to know Him!

The whole range of grace is open to us here in His work and its divine extent, in that which regards its application to the individual, and the personal intelligence we may have respecting it. It is not precisely pardon, nor redemption, nor the assembly. It is grace flowing in the Person of Christ; and the conversion of the sinner, in order that he may enjoy it in himself, and be capable of knowing God and of worshipping the Father of grace. But how entirely have we broken out in principle from the narrow limits of Judaism!

In Galilee: the Lord's second miracle and the great truths it set forth

Nevertheless in His personal ministry, the Lord, always faithful, putting Himself aside in order to glorify His Father by obeying Him, repairs to the sphere of labor appointed Him of God. He leaves the Jews, for no prophet is received in his own country, and goes into Galilee, among the despised of His people, the poor of the flock, where obedience, grace, and the counsels of God alike placed Him. In that sense, He did not forsake His people, perverse as they were. There He works a miracle which expresses the effect of His grace in connection with the believing remnant of Israel, feeble as their faith might be. He comes again to the place where He had turned the water of purification into the wine of joy ("which cheereth God and man"). By that miracle He had, in figure, displayed the power which should deliver the people, and by which, being received, He would establish the fulness of joy in Israel, creating by that power the good wine of the nuptials of Israel with their God. Israel rejected it all. The Messiah was not received. He retires among the poor of the flock in Galilee, after having shown to Samaria (in passing) the grace of the Father, which went beyond all promises to, and dealings with, the Jew, and in the Person and the humiliation of Christ led converted souls to worship the Father (outside all Jewish system, true or false) in spirit and in truth; and there, in Galilee, He works a second miracle in the midst of Israel, where He still labors, according to His Father's will, that is to say, wherever there is faith; not yet, perhaps, in His power to raise the dead, but to heal and save the life of that which was ready to perish. He fulfilled the desire of that faith, and restored the life of one who was at the point of death. It was this, in fact, which He was doing in Israel while here below. These two great truths were set forth—that which He was going to do according to the purposes of God the Father, as being rejected; and that which He was doing at the time for Israel, according to the faith He found among them.

Outline of Chapters 5 to 21

In the chapters that follow we shall find the rights and the glory shown forth that attach to His Person; the rejection of His Word and of His work; the sure salvation of the remnant, and of all His sheep wherever they may be. Afterwards—acknowledged by God, as manifested on earth, the Son of God, of David, and of Man—that which He will do when gone away, and the gift of the Holy Ghost, are unfolded; also the position in which He placed the disciples before the Father, and with regard to Himself. And then—after the history of Gethsemane, the giving of His own life, His death as giving His life for us—the whole result, in the ways of God, until His return, is briefly given in the chapter that closes the book.

We may go more rapidly through the chapters till the tenth, not as of little importance—far from it—but as containing some great principles which may be pointed out, each in its place, without requiring much explanation.

Chapter 5

The quickening power of Christ contrasted with the powerlessness of legal ordinances

CHAPTER 5 contrasts the quickening power of Christ, the power and the right of giving life to the dead, with the powerlessness of legal ordinances. They required strength in the person that was to profit by them. Christ brought with Him the power that was to heal, and indeed to quicken. Further, all judgment is committed to Him, so that those who had received life would not come into judgment. The end of the chapter sets forth the testimonies that have been borne to Him, and the guilt therefore of those who would not come to Him to have life. One is sovereign grace, the other responsibility because life was there. To have life His divine power was needed; but in rejecting Him, in refusing to come unto Him that they might have life, they did so in spite of the most positive proofs.

The impotent man: strength imparted by Christ

Let us go a little into the details. The poor man who had an infirmity for thirty-eight years was absolutely hindered, by the nature of his disease, from profiting by means that required strength to use them. This is the character of sin, on the one hand, and of law on the other. Some remains of blessing still existed among the Jews. Angels, ministers of that dispensation, still wrought among the people. Jehovah did not leave Himself without testimony. But strength was needed to profit by this instance of their ministry. That which the law could not do, being weak through the flesh, God has done through Jesus. The impotent man had desire, but not strength; to will was present with him, but no power to perform. The Lord's question brings this out. A single word from Christ does everything. "Rise, take up thy bed and walk." Strength is imparted. The man rises, and goes away, carrying his bed.[24]

The Sabbath: God beginning to work again in power and love

It was the Sabbath—an important circumstance here, holding a prominent place in this interesting scene. The Sabbath was given as a token of the covenant between the Jews and the Lord.[25] But it had been proved that the law did not give God's rest to man. The power of a new life was needed; grace was needed, that man might be in relationship with God. The healing of this poor man was an operation of this same grace, of this same power, but wrought in the midst of Israel. The pool of Bethesda supposed power in man; the act of Jesus employed power, in grace, on behalf of one of the Lord's people in distress. Therefore, as dealing with His people

[24] Christ brings the strength with Him which the law requires in man himself to profit by it.

[25] The Sabbath is introduced, whatever new institution or arrangement is established under the law. And in truth, a part in the rest of God is, in certain aspects, the highest of our privileges. (See Heb. 4.) The Sabbath was the close of the first or this creation, and will be so when fulfilled. Our rest is in the new one, and that not in the first man's creation state but risen, Christ the second Man being its beginning and head. Hence the first day of the week.

in government, He says to the man, "Sin no more, lest a worse thing come unto thee." It was Jehovah acting by His grace and blessing among His people; but it was in temporal things, the tokens of His favor and loving-kindness, and in connection with His government in Israel. Still it was divine power and grace. Now, the man told the Jews that it was Jesus. They rise up against Him under the pretence of a violation of the Sabbath. The Lord's answer is deeply affecting, and full of instruction—a whole revelation. It declares the relationship, now openly revealed by His coming, that existed between Himself (the Son) and His Father. It shows—and what depths of grace!—that neither the Father nor Himself could find their Sabbath[26] in the midst of misery and of the sad fruits of sin. Jehovah in Israel might impose the Sabbath as an obligation by the law, and make it a token of the precious truth that His people should enter into the rest of God. But, in fact, when God was truly known, there was no rest in existing things; nor was this all—He wrought in grace, His love could not rest in misery. He had instituted a rest in connection with the creation, when it was very good. Sin, corruption, and misery had entered into it. God, the holy and the just, no longer found a Sabbath in it, and man did not really enter into God's rest. (Compare Heb. 4.) Of two things, one: either God must, in justice, destroy the guilty race; or—and this is what He did, according to His eternal purposes—He must begin to work in grace, according to the redemption which the state of man required—a redemption in which all His glory is unfolded. In a word, He must begin to work again in love. Thus the Lord says, "My Father worketh hitherto, and I work." God cannot be satisfied where there is sin. He cannot rest with misery in sight. He has no Sabbath, but still works in grace. How divine an answer to their wretched cavils!

[26] God's sabbath is a sabbath of love and holiness.

The Lord putting Himself on an equality with the Father

Another truth came out from that which the Lord said: He put Himself on an equality with His Father. But the Jews, jealous for their ceremonies—for that which distinguished them from other nations—saw nothing of the glory of Christ, and seek to kill Him, treating Him as a blasphemer. This gives Jesus occasion to lay open the whole truth on this point. He was not like an independent being with equal rights, another God who acted on His own account, which, moreover, is impossible. There cannot be two supreme and omnipotent beings. The Son is in full union with the Father, does nothing without the Father, but does whatsoever He sees the Father do. There is nothing that the Father does which He does not in communion with the Son; and greater proofs of this should yet be seen, that they might marvel. This last sentence of the Lord's words, as well as the whole of this Gospel, shows that, while revealing absolutely that He and the Father are one, He reveals it, and speaks of it as in a position in which He could be seen of men. The thing of which He speaks is in God; the position in which He speaks of it is a position taken, and, in a certain sense, inferior. We see everywhere that He is equal to, and one with, the Father. We see that He receives all from the Father, and does all after the Father's mind. (This is shown very remarkably in chapter 17.) It is the Son, but the Son manifested in the flesh, acting in the mission which the Father sent Him to fulfil.

The Son as the Giver of life and the Judge of all

Two things are spoken of in this chapter (vers. 21, 22) which demonstrate the glory of the Son. He quickens and He judges. It is not healing that is in question—a work which, at bottom, springs from the same source, and has its occasion in the same evil: but the giving of life in a manner evidently divine. As the Father raises the dead and quickens them, so the Son *quickens whom He will*. Here we have the first proof of His divine rights, He gives life, and He gives it to whom He will. But, being incarnate, He may be personally dishonored, disallowed, despised of men. Consequently all judgment is committed unto Him, the Father judging no man, in order that all, even those who have rejected the Son, should honor Him, even as they honor the Father whom they own as God. If they refuse when He acts in grace, they shall be compelled when He acts in judgment. In life, we have communion by the Holy Ghost with the Father and the Son (and quickening or giving life is the work alike of the Father and the Son); but in the judgment, unbelievers will have to do with the Son of Man whom they have rejected. The two things are quite distinct. He whom Christ has quickened will not need to be compelled to honor Him by undergoing judgment. Jesus will not call into judgment one whom He has saved by quickening him.

Grace gives eternal life and secures from judgment

How may we know, then, to which of these two classes we belong? The Lord (praised be His name!) replies, He that hears His word, and believes Him who sent Him (believes the Father by hearing Christ), *has everlasting* life (such is the quickening power of His Word), and *shall not come into judgment*. He *is* passed from death into life. Simple and wonderful testimony![27] The judgment will glorify the Lord in the case of those who have

---

[27] Remark how full the bearing of this is. If they do not come into judgment to settle their state, as man would put it, they are shown to be wholly dead in sin. Grace in Christ does not contemplate an uncertain state which judgment will determine. It gives life and secures from judgment. But while He judges as Son of Man according to the deeds done in the body, He shows us here that all were dead in sin to begin with.

despised Him here. The possession of eternal life, that they may not come into judgment, is the portion of those who *believe*.

Two distinct periods in the Lord's exercise of power: (1) souls quickened by the Son of God

The Lord then points out two distinct periods, in which the power that the Father committed to Him as having come down to the earth, is to be exercised. The hour was coming—was already come—in which the dead should hear the voice of the Son of God, and those that heard should live. This is the communication of spiritual life by Jesus, the Son of God, to man, who is dead by sin, and that by means of the Word which he should hear. For the Father has given to the Son, to Jesus, thus manifested on earth, to have life in Himself. (Compare 1 John 1: 1, 2.) He has also given Him authority to execute judgment, because He is the Son of Man. For the kingdom and the judgment, according to the counsels of God, belong to Him as Son of Man—in that character in which He was despised and rejected when He came in grace.

This passage also shows us that, although He was the Eternal Son, one with the Father, He is always looked upon as manifested here in the flesh, and, therefore, as receiving all from the Father. It is thus that we have seen Him at the well of Samaria—the God who gave, but the One who asked the poor woman to give Him to drink.

(2) Bodies raised from death

Jesus, then, quickened souls at that time. He still quickens. They were not to marvel. A work, more wonderful in the eyes of men, should be accomplished. All those that were in the grave should come forth. This is the second period of which He speaks. In the one He quickens souls; in the other, He raises up bodies from death. The one has lasted during the ministry of Jesus and 1800 years since His death; the other is not yet come, but during its continuance two things will take place. There will be a resurrection of those who have done good (this will be a resurrection of life, the Lord will complete His quickening work), and there will be a resurrection of those who have done evil (this will be a resurrection for their judgment). This judgment will be according to the mind of God, and not according to any separate personal will of Christ. Thus far it is sovereign power, and as regards life sovereign grace—He quickens whom He will. What follows is man's responsibility as regards the obtaining eternal life. It was there in Jesus, and they would not come to Him to have it.

Four testimonies to the Lord's glory and Person leaving man without excuse

The Lord goes on to point out to them four testimonies rendered to His glory and to His Person, which left them without excuse:—John, His own works, His Father, and the Scriptures. Nevertheless, while pretending to receive the latter, as finding in them eternal life, they would not come to Him that they might have life. Poor Jews! The Son came in the name of the Father, and they would not receive Him; another shall come in his own name, and him they will receive. This better suits the heart of man. They sought honor from one another: how could they believe? Let us remember this. God does not accommodate Himself to the pride of man—does not arrange the truth so as to feed it. Jesus knew the Jews. Not that He would accuse them to the Father: Moses, in whom they trusted, would do that; for if they had believed Moses, they would have believed Christ. But if they did not credit the writings of Moses, how would they believe the words of a despised Saviour?

In result, the Son of God gives life, and He executes

judgment. In the judgment that He executes, the testimony which had been rendered to His Person leaves man without excuse on the ground of his own responsibility. In chapter 5 Jesus is the Son of God who, with the Father gives life, and as Son of Man judges. In chapter 6 He is the object of faith, as come down from heaven and dying. He just alludes to His going on high as Son of Man.

Chapter 6

The Bread of Life: the incarnate Lord put to death and ascended again to heaven

IN chapter 6, then, it is the Lord come down from heaven, humbled and put to death, not now as the Son of God, one with the Father, the source of life; but as He who, although He was Jehovah and at the same time the Prophet and the King, would take the place of Victim, and that of Priest in heaven: in His incarnation, the bread of life; dead, the true nourishment of believers; ascended again to heaven, the living object of their faith. But He only glances at this last feature: the doctrine of the chapter is that which goes before. It is not the divine power that quickens, but the Son of Man come in flesh, the object of faith, and so the means of life; and, though, as plainly declared by the calling of grace, yet it is not the divine side, quickening whom He will, but faith in us laying hold of Him. In both He acts independently of the limits of Judaism. He quickens whom He will, and comes to give life to the world.

The Lord in contrast with Judaism: earthly blessings and the new position and doctrine

It was on the occasion of the Passover, a type which the Lord was to fulfil by the death of which He spoke. Observe, here, that all these chapters present the Lord, and the truth that reveals Him, in contrast with Judaism, which He forsook and set aside. Chapter 5 was the impotence of the law and its ordinances; here it is the blessings promised by the Lord to the Jews on earth (Psalm 132: 15), and the characters of Prophet and King fulfilled by the Messiah on earth in connection with the Jews, that are seen in contrast with the new position and the doctrine of Jesus. That of which I here speak characterizes every distinct subject in this Gospel.

The Prophet, Priest and King in respect to Israel

First, Jesus blesses the people, according to the promise of that which Jehovah should do, given them in Psalm 132, for He was Jehovah. On this, the people acknowledge Him to be "that Prophet," and desire by force to make Him their King. But this He declines now—could not take it in this carnal way. Jesus leaves them, and goes up by Himself into a mountain. This was, figuratively, His position as Priest on high. These are the three characters of the Messiah in respect of Israel; but the last has full and special application to the saints now also, as walking on the earth, who continue as to this the position of the remnant. The disciples enter a ship, and, without Him, are tossed upon the waves. Darkness comes on (this will happen to the remnant down here), and Jesus is away. Nevertheless He rejoins them, and they receive Him joyfully. Immediately the ship is at the place to which they were going. A striking picture of the remnant journeying on earth during the absence of Christ, and their every wish fully and immediately satisfied—full blessing and rest—when He rejoins them.[28]

---

[28] The direct application of this is to the remnant; but then, as hinted in the text, we, as to our path on earth, are, so to speak, the continuation of that remnant, and Christ is on high for us, while we are on the waves below. The subsequent part of the chapter, of the bread of life, is properly for us. The world, not Israel, is in question. Indeed though Christ is Aaron within the veil for Israel, while He is there the saints have properly their heavenly character.

The Son of Man in humiliation here

This part of the chapter, having shown us the Lord as already the Prophet here below, and refusing to be made King, and also that which will yet take place when He returns to the remnant on earth—the historical framework of what He was and will be—the remainder of the chapter gives us that which He is meanwhile to faith, His true character, the purpose of God in sending Him, outside Israel, and in connection with sovereign grace. The people seek Him. The true work, which God owns, is to believe in Him whom He has sent. This is that meat which endures unto everlasting life, which is given by the Son of Man (it is in this character we find Jesus here, as in chapter 5 it was the Son of God), for He it is whom God the Father has sealed. Jesus had taken this place of Son of Man in humiliation here below. He went to be baptized of John the Baptist; and there, in this character, the Father sealed Him, the Holy Ghost coming down upon Him.

The true Bread from heaven set before faith

The multitude ask Him for a proof like the manna. He was Himself the proof—the true manna. Moses did not give the heavenly bread of life. Their fathers died in the very wilderness in which they had eaten the manna. The Father now gave them the true bread from heaven. Here, observe, it is not the Son of God who gives, and who is the sovereign Giver of life to whom He will. He is the object set before faith; He is to be fed upon. Life is found in Him; he that eats Him shall live by Him, and shall never hunger. But the multitude did not believe in Him; in fact, the mass of Israel, as such, were not in question. Those that the Father gave Him should come unto Him. He was there the passive object, so to say, of faith. It is no longer to whom He will, but to receive those whom the Father brought Him. Therefore, be it who it might, He would in no wise cast them out: enemy, scoffer, Gentile, they would not come if the Father had not sent them. The Messiah was there to do His Father's will, and whomsoever the Father brought Him He would receive for life eternal. (Compare chap. 5: 21.) The Father's will had these two characters. Of all whom the Father should give Him, He would lose none. Precious assurance! The Lord saves assuredly to the end those whom the Father has given Him; and then every one that should see the Son and believe on Him should have everlasting life. This is the gospel for every soul, as the other is that which infallibly assures the salvation of every believer.

A new dispensation: resurrection and eternal life

But this is not all. The subject of hope was not now the fulfilment on earth of the promises made to the Jew, but being raised from the dead, having part in everlasting life—in resurrection at the last day (that is, of the age of the law in which they were). He did not crown the dispensation of the law; He was to bring in a new dispensation, and with it resurrection. The Jews [29] murmur at His saying that He came down from heaven. Jesus replies by the testimony that their difficulty was easy to be understood: no one could come unto Him except the Father brought him. It was grace that produced this effect; whether they were Jews or not made no difference. It was a question of eternal life, of being raised from the dead by Him; not of performing the promises as Messiah, but of bringing in the life of a widely different world to be enjoyed by faith—the Father's grace having led the soul to find it in Jesus. Moreover, the prophets had said they should all be taught of God. Every one, there-

[29] In John, the Jews are always distinguished from the multitude. They are the inhabitants of Jerusalem and Judea. It would, perhaps, be easier to understand this Gospel, if the words were rendered "those of Judea," which is the true sense.

fore, who had learned of the Father came unto Him. No man, doubtless, had seen the Father excepting Him who was of God—Jesus; He had seen the Father. He that believed in Him was already in possession of eternal life, for He was the bread come down from heaven, that a man might eat thereof and not die.

The death of Christ as the believer's life

But this was not only by the incarnation, but by the death of Him who came down from heaven. He would give His life; His blood should be taken from the body which He had assumed. They should eat His flesh; they should drink His blood. Death should be the believer's life. And, in fact, it is in a dead Saviour that we see the sin taken away which He bore for us, and death for us is death to the sinful nature in which evil and our separation from God lay. There He made an end of sin—He who knew no sin. Death, which sin brought in, puts away the sin that attached to the life, which there comes to its end. Not that Christ had any sin in His own Person; but He took sin, He was made sin, on the cross, for us. And he who is dead is justified from sin. I feed, therefore, on the death of Christ. Death is mine; it is become life. It separates me from sin, from death, from the life in which I was separated from God. In it sin and death have finished their course. They were attached to my life. Christ, in grace, has borne them, and He has given His flesh for the life of the world; and I am freed from them; and I feed on the infinite grace that is in Him who has accomplished this. The expiation is complete, and I live, being happily dead to all that separated me from God. It is death as fulfilled in Him that I feed upon, first *for* me, and entering withal into it by faith. He needed to live as Man in order to die, and He has given His life. Thus His death is efficacious; His love infinite; the expiation total, absolute, perfect. That which was between me and God exists no longer, for Christ died, and it all passed away with His life here on earth—life as He had it before expiring on the cross. Death could not hold Him. To perform this work, He needed to possess a power of divine life which death could not touch; but this is not the truth expressly taught in the chapter before us, although it is implied.

The One who died as the object of faith

In speaking to the multitude, the Lord, while rebuking them for their unbelief, presents Himself, come in the flesh, as the object of their faith at that moment (vers. 32-35). To the Jews, in laying open the doctrine, He repeats that He is the living bread come down from heaven, of which if any man eat he should live for ever. But He makes them understand that they could not stop there—they must receive His death. He does not say here, "He that eateth *Me*," but it was to eat His flesh and drink His blood, to enter fully into the thought— the reality—of His death; to receive a dead (not a living) Messiah, dead for men, dead before God. He does not exist now as a dead Christ; but we must acknowledge, realize, feed upon, His death—identify ourselves with it before God, participating in it by faith, or we have no life in us.[30]

---

[30] This truth is of vast importance as regards the sacramental question. Sacraments are declared by the Puseyite school to be the continuation of the incarnation. This is in every respect error, and, in truth, a denial of the faith. Both sacraments signify death. We are baptized to Christ's death; and the Lord's Supper is confessedly emblematic of His death. I say "denial of the faith;" because, as the Lord shows, if they do not eat His flesh and blood, they have no life in them. As incarnate Christ is alone. His presence in flesh on earth showed that God and sinful men could not be united. His presence as Man in the world resulted in His rejection—proved the impossibility of union or fruit on that ground. Redemption must come in, His blood be shed, Himself lifted up from the earth, and so draw men to Him: death must come in, or He abode alone. They could not eat the bread unless they ate the flesh and drank the blood. A meat-offering without a bloody offering was null, or rather a Cain offering. Further, the Lord's Supper presents a dead Christ, and a dead Christ only—the blood apart from the body. No such Christ exists; and therefore transubstantiation

Life by Christ through feeding on Him

Thus it was for the world. Thus they should live, not of their own life, but by Christ, through feeding on Him. Here He returns to His own Person, faith in His death being established. Moreover, they should dwell in Him (ver. 56)—should be in Him before God according to all His acceptance before God, all the efficacy of His work in dying. [31] And Christ should dwell in them according to the power and grace of that life in which He had gained the victory over death, and in which, having gained it, He now lives. As the living Father had sent Him, and He lived, not by an independent life which had not the Father for its object or source, but by reason of the Father, so he that thus ate Him should live because of Him. [32]

The Lord's ascension again to heaven: the food of faith during His absence

Afterwards, in reply to those who murmured at this fundamental truth, the Lord appeals to His ascension. He had come down from heaven—this was His doctrine; He would ascend thither again. Material flesh profited nothing. It was the Spirit who gave life, by realizing in the soul the mighty truth of that which Christ was, and of His death. But He returns to that which He had told them before; in order to come to Him thus revealed in truth, they must be led of the Father. There is such a

and consubstantiation and all such thoughts are a blundering fable. We are united to a glorified Christ by the Holy Ghost; and we celebrate that most precious death upon which all our blessing is founded, through which we got there. We do it in remembrance of Him, and in our hearts feed on Him, so given, and shedding His blood.

[31] Abiding imports constancy of dependence, confidence, and living by the life in which Christ lives. "Dwelling" and "abiding," though the word be changed in English, are the same in the original: so in chapter 15 and elsewhere.

[32] It may be well to note that in this passage, in verses 51 and 53, eating is in the aorist—whosoever has done so. In verses 54, 56, and 57, it is the present—a present continuous action.

thing as faith that is ignorant perhaps, although through grace real. Such was that of the disciples. They knew that He, and He only, had the words of eternal life. It was not only that He was the Messiah, which they indeed believed, but His words had laid hold of their hearts with the power of the divine life which they revealed and through grace communicated. Thus they acknowledged Him as the Son of God, not only officially, so to speak, but according to the power of divine life. He was the Son of the living God. Nevertheless there was one among them who was of the devil.

Jesus therefore, come down to earth, put to death, ascending again to heaven, is the doctrine of this chapter. As come down and put to death, He is the food of faith during His absence on high. For it is on His death we must feed, in order to dwell spiritually in Him and He in us.

Chapter 7

The future typical fulfilment of the feast of tabernacles

IN chapter 7 His brethren after the flesh, still sunk in unbelief, would have Him show Himself to the world, if He did these great things; but the time for this was not yet come. At the fulfilment of the type of the feast of tabernacles He will do so. The Passover had its antitype at the cross, Pentecost at the descent of the Holy Ghost. The feast of tabernacles, as yet, has had no fulfilment. It was celebrated after the harvest and the vintage, and Israel joyfully commemorated, in the land, their pilgrimage before entering on the rest which God had given them in Canaan. Thus the fulfilment of this type will be when, after the execution of judgment (whether in discerning between the wicked and the good, or simply in vengeance [33]), Israel, restored to their land, shall be in possession of all their promised blessing. At that time Jesus will show Himself to the world; but at the time of which we are speaking His hour was not yet come. Meanwhile, having gone away (vers. 33, 34), He gives the Holy Ghost to believers (vers. 38, 39).

Remark here, there is no Pentecost brought in. We pass from the Passover in chapter 6 to the tabernacles in chapter 7, in lieu of which believers would receive the Holy Ghost. As I have remarked, this Gospel treats of a divine Person on earth, not of the Man in heaven. The coming of the Holy Ghost is spoken of as substituted for the last or eighth day of the feast of tabernacles. Pentecost supposes Jesus on high.

The Holy Spirit presented as the hope of faith at that time: thirst quenched and abundance of living water for others

But He presents the Holy Ghost in such a way as to make Him the hope of faith at the time in which He spoke, if God created a sense of need in the soul. If any one thirsted, let him come to Jesus and drink. Not only should his thirst be quenched, but from the inner man of his soul should flow forth streams of living water. So that coming to Him by faith to satisfy the need of their soul, not only should the Holy Ghost be in them a well of water springing up into everlasting life, but living water should also flow forth from them in abundance to refresh all those who thirsted. Observe here, that Israel drank water in the wilderness before they could keep the feast of tabernacles. But they only drank. There was

---

[33] The harvest is discriminating judgment, there are tares and wheat. The winepress is the destructive judgment of vengeance. In the former there will be two in one bed, one taken and another left, but the winepress is simple wrath, as Isaiah 63. So in Revelation 14.

no well in them. The water flowed from the rock. Under grace every believer is not doubtless a source in himself; but the full stream flows from him. This however would only take place when Jesus was glorified, and in those who were *already believers*, previous to their receiving it. What is spoken of here is not a work that quickens. It is a gift to those who believe. Moreover at the feast of tabernacles Jesus will show Himself to the world; but this is not the subject of which the Holy Ghost thus received is especially the witness. He is given in connection with the glory of Jesus, while He is hidden from the world. It was also on the eighth day of the feast, the sign of a portion beyond the sabbath rest of this world, and which began another period—a new scene of glory.

Observe also that, practically, although the Holy Ghost is presented here as power acting in blessing outside the one in whom He dwells, His presence in the believer is the fruit of a personal thirst of need felt in the soul—need for which the soul had sought an answer in Christ. He who thirsts, thirsts for himself. The Holy Ghost in us, revealing Christ, becomes, by dwelling in us when we have believed, a river in us, and thus *for* others.

The spirit of the Jews plainly shown

The spirit of the Jews plainly showed itself. They sought to kill the Lord; and He tells them that His relationship with them on earth would soon be ended (ver. 33). They need not hasten so much to get rid of Him: soon they would seek Him and not be able to find Him. He was going away to His Father.

We see clearly the difference here between the multitude and the Jews—two parties always distinguished from each other in this Gospel. The former did not understand why He spoke of the desire to kill Him. Those of Judea were astonished at His boldness, knowing that at Jerusalem they were conspiring against His life.

His time was not yet come. They send officers to take Him; and these return, struck with His discourse, without laying hands on Him. The Pharisees are angry, and express their contempt for the people. Nicodemus hazards a word of justice according to the law, and brings their contempt on himself. But each one goes away to his home. Jesus, who had no home until He went back to heaven whence He came, goes to the Mount of Olives, the witness of His agony, His ascension, and His return—a place which He habitually frequented, when at Jerusalem, during the time of His ministry on earth.

Chapter 8

Outside Judaism as shown in Chapters 5, 6, 7

THE contrast of this chapter with Judaism, even with its best hopes in the future that God has prepared for His earthly people, is too evident to be dwelt upon. This Gospel, throughout, reveals Jesus outside all that belonged to that earthly system. In chapter 6 it was death here below on the cross. Here it is glory in heaven, the Jews being rejected, and the Holy Ghost given to the believer. In chapter 5 He gives life, as the Son of God; in chapter 6 He is the same Son, but not as divinely quickening and judging as being Son of Man, but as come down from heaven, the Son in humiliation here, but the true bread from heaven which the Father gave. But in that lowly One, they must see the Son, to live. Then, as so come, and having taken the form of a servant, and being found in fashion as a man, He (ver. 53) humbles Himself, and suffers on the cross, as Son of Man; in chapter 7 He, when glorified, sends the Holy Ghost. Chapter 5 displays His titles of personal glory; chapters 6, 7, His work and the giving of the Spirit to believers consequent on His present glory in heaven,[34] to which the presence of the Holy Ghost answers on earth. In chapters 8, 9 [35] we shall find His testimony and His works rejected, and the question decided between Him and the Jews. It will be observed also, that chapters 5, 6 treat of the life. In chapter 5 it is given sovereignly and divinely by Him who possesses it; in chapter 6, the soul, receiving and being occupied with Jesus by faith, finds life, and feeds upon Him by the grace of the Father: two things distinct in their nature—God gives; man, by grace, feeds. On the other hand, chapter 7 is Christ's going to Him that sent Him, and meanwhile the Holy Ghost, who unfolds the glory He is gone into, in us and by us, in its heavenly character. In chapter 5 Christ is the Son of God, who quickens in abstract divine power and will, what He is, not the place He is in, but alone judges, being Son of Man; in chapter 6, the same Son, but come down from heaven, the object of faith in His humiliation, then the Son of Man, dying, and returning again; in chapter 7, not yet revealed to the world. The Holy Ghost is given instead when He is glorified above, the Son of Man in heaven—at least contemplating His going there.

The Word and works of Jesus rejected: His personal glories putting men to the test

In chapter 8, as we have said, the word of Jesus is rejected; and, in chapter 9, His works. But there is much more than that. The personal glories of chapter 1 are reproduced and developed in all these chapters separately (leaving out for the moment from verse 36 to 51 of chapter 1): we have found again the verses 14-34 in

---

[34] This glory, however, is only supposed, not taught. He cannot be at the feast of tabernacles, Israel's rest, nor show Himself, as He will then, to the world; but gives the Holy Ghost instead. This we know supposes His present position, just referred to in chapter 6.

[35] The doctrine of chapter 9 continues to the 30th verse of chapter 10.

chapters 5, 6, 7. The Holy Ghost now returns to the subject of the first verses in the chapter. Christ is the Word; He is the life, and the life which is the light of men. The three chapters that I have now pointed out speak of what He is in grace for men, while still declaring His right to judge. The Spirit here (in chap. 8) sets before us that which He is in Himself, and that which He is to men (thus putting them to the test, so that in rejecting Him they reject themselves, and show themselves to be reprobate).

The woman taken in adultery: the contrast with Judaism

Let us now consider our chapter. The contrast with Judaism is evident. They bring a woman whose guilt is undeniable. The Jews, in their wickedness, bring her forward in the hope of confounding the Lord. If He condemned her, He was not a Saviour—the law could do as much. If He let her go, He despised and disallowed the law. This was clever; but what avails cleverness in the presence of God who searches the heart? The Lord allows them to commit themselves thoroughly by not answering them for awhile. Probably they thought He was entangled. At last He says, "He that is without sin among you, let him first cast the stone." Convicted by their conscience, without honesty and without faith, they quit the scene of their confusion, separating from each other, each caring for himself, caring for character not conscience, and departing from Him who had convicted them; he who had the most reputation to save going out first. What a sorrowful picture! What a mighty word! Jesus and the woman are left together alone. Who can stand unconvicted in His presence? With regard to the woman, whose guilt was known, He does not go beyond the Jewish position, except to preserve the rights of His own Person in grace.

The glory of the Light

This is not the same thing as in Luke 7, plenary pardon
and salvation. The others could not condemn her—He
would not. Let her go, and let her sin no more. It is
not the grace of salvation that the Lord exhibits here. He
does not judge, He was not come for this; but the efficacy
of the pardon is not the subject of these chapters—it is
the glory here of His Person, in contrast with all that is
of the law. He is the light, and by the power of His
Word He entered as light into the conscience of those
who had brought the woman.

The Light of the world

For the Word was light; but that was not all. Coming
into the world, He was (chap. 1: 4-10) the light. Now
it was the life that was the light of men. It was not
a law that made demands, and condemned; or that promised life on obedience to its precepts. It was the Life
itself which was there in His Person, and that life was
the light of men, convincing them, and, perhaps, judging
them; but it was as light. Thus Jesus says here—in contrast with the law, brought by those who could not stand
before the light—"I am the light of the world" (not
merely of the Jews). For in this Gospel we have what
Christ is essentially in His Person, whether as God, the
Son come from the Father, or Son of Man—not what
God was in special dealings with the Jews. Hence he was
the object of faith in His Person, not in dispensational
dealings. Whoso followed Him should have the light
of life. But it was in Him, in His Person, that it
was found. And He could bear record of Himself, because, although He was a Man there, in this world, He
knew whence He came and whither He was going. It
was the Son, who came from the Father and was returning to Him again. He knew it, and was conscious of
it. His testimony, therefore, was not that of an interested

person which one might hesitate to believe. There was, in proof that this Man was the One whom He represented Himself to be, the testimony of the Son (His own), and the testimony of the Father. If they had known Him, they would have known the Father.

Opposition plainly declared: the true setting free

At that time—in spite of such testimony as this—no one laid hands on Him: His hour was not yet come. That only was wanting; for their opposition to God was certain, and known to Him. This opposition was plainly declared (vers. 19-24); consequently, if they believed not, they would die in their sins. Nevertheless He tells them that they shall know who He is, when He shall have been rejected and lifted up on the cross, having taken a very different position as the Saviour, rejected by the people and unknown of the world; when no longer presented to them as such, they should know that He was indeed the Messiah, and that He was the Son who spoke to them from the Father. As He spake these words, many believed on Him. He declares to them the effect of faith, which gives occasion to the true position of the Jews being manifested with terrible precision. He declares that the truth would set them free, and that if the Son (who is the truth) should set them free, they would be free indeed. The truth sets free morally before God. The Son, by virtue of the rights that were necessarily His, and by inheritance in the house, would place them in it according to those rights, and that in the power of divine life come down from heaven—the Son of God with power as resurrection declared it. In this was the true setting free.

Servants of sin, not children of God

Piqued at the idea of bondage, which their pride could not bear, they declare themselves to be free, and never

to have been in bondage to any one. In reply, the
Lord shows that those who commit sin are the servants
(slaves) of sin. Now, as being under the law, as being
Jews, they were servants in the house: they should be
sent away. But the Son had unalienable rights; He was
of the house and would abide in it for ever. Under sin,
and under the law, was the same thing for a child of
Adam; he was a servant. The apostle shows this in
Romans 6 (compare chaps. 7 and 8) and in Galatians
4 and 5. Moreover, they were neither really, nor morally,
the children of Abraham before God, although they were
so according to the flesh; for they sought to kill Jesus.
They were not children of God; had they been, they
would have loved Jesus who came from God. They
were the children of the devil and would do his works.

Observe here, that to understand the meaning of the
word is the way to apprehend the force of the words.
One does not learn the definition of words and then the
things; one learns the things, and then the meaning of the
words is evident.

The revelation that God Himself was there

They begin to resist the testimony, conscious that He
was making Himself greater than all those whom they
had leant upon. They rail upon Him because of His
words; and by their opposition the Lord is induced to
explain Himself more clearly; until, having declared that
Abraham rejoiced to see His day, and the Jews applying
this to His age as man, He announces positively that He
is the One who calls Himself *I am*—the supreme name
of God, that He is God Himself—He whom they pretended to know as having revealed Himself in the bush.

Wondrous revelation! A despised, rejected Man, despised and rejected by men, contradicted, ill-treated, yet
it was God Himself who was there. What a fact! What
a total change! What a revelation to those who acknowl-

edged Him, or who know Him! What a condition is
theirs who have rejected Him, and that because their
hearts were opposed to all that He was, for He did not
fail to manifest Himself! What a thought, that God
Himself has been here! Goodness itself! How everything vanishes before Him!—the law, man, his reasonings.
Everything necessarily depends on this great fact. And—
blessed be His name!—this God is a Saviour. We are
indebted to the sufferings of Christ for knowing it. And
note here, how the setting aside formal dispensations
from God, if true, is by the revelation of Himself, and so
introduces infinitely greater blessing.

The character in which the Lord presented Himself

But here He presents Himself as the Witness, the
Word, the Word made flesh, the Son of God, but still
the Word, God Himself. In the narrative at the beginning
of the chapter He is a testimony to the conscience, the
Word that searches and convicts. Verse 18, He bears
testimony with the Father. Verse 26, He declares in the
world that which He has received of the Father, and as
taught of God He has spoken. Moreover the Father
was with Him. Verses 32, 33, the truth was known by
His word, and the truth made them free. Verse 47, He
spoke the words of God. Verse 51, His word, being kept,
preserved from death. Verse 58, it was God Himself, the
Jehovah whom the fathers knew, that spoke.

The source and character of opposition to the truth

Opposition arose from its being the word of truth
(ver. 45). Opposers were of the adversary. He was a
murderer from the beginning, and they would follow
him; but as the truth was the source of life, so that
which characterized the adversary was, that he abode not
in the truth: there is no truth in him. He is the father
and the source of lies, so that, if falsehood speaks, it is

one belonging to him that speaks. Sin was bondage, and they were in bondage by the law. (Truth, the Son Himself, made free.) But, more than that, the Jews were enemies, children of the enemy, and they would do his works, not believing the words of Christ *because* He spoke the truth. There is no miracle here; it is the power of the Word, and the living Word is God Himself: rejected by men, He is, as it were, compelled to speak the truth, to reveal Himself, hidden at once and manifested, as He was in the flesh—hidden as to His glory, manifested as to all that He is in His Person and in His grace.

Chapter 9

The testimony of the Lord's works that men may see Him

IN chapter 9 we come to the testimony of His works, but as down here as a Man in lowliness. It is not the Son of God quickening whom He will as the Father, but by the operation of His grace down here, the eye opened to see in the lowly Man the Son of God. In chapter 8 it is that which He is towards men; in chapter 9 it is that which He does in man, that man may see Him. Thus we shall find Him presented in His human character, and (the Word being received) acknowledged to be the Son of God; and in this way the remnant separated, the sheep restored to the good Shepherd. He is the light of the world while He is in it; but where, through grace received in His humiliation, He communicates the power to see the light, and to see all things by it.

Observe here, that when it is the Word (the manifestation in testimony of what Christ is), man is manifested as he is in himself, a child—in his nature—of the devil, who is a murderer and a liar from the beginning, the inveterate enemy of Him who can say, "I am."[36] But when the Lord works, He produces something in man that he had not previously. He bestows sight on him, attaching him thus to the One who had enabled him to see. The Lord is not here understood or manifested in apparently as exalted a manner, because He comes down to the wants and circumstances of man, in order that He may be more closely known; but, in result, He brings the soul to the knowledge of His glorious Person. Only, instead of being the Word and the testimony—the Word of God—to show as light what man is, He is the Son, one with the Father,[37] giving eternal life to His sheep, and preserving them in this grace for ever. For, as to the blessing that flows from thence, and the full doctrine of His true position with regard to the sheep in blessing, chapter 10 goes with chapter 9. Chapter 10 is the continuation of the discourse begun at the end of chapter 9.

The man born blind: the power of the Spirit and Word making Christ known

Chapter 9 opens with the case of a man that gives rise to a question from the disciples, in relation to the government of God in Israel. Was it his parents' sin that brought this visitation on their child, according to the principles God had given them in Exodus? Or was it his own sin, known to God though not manifested to men, that had procured him this judgment? The Lord replies, that the man's condition did not depend on the government of God with respect to the sin either of himself or of his parents. His case was but the misery which gave room for the mighty operation of God in grace. It is the contrast that we have continually seen; but here it is in order to set forth the works of God.

[36] Chapter 8 is practically chapter 1: 5; only that there is, besides that, enmity, hostility against Him who was light.
[37] This distinction of grace and responsibility (in connection with the names "Father" and "Son," and "God") has been already noticed.

God acts. It is not only that which He *is*, nor even simply an object of faith. The presence of Jesus on earth made it *day*. It was therefore the time of work to do the works of Him that sent Him. But He who works here, works by means that teach us the union which exists between an object of faith and the power of God who works. He makes clay with His spittle and the earth, and puts it on the eyes of the man who was born blind. As a figure, it pointed to the humanity of Christ in earthly humiliation and lowliness, presented to the eyes of men, but with divine efficacy of life in Him. Did they see any the more? If possible, their eyes were the more completely closed. Still the object was there; it touched their eyes, and they could not see it. The blind man then washes in the pool that was called "Sent," and is enabled to see clearly. The power of the Spirit and of the Word, making Christ known as the One sent by the Father, gives him sight. It is the history of divine teaching in the heart of man. Christ, as Man, touches us. We are absolutely blind, we see nothing. The Spirit of God acts, Christ being there before our eyes; and we see plainly.

Hostility of the Jews: deciding their own fate and judging their own condition

The people are astonished and know not what to think. The Pharisees oppose. Again the sabbath is in question. They find (it is always the story) good reasons for condemning Him who bestowed sight, in their pretended zeal for God's glory. There was positive proof that the man was born blind, that he now saw, that Jesus had done it. The parents testify to the only thing that was important on their part. As to who it was that had given him sight, others knew more than they; but their fears bring out in evidence, that it was a settled thing to cast out, not only Jesus, but all who should confess Him. Thus the Jewish leaders brought the thing to a decisive point. They not only rejected Christ, but they cast out from the privileges of Israel, as to their ordinary worship, those who confessed Him. Their hostility distinguished the manifested remnant and put them apart; and that, by using confession of Christ as a touchstone. This was deciding their own fate, and judging their own condition.

The once-blind man cast out by the Jews, but found by the rejected Son of God: the effects

Observe, that proofs here went for nothing; the Jews, the parents, the Pharisees, had them before their eyes. Faith came through being personally the subject of this mighty operation of God, who opened the eyes of men to the glory of the Lord Jesus. Not that the man understood it all. He perceives that he has to do with some one sent of God. To him Jesus is a prophet. But thus the power which He had manifested in giving sight to this man enables him to trust the Lord's word as divine. Having gone so far, the rest is easy: the poor man is led much farther, and finds himself on ground that sets him free from all his former prejudices, and that gives a value to the Person of Jesus which overcomes all other considerations. The Lord develops this in the next chapter.

In truth, the Jews had made up their mind. They would have nothing to do with Jesus. They were all agreed to cast out those who believed in Him. Consequently, the poor man having begun to reason with them on the proof that existed in his own person of the Saviour's mission, they cast him out. Thus cast out, the Lord—rejected before him—finds and reveals Himself to him by His personal name of glory. "Dost thou believe on the Son of God?" The man refers it to the Word of Jesus, which to him was divine truth, and He proclaims Himself to him as being Himself the Son of God, and the man worships Him.

Thus the effect of His power was to blind those who saw, who were full of their own wisdom, whose light was darkness; and to give sight to those who were born blind.

Chapter 10

The Good Shepherd contrasted with Israel's shepherds

IN chapter 10 He contrasts Himself with all those who pretended, or had pretended, to be shepherds of Israel. He develops these three points; He comes in by the door; He is the door; and He is the Shepherd of the sheep—the good Shepherd.

The Lord's entrance into the fold: the true Shepherd

He comes in by the door. That is to say, He submits to all the conditions established by Him who built the house. Christ answers to all that is written of the Messiah, and takes the path of God's will in presenting Himself to the people. It is not human energy and power awakening and attracting the passions of men; but the obedient Man who bowed to Jehovah's will, kept the lowly place of a servant, and lived by every word that proceeded out of the mouth of God, bowed in lowliness to the place in which Jehovah's judgment had placed and viewed Israel. All the Lord's quotations in His conflict with Satan are from Deuteronomy. Consequently He who watches over the sheep, Jehovah, acting in Israel by His Spirit and providence, and arranging all things, gives Him access to the sheep in spite of the Pharisees and priests and so many others. The elect of Israel hear His voice. Now Israel was under condemnation: He therefore brings the sheep out, but He goes before them. He leaves that ancient fold, under reproach doubtless, but going before His sheep, in obedience according to the power of God—a security to every one who believed in Him that it was the right road, a warrant for their following Him, come what might, meeting every danger and showing them the way.

The sheep follow Him, for they know His voice. There are many other voices, but the sheep do not know them. Their safety consists, not in knowing them all, but in knowing that they are not the one voice which is life to them—the voice of Jesus. All the rest are the voices of strangers.

The Door for the sheep

He is the door for the sheep. He is their authority for going out, their means of entering in. By entering in, they are saved. They go in and out. It is no longer the yoke of ordinances, which, in guarding them from those without, put them in prison. The sheep of Christ are free: their safety is in the personal care of the Shepherd; and in this liberty they feed in the good and fat pastures which His love supplies. In a word, it is no longer Judaism; it is salvation, and liberty, and food. The thief comes to make his profit on the sheep by killing them. Christ is come that they might have life, and that abundantly; that is, according to the power of this life in Jesus, the Son of God, who would soon have this life (whose power was in His Person) in resurrection beyond death.

The Good Shepherd who gave His life for the sheep

The true Shepherd of Israel—at least of the remnant of the sheep—the door to authorize their coming out of the Jewish fold, and to admit them into the privileges of God by giving them life according to the abundance in

which He was able to bestow it—He was also in special
connection with the sheep thus set apart, the good Shepherd who thus gave His life for the sheep. Others would
think of themselves, He of His sheep. He knew them,
and they knew Him, even as the Father knew Him,
and He knew the Father. Precious principle! They
could have understood an earthly knowledge and interest
on the part of the Messiah on earth with regard to His
sheep. But the Son, although He had given His life and
was in heaven, knows His own, even as the Father knew
Him when He was on the earth.

His "other sheep": one flock and one Shepherd

Thus He laid down His life for the sheep; and He had
other sheep who were not of this fold, and His death
intervened for the salvation of these poor Gentiles. He
would call them. Doubtless He had given His life for the
Jews also—for all the sheep in general, as such (ver. 11).
But He does not speak distinctly of the Gentiles until
after He has spoken of His death. He would bring them
also, and there should be but one flock [38] and one Shepherd.

The intrinsic value of Christ's death in the Father's eyes: His unique power to lay down His life and take it again

Now this doctrine teaches the rejection of Israel, and
the calling out of the elect among that people, presents
the death of Jesus as being the effect of His love for His
own, tells of His divine knowledge of His sheep when He
shall be away from them, and of the call of the Gentiles.
The importance of such instruction at that moment is
obvious. Its importance, thank God, is not lost by the
lapse of time, and is not limited to the fact of a change

[38] Not "one fold." There is no fold now.

of dispensation. It introduces us into the substantial realities of the grace connected with the Person of Christ. But the death of Christ was more than love for His sheep. It had an intrinsic value in the Father's eyes. "Therefore doth the Father love Me, because I lay down My life that I might take it again." He does not say here for His sheep—it is the thing itself that is well-pleasing to the Father. *We* love because God has first loved us, but Jesus, the divine Son, can furnish motives for the Father's love. In laying down His life, He glorified the Father. Death was owned to be the just penalty for sin (being at the same time annulled and he who had the power of it,[39] and eternal life brought in as the fruit of redemption —life from God. Here also the rights of the Person of Christ are set forth. No man takes His life from Him: He lays it down Himself. He had this power (possessed by no other, true only of Him who had divine right) to lay it down, and power to take it again. Nevertheless, even in this, He did not depart from the path of obedience. He had received this commandment from His Father. But who would have been able to perform it save He who could say, "Destroy this temple, and in three days I will raise it again"? [40]

"Never perish": the glory and love of the Son and the Father identified with the safety of the sheep

They discuss what He had been saying. There were some who only saw in Him a man beside himself, and who insulted Him. Others, moved by the power of the miracle He had performed, felt that His words had a different character from that of madness. To a certain point their consciences were reached. The *Jews* surround

[39] 2 Timothy 1: 10; Hebrews 2: 14.
[40] Love and obedience are the governing principles of divine life. This is unfolded in the First Epistle of John as to ourselves. Another mark of it in the creature is dependence, and this was fully manifested in Jesus as Man.

Him, and ask how long He would keep them in suspense. Jesus answers that He had already told them; and that His works bore Him testimony. He appeals to the two testimonies which we have seen brought forward in the previous chapter (8, 9); namely, His Word and His works. But He adds, they were not of His sheep. He then takes occasion, without noticing their prejudices, to add some precious truths respecting His sheep. They hear His voice; He knows them; they follow Him; He gives them eternal life; they shall never perish. On the one hand, there shall be no perishing of life as within; on the other, no one shall pluck them out of the Saviour's hand—force from without shall not overcome the power of Him who keeps them. But there is another and an infinitely precious truth which the Lord in His love reveals to us. The Father has given us to Jesus, and He is greater than all who would seek to pluck us out of His hand. And Jesus and the Father are one. Precious teaching, in which the glory of the Person of the Son of God is identified with the safety of His sheep, with the height and depth of the love of which they are the objects. Here it is not a testimony which, as altogether divine, sets forth what man is. It is the work and the efficacious love of the Son, and at the same time that of the Father. It is not "I am;" but "I and the Father are one." If the Son has accomplished the work, and takes care of the sheep, it was the Father who gave them to Him. The Christ may perform a divine work, and furnish a motive for the Father's love, but it was the Father who gave it Him to do. Their love to the sheep is one, as those who bear that love are one.

The subjects of Chapters 8, 9, 10

Chapter 8, therefore, is the manifestation of God in testimony, and as light; chapters 9 and 10, the efficacious grace which gathers the sheep under the care of the Son, and of the Father's love. John speaks of God when he speaks of a holy nature, and man's responsibility—of the Father and the Son, when he speaks of grace in connection with the people of God.

Observe, that the wolf may come and catch [41] the sheep, if the shepherds are hirelings; but he cannot catch [41] them out of the Saviour's hands.

Active rejection of the Lord: Israel definitely left by Him

At the end of the chapter, the Jews having taken up stones to stone Him, because He made Himself equal with God, the Lord does not seek to prove to them the truth of what He is, but shows that, according to their own principles and the testimony of the Scriptures, they were wrong in this case. He appeals again to His own words and works, as proving that He was in the Father and the Father in Him. Again they take up stones, and Jesus definitely leaves them. It was all over with Israel.

Chapter 11

The death of Lazarus: man's real state: evil allowed to go on to the end

WE come now to the testimony which the Father renders to Jesus in answer to His rejection. In this chapter the power of resurrection and of life in His own Person are presented to faith.[42] But here it is not simply that He is rejected: man is looked upon as dead,

---

[41] The words in verses 12, 28 and 29 are the same in the original.

[42] It is very striking to see the Lord in the lowliness of obedient service, allowing evil to have its full way in man's failure (death) and Satan's power, till His Father's will called Him to meet it. Then no danger hinders, and then He is the resurrection and the life in personal presence and power, and then giving Himself—being such—up to death for us.

and Israel also. For it is man in the person of Lazarus. This family was blessed; it received the Lord into its bosom. Lazarus falls sick. All the Lord's human affections would be naturally concerned. Martha and Mary feel this; and they send Him word that he whom He loved was sick. But Jesus stays where He is. He might have said the word, as in the case of the centurion, and of the sick child at the beginning of this Gospel. But He did not. He had manifested His power and His goodness in healing man as he is found on earth, and delivering him from the enemy, and that in the midst of Israel. But this was not His object here—far from it— or the limits of what He was come to do. It was a question of bestowing life, or raising up again that which was dead before God. This was the real state of Israel; it was the state of man. Therefore He allows the condition of man under sin to go on and manifest itself in all the intensity of its effects down here, and permits the enemy to exercise his power to the end. Nothing remained but the judgment of God; and death, in itself, convicted man of sin while conducting him to judgment. The sick may be healed—there is no remedy for death. All is over for man, as man here below. Nothing remains but the judgment of God. It is appointed unto men once to die, but after this the judgment. The Lord therefore does not heal in this instance. He allows the evil to go on to the end—to death. That was the true place of man. Lazarus once fallen asleep, He goes to awaken him. The disciples fear the Jews, and with reason. But the Lord, having waited for His Father's will, does not fear to accomplish it. It was *day* to Him.

In fact, whatever might be His love for the nation, He must needs let it die (indeed, it was dead), and wait for the time appointed by God to raise it up again. If He must die Himself to accomplish it, He commits Himself to His Father.

Lazarus' death not prevented: Christ who died shown to be the Resurrection and the Life

But let us follow out the depths of this doctrine. Death has come in; it must take effect. Man is really in death before God; but God in grace comes in. Two things are presented in our history. He might have healed. The faith and hope of neither Martha, Mary, nor the Jews, went any farther. Only Martha acknowledges that, as the Messiah, favored of God, He would obtain from Him whatsoever He asked. But He had not prevented the death of Lazarus. He had done so many times, even for strangers, for whosoever desired it. In the second place, Martha knew that her brother would rise again at the last day; but true as it was, this truth availed nothing. Who would answer for man, dead through judgment on sin? To rise again and appear before God was not an answer to death come in by sin. The two things were true. Christ had often delivered mortal man from his sufferings in flesh, and there shall be a resurrection at the last day. But these things were of no value in the presence of death. Christ was, however, there; and He is— thanks be to God!—the resurrection and the life. Man being dead, resurrection comes first. But Jesus is the resurrection and the life in the present power of a divine life. And observe that life, coming by resurrection, delivers from all that death implies, and leaves it behind [43]

[43] Christ took human life in grace and sinless; and as alive in this life He took sin upon Him. Sin belongs, so to speak, to this life in which Christ knew no sin, but was made sin for us. But He dies—He quits this life. He is dead to sin; He has done with sin in having done with the life to which sin belonged, not in Him indeed but in us, and alive in which He was made sin for us. Raised up again by the power of God, He lives in a new condition, into which sin cannot enter, being left behind with the life that He left. Faith brings us into it by grace.

It has been pretended that these thoughts affect the divine and eternal life which was in Christ. But this is all idle and evil cavil. Even in an unconverted sinner, dying or laying down life has nothing to do with ceasing to exist as to the life of the man within. All live to God, and divine life in Christ never could cease or be changed. He never laid that down, but in the power of that, laid down His life as He possessed it here as man, to take it up in an entirely new way in

—sin, death, all that belongs to the life that man has
lost. Christ, having died for our sins, has borne their
punishment—has borne *them*. *He has died*. All the
power of the enemy, all its effect on mortal man, all the
judgment of God, He has borne it all, and has come up
from it, in the power of a new life in resurrection, which
is imparted to us; so that we are in spirit alive from
among the dead, as He is alive from among the dead.
Sin (as made sin, and bearing our sins in His own body
on the tree), death, Satan's power, God's judgment, are
all past through and left behind, and man is in a wholly
new state, in incorruption. It will be true of us, if we
die (for we shall not all die), as to the body, or, being
changed, if we do not die. But in the communication of
His life who is risen from the dead, God has quickened us
with Him, having forgiven us all our trespasses.

Life communicated by Christ to the believer: death cannot subsist before Him

Jesus here manifested His own divine power to this
effect; the Son of God was glorified in it, for we know
He had not yet died for sin; but it was this same power
in Him that was manifested.[44] The believer, even if he

resurrection beyond the grave. The cavil is a very evil cavil. In this
present edition I have changed nothing in this note, but have added a few
words in the hope that it may be clear to all. The doctrine itself is
vital truth. In the text I have erased or altered a part for another
reason, namely, that there was confusion between the divine power of
life in Christ, and God's raising Him viewed as a dead man from the
grave. Both are true and blessedly so, but they are different and were
here confounded together. In Ephesians Christ as man is raised by God.
In John it is the divine and quickening power in Himself.

[44] Resurrection has a double character: divine power, which He could
exercise and did exercise as to Himself (chap. 2: 19), and here as to
Lazarus, both the proof of divine Sonship; and the deliverance of a dead
man from his state of death. Thus God raised Christ from the dead,
so here Christ raises Lazarus. In Christ's resurrection both were
united in His own Person. Here, of course, they were separate. But
Christ has life in Himself and that in divine power. But He laid down
His life in grace. We are quickened together with Him in Ephesians 2.
But it seems avoided saying, He was quickened, when speaking of Him
alone in chapter 1.

were dead, shall rise again; and the living who believe in Him shall not die. Christ has overcome death; the power for this was in His Person, and the Father bore Him witness of it. Are any that are His alive when the Lord exercises this power? They will never die—death exists no more in His presence. Have any died before He exercises it? They shall live—death cannot subsist before Him. All the effect of sin upon man is completely destroyed by resurrection, viewed as the power of life in Christ. This refers of course to the saints, to whom life is communicated. The same divine power is, of course, exercised as to the wicked; but it is not the communication of life from Christ, nor being raised with Him, as is evident.[45]

Death the end of natural life: resurrection the end of death

Christ exercised this power in obedience and in dependence on His Father, because He was Man, walking before God to do His will; but *He is* the resurrection and the life. He has brought the power of divine life into the midst of death; and death is annihilated by it, for in life death is no more. Death was the end of natural life to sinful man. Resurrection is the end of death, which has thus no longer anything in us. It is our advantage that, having done all it could do, it is finished. We live in the life [46] that put an end to it. We come out from all that could be connected with a life that no longer

[45] The cavil I have referred to in the note to page 481 sanctions (most unwittingly, I gladly admit) the pestiferous doctrine of annihilation, as if laying down life, or death, that is the end of natural life, were ceasing to exist. I notice it, because this form of evil doctrine is one very current now. It subverts the whole substance of Christianity.

[46] Observe the sense which the apostle had of the power of this life, when he says, "That mortality might be swallowed up of life." Consider, in this point of view, the first five chapters of 2 Corinthians.

exists. What a deliverance! Christ is this power. He became this for us in its full display and exercise in His resurrection.

The need and sorrow of Martha and Mary: the Lord's sympathy

Martha, while loving Him and believing in Him, does not understand this; and she calls Mary, feeling that her sister would better understand the Lord. We will speak a little of these two presently. Mary, who waited for the Lord's own calling her to Him, modestly though sorrowfully leaving the initiative with Him, believing thus that the Lord had called her, goes to Him directly. Jews and Martha and Mary all had seen miracles and healings that had arrested the power of death. To this they all refer. But here life had passed away. What now could help? If He had been there, His love and power they could have counted on. Mary falls down at His feet weeping. On the point of resurrection power she understood no more than Martha; but her heart is melted under the sense of death in the presence of Him who had life. It is an expression of need and sorrow rather than a complaint that she utters. The Jews also weep: the power of death was on their hearts. Jesus enters into it in sympathy. He was troubled in spirit. He sighs before God; He weeps with man; but His tears turn into a groan, which was, though inarticulate, the weight of death, felt in sympathy, and presented to God by this groan of love which fully realized the truth; and that in love to those who were suffering the ill that His groan expressed.

The need brings the Lord's power to meet it

He bore death before God in His spirit as the misery of man—the yoke from which man could not deliver

himself, and He is heard. The need brings His power
into action. It was not His part now patiently to explain
to Martha what He was. He feels and acts upon the
need to which Mary had given expression, her heart being
opened by the grace that was in Him.

Man's sympathy and the exercise of the power of life by the Son of God

Man may sympathize: it is the expression of his powerlessness. Jesus enters into the affliction of mortal man,
puts Himself under the burden of death that weighs upon
man (and that more thoroughly than man himself can
do), but He takes it away with its cause. He does more
than take it away; He brings in the power that is able
to take it away. This is the glory of God. When Christ
is present, if we die, we do not die for death, but for
life: we die that we may live in the life of God, instead
of in the life of man. And wherefore? That the Son of
God may be glorified. Death came in by sin; and man
is under the power of death. But this has only given
room for our possessing life according to the second
Adam, the Son of God, and not according to the first
Adam, the sinful man. This is grace. God is glorified
in this work of grace, and it is the Son of God whose
glory shines brightly forth in this divine work.

Martha and Mary and what marked them: Mary at Jesus' feet

And, observe, that this is not grace offered in testimony, it is the exercise of the power of life. Corruption
itself is no hindrance to God. Why did Christ come?
To bring the words of eternal life to dead man. Now
Mary fed upon those words. Martha served—cumbered
her heart with many things. She believed, she loved
Jesus, she received Him into her house: the Lord loved

her. Mary listened to Him: this was what He came for;
and He had justified her in it. The good part which
she had chosen should not be taken from her.

When the Lord arrives, Martha goes of her own accord
to meet Him. She withdraws when Jesus speaks to her
of the present power of life. We are ill at ease when,
although Christians, we feel unable to apprehend the
meaning of the Lord's words, or of what His people say
to us. Martha felt that this was rather Mary's part than
hers. She goes away and calls her sister, saying, that
the Master (He who taught—observe this name that she
gives Him) was come, and *called for her*. It was her own
conscience that was to her the voice of Christ. Mary
instantly arises and comes to Him. She understood no
more than Martha. Her heart pours out its need at the
feet of Jesus, where she had heard His words and learnt
His love and grace; and Jesus asks the way to the grave.
To Martha, ever occupied with circumstances, her brother
stank already.

The family at Bethany

Afterwards (Martha served, and Lazarus was present),
Mary anoints the Lord, in the instinctive sense of what
was going on; for they were consulting to put Him to
death. Her heart, taught by love to the Lord, felt the
enmity of the Jews; and her affection, stimulated by deep
gratitude, expends on Him the most costly thing she had.
Those present blame her; Jesus again takes her part.
It might not be reasonable, but she had apprehended His
position. What a lesson! What a blessed family was
this at Bethany, in which the heart of Jesus found (as
far as could be on earth) a relief that His love accepted!
With what love have we to do! Alas, with what hatred!
For we see in this Gospel the dreadful opposition between
man and God.

God's testimony of His grace thrown over His feeblest servants—Thomas, Mark and Barnabas

There is an interesting point to be observed here before we pass on. The Holy Ghost has recorded an incident, in which the momentary but guilty unbelief of Thomas was covered by the Lord's grace. It was needful to relate it; but the Holy Ghost has taken care to show us, that Thomas loved the Lord, and was ready, at heart, to die with Him. We have other instances of the same kind. Paul says, "Take Mark, and bring him with thee; for he is profitable to me for the ministry." Poor Mark, this was necessary on account of what took place at Perga! Barnabas also has the same place in the apostle's affection and remembrance. We are weak: God does not hide it from us; but He throws the testimony of His grace over the feeblest of His servants.

Jesus' death proposed by the high priest: the Lord quietly in the place of service

But to continue. Caiaphas, the chief of the Jews, as high priest, proposes the death of Jesus, because He had restored Lazarus to life. And from that day they conspire against Him. Jesus yields to it. He came to give His life a ransom for many. He goes on to fulfil the work His love had undertaken, in accordance with His Father's will, whatever might be the devices and the malice of men. The work of life and of death, of Satan and of God, were face to face. But the counsels of God were being accomplished in grace, whatever the means might be. Jesus devotes Himself to the work by which they were to be fulfilled. Having shown the power of resurrection and of life in Himself, He is again, when the time comes, quietly in the place to which His service led Him; but He no longer goes in the same manner as before into the temple. He goes thither indeed; but the question between God and man was morally settled already.

Chapter 12

The Bethany family a sample of the three different classes of the true remnant

HIS place now is with the remnant, where His heart found rest—the house of Bethany. We have, in this family, a sample of the true remnant of Israel, three different cases with regard to their position before God. Martha had faith which, no doubt, attached her to Christ, but which did not go beyond that which was needed for the kingdom. Those who will be spared for the earth in the last days will have the same. Their faith will at length acknowledge Christ the Son of God. Lazarus was there, living by that power which could have also raised up all the dead saints in the same way,[47] which, by grace, at the last day, will call up Israel, morally, from their state of death. In a word, we find the remnant, who will not die, spared through true faith (but faith in a living Saviour, who should deliver Israel), and those who shall be brought back as from the dead, to enjoy the kingdom. Martha served; Jesus is in company with them; Lazarus sits at the table with Him.

Mary's true appreciation of Christ: God's gracious remembrance of her

But there was also the representative of another class. Mary, who had drunk at the fountain of truth, and had

[47] I speak only of the power needed to produce this effect; for in truth, the sinful condition of man, whether Jew or Gentile, required expiation; and there would have been no saints to call out from among the dead, if the grace of God had not acted by virtue, and in view, of that expiation. I speak merely of the power that dwelt in the Person of Christ, that overcame all the power of death, which could do nothing against the Son of God. But man's condition, which made the death of Christ necessary, was only demonstrated by His rejection, which proved that all means were unavailing to bring back man, as he was, to God.

received that living water into her heart, had understood that there was something more than the hope and the blessing of Israel—namely, Jesus Himself. She does that which is suitable to Jesus in His rejection—to Him who is resurrection before He is our life. Her heart associates her with that act of His, and she anoints Him for His burial. To her it is Jesus Himself who is in question—and Jesus rejected; and faith takes its place in that which was the seed of the assembly, still hidden in the soil of Israel and of this world, but which, in the resurrection, would come forth in all the beauty of the life of God—of eternal life. It is a faith that expends itself on Him, on His body, in which He was about to undergo the penalty of sin for our salvation. The selfishness of unbelief, betraying its sin in its contempt of Christ, and in its indifference gives the Lord occasion to attach its true value to this action of His beloved disciple. Her anointing His feet is pointed out here, as showing that all that was of Christ, that which was Christ, had to her a value which prevented her regarding anything else. This is a true appreciation of Christ. The faith that knows His love which passes knowledge—this kind of faith is a sweet odor in the whole house. And God remembers it according to His grace. Jesus understood her: that was all she wanted. He justifies her: who should rise up against her? This scene is over, and the course of events is resumed.

Deliberate rejection of the King of Israel, the true Son of David

The enmity of the Jews (alas, that of man's heart, thus given up to itself, and consequently to the enemy who is a murderer by nature and the enemy of God—an enemy that nothing merely human can subdue) would fain kill Lazarus also. Man is indeed capable of this: but capable of what? Everything yields to hatred—to this kind of hatred of God who manifests Himself. But for this it would in fact be inconceivable. They must now either believe in Jesus or reject Him: for His power was so evident that they must do the one or the other—a man publicly raised from the dead after four days, and alive among the people, left no longer any possibility of indecision. Jesus knew it divinely. He presents Himself as King of Israel to assert His rights, and to offer salvation and the promised glory to the people and to Jerusalem.[48] The people understand this. It must be a deliberate rejection, as the Pharisees are well aware. But the hour was come: and although they could do nothing, for the world went after Him, Jesus is put to death, for "He gave Himself."

Jesus taking His place as the Son of Man

The second testimony of God to Christ has now been borne to Him, as the true Son of David. He has been witnessed to as the Son of God in raising Lazarus (chap. 11: 4), and Son of David in riding into Jerusalem on the ass's colt. There was yet another title to be acknowledged. As Son of Man He is to possess all the kingdoms of the earth. The Greeks [49] come (for His fame had gone abroad), and desire to see Him. Jesus says, "The hour is come for the Son of Man to be glorified." But now He returns to the thoughts of which Mary's ointment was the expression to His heart. He should have been received as the Son of David; but, in taking His place as the Son of Man, a very different thing necessarily opens before Him. How could He be seen as Son of Man, coming in the clouds of heaven to take possession of all

---

[48] In this Gospel the occasion of the assembling of the crowd to meet and to accompany Jesus, was the raising of Lazarus—the testimony to His being Son of God.

[49] Greeks properly speaking: not Hellenists, that is, Jews who spoke the Greek language, and belonged to foreign countries, being of the dispersion.

things according to the counsels of God, without dying? If His human service on earth was finished, and He had gone out free, calling, if need were, for twelve legions of angels, no one could have had any part with Him: He would have remained alone. "Except the corn of wheat fall into the ground and die, it abideth alone; if it die, it bringeth forth much fruit." If Christ takes His heavenly glory, and is not alone in it, He dies to attain it, to bring with Him the souls whom God has given Him. In fact the hour was come: it could no longer tarry. Everything was now ready for the end of the trial of this world, of man, of Israel; and, above all, the counsels of God were being fulfilled.

The corn of wheat: the necessity for the Lord's death

Outwardly all was testimony to His glory. He enters Jerusalem in triumph—the multitude proclaiming Him King. What were the Romans about? They were silent before God. The Greeks came to seek Him. All is ready for the glory of the Son of Man. But the heart of Jesus well knew that for this glory—for the accomplishment of the work of God, for His having one human being with Him in the glory, for the granary of God to be filled according to the counsels of grace—He must die. No other way for guilty souls to come to God. That which Mary's affection foresaw, Jesus knows according to the truth; and according to the mind of God He feels it, and submits to it. And the Father responds at this solemn moment, by bearing testimony to the glorious effect of that which His sovereign majesty at the same time required—majesty which Jesus fully glorified by His obedience: and who could do this, excepting Him who, by that obedience, brought in the love and the power of God which accomplished it?

Serving and following: loving one's life, to lose it; hating it, to keep it

In that which follows, the Lord introduces a great principle connected with the truth contained in His sacrifice. There was no link between the natural life of man and God. If in the Man Christ Jesus there was a life in entire harmony with God, He must needs lay it down on account of this condition of man. Being of God, He could not remain in connection with man. Man would not have it. Jesus would rather die than not fulfil His service by glorifying God—than not be obedient unto the end. But if any one loved his life of this world, he lost it; for it was not in connection with God. If any one by grace hated it—separated himself in heart from this principle of alienation from God, and devoted his life to Him, he would have it in the new and eternal state. To serve Jesus therefore was to follow Him; and where He was going, there should His servant be. The result of association of heart with Jesus here, shown in following Him, passes out of this world, as He was indeed doing, and Messiah blessings, into the heavenly and eternal glory of Christ. If any one served Him, the Father would remember it, and would honor him. All this is said in view of His death, the thought of which comes over His mind; and His soul is troubled. And in the just dread of that hour which, in itself, is the judgment of God, and the end of man as God created him here on earth, He asks God to deliver Him from that hour. And, in truth, He had come—not then to be (although He was) the Messiah, not then (although it was His right) to take the kingdom; but He had come for this very hour—by dying to glorify His Father. This He desires, involve what it may. "Father, glorify Thy name," is His only prayer. This is perfectness—He feels what death is: there would have been no sacrifice if He had not felt it. But while feeling it, His only desire was to glorify His Father. If that cost Him everything, the work was perfect in proportion.

The Father's name glorified in resurrection

Perfect in this desire, and that unto death, the Father could not but answer Him. In His answer, as it appears to me, the Father announces the resurrection. But what grace, what marvel, to be admitted into such communications! The heart is astounded, while filled with worship and with grace, in beholding the perfection of Jesus, the Son of God, unto death; that is to say, absolute; and in seeing Him, with the full sense of what death was, seeking the sole glory of the Father; and the Father answering—an answer morally needful to this sacrifice of the Son, and to His own glory. Thus He said, "I have both glorified it, and will glorify it again." I believe that He had glorified it in the resurrection of Lazarus;[50] He would do so again in the resurrection of Christ—a glorious resurrection which, in itself, implied ours; even as the Lord had said, without naming His own.

The coming glory of the Son of Man and the truths connected with it

Let us now observe the connection of the truths spoken of in this remarkable passage. The hour was come for the glory of the Son of Man. But, in order to this, it needed that the precious corn of wheat should fall into the ground and die; else it would remain alone. This was the universal principle. The natural life of this world in us had no part with God. Jesus must be followed. We should *thus* be with Him: this was serving Him. Thus also we should be honored by the Father. Christ,

[50] Resurrection follows the condition of Christ. Lazarus was raised while Christ was living here in the flesh, and Lazarus is raised to life in the flesh. When Christ in glory raises us, He will raise us in glory. And even now that Christ is hid in God, our life is hid with Him there.

for Himself, looks death in the face, and feels all its import. Nevertheless He gives Himself to one only thing—the glory of His Father. The Father answers Him in this. His desire should be fulfilled. He should not be without an answer to His perfection. The people hear it as the voice of the Lord God, as described in the Psalms. Christ (who, in all this, had put Himself entirely aside, had spoken only of the glory of His followers and of His Father) declares that this voice came for the people's sake, in order that they might understand what He was for their salvation. Then there opens before Him, who had put Himself aside and submitted to everything for His Father's sake, not the future glory, but the value, the import, the glory, of the work He was about to do. The principles of which we have spoken are here brought to the central point of their development. In His death the *world* was judged: Satan was its prince, and he is cast out: in appearance it is Christ who was so. By death He morally and judicially destroyed him who had the power of death. It was the total and entire annihilation of all the rights of the enemy, over whomsoever and whatsoever it might be, when the Son of God and Son of Man bore the judgment of God as Man in obedience unto death. All the rights that Satan possessed through man's disobedience and the judgment of God upon it, were only rights in virtue of the claims of God upon man, and come back to Christ alone. And being lifted up between God and the world, in obedience, on the cross, bearing that which was due to sin, Christ became the point of attraction for all men living, that through Him they might draw nigh to God. While living, Jesus ought to have been owned as the Messiah of promise; lifted up from the earth as a victim before God, being no longer of the earth as living upon it, He was the point of attraction towards God for all those who, living on earth, were alienated from God, as we have seen, that they might come to Him there (by grace), and have life through

the Saviour's death. Jesus warns the people that it was
only for a little time that He, the light of the world,
would remain with them. They should believe while it
was yet time. Soon would the darkness come, and they
would not know whither they went. We see that, whatever might be the thoughts that occupy His heart, the
love of Jesus never grows cold. He thinks of those
around Him—of men according to their need.

Isaiah's prophetic warning of the results of unbelief

Nevertheless they did not believe according to the testimony of the prophet, given in view of His humiliation
unto death, given in sight of the vision of His divine
glory, which could but bring judgment on a rebellious
people (Isa. 53 and 6).

God's counsels of grace: His long-suffering

Nevertheless, such is grace, His humiliation should be
their salvation; and, in the glory that judged them, God
would remember the counsels of His grace, as sure a fruit
of that glory as was the judgment which the Holy, Holy,
Holy, Jehovah of Hosts must pronounce against evil—a
judgment suspended, by His long-suffering, during cen-
turies, but now fulfilled when these last efforts of His
mercy were despised and rejected. They preferred the
praise of men.

The Saviour and His Word

At last Jesus declares that which His coming really
was—that, in fact, they who believed in Him, in the
Jesus whom they saw on the earth, believed in His Father,
and saw His Father. He was come as the light, and they
who believed should not walk in darkness. He did not
judge; He was come to save; but the Word which He
had spoken should judge those who heard, for it was the
Father's Word, and it was life everlasting.

Chapter 13

Man's unceasing hatred: the Lord's unchanging love

NOW, then, the Lord has taken His place as going to the Father. The time was come for it. He takes His place above, according to the counsels of God, and is no longer in connection with a world that had already rejected Him; but He loves His own unto the end. Two things are present to Him: on the one hand, sin taking the form most painful to His heart; and on the other, the sense of all glory being given to Him as Man, and of whence He came and whither He was going: that is, His personal and heavenly character in relationship with God, and the glory that was given Him. He came from God and went to God; and the Father had put all things into His hands.

The service of love: our Advocate on high

But neither His entrance into glory, nor the heartlessness of man's sin, takes His heart away from His disciples or even from their wants. Only He exercises His love, to put them in connection with Himself in the new position He was creating for them by entering thus into it. He could no longer remain with them on earth; and if He left them, and must leave them, He would not give them up, but fit them for being where He was. He loved them with a love that nothing stopped. It went on to perfect its results; and He must fit them to be with Him. Blessed change that love accomplished even from His being with them here below! They were to have a part with Him who came from God and went to God, and into whose hands the Father had put all things; but then they must be fit to be with Him there. To this end He is still their servant in love, and even more so than ever. No doubt He had been so in His perfect grace, but it was

while among them. They were thus in a certain sense
companions. They were all supping together here at the
same table. But He quits this position, as He did His
personal association with His disciples by ascending to
heaven, by going to God. But, if He does, He still girds
Himself for their service, and takes water[51] to wash
their feet. Although in heaven, He is still serving us.[52]
The effect of this service is, that the Holy Ghost takes
away practically by the Word all the defilement that we
gather in walking through this world of sin. On our
way we come in contact with this world that rejected
Christ. Our advocate on high (compare 1 John 2), He
cleanses us from its defilement by the Holy Ghost and
the Word; He cleanses us in view of the relationships
with God His Father, into which He has brought us by
entering into them Himself as Man on high.

Washing the disciples' feet; the means

A purity was needed that should befit the presence of
God, for He was going there. However it is only the feet
that are in question. The priests that served God in the
tabernacle were washed at their consecration. That washing was not repeated. So, when once spiritually renewed
by the Word, this is not repeated for us. In "he that is
washed" it is a different word from "save to wash his

[51] It is not blood here. That assuredly there must be. He came not
by water only, but by water and blood; but here the washing is in every
repect that of water. The washing from sins in His own blood is
never repeated at all in any way. Christ must have suffered often in
that case. See Hebrews 9, 10. In respect of imputation, there is no
more conscience of sins.

[52] The Lord in becoming a Man took on Him the form of a servant.
(Phil. 2.) This He never gives up. It might have been thought so
when He went into glory, but He is showing here that it is not so. He
is now, as in Exodus 21, saying, "I love my master, I love my wife, I
love my children; I will not go out free;" and becoming a servant for
ever, even if He could have had twelve legions of angels. Here He is a
servant to wash their feet, defiled in passing through this world. In
Luke 12 we see that He keeps the place of service in glory. It is a
sweet thought that even there He ministers heaven's best blessedness
to our happiness.

feet." The first is bathing the whole body; the latter
washing hands or feet. We need the latter continually,
but are not, once born of water by the Word, washed
over again, any more than the priests' first consecration
was repeated. The priests washed their hands and their
feet every time they engaged in service—that they drew
near to God. Our Jesus restores communion and power
to serve God, when we have lost it. He does it, and with
a view to communion and service; for before God we are
entirely clean personally. The service was the service of
Christ—of His love. He wiped their feet with the towel
wherewith He was girded (a circumstance expressive of
service). The means of purification was water—the
Word, applied by the Holy Ghost. Peter shrinks from
the idea of Christ thus humbling Himself: but we must
submit to this thought, that our sin is such that nothing
less than the humiliation of Christ can in any sense
cleanse us from it. Nothing else will make us really know
the perfect and dazzling purity of God, or the love and
devotedness of Jesus: and in the realization of these consists the having a heart sanctified for the presence of
God. Peter, then, would have the Lord to wash also his
hands and his head. But this is already accomplished.
If we are His, we are born again and cleansed by the
Word which He has already applied to our souls; only we
defile our feet in walking. It is after the pattern of this
service of Christ in grace that we are to act with regard
to our brethren.

Judas' treachery known to the Lord

Judas was not clean; he had not been born again,
was not clean through the Word Jesus had spoken. Nevertheless, being sent of the Lord, they who had received
him had received Christ. And this is true also of those
whom He sends by His Spirit. This thought brings the
treachery of Judas before the Lord's mind; His soul is

troubled at the thought, and He unburdens His heart by declaring it to His disciples. What His heart is occupied with here is, not His knowledge of the individual, but of the fact that *one of them* should do it, one of those who had been His companions.

The love of John and Peter to their Lord

Therefore it was, because of His saying this, that the disciples looked upon another. Now there was one near Him, the disciple whom Jesus loved; for we have, in all this part of the Gospel of John, the testimony of grace that answers to the diverse forms of malice and wickedness in man. This love of Jesus had formed the heart of John—had given him confidingness and constancy of affection; and consequently, without any other motive than this, he was near enough to Jesus to receive communications from Him. It was not in order to receive them that he placed himself close to Jesus: he was there because he loved the Lord, whose own love had thus attached him to Himself; but, being there, he was able to receive them. It is thus that we may still learn of Him.

Peter loved Him; but there was too much of Peter, not for service, if God called him to it—and He did in grace, when He had thoroughly broken him down, and made him know himself—but for intimacy. Who, among the twelve, bore testimony like Peter, in whom God was mighty towards the circumcision? But we do not find in his epistles that which is found in John's.[53] Moreover each one has his place, given in the sovereignty of God. Peter loved Christ; and we see that, linked also with John by this common affection, they are constantly together; as also at the end of this Gospel he is anxious to know the fate of John. He uses John, therefore, to

[53] On the other hand, Peter died for the Lord. John was left to care for the assembly: it does not appear that he became a martyr.

ask the Lord, which it was among them that should betray Him, as He had said. Let us remember that being
near Jesus for His own sake is the way of having His
mind when anxious thoughts arise.

Judas possessed by Satan: darkness and despair

Jesus points out Judas by the sop, which would have
checked any other, but which to him was only the seal
of his ruin. It is indeed thus in degree with every favor
of God that falls upon a heart that rejects it. After the
sop Satan enters into Judas. Wicked already through
covetousness, and yielding habitually to ordinary temptations; although he was with Jesus, hardening his heart
against the effect of that grace which was ever before his
eyes and at his side, and which, in a certain way, was
exercised towards him, he had yielded to the suggestion
of the enemy, and made himself the tool of the high
priests to betray the Lord. He knew what they desired,
and goes and offers himself. And when, by his long
familiarity with the grace and presence of Jesus while
addicting himself to sin, that grace and the thought of the
Person of Christ had entirely lost their influence, he was
in a state to feel nothing at betraying Him. The knowledge he had of the Lord's power, helped him to give himself up to evil, and strengthened the temptation of Satan;
for evidently he made sure that Jesus would always succeed in delivering Himself from His enemies; and, as far
as power was concerned, Judas was right in thinking that
the Lord could have done so. But what knew he of the
thoughts of God? All was darkness, morally, in his soul.

And now, after this last testimony, which was both
a token of grace and a witness to the true state of his
heart that was insensible to it (as expressed in the Psalm
here fulfilled), Satan enters into him, takes possession
of him so as to harden him against all that might have
made him feel, even as a man, the horrid nature of what

he was doing, and thus enfeeble him in accomplishing the evil; so that neither his conscience nor his heart should be awakened in committing it. Dreadful condition! Satan possesses him, until forced to leave him to the judgment from which he cannot shelter him, and which will be his own at the time appointed of God—judgment that manifests itself to the conscience of Judas when the evil was done, when too late (and the sense of which is shown by a despaire that his link with Satan did but augment), but which is forced to bear testimony to Jesus before those who had profited by his sin and who mocked at his distress. For despair speaks the truth; the veil is torn away; there is no longer self-deception; the conscience is laid bare before God, but it is before His judgment. Satan does not deceive there; and not the grace, but the perfection of Christ is known. Judas bore witness to the innocence of Jesus, as did the thief on the cross. It is thus that death and destruction heard the fame of His wisdom: only God knows it. (Job 28: 22, 23.)

The Lord's omniscience

Jesus knew his condition. It was but the accomplishing that which He was going to do, by means of one for whom there was no longer any hope. "That thou doest," said Jesus, "do quickly." But what words, when we hear them from the lips of Him who was love itself! Nevertheless, the eyes of Jesus were now fixed upon His own death. He is alone. No one, not even His disciples, had any part with Him. These could no more follow Him whither He was now going, than the Jews themselves. Solemn but glorious hour! A Man, He was going to meet God in that which separated man from God—to meet Him in judgment. This, in fact, is what He says, as soon as Judas is gone out. The door which closed on Judas separated Christ from this world.

The cross the brightest manifestation of God's glory, the centre of the history of eternity

"Now," He says, "is the Son of Man glorified." He had said this when the Greeks arrived; but then it was the glory to come—His glory as the head of all men, and, in fact, of all things. But this could not yet be; and He said, "Father, glorify Thy name." Jesus must die. It was *that* which glorified the name of God in a world where sin was. It was the glory of the Son of Man to accomplish it there, where all the power of the enemy, the effect of sin, and the judgment of God upon sin, were displayed; where the question was morally settled; where Satan (in his power over sinful man—man under sin, and that fully developed in open enmity against God), and God met, not as in the case of Job, as an instrument in God's hand for discipline, but for justice— that which God was against sin, but that in which, through Christ's giving Himself, all His attributes should be in exercise, and be glorified, and by which, in fact, through that which took place, all the perfections of God have been glorified, being manifested through Jesus, or by means of that which Jesus did and suffered.

These perfections had been directly unfolded in Him, as far as grace went; but now that the opportunity of the exercise of all of them was afforded, by His taking a place which put Him to the proof according to the attributes of God, their divine perfection could be displayed through man in Jesus there where He stood in the place of man; and (made sin, and, thank God, for the sinner) God was glorified in Him. For see what in fact met in the cross: Satan's complete power over men, Jesus alone excepted; man in open perfect enmity against God in the rejection of His Son; God manifest in grace: then in Christ, as Man, perfect love to His Father, and perfect obedience, and that in the place of sin, that is, as made it (for the perfection of love to His Father and obedience were when

He was as sin before God on the cross); then God's majesty made good, glorified (Heb. 2:10); His perfect, righteous judgment against sin as the Holy One; but therein His perfect love to sinners in giving His only-begotten Son. For hereby know we love. To sum it up: at the cross we find man in absolute evil—the hatred of what was good; Satan's full power over the world—the prince of this world; man in perfect goodness, obedience, and love to the Father at all cost to Himself; God in absolute, infinite, righteousness against sin, and infinite divine love to the sinner. Good and evil were fully settled for ever, and salvation wrought, the foundation of the new heavens and the new earth laid. Well may we say, "Now is the Son of Man glorified, and God is glorified in Him." Utterly dishonored in the first, He is infinitely more glorified in the Second, and therefore puts Man (Christ) in glory, and straightway, not waiting for the kingdom. But this requires some less abstract words; for the cross is the centre of the universe, according to God, the basis of our salvation and our glory, and the brightest manifestation of God's own glory, the centre of the history of eternity.

"The Son of Man glorified" in Jesus on the cross, and "God glorified in Him" there

The Lord had said, when the Greeks desired to see Him, that the hour was come for the Son of Man to be glorified. He spoke then of His glory as Son of Man, the glory which He should take under that title. He felt indeed that in order to bring men into that glory, He must needs pass through death Himself. But He was engrossed by one thing which detached His thoughts from the glory and from the suffering—the desire which possessed His heart that His Father should be glorified. All was now come to the point at which this was to be accomplished; and the moment had arrived when Judas (overstepping the limits of God's just and perfect patience) was gone out, giving the reins to his iniquity, to consummate the crime which would lead to the wonderful fulfilment of the counsels of God.

Now, in Jesus on the cross, the Son of Man has been glorified in a much more admirable way than He will be even by the positive glory that belongs to Him under that title. He will, we know, be clothed with that glory; but, on the cross, the Son of Man bore all that was necessary for the perfect display of all the glory of God. The whole weight of that glory was brought to bear upon Him, to put Him to the proof, that it might be seen whether He could sustain it, verify, and exalt it; and that by setting it forth in the place where, but for this, sin concealed that glory, and, so to speak, gave it impiously the lie. Was the Son of Man able to enter into such a place, to undertake such a task, and to accomplish the task, and maintain His place without failure to the end? This Jesus did. The majesty of God was to be vindicated against the insolent rebellion of His creature; His truth, which had threatened Him with death, maintained; His justice established against sin (who could withstand it?); and, at the same time, His love fully demonstrated. Satan having here all the sorrowful rights that he had acquired through our sin, Christ—perfect as a Man, alone, apart from all men, in obedience, and having as Man but one object, that is, the glory of God, thus divinely perfect, sacrificing *Himself* for this purpose—fully glorified God. God was glorified *in Him*. His justice, His majesty, His truth, His love—all was verified on the cross as they are in Himself, and revealed only there; and that with regard to sin.

All God's attributes freely and fully displayed to the sinner

And God can now act freely, according to that which He is consciously to Himself, without any one attribute hiding, or obscuring, or contradicting another. Truth condemned man to death, justice for ever condemned the sinner, majesty demanded the execution of the sentence. Where, then, was love? If love, as man would conceive it, were to pass over all, where would be His majesty and His justice? Moreover, that could not be; nor would it really then be love, but indifference to evil. By means of the cross, He is just, and He justifies in grace; He is love, and in that love He bestows His righteousness on man. The righteousness of God takes the place of man's sin to the believer. The righteousness, as well as the sin, of man vanishes before the bright light of grace, and does not becloud the sovereign glory of a grace like this towards man, who was really alienated from God.

God glorifying the Son of Man in Himself

And who had accomplished this? Who had thus established (as to its manifestation, and the making it good where it had been, as to the state of things, compromised by sin) the whole glory of God? It was the Son of Man. Therefore God glorifies Him with His own glory; for it was indeed that glory which He had established and made honorable, when before His creatures it was effaced by sin—it cannot be so in itself. And not only was it established, but it was thus realized as it could have been by no other means. Never was love like the gift of the Son of God for sinners; never justice (to which sin is insupportable) like that which did not spare even the Son Himself when He bore sin upon Him; never majesty like that which held the Son of God Himself responsible for the full extent of its exigencies (compare Heb. 2); never truth like that which did not yield before the necessity of the death of Jesus. We now know God. God, being glorified in the Son of Man, glorifies Him in Himself. But, consequently, He does not wait for the day of His glory with man, according to the thought of

chapter 12. God calls Him to His own right hand, and
sets Him there at once and alone. Who could be there
(save in spirit) excepting He? Here His glory is connected with that which He alone could do—with that
which He must have done alone; and of which He must
have the fruit alone with God, for He was God.

Alone on the cross, unique and pre-eminent in glory

Other glories shall come in their time. He will share
them with us, although in all things He has the pre-
eminence. Here He is, and must ever be, alone (that
is, in that which is personal to Himself). Who shared
the cross with Him, as suffering for sin, and fulfilling
righteousness? We, indeed, share it with Him so far as
suffering for righteousness' sake, and for the love of Him
and His people, even unto death: and thus we shall share
His glory also. But it is evident that we could not glorify
God for sin. He who knew no sin could alone be made
sin. The Son of God alone could bear this burden.

The new commandment given to the disciples: brotherly love

In this sense the Lord—when His heart found relief
in pouring out these glorious thoughts, these marvellous
counsels—addressed His disciples with affection, telling
them that their connection with Him here below would
soon be ended, that He was going where they could not
follow Him, any more than could the unbelieving Jews.
Brotherly love was, in a certain sense, to take His place.
They were to love one another as He had loved them,
with a love superior to the faults of the flesh in their
brethren—brotherly love gracious in these respects. If
the main pillar were taken away against which many
around it were leaning, they would support each other,
although not by their strength. And thus should the
disciples of Christ be known.

Simon Peter's self-confidence

Now Simon Peter desires to penetrate into that which no man, save Jesus, could enter—God's presence by the path of death. This is fleshly confidence. The Lord tells him, in grace, that it could not be so now. He must dry up that sea fathomless to man—death—that over-flowing Jordan; and then, when it was no longer the judgment of God, nor wielded by the power of Satan (for in both these characters Christ has entirely destroyed its power for the believer), then His poor disciple might pass through it for the sake of righteousness and of Christ. But Peter would follow Him in his own strength, declaring himself able to do exactly that which Jesus was going to do for him. Yet, in fact, terrified at the first movement of the enemy, he draws back before the voice of a girl, and denies the Master whom he loved. In the things of God, fleshly confidence does but lead us into a position in which it cannot stand. Sincerity alone can do nothing against the enemy. We must have the strength of God.

Chapter 14

In view of His departure the Lord alone an object of faith

THE Lord now begins to discourse with them in view of His departure. He was going where they could not come. To human sight they would be left alone upon the earth. It is the sense of this apparently deso-late condition that the Lord addresses Himself, showing them that *He* was an object for faith, even as God was. In doing this, He opens to them the whole truth with respect to their condition. His work is not the subject treated of, but their position by virtue of that work. His

Person should have been for them the key to that position,
and would be so now: the Holy Ghost, the Comforter,
who should come, would be the power by which they
should enjoy it, and indeed more yet.

The revelation of what is beyond death for faith: what the Lord's departure meant for His disciples: with Him

To Peter's question, "Whither goest Thou?" the Lord
replies. Only when the desire of the flesh seeks to enter
into the path on which Jesus was then entering, the Lord
could but say that the strength of the flesh was unavailing there; for, in fact, he proposed to follow Christ in
death. Poor Peter!

But when the Lord has written the sentence of death
upon the flesh for us, by revealing its impotency, He
can then (chap. 14) reveal that which is beyond it for
faith; and that which belongs to us through His death
throws its light back, and teaches who He was, even
when on earth, and always, before the world was. He
did but return to the place from which He came. But
He begins with His disciples where they were, and meets
the need of their hearts by explaining to them in what
manner—better, in a certain sense, than by following
Him here below—they should be with Him when absent
where He would be. They did not see God corporeally
present with them: to enjoy His presence they believed
in Him. It was to be the same thing with regard to
Jesus. They were to believe in Him. He did not forsake
them in going away, as though there were only room for
Himself in His Father's house. (He alludes to the temple
as a figure.) There was room for them all. The going
thither, observe, was still His thought—He is not here as
the Messiah. We see Him in the relationships in which
He stood according to the eternal truths of God. He
had always His departure in view: had there been no

room for them, He would have told them so. Their place was with Him. But He was going to prepare a place for them. Without presenting redemption there, and presenting Himself as the new man according to the power of that redemption, there was no place prepared in heaven. He enters it in the power of that life which should bring them in also. But they should not go alone to rejoin Him, nor would He rejoin them down here. Heaven, not earth, was in question. Nor would He simply send others for them; but as those He dearly valued, He would come for them Himself, and receive them unto Himself, that where He was there should they be also. He would come from the Father's throne: there, of course, they cannot sit; but He will receive them there, where He shall be in glory before the Father. They should be with Him—a far more excellent position than His remaining with them here below, even as Messiah in glory on the earth.

Going to the Father: Himself the Way

Now, also, having said where He was going, that is, to His Father (and speaking according to the effect of His death for them), He tells them that they knew whither He was going, and the way. For He was going to the Father, and they had seen the Father in seeing Him; and thus, having seen the Father in Him, they knew the way; for in coming to Him, they came to the Father, who was in Him as He was in the Father. He was, then, Himself the way. Therefore He reproaches Philip with not having known Him. He had been long with them, as the revelation in His own Person of the Father; and they ought to have known Him, and to have seen that He was in the Father, and the Father in Him, and thus have known where He was going, for it was to the Father. He had declared the name of the Father; and if they were unable to see the Father in Him, or to

be convinced of it by His words, they ought to have
known it by His works; for the Father who dwelt in
Him—He it was who did the works. This depended on
His own Person, being still in the world; but a striking
proof was connected with His departure. After He was
gone, they would do even greater works than He did,
because they should act in connection with His greater
nearness to the Father. This was requisite to His glory.
It was even unlimited. He placed them in immediate
connection with the Father by the power of His work and
of His name; and whatsoever they should ask the Father
in His name, Christ Himself would do it for them. Their
request should be heard and granted by the Father—
showing what nearness He had acquired for them; and
He (Christ) would do all they should ask. For the power
of the Son was not, and could not be, wanting to the
Father's will: there was no limit to His power.

Discipleship characterized by obedience: the promise of the Holy Spirit, to abide forever

But this led to another subject. If they loved Him, it
was to be shown, not in regrets, but in keeping His commandments. They were to walk in obedience. This
characterizes discipleship up to the present time. Love
desires to be with Him, but shows itself by obeying His
commands; for Christ also has a right to command. On
the other hand He would seek their good on high, and
another blessing should be granted them; namely, the
Holy Ghost Himself, who should never leave them, as
Christ was about to do. The world could not receive
Him. Christ, the Son, had been shown to the eyes of the
world, and ought to have been received by it. The Holy
Ghost would act, being invisible; for by the rejection of
Christ, it was all over with the world in its natural and
creature relationships with God. But the Holy Ghost
should be known by the disciples; for He should not

only remain with them, as Christ could not, but be in them, not with them as He was. The Holy Ghost would not be seen then or known by the world.

The Way, the Truth, and the Life

Until now, in His discourse, He had led His disciples to follow Him (in spirit) on high, through the knowledge which acquaintance with His Person (in which the Father was revealed) gave them of whither He was going, and of the way. He was Himself the way, as we have seen. He was the truth itself, in the revelation (and the perfect revelation) of God and of the soul's relationship to Him; and, indeed, of the real condition and character of all things, by bringing out the perfect light of God in His own Person who revealed Him. He was the life, in which God and the truth could thus be known. Men came by Him; they found the Father revealed in Him; and they possessed in Him that which enabled them to enjoy, and in the reception of which they came in fact to, the Father.

The stream of blessing flowing for the disciples in this world: life in Christ

But, now, it is not what is objective which He presents; not the Father in Him (which they ought to have known) and He in the Father, when here below. He does not, therefore, raise their thoughts to the Father through Himself and in Himself, and He in the Father in heaven. He sets before them that which should be given them down here—the stream of blessing that should flow for them in this world, by virtue of that which Jesus was, and was for them, in heaven. The Holy Ghost once introduced as sent, the Lord says, "I will not leave you orphans, I will come to you." His presence, in spirit, here below, is the consolation of His people. They should see Him; and this is much more true than seeing Him

with the eyes of flesh. Yes, more true; it is knowing Him
in a much more real way, even though by grace they had
believed in Him as the Christ, the Son of God. And,
moreover, this spiritual sight of Christ by the heart,
through the presence of the Holy Ghost, is connected
with life. "Because I live, ye shall live also." We see
Him, because we have life, and this life is in Him, and He
in this life. "This life is in the Son." It is as sure as
His duration. It is derived from Him. *Because* He
lives, we shall live. Our life is, in everything, the manifestation of Himself who is our life. Even as the apostle
expresses it, "That the life of Jesus may be manifested in
our mortal bodies." Alas, the flesh resists; but this is our
life in Christ.

The disciples in Christ in virtue of the Holy Spirit's presence

But this is not all. The Holy Ghost dwelling in us,
we know that we are in Christ.[54] At that day ye shall
know that I am in My Father, and ye in Me, and I in
you." It is not, "The Father in Me [which, however,
was always true], and I in Him"—words, the first of
which, here omitted, expressed the reality of His manifestation of the Father here on earth. The Lord only
expresses that which belongs to His being really and
divinely one with the Father—"I am in My Father."
It is this last part of the truth (implied, doubtless, in the
other when rightly understood) of which the Lord here
speaks. It could not really be so; but men might imagine
such a thing as a manifestation of God in a man, without

[54] Note, this is individual, not the union of the members of the body
with Christ; nor is union indeed an exact term for it. We are *in* Him.
This is more than union, but not the same thing. It is nature and life,
and position in it, our place in that nature and life. When He was on
earth, and they had not the Holy Ghost, they should have known that
He was in the Father and the Father in Him. When He was in heaven,
and they had the Holy Ghost, they would know they were in Him and
He in them.

this man being really such—so truly God, that is to say,
in Himself—that it must also be said, He is in the Father.
People dream of such things; they speak of the manifestation of God in flesh. We speak of God manifest in the
flesh. But here all ambiguity is obviated—He was in the
Father, and it is this part of the truth which is repeated
here; adding to it, in virtue of the presence of the Holy
Ghost, that while the disciples should indeed fully know
the divine Person of Jesus, they should moreover know
that they were themselves in Him. He who is joined to
the Lord is one spirit. Jesus did not say that they ought
to have known *this* while He was with them on earth.
They ought to have known that the Father was in Him
and He in the Father. But in that He was alone. The
disciples, however, having received the Holy Ghost, should
know their own being in Him—a union of which the
Holy Ghost is the strength and the bond. The life of
Christ flows from Him in us. He is in the Father, we
in Him, and He also in us, according to the power of
the presence of the Holy Ghost.

Continual guardianship and government: the child's love, the Father's love, and that of Christ, shown in the path of obedience

This is the subject of the common faith, true of all.
But there is continual guardianship and government, and
Jesus manifests Himself to us in connection with, and in
a manner dependent on, our walk. He who is mindful
of the Lord's will possesses it, and observes it. A *good* child
not only obeys when he knows his father's will, but he
acquires the knowledge of that will by giving heed to it.
This is the spirit of obedience in love. If we act thus
with regard to Jesus, the Father, who takes account of all
that relates to His Son, will love us. Jesus will also love
us, and will manifest Himself to us. Judas (not Iscariot)

did not understand this, because he saw no farther than a bodily manifestation of Christ, such as the world also could perceive. Jesus therefore adds, that the truly obedient disciple (and here He speaks more spiritually and generally of His Word, not merely of His commandments) should be loved of the Father, and that the Father and Himself would come and make their abode with him. So that, if there be obedience, while waiting for the time when we shall go and dwell with Jesus in the Father's presence, He and the Father dwell in us. The Father and the Son manifest themselves in us, in whom the Holy Ghost is dwelling, even as the Father and the Holy Ghost were present, when the Son was here below— doubtless in another way, for He was the Son, and we only live by Him — the Holy Ghost only dwelling in us. But with respect to those glorious Persons they are not disunited. The Father did the works in Christ, and Jesus cast out devils by the Holy Ghost; nevertheless, the Son wrought. If the Holy Ghost is in us, the Father and the Son come and make their abode in us. Only it will be observed here that there is government. We are, according to the new life, sanctified unto obedience. It is not here a question of the love of God in sovereign grace to a sinner, but of the Father's dealings with His children. Therefore it is in the path of obedience that the manifestations of the Father's love and the love of Christ are found. We love, but do not caress, our naughty children. If we grieve the Spirit, He will not be in us the power of the manifestation to our souls of the Father and the Son in communion, but will rather act on our consciences in conviction, though giving the sense of grace. God may restore us by His love, and by testifying when we have wandered; but communion is in obedience. Finally, Jesus was to be obeyed; but it was the Father's word to Jesus, observe, as He was here below. His words were the words of the Father.

Christ truly and ever Man, but God manifest in flesh

The Holy Ghost bears testimony to that which Christ was, as well as to His glory. It is the manifestation of the perfect life of Man, of God in Man, of the Father in the Son—the manifestation of the Father by the Son who is in the bosom of the Father. Such were the words of the Son here below; and when we speak of His commandments, it is not only the manifestation of His glory by the Holy Ghost, when He is on high, and its results; but His commandments when He spoke here below, and spoke the words of God; for He had not the Holy Ghost by measure, so that His words would have been mingled, and partly imperfect, or at least not divine. He was truly Man, and ever Man; but it was God manifest in the flesh. The old commandment from the beginning is new, inasmuch as this same life, which expressed itself in His commandments, now moves in and animates us—true in Him and in us. (Compare 1 John 2.) The commandments are those of the Man Christ, yet they are the commandments of God and the words of the Father, according to the life that has been manifested in this world in the Person of Christ. They express in Him, and form and direct in us, that eternal life which was with the Father, and which has been manifested to us in man —in Him whom the apostles could see, hear, and touch; and which life we possess in Him. Nevertheless the Holy Ghost has been given us to lead us into all truth, according to this same chapter of John's Epistle—"Ye have an unction from the Holy One, and ye know all things."

The difference between Christ's commandments and the law

To direct life is different from knowing all things. The two are connected, because, in walking according to that life, we do not grieve the Holy Spirit, and we are in the light. To direct life, where it exists, is not the same thing as to give a law imposed on man in the flesh (right-eously, no doubt), promising him life if he keep these commandments. This is the difference between the commandments of Christ and the law: not as to authority—divine authority is always the same in itself—but that the law offers life, and is addressed to man responsible in flesh, offering him life as the result; while the commandments of Christ express and direct the life of one who lives through the Spirit, in connection with his being in Christ, and Christ in him. The Holy Ghost (who, besides this, teaches all things) brought to remembrance the commandments of Christ—all things that He had said to them. It is the same thing in detail, by His grace, with Christians individually now.

The Lord's gift of His own peace

Finally, the Lord, in the midst of this world, left peace to His disciples, giving them His own peace. It is when going away, and in the full revelation of God, that He could say this to them; so that He possessed it in spite of the world. He had gone through death and the drinking of the cup, put away sin for them, destroyed the power of the enemy in death, made propitiation by fully glorifying God. Peace was made, and made for them before God, and all that they were brought into—the light as He was, so that this peace was perfect in the light; and it was perfect in the world, because it brought them so into connection with God that the world could not even touch or reach their source of joy. Moreover Jesus had so accomplished this for them, and He bestowed it on them in such a way, that He gave them the peace which He Himself had with the Father, and in which, consequently He walked in this world. The world gives a part of its goods while not relinquishing the mass; but what it gives, it gives away and has no longer. Christ introduces into the enjoyment of that which is His own—

of His own position before the Father.[55] The world does not and cannot give in this manner. How perfect must that peace have been which He enjoyed with the Father —that peace He gives to us—His own!

In the Lord's glory and happiness we find our own

There remains yet one precious thought—a proof of unspeakable grace in Jesus. He so reckons upon our affection, and this as personal to Himself, that He says to them, "If ye loved Me ye would rejoice, because I said, I go unto the Father." He gives us to be interested in His own glory, in His happiness, and, in it, to find our own.

The desire of the Christian's heart

Good and precious Saviour, we do indeed rejoice that Thou who hast suffered so much for us, hast now fulfilled all things, and art at rest with Thy Father, whatever may be thine active love for us. Oh, that we knew and loved Thee better! But still we can say in fulness of heart, Come quickly, Lord! Leave once more the throne of Thy rest and of Thy personal glory, to come and take us to Thyself, that all may be fulfilled for us also, and that we may be with Thee and in the light of Thy Father's countenance and in His house. Thy grace is infinite, but Thy presence and the joy of the Father shall be the rest of our hearts, and our eternal joy.

[55] This is blessedly true in every respect, except of course essential Godhead and oneness with the Father: in this He remains divinely alone. But all He has as Man, and as Son in manhood, He introduces into "My Father and your Father, My God and your God." His peace, His joy, the words the Father gave to Him, He has given to us; the glory given to Him He has given to us; with the love wherewith the Father has loved Him we are loved. The counsels of God were not merely to meet our responsibility as children of Adam, but before the world to put us into the same position with the second Adam, His own Son. And Christ's work has made that to be righteousness.

The fulness of grace and perfection shown in the Person of Christ

Here the Lord closes this part of His discourse.[56]　He had shown them as a whole all that flowed from His departure and from His death.　The glory of His Person, observe, is always here the subject; for, even with regard to His death, it is said, "Now is the Son of Man glorified." Nevertheless He had forewarned them of it, that it might strengthen and not weaken their faith, for He would not talk much more with them.　The world was under the power of the enemy, and he was coming: not because he had anything in Christ—he had nothing—therefore he had not even the power of death over Him.　His death was not the effect of the power of Satan over Him, but thereby He showed the world that He loved the Father; and He was obedient to the Father, cost what it would. And this was absolute perfection in Man.　If Satan was the prince of this world, Jesus did not seek to maintain His Messiah glory in it.　But He showed to the world, there where Satan's power was, the fulness of grace and of perfection in His own Person; in order that the world might come from itself (if I may use such an expression) —those at least, who had ears to hear.

The Lord then ceases to speak, and goes forth.　He is no longer seated with His own, as of this world.　He arises and quits it.

Summary of the Lord's discourse in Chaps. 14, 15, 16

That which we have said of the Lord's commandments, given during His sojourn here below (a thought to which the succeeding chapters will give interesting development)

[56] Chapter 14 gives to us the Son's personal relationship with the Father, and our place in Him who is in it, known by the Holy Ghost given.　In chapter 15 we have His place and standing on earth, the true Vine, and then His state of glory as exalted and sending the Comforter to reveal that.

helps us much in understanding the Lord's whole discourse here to the end of chapter 16. The subject is
divided into two principal parts:—The action of the Holy
Ghost when the Lord should be away; and the relationship of the disciples to Him during His stay upon the
earth. On the one hand, that which flowed from His
exaltation to the right hand of God (which raised Him
above the question of Jew and Gentile); and, on the other,
that which depended on His presence upon earth, as
necessarily centering all the promises in His own Person,
and the relations of His own with Himself, viewed as in
connection with the earth and themselves in it, even when
He should be absent. There were, in consequence, two
kinds of testimony: that of the Holy Ghost, strictly
speaking (that is, what He revealed in reference to Jesus
on high); and that of the disciples themselves, as eye-
witnesses to all that they had seen of Jesus on the earth.
(Chap. 15: 26, 27.) Not that for this purpose they were
without the help of the Holy Ghost; but the latter was
not the new testimony of the heavenly glory by the Holy
Ghost sent down from heaven. He brought to their remembrance that which Jesus had been, and that which
He had spoken, while on earth. Therefore, in the passage
we have been reading, His work is thus described (chap.
14: 26): "He shall teach you all things, and *bring all
things to your remembrance whatsoever I have said unto
you.*" (Compare ver. 25.) The two works of the Holy
Ghost are here presented. Jesus had spoken many things
unto them. The Holy Ghost would teach them all things;
moreover, He would bring to their remembrance all that
Jesus had said. In chapter 16: 12, 13, Jesus tells them
that He had many things to say, but that they could not
bear them then. Afterwards, the Spirit of truth should
lead them into all truth. He should not speak from Himself; but whatsoever He should hear, that should He
speak. He was not like an individual spirit, who speaks
on his own account. *One* with the Father and the Son,

and come down to reveal the glory and the counsels of God, all His communications would be in connection with them, revealing the glory of Christ ascended on high—of Christ, to whom belonged all that the Father had.   Here it is no question of recalling all that Jesus had said upon earth: all is heavenly, in connection with that which is on high, and with the full glory of Jesus, or else relates to the future purposes of God.   We shall return to this subject by-and-by.   I have said these few words to mark the distinctions which I have pointed out.

Chapter 15

The true Vine: Christ on earth in contrast with Israel

THE beginning of this chapter, and that which relates to the vine, belongs to the earthly portion—to that which Jesus was on earth—to His relationship with His disciples as on the earth, and does not go beyond that position.

"I am the true Vine."   Jehovah had planted a vine brought out of Egypt.   (Psalm 80: 8.)   This is Israel after the flesh; but it was not the true Vine.   The true Vine was His Son, whom He brought up out of Egypt—Jesus.[57] He presents Himself thus to His disciples.   Here it is not that which He will be after His departure; He was this upon earth, and distinctively upon earth.   We do not speak of planting vines in heaven, nor of pruning branches there.

The fruit-bearing of the branches: the disciples' personal responsibility

The disciples would have considered Him as the most

---

[57] Compare, for this substitution of Christ for Israel, Isaiah 49.   He began Israel over again in blessing, as He did man.

excellent branch of the Vine; but thus He would have been only a member of Israel, whereas He was Himself the vessel, the source of blessing, according to the promises of God. The true Vine, therefore, is not Israel; quite the contrary, it is Christ in contrast with Israel, but Christ planted on earth, taking Israel's place, as the *true* Vine. The Father cultivates this plant, evidently on the earth. There is no need of a husbandman in heaven. Those who are attached to Christ, as the remnant of Israel, the disciples, need this culture. It is on the earth that fruit-bearing is looked for. The Lord therefore says to them, "Ye *are* clean *already*, through the Word which I have spoken unto you;" "Ye are the branches." Judas, perhaps it may be said, was taken away, so the disciples who walked no more with Him. The others should be proved and cleansed, that they might bear more fruit.

I do not doubt that this relationship, in principle and in a general analogy, still subsists. Those who make a profession, who attach themselves to Christ in order to follow Him, will, if there is life, be cleansed; if not, that which they have will be taken away. Observe therefore here, that the Lord speaks only of His Word—that of the true prophet—and of judgment, whether in discipline or in cutting off. Consequently He speaks not of the power of God, but of the responsibility of man—a responsibility which man will certainly not be able to meet without grace; but which has nevertheless that character of personal responsibility here.

Pruned by the Father: fruit as the proof of a vital and eternal link

Jesus was the source of all their strength. They were to abide in Him; thus—for this is the order—He would abide in them. We have seen this in chapter 14. He does not speak here of the sovereign exercise of love in salvation, but of the government of children by their

Father; so that blessing depends on walk (vers. 21, 23).
Here the husbandman seeks for fruit; but the instruction
given presents entire dependence on the Vine as the means
of producing it. And He shows the disciples that, walking
on earth, they should be pruned by the Father, and a
man (for in verse 6 He carefully changes the expression,
for He knew the disciples and had pronounced *them* already clean)—a man, any one who bore no fruit, would
be cut off. For this subject here is not that relationship
with Christ in heaven by the Holy Ghost, which cannot
be broken, but of that link which even then was formed
here below, which might be vital and eternal, or which
might not. Fruit should be the proof.

In the former vine this was not necessary; they were
Jews by birth, they were circumcised, they kept the ordinances, and abode in the vine as good branches, without
bearing any fruit at all. They were only cut off from
Israel for wilful violation of the law. Here it is not a
relationship with Jehovah founded on the circumstance
of being born of a certain family. That which is looked
for is the glorifying the Father by fruit-bearing. It is
this which will show that they are the disciples of Him
who has borne so much.

What precedes fruit: the source of strength and fruit: abiding in Christ

Christ, then, was the true Vine; the Father, the Husbandman; the eleven were the branches. They were to
abide in Him, which is realized by not thinking to produce
any fruit except as in Him, looking to Him first. Christ
precedes fruit. It is dependence, practical habitual nearness of heart to Him, and trust in Him, being attached
to Him through dependence on Him. In this way Christ
in them would be a constant source of strength and of
fruit. He would be in them. Out of Him they could do
nothing. If, by abiding in Him, they had the strength of

His presence, they should bear much fruit. Moreover, "if a man" (He does not say "they;" He knew them as true branches and clean) did not abide in Him, he should be cast forth to be burnt. Again, if they abode in Him (that is, if there was the constant dependence that draws from the source), and if the words of Christ abode in them, directing their hearts and thoughts, they should command the resources of divine power; they should ask what they would, and it should be done. But, further, the Father had loved the Son divinely while He dwelt on earth. Jesus did the same with regard to them. They were to abide in His love. In the former verses it was in Him, here it is in His love.[58] By keeping His Father's commandments, He had abode in His love; by keeping the commandments of Jesus, they should abide in *His*. Dependence (which implies confidence, and reference to Him on whom we depend for strength, as unable to do anything without Him, and so clinging close to Him) and obedience, are the two great principles of practical life here below. Thus Jesus walked as Man: He knew by experience the true path for His disciples. The commandments of His Father were the expression of what the Father was; by keeping them in the spirit of obedience, Jesus had ever walked in the communion of His love; had maintained communion with Himself. The commandments of Jesus when on earth were the expression of what *He* was, divinely perfect in the path of man. By walking in them, His disciples should be in the communion of *His* love. The Lord spoke these things to His disciples, in order that His joy [59] should abide in them, and that their joy should be full.

[58] There are the three exhortations: "Abide in Me;" "If ye abide in Me, and My words abide in you, ye shall ask what ye will;" "Abide in My love."

[59] Some have thought that this means the joy of Christ in the faithful walk of a disciple: I do not think so. It is the joy He had down here, just as He left us His own peace, and will give us His own glory.

The path of a disciple, not the salvation of a sinner, treated here

We see that it is not the salvation of a sinner that is the subject treated of here, but the path of a disciple, in order that he may fully enjoy the love of Christ, and that his heart may be unclouded in the place where joy is found.

Obedience the means of abiding in the Lord's love

Neither is the question entered on here, whether a real believer can be separated from God, because the Lord makes obedience the means of abiding in His love. Assuredly *He* could not lose the favor of His Father, or cease to be the object of His love. That was out of the question; and yet He says, "I have kept My Father's commandments, and abide in His love." But this was the divine path in which He enjoyed it. It is the walk and the strength of a disciple that is spoken of, and not the means of salvation.

Love one to another: its measure

At verse 12 another part of the subject begins. He wills (*this* is His commandment) that they should love one another, as He had loved them. Before, He had spoken of the Father's love for Him, which flowed from heaven into His heart here below.[60] He had loved them in this same way; but He had also been a companion, a servant, in this love. Thus the disciples were to love one another with a love that rose above all the weaknesses of others, and which was at the same time brotherly, and caused the one who felt it to be the servant of his brother.

---

[60] He does not say, "loveth Me," but "hath loved Me;" that is, He does not speak merely of the eternal love of the Father for the Son, but of the Father's love displayed towards Him in His humanity here on earth.

It went so far as to lay down life itself for one's friends. Now, to Jesus, he who obeyed Him was His friend. Observe, He does not say that He would be their Friend. He was *our* Friend when He gave His life for sinners: we are His friends when we enjoy His confidence, as He here expresses it—"I have told you all things that I have heard of My Father."   Men speak of their affairs, according to the necessity of doing so which may arise, to those who are concerned in them. I impart all my own thoughts to one who is my friend. "Shall I hide from Abraham the thing that I will do?" and Abraham was called the "friend of God."   Now it was not things concerning Abraham himself that God then told Abraham (He had done so as God), but things concerning the world— Sodom.   God does the same with respect to the assembly, practically with respect to the obedient disciple: such a one should be the depositary of His thoughts.   Moreover, He had chosen them for this.   It was not they who had chosen Him by the exercise of their own will.   He had chosen them and ordained them to go and bring forth fruit, and fruit that should remain; so that, being thus chosen of Christ for the work, they should receive from the Father, who could not fail them in this case, whatsoever they should ask.   Here the Lord comes to the source and certainty of grace, in order that the practical responsibility, under which He puts them, should not cloud the divine grace which acted towards them and placed them there.

Hated by the world: in the same position as their Master

They were therefore to love one another.[61]   That the world should hate them was but the natural consequence

---

[61] By choosing them and setting them apart to enjoy together this relationship with Him outside the world, He had put them in a position of which mutual love was the natural consequence; and, in fact, the sense of this position and love go together.

of its hatred to Christ; it sealed their association with Him. The world loves that which is of the world: this is quite natural. The disciples were not of it; and, besides, the Jesus whom it had rejected had chosen them and separated them from the world: therefore it would hate them because so chosen in grace. There was, besides, the moral reason, namely, that they were not of it; but this demonstrated their relationship to Christ, and His sovereign rights, by which He had taken them to Himself out of a rebellious world. They should have the same portion as their Master: it should be for His name's sake, because the world—and He speaks especially of the Jews, among whom He had labored—knew not the Father who had sent Him in love. To make their boast of Jehovah, as *their* God, suited them very well. They would have received the Messiah on that footing. To know the Father, revealed in His true character by the Son, was quite a different thing. Nevertheless the Son had revealed Him, and, both by His words and His works, had manifested the Father and His perfections.

Fallen creatures in the presence of mercy and grace proving they preferred sin to God: the Father and Son seen and hated

If Christ had not come and spoken unto them, God would not have had to reproach them with sin. They might still drag on, even if in an unpurged state, without any proof (though there was plenty of sin and transgression as men and as a people under the law) that they would not have God—would not even by mercy return. The fruit of a fallen nature was there, no doubt, but not the proof that that nature preferred sin to God, when God was there in mercy, not imputing it. Grace was dealing with them, not imputing sin to them. Mercy had been treating them as fallen, not as wilful creatures. God was not taking the ground of law, which imputes, or of judgment, but of grace in the revelation of the Father by the Son. The words and works of the Son revealing the Father in grace, rejected, left them without hope. (Compare chap. 16: 9.) Their real condition would otherwise not have been thoroughly tested, God would have had still a means to use; He loved Israel too much to condemn them while there was one left untried.

If the Lord had not done among them the works which no other man had done, they might have remained as they were, refused to believe in Him, and not have been guilty before God. They would have been still the object of Jehovah's long-suffering; but in fact they had seen and hated both the Son and the Father. The Father had been fully manifested in the Son—in Jesus; and if, when God was fully manifested, and in grace, they rejected Him, what could be done except to leave them in sin, afar from God? If He had been manifested only in part, they would have had an excuse; they might have said, "Ah! if He had shown grace, if we had known Him as He is, we would not have rejected Him." They could not now say this. They had seen the Father and the Son in Jesus. Alas, they had seen and hated! [62]

But this was only the fulfilment of that which was foretold of them in their law. As to the testimony borne to God by the people, and of a Messiah received by them, all was over. They had hated Him without a cause.

The promised Holy Spirit: new testimony to be rendered to the Son of God

The Lord now turns to the subject of the Holy Ghost who should come to maintain His glory, which the people

[62] Remark, that His Word and His works are here again referred to.

had cast down to the ground. The Jews had not known the Father manifested in the Son; the Holy Ghost should now come from the Father to bear witness of the Son. The Son should send Him from the Father. In chapter 14 the Father sends Him in Jesus' name for the personal relationship of the disciples with Jesus. Here Jesus, gone on high, sends Him the witness of His exalted glory, His heavenly place. This was the new testimony, and was to be rendered unto Jesus, the Son of God, ascended up to heaven. The disciples *also* should bear witness of Him, because they had been with Him from the beginning. They were to testify with the help of the Holy Ghost, as eye-witnesses of His life on earth, of the manifestation of the Father in Him. The Holy Ghost, sent by Him, was the witness to His glory with the Father, whence He Himself had come.

The disciples' position after Christ's departure

Thus in Christ, the true Vine, we have the disciples, the branches, clean already, Christ being still present on the earth. After His departure they were to maintain this practical relationship. They should be in relationship with Him, as He, here below, had been with the Father. And they were to be with one another as He had been with them. Their position was outside the world. Now the Jews had *hated* both the Son and the Father; the Holy Ghost should bear witness to the Son as with the Father, and in the Father; and the disciples should testify also of that which He had been on earth.

The Holy Ghost, and, in a certain sense, the disciples take the place of Jesus, as well as of the old vine, on the earth.

The presence and testimony of the Holy Spirit on earth

The presence and the testimony of the Holy Ghost on earth are now developed.

It is well to notice the connection of the subjects in the passages we are considering. In chapter 14 we have the Person of the Son revealing the Father, and the Holy Ghost giving the knowledge of the Son's being in the Father and the disciples in Jesus on high. This was the personal condition both of Christ and the disciples, and is all linked together; only first the Father, the Son being down here, and then the Holy Ghost sent by the Father. In chapters 15, 16 you get the distinct dispensations— Christ the true Vine on earth, and then the Comforter come on earth sent down by the exalted Christ. In chapter 14 Christ prays the Father, who sends the Spirit in Christ's name. In chapter 15 Christ exalted sends the Spirit from the Father, a witness of His exaltation, as the disciples, led by the Spirit, were of His life of humiliation, but as Son on earth.

The Spirit sent by the Father in Christ's name as an abiding Comforter on the Lord's departure

Nevertheless there is development as well as connection. In chapter 14 the Lord, although quitting the earth, speaks in connection with that which He was upon earth. It is (not Christ Himself) the Father who sends the Holy Ghost at His request. He goes from earth to heaven on their part as Mediator. He would pray the Father, and the Father would give them another Comforter, who should continue with them, not leaving them as He was doing. Their relationship to the Father depending on Him, it would be as believing in Him that He would be sent to them—not to the world—not upon Jews, as such. It should be *in His name*. Moreover the

Holy Ghost would Himself teach them, and He would
recall to their mind the commandments of Jesus—all that
He had said unto them. For chapter 14 gives the whole
position that resulted from the manifestation [63] of the
Son, and that of the Father in Him, and from His departure (that is to say, its result with regard to the
disciples).

The Spirit to be sent by Christ also from heaven, a witness to His exaltation

Now, in chapter 15 He had exhausted the subject of
commandments in connection with the life manifested in
Himself here below; and at the close of this chapter He
considers Himself as ascended, and He adds, "But when
the Comforter is come, whom I will send unto you from
the Father." He comes, indeed, from the Father; for our

[63] Observe here the practical development, with respect to life, of this
most deeply interesting subject, in 1 John 1, 2. The eternal life which
was with the Father had been manifested (for in Him, in the Son, was
life, He was also the Word of life, and God was light. Compare John 1).
They were to keep His commandments. (Chap. 2: 3-5.) It was an old
commandment which they had had from the beginning—that is, from
Jesus on earth, from Him whom their hands had handled. But now
this commandment was true in Him and in them: that is to say, this
life of love (of which these commandments were the expression) as
well as that of righteousness reproduced itself in them, by virtue of their
union with Him, through the Holy Ghost, according to John 14: 20.
They also abide in Jesus. (1 John 2: 6.) In John 1 we find the Son
who is in the bosom of the Father, who declares Him. He reveals Him
as He has thus known Him—as that which the Father was to Himself.
And He has brought this love (of which He was the object) down into
the bosom of humanity, and placed it in the heart of His disciples (see
chapter 17: 26); and this is known now in perfection by God dwelling
in us, and His love being perfect in us, while we dwell in brotherly
love. (1 John 4: 12; compare John 1: 18.) The manifestation of our
having been thus loved will consist in our appearing in the same glory
as Christ. (Chap. 17: 22, 23.) Christ manifests this love by coming
from the Father. His commandments teach us us; the life which we have
in Him reproduces it. His precepts give form to this life, and guide it
through the ways of the flesh, and the temptations in the midst of
which He, without sin, lived by this life. The Holy Ghost is its strength,
as being the mighty and living link with Him, and He by whom we are
consciously in Him and He in us. (Union, as the body to the Head, is
another thing, which is never the subject of John's teaching.) Of His
fulness we receive grace upon grace. Therefore it is that we ought to
walk as He walked (not to be what He was); for we ought not to walk
in the flesh, although it is in us and was not in Him.

relationship is, and ought to be, immediate to Him. It is there that Christ has placed us. But in this verse it is not the Father who sends Him at the request of Jesus, and in His name. Christ has taken His place in glory as Son of Man, and according to the glorious fruits of His work, and *He* sends Him. Consequently He bears witness to that which Christ is in heaven. No doubt He makes us perceive what Jesus was here below, where in infinite grace He manifested the Father, and perceive it much better than they did, who were with Him during His sojourn on earth. But this is in chapter 14. Nevertheless the Holy Ghost is sent by Christ from heaven, and He reveals to us the Son, whom now we know as having perfectly and divinely (albeit as man and amid sinful men) manifested the Father. We know, I repeat, the Son, as with the Father, and in the Father. From thence it is He has sent us the Holy Ghost.

Chapter 16

The Holy Spirit looked up as already here: sufferings and joy predicted

IN chapter 16 a further step is taken in the revelation of this grace. The Holy Ghost is looked upon as already here below.

In this chapter the Lord declares that He has set forth all His instruction with regard to His departure; their sufferings in the world as holding His place; their joy, as being in the same relationship to Him as that in which He had been while on earth to His Father; their knowledge of the fact that He was in the Father and they in Him, and He Himself in them; the gift of the Holy Ghost, in order to prepare them for all that would happen when He was gone, that they might not be offended. For they should be cast out of the synagogues, and he who should kill them would think that he was serving God. This would be the case with those who, resting in their old doctrines as a form, and rejecting the light, would only use the form of truth by which they accredited the flesh as orthodox to resist the light which, according to the Spirit, would judge the flesh. This would they do, because they knew neither the Father nor Jesus, the Son of the Father. It is fresh truth which tests the soul, and faith. Old truth, generally received and by which a body of people are distinguished from those around them, may be a subject of pride to the flesh, even where it is the truth, as was the case with the Jews. But fresh truth is a question of faith in its source: there is not the support of a body accredited by it, but the cross of hostility and isolation. They thought they served God. They knew not the Father and the Son.

Nature's sorrow at the Lord's departure: faith's gain

Nature is occupied with that which it loses. Faith looks at the future into which God leads. Precious thought! Nature acted in the disciples: they loved Jesus; they grieved at His going away. We can understand this. But faith would not have stopped there. If they had apprehended the necessary glory of the Person of Jesus, if their affection, animated by faith, had thought of Him and not of themselves, they would have asked, "Whither goest Thou?" Nevertheless He who thought of them assures them that it would be gain to them even to lose Him. Glorious fruit of the ways of God! Their gain would be in this, that the Comforter should be here on earth with them and in them. Here, observe, Jesus does not speak of the Father. It was the Comforter here below in His stead, to maintain the testimony of His love for the disciples, and His relationship to them. Christ was going away: for if He went not away, the Comforter would not come; but if He departed, He would send Him. When He was come, He would act in demonstration of the truth with regard to the world that rejected Christ and persecuted His disciples; and He would act for blessing in the disciples themselves.

The Comforter's testimony to the world: its sin in the rejection of Christ

With regard to the world, the Comforter had one only subject of testimony, in order to demonstrate the sin of the world. It had not believed in Jesus—in the Son. Doubtless there was sin of every kind, and, to speak truth, nothing but sin—sin that deserved judgment; and in the work of conversion, He brings these sins home to the soul. But the rejection of Christ put the whole world under one common judgment. No doubt every one shall answer for his sins; and the Holy Ghost makes one feel them. But, as a system responsible to God, the world had rejected His Son. This was the ground on which God dealt with the world now; this it was which made manifest the heart of man. It was the demonstration that, God being fully revealed in love such as He was, man would not receive Him. He came, not imputing their trespasses unto them; but they rejected Him. The presence of Jesus was not the Son of God Himself manifested in His glory, from which man might shrink with fear, though he could not escape; it was what He was morally, in His nature, in His character. Man hated Him: all testimony to bring man to God was unavailing. The plainer the testimony, the more he turned from it and opposed it. The demonstration of the sin of the world was its having rejected Christ. Terrible testimony, that God in goodness should excite detestation because He was perfect, and perfectly good! Such is man. The testimony of the Holy Ghost to the world, as God's to Cain of old, would be, Where is My Son? It was not that man was

guilty; that he was when Christ came; but he was lost,
the tree was bad.[64]

The demonstration of righteousness—Christ at God's right hand

But this was God's path to something altogether different—the demonstration of righteousness, in that Christ
went to His Father, and the world saw Him no more.
It was the result of Christ's rejection. Human righteousness there was none. Man's sin was proved by the rejection of Christ. The cross was indeed judgment executed
upon sin. And in that sense it was righteousness; but
in this world it was the only righteous One condemned by
man forsaken by God; it was not the manifestation of
righteousness. It was a final judicial separation between
man and God. (See chapters 11, 12: 31.) If Christ had
been delivered there, and had become the King of Israel,
this would not have been an adequate consequence of His
having glorified God. Having glorified God His Father,
He was going to sit at His right hand, at the right hand
of the Majesty on high, to be glorified in God Himself,
to sit on the Father's throne. *To set Him there was
divine righteousness.*[65] This same righteousness deprived
the world, as it is, of Jesus for ever. Man saw Him no
more. Righteousness in favor of men was in Christ at
God's right hand—in judgment as to the world, in that
it had lost Him hopelessly and for ever.

Satan, the prince of this world, judged

Moreover Satan had been proved to be the prince of
this world by leading all men against the Lord Jesus. To
accomplish the purposes of God in grace, Jesus does not
resist. He gives Himself up to death. He who has the

[64] Man is judged for what he has done; he is lost by what he is.
[65] Chapters 13: 31, 32; 17: 1, 4, 5.

power of death committed himself thoroughly. In his desire to ruin man he had to hazard everything in his enterprise against the Prince of Life. He was able to associate the whole world with himself in this, Jew and Gentile, priest and people, governor, soldier, and subject. The world was there, headed by its prince, on that solemn day. The enemy had everything at stake, and the world was with him. But Christ has risen, He has ascended to His Father, and has sent down the Holy Ghost. All the motives that govern the world, and the power by which Satan held men captive, are shown to be of him; he is judged. The power of the Holy Ghost is the testimony of this, and surmounts all the powers of the enemy. The world is not yet judged, that is, the judgment executed— it will be in another manner; but it is morally, its prince is judged. All its motives, religious and irreligious, have led it to reject Christ, placing it under Satan's power. It is in that character that he has been judged; for he led the world against Him who is manifested to be the Son of God by the presence of the Holy Ghost, consequent on His breaking the power of Satan in death.

The Holy Spirit's presence here the proof of the world's rejection of the Son of God

All this took place through the presence on earth of the Holy Ghost, sent down by Christ. His presence in itself was the demonstration of these three things. For, if the Holy Ghost was here, it was because the world had rejected the Son of God. Righteousness was evidenced by Jesus being at the right hand of God, of which the presence of the Holy Ghost was the proof, as well as in the fact that the world had lost Him. Now the world which rejected Him was not outwardly judged, but, Satan having led it to reject the Son, the presence of the Holy Ghost proved that Jesus had destroyed the power of death; that he who had possessed that power was thus judged; that he had shown himself to be the enemy of Him whom the Father had owned; that his power was gone, and victory belonged to the Second Adam, when Satan's whole power had been arrayed against the human weakness of Him who in love had yielded to it. But Satan, thus judged, was the prince of this world.

The Holy Spirit's work in and for the disciples

The presence of the Holy Ghost should be the demonstration not of Christ's rights as Messiah, true as they were, but of those truths that related to man—to the world, in which Israel was now lost, having rejected the promises, although God would preserve the nation for Himself. But the Holy Ghost was doing something more than demonstrating the condition of the world. He would accomplish a work in the disciples; He would lead them into all truth, and He would show them things to come; for Jesus had many things to tell them which they were not yet able to bear. When the Holy Ghost should be in them, He should be their strength in them as well as their teacher; and it would be a wholly different state of things for the disciples. Here He is considered as present on the earth in place of Jesus, and dwelling in the disciples, not as an individual spirit speaking from Himself, but even as Jesus said, "As I hear I judge," with a judgment perfectly divine and heavenly: so the Holy Ghost, acting in the disciples, would speak that which came from above, and of the future, according to divine knowledge. It should be heaven and the future of which He would speak, communicating what was heavenly from above, and revealing events to come upon the earth, the one and the other being witnesses that it was a knowledge which belonged to God. How blessed to have that which He has to give!

The Holy Spirit taking the place of Christ here

But, further, He takes here the place of Christ. Jesus had glorified the Father on earth. The Holy Ghost would glorify Jesus, with reference to the glory that belonged to His Person and to His position. He does not here speak directly of the glory of the Father. The disciples had seen the glory of the life of Christ on earth; the Holy Ghost would unfold to them His glory in that which belonged to Him as glorified with the Father—that which was His own.

They would learn "in part." This is man's measure when the things of God are in question, but its extent is declared by the Lord Himself: "He shall glorify Me, for He shall receive of Mine, and shall show it unto you. *All that the Father hath* is Mine: therefore, said I, He shall take of Mine, and shall show it unto you."

Christ's name and glory: His position in virtue of His work as Son of Man: His rights as Son of the Father

Thus we have the gift of the Holy Ghost variously presented in connection with Christ. In dependence on His Father, and representing His disciples as gone up from among them, on their behalf, He addresses Himself to the Father; He asks the Father to send the Holy Ghost. (Chap. 14: 16.) Afterwards we find that His own name is all powerful. All blessing from the Father comes in His name. It is on His account, and according to the efficacy of His name, of all that in Him is acceptable to the Father, that good comes to us. Thus the Father will send the Holy Ghost in His name. (Chap. 14: 26.) And Christ being glorified on high, and having taken His place with His Father, He Himself sends the Holy Ghost (chap. 15: 26) from the Father, as proceeding from Him. Finally, the Holy Ghost is present here in this world, in and with the disciples, and He glorifies Jesus, and takes of His and reveals it to His own. (Chap. 16: 13-15.) Here all the glory of the Person of Christ is set forth, as well as the rights belonging to the position

He has taken. "All things that the Father hath" are His. He has taken His position according to the eternal counsels of God, in virtue of His work as Son of Man. But if He has entered into possession in this character, all that He possesses in it is His, as a Son to whom (being one with the Father) all that the Father has belongs.

The Lord's coming departure to His Father: the disciples encouraged to draw nigh to the Father

There He should be hidden for a while: the disciples should afterwards see Him, for it was only the accomplishment of the ways of God; it was no question of being, as it were, lost by death. He was going to His Father. On this point the disciples understood nothing. The Lord develops the fact and its consequences, without yet showing them the whole import of what He said. He takes it up on the human and historical side. The world would rejoice at having got rid of Him. Miserable joy! The disciples would lament, although it was the true source of joy for them; but their sorrow should be turned into joy. As testimony, this took place when He showed Himself to them after His resurrection; it will be fully accomplished when He shall return to receive them unto Himself. But when they had seen Him again, they should understand the relationship in which He has placed them with His Father, they should enjoy it by the Holy Ghost. It should not be as though they could not themselves draw nigh to the Father, while Christ could do so (as Martha said, "I know that whatsoever Thou wilt ask of God, He will give it Thee"). They might themselves go *directly* to the Father, who loved them, because they had believed in Jesus, and had received Him when He had humbled Himself in this world of sin (in principle it is always thus); and asking what they would in His name they should receive it, so that their joy might be full in the consciousness of the blessed position of unfailing favor into which they were brought, and of the value of all that they possessed in Christ.

The disciples' limited apprehension of the Lord's meaning

Nevertheless the Lord already declares to them the basis of the truth—He came from the Father, He was going away to the Father. The disciples think they understand that which He had thus spoken without a parable. They felt that He had divined their thought, for they had not expressed it to Him. Yet they did not rise really to the height of what He said. He had told them that they had believed in His having come "from God." This they understood; and that which had taken place had confirmed them in this faith, and they declare their conviction with regard to this truth; but they do not enter into the thought of coming "from the Father," and going away "to the Father." They fancied themselves quite in the light; but they had apprehended nothing that raised them above the effect of Christ's rejection, which the belief that He came from the Father and was going to the Father would have done. Jesus therefore declares to them, that His death would scatter them, and that they would forsake Him. His Father would be with Him; He should not be alone. Nevertheless He had explained all these things to them, in order that they should have peace in Him. In the world that rejected Him they should have tribulation; but He had overcome the world, they might be of good cheer.

Chapter 17

The Lord's intercessory prayer

THIS ends the conversation of Jesus with His disciples on earth. In this next chapter (17) He addresses His Father as taking His own place in departing, and giving

His disciples theirs (that is, His own), with regard to
the Father and to the world, after He had gone away to
be glorified with the Father. The whole chapter is
essentially putting the disciples in His own place, after
laying the ground for it in His own glorifying and work.
It is, save the last verses, His place on earth. As He was
divinely in heaven, and so showed a divine heavenly
character on earth, so (He being glorified as Man in
heaven) they, united with Him, were in turn to display
the same. Hence we have first the place He personally
takes, and the work which entitles them to be in it.

Outline and divisions of Chapter 17

Chapter 17 is divided thus: Verses 1-5 relate to Christ
Himself, to His taking His position in glory, to His work,
and to that glory as belonging to His Person, and the
result of His work. Verses 1-3 present His new position
in two aspects: "Glorify Thy Son"—power over all flesh,
for eternal life to those given to Him; verses 4, 5, His
work and its results. In verses 6-13 He speaks of His
disciples as put into this relationship with the Father by
His revealing His name to them, and then His having
given them the words which He had Himself received,
that they might enjoy all the full blessedness of this relationship. He also prays for them that they may be
one as He and the Father were. In verses 14-21 we find
their consequent relationship to the world; in verses 20,
21, He introduces those who should believe through their
means into the enjoyment of their blessing. Verses 22-26
make known the result, both future, and in this world, for
them: the possession of the glory which Christ Himself
had received from the Father—to be with Him, enjoying
the sight of His glory—that the Father's love should be
with them here below, even as Christ Himself had been
its object—and that Christ Himself should be in them.
The last three verses alone take the disciples up to heaven
as a supplemental truth.

This is a brief summary of this marvellous chapter, in which we are admitted, not to the discourse of Christ with man, but to hear the desires of His heart, when He pours it out to His Father for the blessing of those that are His own. Wonderful grace that permits us to hear these desires, and to understand all the privileges that flow from His thus caring for us, from our being the subject of intercourse between the Father and the Son, of their common love towards us, when Christ expresses His own desires—that which He has at heart, and which He presents to the Father as His own personal wishes!

Some explanations may assist in apprehending the meaning of certain passages in this marvellous and precious chapter. May the Spirit of God aid us!

Christ's new position in glory: power over all flesh, the gift of eternal life to those given Him

The Lord, whose looks of love had until then been directed towards His disciples on the earth, now lifts His eyes to heaven as He addresses His Father. The hour was come to glorify the Son, in order that from the glory He might glorify the Father. This is, speaking generally, the new position. His career here was finished, and He had to ascend on high. Two things were connected with this—power over *all flesh,* and the gift of eternal life to as many as the Father had given Him. "The head of *every man* is Christ." Those whom the Father had given Him receive eternal life from Him who has gone up on high. Eternal life was the knowledge of the Father, the only true God, and of Jesus Christ, whom He had sent. The knowledge of the Almighty gave assurance to the pilgrim of faith; that of Jehovah, the certainty of the fulfilment of the promises of God to Israel; that of the Father, who sent the Son, Jesus Christ (the Anointed Man and the Saviour), who was that life itself, and so received as a present thing (1 John 1: 1-4), was life

eternal. True knowledge here was not outward protection
or future hope, but the communication, in life, of communion with the Being thus known to the soul—of communion with God Himself fully known as the Father
and the Son. Here it is not the divinity of His Person
that is before us in Christ, though a divine Person alone
could be in such a place and so speak, but the place that
He had taken in fulfilling the counsels of God. That
which is said of Jesus in this chapter could only be said
of One who is God; but the point treated is that of His
place in the counsels of God, and not the revelation of His
nature. He receives all from His Father—He is sent by
Him, His Father glorifies Him.[66] We see the same truth
of the communication of eternal life in connection with
His divine nature and His oneness with the Father in
1 John 5: 20. Here He fulfils the Father's will, and is
dependent on Him in the place that He has taken, and
that He is going to take, even in the glory, however
glorious His nature may be. So, also, in chapter 5 of
our Gospel, He quickens whom He will; here it is those
whom the Father has given Him. And the life He gives
is realized in the knowledge of the Father, and of Jesus
Christ whom He has sent.

Christ's work and its results

He now declares the conditions under which He takes
this place on high. He had perfectly glorified the Father
on earth. Nothing that manifested God the Father had
been wanting, whatever might be the difficulty; the con-

[66] The more we examine the Gospel of John, the more we shall see
One who speaks and acts as a divine Person—one with the Father—
alone could do, but yet always as One who has taken the place of a
servant, and takes nothing to Himself, but receives all from His Father.
"I have glorified Thee;" "now glorify Me." What language of equality
of nature and love! But He does not say, "And now I will glorify
Myself." He has taken the place of Man to receive all, though it be a
glory He had with the Father before the world was. This is of exquisite
beauty. I add, it was out of this the enemy sought to seduce Him, in
vain, in the wilderness.

tradition of sinners was but an occasion of so doing. But this very thing made the sorrow infinite. Nevertheless Jesus had accomplished that glory on the earth in the face of all that opposed itself. His glory with the Father in heaven was but the just consequence—the necessary consequence, in mere justice. Moreover Jesus had had this glory with His Father before the world was. His work and His Person alike gave Him a right to it. The Father glorified on earth by the Son: the Son glorified with the Father on high: such is the revelation contained in these verses—a right, proceeding from His Person as Son, but to a glory into which He entered as man, in consequence of having, as such, perfectly glorified His Father on earth. These are the verses that relate to Christ. This, moreover, gives the *relationship* in which He enters into this new place as Man, His Son, and the work by which He does so in righteousness, and thus gives us a *title*, and the character in which we have a place there.

The Lord's disciples in relationship with the Father by the revelation of His name and Word

He now speaks of the disciples; how they entered into their peculiar place in connection with this position of Jesus—into this relationship with His Father. He had manifested the Father's name to those whom the Father had given Him out of the world. They belonged to the Father, and the Father had given them to Jesus. They had kept the Father's Word. It was faith in the revelation which the Son had made of the Father. The words of the prophets were true. The faithful enjoyed them: they sustained their faith. But the Word of the Father, by Jesus, revealed the Father Himself, in Him whom the Father had sent, and put him who received them into the place of love, which was Christ's place; and to know the Father and the Son was life eternal. This was quite another thing from hopes connected with the Messiah or what Jehovah had given Him. It is thus, also, that the disciples are presented to the Father; not as receiving Christ in the character of Messiah, and honoring Him as possessing His power by that title. They had known that all which Jesus had was of the Father. He was then the Son; His relationship to the Father was acknowledged. Dull of comprehension as they were, the Lord recognizes them according to His appreciation of their faith, according to the object of that faith, as known to Himself, and not according to their intelligence. Precious truth! (Compare chap. 14: 7.)

They acknowledged Jesus, then, as receiving all from *the Father*, not as Messiah from Jehovah; for Jesus had given them all the words that the Father had given Him. Thus He had brought them in their own souls into the consciousness of the relationship between the Son and the Father, and into full communion, according to the communications of the Father to the Son in that relationship. He speaks of their position through faith—not of their realization of this position. Thus they had acknowledged that Jesus came forth from the Father, and that He came with the Father's authority—the Father had sent Him. It was from thence He came, and He came furnished with the authority of a mission from the Father. This was their position by faith.

The Lord's prayer for the disciples as distinguished from the world

And now—the disciples being already in this position— He places them, according to His thoughts and His desires, before the Father in prayer. He prays for them, distinguishing them completely from the world. The time would come when (according to Psalm 2) He would ask of the Father with reference to the world; He was not doing so now, but for those out of the world, whom the

Father had given Him. For they were the Father's. For all that is the Father's is in essential opposition to the world. (Compare 1 John 2: 16.)

The motives for the Lord's request

The Lord presents to the Father two motives for His request: 1st, They were the Father's, so that the Father, for His own glory, and because of His affection for that which belonged to Him, should keep them; 2nd, Jesus was glorified in them, so that if Jesus was the object of the Father's affection, for that reason also the Father should keep them. Besides, the interests of the Father and the Son could not be separated. If they were the Father's, they were, in fact, the Son's; and it was but an example of that universal truth—all that was the Son's was the Father's, and all that was the Father's was the Son's. What a place for us!—to be the object of this mutual affection, of these common and inseparable interests of the Father and the Son! This is the great principle—the great foundation of the prayer of Christ. He prayed the Father for His disciples, because they belonged to the Father; Jesus must needs, therefore, seek their blessing. The Father would be thoroughly interested for them, because in them the Son was to be glorified.

The circumstances to which the prayer applied

He then presents the circumstances to which the prayer applied. He was no longer in this world Himself. They would be deprived of His personal care as present with them, but they would be in this world, while He was coming to the Father. This is the ground of His request with regard to their position. He puts them in connection, therefore, with the Holy Father—all the perfect love of such a Father—the Father of Jesus and their Father, maintaining (it was their blessing) the holiness that His nature required, if they were to be in relationship with

Him. It was direct guardianship. The Father would keep in His own name those whom He had given to Jesus. The connection thus was direct. Jesus committed them to Him, and that, not only as belonging to the Father, but now as His own, invested with all the value which that would give them in the Father's eyes.

Oneness and its bond

The object of His solicitude was to keep them in unity, even as the Father and the Son are one. One only divine Spirit was the bond of that oneness. In this sense the bond was truly divine. So far as they were filled with the Holy Spirit, they had but one mind, one counsel, one aim. This is the unity referred to here. The Father and the Son were their only object; the accomplishing their counsels and objects their only pursuit. They had only the thoughts of God; because God Himself, the Holy Ghost, was the source of their thoughts. It was one only divine power and nature that united them—the Holy Ghost. The mind, the aim, the life, the whole moral existence, were consequently one. The Lord speaks, necessarily, at the height of His own thoughts, when He expresses His desires for them. If it is a question of realization, we must then think of man; yet of a strength also that is perfected in weakness.

The sum of the Lord's desires—the disciples' relationship to the Father as sons, saints, under His care

This is the sum of the Lord's desires—sons, saints, under the Father's care; one, not by an effort or by agreement, but according to divine power. He being here, had kept them in the Father's name, faithful to accomplish all that the Father had committed to Him, and to lose none of those that were His. As to Judas, it was only the fulfilment of the Word. The guardianship of Jesus present in the world could now no longer exist. But He spoke these things, being still here, the disciples hearing them, in order that they might understand that they were placed before the Father in the same position that Christ had held, and that they might thus have fulfilled in themselves, in this same relationship, the joy which Christ had possessed. What unutterable grace! They had lost Him, visibly, to find themselves (by Him and in Him) in His own relationship with the Father, enjoying all that He enjoyed in that communion here below, as being in His place in their own relationship with the Father. Therefore He had imparted to them all the words that the Father had given Him—the communications of His love to Himself, when walking as Son in that place here below; and, in the especial name of "Holy Father," by which the Son Himself addressed Him from the earth, the Father was to keep those whom the Son had left there. Thus should they have His joy fulfilled in themselves.

This was their relationship to the Father, Jesus being away. He turns now to their relationship with the world, in consequence of the former.

The disciples' relationship with the world: set apart by the Word

He gave them the Word of His Father—not the words to bring them into communion with Him, but His Word —the testimony of what He was. And the world had hated them as it had hated Jesus (the living and personal testimony of the Father) and the Father Himself. Being thus in relationship with the Father, who had taken them out from the men of the world, and having received the Father's word (and eternal life in the Son in that knowledge), they were not of the world even as Jesus was not of the world: and therefore the world hated them. Nevertheless the Lord does not pray that they might be taken out of it; but that the Father should keep

them from the evil. He enters into the detail of His
desires in this respect, grounded on their not being of the
world. He repeats this thought as the basis of their
position here below. "They are not of the world, even
as I am not of the world." What then were they to be?
By what rule, by what model, were they to be formed?
By the truth, and the Father's Word is truth. Christ
was always the Word, but the living Word among men.
In the Scriptures we possess it, written and stedfast: they
reveal Him, bear witness to Him. It was thus that the
disciples were to be set apart. "Sanctify them by Thy
truth: Thy Word is the truth." It was this, personally,
that they were to be formed by, the Father's Word, as
He was revealed in Jesus.

The disciples sent into the world: their mission and testimony

Their mission follows. Jesus sends them into the world,
as the Father had sent Him into the world; into the world
—in no wise of the world. They are sent into it on the
part of Christ: were they of it, they could not be sent
into it. But it was not only the Father's Word which
was the truth, nor the communication of the Father's
Word by Christ present with His disciples (points of
which from verse 14 till now Jesus had been speaking,
"I have given them Thy Word"): He sanctified Himself.
He set Himself apart as a heavenly Man above the
heavens, a glorified Man in the glory, in order that all
truth might shine forth in Him, in His Person, raised up
from the dead by the glory of the Father—all that the
Father is being thus displayed in Him; the testimony of
divine righteousness, of divine love, of divine power,
totally overturning the lie of Satan, by which man had
been deceived and falsity brought into the world; the
perfect model of that which man was according to the
counsels of God, and as the expression of His power

morally and in glory—the image of the invisible God, the
Son, and in glory. Jesus set Himself apart, in this place,
in order that the disciples might be sanctified by the communication to them of what He was; for this communication was the truth, and created them in the image of
that which it revealed. So that it was the Father's glory,
revealed by Him on earth, and the glory into which He
had ascended as Man; for this is the complete result—
the illustration in glory of the way in which He had
set Himself apart for God, but on behalf of His own.
Thus there is not only the forming and governing of the
thoughts by the Word, setting us apart morally to God,
but the blessed affections flowing from our having this
truth in the Person of Christ, our hearts connected with
Him in grace. This ends the second part of that which
related to the disciples, in communion and in testimony.

The Lord's prayer for believers, not limited to the twelve: unity in communion with the Father and the Son

In verse 20, He declares that He prays also for those
who should believe on Him through their means. Here
the character of the unity differs a little from that in
verse 11. There, in speaking of the disciples, He says
"*as We are;*" for the oneness of the Father and the Son
showed itself in fixed purpose, object, love, work, everything. Therefore the disciples were to have that kind
of unity. Here those who believed, inasmuch as receiving
and taking part in that which was communicated, had
their oneness in the power of the blessing into which they
were brought. By one Spirit, in which they were necessarily united, they had a place in communion with the
Father and the Son. It was the communion of the Father
and of the Son. (Compare 1 John 1: 3; and how similar
the language of the apostle is to that of Christ!) Thus,
the Lord asks that they may be one in them—the Father

and the Son. This was the means to make the world
believe that the Father had sent the Son; for here were
those that had believed it, who, however opposed their
interests and habits might be, however strong their prejudices, yet were *one* (by this powerful revelation and by
this work) in the Father and the Son.

Converse with His Father: the glory He has given His Son

Here His prayer ends, but not all His converse with His
Father. He gives us (and here the witnesses and the
believers are together) the glory which the Father has
given Him. It is the basis of another, a third,[67] mode of
oneness. All partake, it is true, in glory, of this absolute
oneness in thought, object, fixed purpose, which is found
in the oneness of the Father and the Son. Perfection
being come, that which the Holy Ghost had produced
spiritually, His absorbing energy shutting out every other,
was natural to all in glory.

A unity in manifestation in glory

But the principle of the existence of this unity, added
yet another character to that truth—that of manifestation,
or at least of an inward source which realized its manifestation in them: "I in them," said Jesus, "and Thou
in Me." This is not the simple, perfect oneness of verse
11, nor the mutuality and communion of verse 21. It

[67] There are three unities spoken of. First of the disciples, "as we
are," unity by the power of one Spirit in thought, purpose, mind, service,
the Holy Ghost making them all one, their path in common, the expression of His mind and power, and of nothing else. Then, of those
who should believe through their means, unity in communion with the
Father and the Son, "one in Us"—still by the Holy Ghost but, as brought
into that, as already said above, as in 1 John 1: 3. Then unity in glory,
"perfect in one, in manifestation and descending revelation, the Father
in the Son, and the Son in all of them. The second was for the world's
believing, the third for its knowing. The two first were literally accomplished according to the terms in which they are expressed. How
far believers are departed from them since need not be said.

is Christ in all believers, and the Father in Christ, a unity
in manifestation in glory, not merely in communion—
a oneness in which all is perfectly connected with its
source. And Christ, whom alone they were to manifest,
is in them; and the Father, whom Christ had perfectly
manifested, is in Him. The world (for this will be in the
millennial glory, and manifested to the world) will then
know (He does not say, "That it may believe") that
Jesus had been sent by the Father (How deny it, when
He should be seen in glory?) and, moreover, that the
disciples had been loved by the Father, even as Jesus
Himself was loved. The fact of their possessing the same
glory as Christ would be the proof.

With Christ, to see His glory, the secret for those who love Him

But there was yet more. There is that which the world
will not see, because it will not be in it. "Father, I will
that they whom Thou hast given Me be with Me where
I am." There we are not only like Christ (conformed to
the Son, bearing the image of the heavenly man before
the eyes of the world), but *with Him* where He is. Jesus
desires that we should see His glory.[68] Solace and encouragement for us, after having partaken of His shame:
but yet more precious, inasmuch as we see that He who
has been dishonored as Man, and because He became
Man for our sake, shall, even on that account, be glorified
with a glory above all other glory, save His who has put
all things under Him. For He speaks here of given glory.
It is this which is so precious to us, because He has
acquired it by His sufferings for us, and yet it is what
was perfectly due to Him—the just reward for having, in
them, perfectly glorified the Father. Now, this is a
peculiar joy, entirely beyond the world. The world will

---

[68] This answers to Moses and Elias entering into the cloud, besides
their display in the same glory as Christ, standing on the mountain.

see the glory that we have in common with Christ, and will know that we have been loved as Christ was loved. But there is a secret for those who love Him, which belongs to His Person and to our association with Himself. The Father loved Him before the world was—a love in which there is no question of comparison, but of that which is infinite, perfect, and thus in itself satisfying. We shall share this in the sense of seeing our Beloved in it, and of being with Him, and of beholding the glory which the Father has given Him, according to the love wherewith He loved Him before the world had any part whatever in the dealings of God. Up to this we were in the world; here in heaven, out of all the world's claims or apprehension (Christ seen in the fruit of that love which the Father had for Him before the world existed). Christ, then, was the Father's delight. We see Him in the eternal fruit of that love as Man. We shall be in it with Him for ever, to enjoy His being in it—that our Jesus, our Beloved, is in it, and is what He is.

The righteousness of the Father

Meantime, being such, there was justice in the dealings of God with regard to His rejection. He had fully, perfectly, manifested the Father. The world had not known Him, but Jesus had known Him, and the disciples had known that the Father had sent Him. He appeals here, not to the holiness of the Father, that He might keep them according to that blessed name, but to the righteousness of the Father, that He might make a distinction between the world on one side, and Jesus with His own on the other; for there was the moral reason as well as the ineffable love of the Father for the Son. And Jesus would have us enjoy, while here below, the consciousness that the distinction has been made by the communications of grace, before it is made by judgment.

The Father's name declared: His love to be known and enjoyed

He had declared unto them the Father's name, and would declare it, even when He had gone up on high, in order that the love wherewith the Father had loved Him might be in them (that their hearts might possess it in this world—what grace!) and Jesus Himself in them the communicator of that love, the source of strength to enjoy. it, conducting it, so to speak, in all the perfection in which He enjoyed it, into their hearts, in which He dwelt —Himself the strength, the life, the competency, the right, and the means of enjoying it thus, and as such, in the heart. For it is in the Son who declares it to us, that we know the name of the Father whom He reveals to us. That is, He would have us enjoy now that relationship in love in which we shall see Him in heaven. The world will know we have been loved as Jesus when we appear in the same glory with Him; but our part is to know it now, Christ being in us.

Chapter 18

The Lord's personal glory brought out in the history of His last moments

THE history of our Lord's last moments begins after the words that He addressed to His Father. We shall find even in this part of it, the general character of that which is related in this Gospel (according to all that we have seen in it), that the events bring out the personal glory of the Lord. We have, indeed, the malice of man strongly characterized; but the principal object in the picture is the Son of God, not the Son of Man suffering under the weight of that which is come upon Him. We have not the agony in the garden. We have not the ex-

pression of His feeling Himself forsaken by God. The
Jews too are put in the place of utter rejection.

Judas' iniquity: the malice of a hardened heart

The iniquity of Judas is as strongly marked here as in
chapter 13. He well knew the place; for Jesus was in
the habit of resorting thither with His disciples. What a
thought—to choose such a place for His betrayal! What
inconceivable hardness of heart! But alas, he had, as it
were, given himself up to Satan, the tool of the enemy,
the manifestation of his power and of his true character!

Divine glory displayed: the Good Shepherd and His sheep

How many things had taken place in that garden!
What communications from a heart filled with God's
own love, and seeking to make it penetrate into the narrow
and too insensible hearts of His beloved disciples! But
all was lost upon Judas. He comes, with the agents
employed by the malice of the priests and Pharisees, to
seize the Person of Jesus. But Jesus anticipates them.
It is He who presents Himself to them. Knowing all
things that should come upon Him, He goes forth, in-
quiring "Whom seek ye?" It is the Saviour, the Son of
God, who offers Himself. They reply, "Jesus of Nazareth."
Jesus says unto them, "I am He." Judas, also, was there,
who knew Him well, and knew that voice, so long familiar
to his ears. No one laid hands on Him: but as soon as
His word echoes in their hearts, as soon as that divine "I
am" is heard within them, they go backward, and fall
to the ground. Who will take Him? He had but to go
away and leave them there. But He came not for this;
and the time to offer Himself up was come. He asks
them again, therefore, "Whom seek ye?" They say, as
before, "Jesus of Nazareth." The first time, the divine
glory of the Person of Christ must needs display it-

Chapter 19

The real authors of the Lord's death

PILATE gives way to his usual inhumanity. In the account, however, given in this Gospel, the Jews are prominent, as the real authors (as far as man was concerned) of the Lord's death. Jealous for their ceremonial purity, but indifferent to justice, they are not content to judge Him according to their own law; [69] they choose to have Him put to death by the Romans, for the whole counsel of God must needs be accomplished.

Pilate's alarm, pride, and injustice: his attempt to make the Jews fully guilty

It is on the repeated demands of the Jews that Pilate delivers Jesus into their hands—thoroughly guilty in so doing, for he had openly avowed His innocence, and had had his conscience decidedly touched and alarmed by the evident proofs there were that he had some extraordinary person before him. He will not show that he is touched, but he is so. (Chap. 19: 8.) The divine glory that pierced through the humiliation of Christ acts upon him, and gives force to the declaration of the Jews that Jesus had made Himself the Son of God. Pilate had scourged Him and given Him up to the insults of the soldiers; and here he would have stopped. Perhaps he hoped also that the Jews would be satisfied with this, and he presents Jesus to them crowned with thorns. Perhaps he hoped that their jealousy with regard to these national insults would induce them to ask for His deliverance. But, ruthlessly pursuing their malicious purpose, they cry out, "Crucify Him, crucify Him!" Pilate objects to this for

---

[69] It is said that their Jewish traditions forbade their putting any one to death during the great feasts. It is possible that this may have influenced the Jews; but however that might be, the purposes of God were thus accomplished. At other times the Jews were not so prompt in submitting to the Roman exigencies that deprived them of the right of life and death.

himself, while giving them liberty to do it, saying that he finds no fault in Him. Upon this they plead their Jewish law. They had a law of their own, say they, and by this law He ought to die, because He made Himself the Son of God. Pilate, already struck and exercised in mind, is the more alarmed; and, going back to the judgment hall again, questions Jesus. He makes no reply. The pride of Pilate awakes, and he asks if Jesus does not know that he has power to condemn or to release Him. The Lord maintains, in replying, the full dignity of His Person. Pilate had no power over Him, were it not the will of God—to this He submitted. It heightened the sin of those who had delivered Him up, to suppose that man could do anything against Him, were it not that the will of God was thus to be accomplished. The knowledge of His Person formed the measure of the sin committed against Him. The not perceiving it caused everything to be falsely judged, and, in the case of Judas, showed the most absolute moral blindness. He knew his Master's power. What was the meaning of delivering Him up to man, if it were not that His hour was come? But, this being the case, what was the betrayer's position?

But Jesus always speaks according to the glory of His Person, and as being thereby entirely above the circumstances through which He was passing in grace, and in obedience to His Father's will. Pilate is thoroughly disturbed by the Lord's reply, yet his feeling is not strong enough to counteract the motive with which the Jews press him, but it has sufficient power to make him throw back upon the Jews all that there was of will in His condemnation, and to make them fully guilty of the Lord's rejection.

The Jews' own condemnation and calamity: Jesus delivered up

Pilate sought to withdraw Him from their fury. At last, fearing to be accused of infidelity to Cæsar, he turns with contempt to the Jews, saying, "Behold your King;" acting—although unconsciously—under the hand of God, to bring out that memorable word from their lips, their condemnation, and their calamity even to this day, "We have no king but Cæsar." They denied their Messiah. The fatal word, which called down the judgment of God, was now pronounced; and Pilate delivers up Jesus to them.

The Lord's title affixed to the cross

Jesus, humbled and bearing His cross, takes His place with the transgressors. Nevertheless He who would that all should be fulfilled ordained that a testimony should be rendered to His dignity; and Pilate (perhaps to vex the Jews, certainly to accomplish the purposes of God) affixes to the cross as the Lord's title, "Jesus of Nazareth, the King of the Jews:" the twofold truth—the despised Nazarene is the true Messiah. Here, then, as throughout this Gospel, the Jews take their place as cast off by God.

Jesus crucified: prophecy fulfilled

At the same time the apostle shows—here, as elsewhere—that Jesus was the true Messiah, by quoting the prophecies which speak of that which happened to Him in general, with regard to His rejection and His sufferings, so that He is proved to be the Messiah by the very circumstances in which He was rejected of the people.

After the history of His crucifixion, as the act of man, we have that which characterizes it in respect to what Jesus was upon the cross. The blood and water flowed from His pierced side.

The devotion of the women at the cross: nature seen in its perfection in the Lord's human feelings

The devotedness of the women who followed Him, less important perhaps on the side of action, shines out in its own way nevertheless in that perseverance of love which

brought them nigh to the cross. The more responsible
position of the apostles as men scarcely allowed it to
them, circumstanced as they were; but this takes nothing
from the privilege which grace attaches to woman when
faithful to Jesus. But it was the occasion for Christ to
give us fresh instruction, by showing Himself such as He
was, and by setting His work before us, above all mere
circumstances, as the effect and the expression of a spiritual energy which consecrated Him, as Man, entirely to
God, offering Himself also to God by the Eternal Spirit.
His work was done. He had offered Himself up. He
returns, so to speak, into His personal relationships.
Nature, in His human feelings, is seen in its perfection;
and, at the same time, His divine superiority, personally,
to the circumstances through which He passed in grace as
the obedient Man. The expression of His filial feelings
shows, that the consecration to God, which removed Him
from all those affections that are alike the necessity and
the duty of the man according to nature, was not the
want of human feeling, but the power of the Spirit of
God. Seeing the women, He speaks to them no longer
as Teacher and Saviour, the resurrection and the life; it
is Jesus, a Man, individually, in His human relationship.

John's commission: the Master's love for John

"Woman," He says, "behold thy son!"—committing
His mother to the care of John, the disciple whom Jesus
loved—and to the disciple, "Behold thy mother!" and
thenceforth that disciple took her to his own home. Sweet
and precious commission! A confidence which spoke that
which he who was thus loved could alone appreciate, as being its immediate object. This shows us also that His love
for John had a character of human affection and attachment, according to God, but not essentially divine, although full of divine grace—a grace which gave it all its
value, but which clothed itself with the reality of the

human heart. It was this, evidently, which bound Peter and John together. Jesus was their only and common object. Of very different characters—and so much the more united on that account—they thought but of one thing. Absolute consecration to Jesus is the strongest bond between human hearts. It strips them of self, and they have but one soul in thought, intent, and settled purpose, because they have only one object. But in Jesus this was perfect, and it was grace. It is not said, "The disciple who loved Jesus;" that would have been quite out of season. It would have been to take Jesus entirely out of His place, and His dignity, His personal glory, and to destroy the value of His love to John. Nevertheless John loved Christ, and consequently appreciated thus his Master's love; and, his heart attached to Him by grace, he devoted himself to the execution of this sweet commission, which he takes pleasure in relating here. It is indeed love that tells it, although it does not speak of itself.

I believe that we again see this feeling (used by the Spirit of God, not evidently as the foundation, but to give its color to the expression of that which he had seen and known) in the beginning of John's first epistle.

Christ acting in accordance with the glory of His Person

We also see here that this Gospel does not show us Christ under the weight of His sufferings, but acting in accordance with the glory of His Person as above all things, and fulfilling all things in grace. In perfect calmness He provides for His mother; having done this, He knows that all is finished. He has, according to human language, entire self-possession.

The Lord laying down His life: a voluntary act

There is yet one prophecy to be fulfilled. He says, "I thirst," and, as God had foretold, they give Him

vinegar. He knows that now there is not one detail left
of all that was to be accomplished. He bows His head,
and Himself gives[70] up His spirit.

Thus, when the whole divine work is accomplished
the divine Man giving up His spirit, that spirit leaves
the body which had been its organ and its vessel. The
time was come for so doing; and by doing it, He secured
the accomplishment of another divine word—"Not one
of His bones shall be broken." But everything bore its
part in the fulfilment of those words, and the purposes of
Him who had pronounced them beforehand.

The tokens of an eternal and perfect salvation from His pierced side: the purpose of the record

A soldier pierces His side with a spear. It is from a
dead Saviour that flow forth the tokens of an eternal and
perfect salvation—the water and the blood; the one to
cleanse the sinner, the other to expiate his sins. The
Evangelist saw it. His love for the Lord makes him like
to remember that he saw Him thus unto the end; he
tells it in order that we may believe. But if we see in the
beloved disciple the vessel that the Holy Ghost uses (and
very sweet it is to see it, and according to the will of
God), we see plainly who it is that uses it. How many
things John witnessed which he did not relate! The cry
of grief and of abandonment—the earthquake—the centurion's confession—the history of the thief: all these

---

[70] This is the force of the expression; which is quite different from
the word *exepneusen* (expired). We learn from Luke that He did this
when He had said, "Father, into Thy hands I commend My spirit."
But in John, the Holy Ghost is setting forth even His death as the
result of a voluntary act, giving up His spirit, and not saying to whom
He committed (as man with absolute and perfect faith) His human
spirit, His soul, in dying. It is His divine competency that is here
shown, and not His trust in His Father. The word is never used in
this way but in this passage as to Christ, in either the New Testament
or the LXX.

things took place before his eyes, which were fixed upon
his Master; yet he does not mention them. He speaks
of that which his Beloved was in the midst of all this.
The Holy Ghost causes him to relate that which belonged
to the personal glory of Jesus. His affections made him
find it a sweet and easy task. The Holy Ghost attached
him to it, employing him in that which he was well suited
to perform. Through grace the instrument lent itself
readily to the work for which the Holy Ghost set it apart.
His memory and his heart were under the dominant and
exclusive influence of the Spirit of God. That Spirit
employed them in His work. One sympathizes with the
instrument; one believes in that which the Holy Ghost
relates by his means, for the words are those of the Holy
Ghost.

Divine grace expressing itself; but Christ's personal dignity never lost

Nothing can be more touching, more deeply interesting,
than divine grace thus expressing itself in human tenderness and taking its form. While possessing the entire
reality of human affection, it had all the power and depth
of divine grace. It was divine grace that Jesus should
have such affections. On the other hand, nothing could be
farther from the appreciation of this sovereign source of
divine love, flowing through the perfect channel which it
made for itself by its own power, than the pretension to
express our love as reciprocal; it would be, on the contrary, to fail entirely in that appreciation. True saints
among the Moravians have called Jesus "brother," and
others have borrowed their hymns or the expression; the
Word never says so. *"He is not ashamed* to call us brethren," but it is quite another thing for us to call Him
so. The personal dignity of Christ is never lost in the
intensity and tenderness of His love.

Joseph of Arimathea and Nicodemus rendering the last honors to the Lord's dead body

But the rejected Saviour was to be with the rich and the honorable in His death, however despised He may previously have been; and two, who dared not confess Him while He lived, awakened now by the greatness of the sin of their nation, and by the event itself of His death—which the grace of God, who had reserved them for this work, made them feel—occupy themselves with the attentions due to His dead body. Joseph, himself a counsellor, comes to ask Pilate for the body of Jesus, Nicodemus joining with him to render the last honors to Him whom they had never followed during His life. We can understand this. To follow Jesus constantly under reproach, and compromise oneself for ever on His account, is a very different thing from acting when some great occasion happens in which there is no longer room for the former, and when the extent of the evil compels us to separate from it; and when the good, rejected because it is perfect in testimony, and perfected in its rejection, forces us to take a part, if through grace any *moral* sense exists in us. God thus fulfilled His words of truth. Joseph and Nicodemus place the Lord's body in a new sepulchre in a garden near the cross; for, on account of it being the Jews' preparation, they could do no more at that moment.

Chapter 20

Summary of Chapters 20, 21

IN chapter 20 we have, in a summary of several of the leading facts among those which took place after the resurrection of Jesus, a picture of all the consequences of that great event, in immediate connection with the grace that produced them, and with the affections that ought to

be seen in the faithful when again brought into relationship with the Lord; and at the same time, a picture of all
God's ways up to the revelation of Christ to the remnant
before the millennium. In chapter 21 the millennium is
pictured to us.

Jesus risen: Mary Magdalene seeking Jesus: Peter and John finding the proofs of His resurrection

Mary Magdalene, out of whom He had cast seven
demons, appears first in the scene—a touching expression
of the ways of God. She represents, I doubt not, the
Jewish remnant of that day, personally attached to the
Lord, but not knowing the power of His resurrection.
She is alone in her love: the very strength of her affection
isolates her. She was not the only one saved, but she
comes alone to seek—wrongly to seek, if you will, but to
seek—Jesus, before the testimony of His glory shines forth
in a world of darkness, because she loved Himself. She
comes before the other women, while it was yet dark. It
is a loving heart (we have already seen it in the believing
women) occupied with Jesus, when the public testimony
of man is still entirely wanting. And it is to this that
Jesus first manifests Himself when He had risen. Nevertheless her heart knew where it would find a response.
She goes away to Peter and to the other disciple whom
Jesus loved, when she does not find the body of Christ.
Peter and the other disciple go, and find the proofs of a
resurrection accomplished (as to Jesus Himself) with all
the composure that became the power of God, great as
the alarm might be that it created in the mind of man.
There had been no haste; everything was in order: and
Jesus was not there.

Mary's affection: the Good Shepherd and His sheep

The two disciples, however, are not moved by the same
attachment as that which filled her heart, who had been

the object of so mighty a deliverance [71] on the Lord's
part. They see, and, on these visible proofs, they believe.
It was not a spiritual understanding of the thoughts of
God by means of His word; they *saw* and believed. There
is nothing in this which gathers the disciples together.
Jesus was away; He had risen. They had satisfied themselves on this point, and they go away *to their home.* But
Mary, led by affection rather than by intelligence, is not
satisfied with coldly recognizing that Jesus was again
risen.[72] She thought Him still dead, because she did not
possess Him. His death, the fact of her not finding Him
again, added to the intensity of her affection, because He
Himself was its object. All the tokens of this affection
are produced here in the most touching manner. She
supposes that the gardener must know who was in question without her telling him, for she only thought of
one (as if I inquired of a beloved object in a family,
"How is he?"). Bending over the sepulchre, she turns
her head when He approaches; but then the Good Shep-

---

[71] "Seven demons." This represents the complete possession of this
poor woman by the unclean spirits to whom she was a prey. It is the
expression of the real state of the Jewish people.

[72] It is impossible to me, in giving great principles for the help of
those who seek to understand the Word, to develop all that is so deeply
touching and interesting in this twentieth chapter, on which I have
often pondered with (through grace) an ever-growing interest. This
revelation of the Lord to the poor woman who could not do without
her Saviour, has a touching beauty, which every detail enhances. But
there is one point of view to which I cannot but call the reader's
attention. There are four conditions of soul presented here which,
taken together, are very instructive, and each in the case of a believer:—

1st. John and Peter, who see and believe, are really believers; but
they do not see in Christ the only centre of all the thoughts of God, for
His glory, for the world, for souls. Neither is He so for their affections,
although they are believers. Having found that He was risen, they do
without Him. Mary, who did not know this, who was even culpably
ignorant, could nevertheless not do without Jesus. She must possess
Himself. Peter and John go to their home; this is the centre of their
interests. They believe indeed, but self and home suffice them.

2nd. Thomas believes, and acknowledges with true orthodox faith,
on incontestable proofs, that Jesus is his Lord and his God. He truly
believes for himself. He has not the communications of the efficacy of
the Lord's work, and of the relationship with His Father into which
Jesus brings His own, the assembly. He has peace perhaps, but he has
missed all the revelation of the assembly's position. How many souls—
saved souls even—are there in these two conditions!

herd, risen from the dead, calls His sheep by her name; and the known and loved voice—mighty according to the grace which thus called her—instantly reveals Him to her who heard it. She turns to Him, and replies, "Rabboni— my Master."

The Lord's new position and relationship with the remnant

But while thus revealing Himself to the beloved remnant, whom He had delivered, all is changed in their position and in His relationship with them. He was not going now to dwell bodily in the midst of His people on earth. He did not come back to re-establish the kingdom in Israel. "Touch Me not," says He to Mary. But by redemption He had wrought a far more important thing. He had placed them in the same position as Himself with His Father and His God; and He calls them—which He never had, and never could have done before—His breth-

---

3rd. Mary Magdalene is ignorant in the extreme. She does not know that Christ is risen. She has so little right sense of His being Lord and God, that she thinks some one might have taken away His body. But Christ is her all, the need of her soul, the only desire of her heart. Without Him she has no home, no Lord, no anything. Now to this need Jesus answers; it indicates the work of the Holy Ghost. He calls His sheep by her name, shows Himself to her first of all, teaches her that His presence was not now to be a Jewish bodily return to earth, that He must ascend to His Father, that the disciples were now His brethren, and that they were placed in the same position as Himself with His God and His Father—as Himself, the risen Man, ascended to His God and Father. All the glory of the new individual position is opened to her.

4th. This gathers the disciples together. Jesus then brings them the peace which He has made, and they have the full joy of a present Saviour who brings it them. He makes this peace (possessed by them in virtue of His work and His victory) their starting-point, sends them as the Father had sent Him, and imparts to them the Holy Ghost as the breath and power of life, that they may be able to bear that peace to others.

These are the communications of the efficacy of His work, as He had given to Mary that of the relationship to the Father which resulted from it. The whole is the answer to Mary's attachment to Christ, or what resulted from it. If through grace there is affection, the answer will assuredly be granted. It is the truth which flows from the work of Christ. No other state than that which Christ here presents is in accordance with what He has done, and with the Father's love. He cannot, by His work, place us in any other.

ren. Until His death the corn of wheat remained alone.
Pure and perfect, the Son of God, He could not stand
in the same relationship to God as the sinner; but, in the
glorious position which He was going to resume as Man,
He could, through redemption, associate with Himself
His redeemed ones, cleansed, regenerated, and adopted in
Him.

The remnant's new position with Him

He sends them word of the new position they were to
have in common with Himself. He says to Mary, "Touch
Me not; but go to My brethren, and tell them that I
ascend to My Father and your Father, to My God and
your God." The will of the Father—accomplished by
means of the glorious work of the Son, who, as Man, has
taken His place, apart from sin, with His God and Father
—and the work of the Son, the source of eternal life to
them, have brought the disciples into the same position
as Himself before the Father.

The risen Lord in the midst of the gathered disciples, bringing peace

The testimony borne to the truth *gathers the disciples
together*. They meet with closed doors, unprotected now
by the care and power of Jesus, the Messiah, Jehovah on
earth. But if they had no longer the shelter of the Messiah's presence, they have Jesus in their midst, bringing
them that which they could not have before His death—
"Peace."

The disciples sent forth into the world for Him with peace as their starting-point

But He did not bring them this blessing merely as their
own portion. Having given them proofs of His resurrection, and that in His body He was the same Jesus, He

sets them in this perfect peace as the starting-point of their mission. The Father, eternal and infinite fountain of love, had sent the Son, who abode in it, who was the witness of that love, and of the peace which He, the Father, shed around Himself, where sin had no existence. Rejected in His mission, Jesus had—on behalf of a world where sin existed—made peace for all who should receive the testimony of the grace which had made it; and He now sends His disciples from the bosom of that peace into which He had brought them, by the remission of sins through His death, to bear testimony to it in the world.

The Holy Spirit given for peace and power

He says *again*, "Peace be unto you," to send them forth into the world clothed and filled with that peace, their feet shod with it, even as the Father had sent Him. He gives them the Holy Ghost for this end, that according to His power they might bear the remission of sins to a world that was bowed down under the yoke of sin.

The distinction between the bestowal of the Holy Spirit here and at Pentecost

I do not doubt that, speaking historically, the Spirit here is distinguished from Acts 2, inasmuch as here it is a breath of inward life, as God breathed into the nostrils of Adam a breath of life. It is not the Holy Ghost sent down from heaven. Thus Christ, who is a quickening Spirit, imparts spiritual life to them according to the power of resurrection.[73] As to the general picture figur-

---

[73] Compare Romans 4 to 8 and Colossians 2, 3. Resurrection was the power of life which brought them out of the dominion of sin, that had its end in death, and that was condemned in the death of Jesus, and they dead to it, but not condemned by it, sin having been condemned in His death. This is a question, not of guilt, but of state. Our guilt, blessed be God, was put away too. But here we die with Christ, and resurrection presents us (Romans, as quoted, unfolds the side of death; Colossians adds resurrection. Romans is death to sin, Colossians to the world) living before God in a life in which Jesus—and we by Him —appeared in His presence according to the perfection of divine righteousness. But this supposed His work also.

atively presented in the passage, it is the Spirit bestowed
on the saints gathered by the testimony of His being
risen and His going to the Father, as the whole scene
represents the assembly in its present privileges. Thus
we have the remnant attached to Christ by love; believers
individually recognized as children of God, and in the
same position before Him as Christ; and then the assembly founded on this testimony gathered together with
Jesus in the midst, in the enjoyment of peace; and its
members, individually constituted, in connection with the
peace which Christ has made, a witness to the world of
the remission of sins—its administration being committed
to them.

Thomas' absence from the first gathering

Thomas represents the Jews in the last days, who will
believe when they see. Blessed are they who have believed
without seeing. But the faith of Thomas is not concerned
with the position of sonship. He acknowledges, as the
remnant will do, that Jesus is his Lord and his God.
He was not with them in their first Church gathering.

The Lord here, by His actions, consecrates the first
day of the week for His meeting together with His own,
in spirit here below.

The Evangelist's object in what he has related

The Evangelist is far from exhausting all that there
was to relate of that which Jesus did. The object of that
which he has related is linked with the communication of
eternal life in Christ; first, that Jesus is the Christ, the
Son of God; and, second, that in believing we have life
through His name. To this the Gospel is consecrated.

Chapter 21

Chapter 21 picturing the millennial work of Christ

THE next chapter, while rendering a fresh testimony to the resurrection of Jesus, gives us—to verse 13—a picture of the millennial work of Christ; from thence to the end, the especial portions of Peter and John in connection with their service to Christ. The application is limited to the earth, for they had known Jesus on earth. It is Paul who will give us the heavenly position of Christ and the assembly. But he has no place here.

The disciples fishing in Galilee: Peter and John in the same circumstances as when first called

Led by Peter, several of the apostles go a fishing. The Lord meets them in the same circumstances as those in which He found them at the beginning, and reveals Himself to them in the same manner. John at once understands that it is the Lord. Peter, with his usual energy, casts himself into the sea to reach Him.

Observe here, that we find ourselves again upon the ground of the historic Gospels—that is to say, that the miracle of the draught of fishes identifies itself with the work of Christ on earth, and is in the sphere of His former association with His disciples. It is Galilee, not Bethany. It has not the usual character of the doctrine of this Gospel, which presents the divine Person of Jesus, outside all dispensation, here below; raising our thoughts above all such subjects. Here (at the end of the Gospel and of the sketch given in chapter 20 of the result of the manifestation of His divine Person and of His work) the Evangelist comes for the first time on the ground of the Synoptics, of the manifestation and coming fruits of Christ's connection with earth. Thus the application of the passage to this point is not merely an idea which the narrative suggests to the mind, but it rests upon the general teaching of the Word.

The difference after the Lord's manifestation: the net unbroken: Christ's millennial work not marred

Still there is a notable difference between that which took place at the beginning and here. In the former scene the ships began to sink, the nets broke. Not so here, and the Holy Ghost marks this circumstance as distinctive: Christ's millennial work is not marred. He is there after His resurrection, and that which He performs does not rest, in itself, on man's responsibility as to its effect here below: the net does not break. Also, when the disciples bring the fish which they had caught, the Lord has some already there. So shall it be on earth at the end. Before His manifestation He will have prepared a remnant for Himself on the earth; but after His manifestation He will gather a multitude also from the sea of nations.

Christ in companionship with His disciples: His three manifestations

Another idea presents itself. Christ is again as in companionship with His disciples. "Come," says He, "and dine." There is no question here of heavenly things, but of the renewing of His connection with His people in the kingdom. All this does not immediately belong to the subject of this Gospel, which leads us higher. Accordingly it is introduced in a mysterious and symbolical manner. This appearance of Christ's is spoken of as His third manifestation. I doubt His manifestation on earth before His death being included in the number. I would rather apply it to that which, first, after His resurrection, gave rise to the gathering together of the saints as an assembly; secondly, to a revelation of Himself to the

Jews after the manner of that which is presented in the
Song of Songs; and lastly here to the public display of
His power, when He shall already have gathered the
remnant together. His appearing like the lightning is
outside all these things. Historically the three appearances were—the day of His resurrection; the following
first day of the week; and His appearance at the Sea of
Galilee.

Peter's restoration: the Lord's sheep committed to his care when humbled

Afterwards, in a passage full of ineffable grace, He
entrusts Peter with the care of His sheep (that is, I doubt
not, of His Jewish sheep; he is the apostle of the circumcision), and leaves to John an indefinite period of
sojourn upon earth. His words apply much more to their
ministry than to their persons, with the exception of one
verse referring to Peter. But this demands a little more
development.

The Lord begins with the full restoration of Peter's
soul. He does not reproach him with his fault, but judges
the source of evil that produced it—self-confidence. Peter
had declared, that if all should deny Jesus, yet he at least
would not deny Him. The Lord therefore asks him,
"Lovest thou Me more than do these?" and Peter is reduced to acknowledge that it required the omniscience of
God to know that he, who had boasted of having more
love than all others for Jesus, had really any affection
for Him at all. And the question thrice repeated must
indeed have searched the depths of his heart. Nor was
it till the third time that he says, "Thou knowest all
things; Thou knowest that I love Thee." Jesus did not
let his conscience go until he had come to this. Nevertheless the grace which did this for Peter's good—the
grace which had followed him in spite of everything, praying for him before he felt his need or had committed the

fault—is perfect here also. For, at the moment when it
might be thought that at the utmost he would be re-
admitted through divine forbearance, the strongest testimony of grace is lavished upon him. When humbled by
his fall, and brought to entire dependence upon grace, all-
abounding grace displays itself. The Lord commits that
which He most loved to him—the sheep whom He had
just redeemed. He commits them to Peter's care. This
is the grace which surmounts all that man is, which is
above all that man is, which consequently produces confidence, not in self, but in God, as One whose grace can
always be trusted in, as being full of grace, and perfect
in that grace which is above everything, and is always
itself; grace which makes us able to accomplish the work
of grace towards—whom?—man who needs it. It creates
confidence in proportion to the measure in which it acts.

I think that the Lord's words apply to the sheep
already known to Peter; and with whom only Jesus had
been in daily connection; who would naturally be before
His mind, and that in the scene which we see this chapter
puts before us—the sheep of the house of Israel.

It appears to me that there is progression in that which
the Lord says to Peter. He asks, "Lovest thou Me more
than do these?" Peter says, "Thou knowest that I have
affection for Thee." Jesus replies, "Feed My lambs."
The second time He says only, "Lovest thou Me?" omit-
ting the comparison between Peter and the rest, and his
former pretension. Peter repeats the declaration of his
affection. Jesus says to him, "Shepherd My sheep." The
third time He says, "Hast thou affection for Me?" using
Peter's own expression; and on Peter's replying, as we
have seen, seizing this use of his words by the Lord, He
says, "Feed My sheep." The links between Peter and
Christ known on earth made him fit to pasture the flock
of the Jewish remnant—to feed the lambs, by showing
them the Messiah as He had been, and to act as a shep-

herd, in guiding those that were more advanced, and in
supplying them with food.

Peter's desire to follow the Lord granted by the will of God

But the grace of the loving Saviour did not stop here.
Peter might still feel the sorrow of having missed such
an opportunity of confessing the Lord at the critical
moment. Jesus assures him that if he had failed in doing
so of his own will, he should be allowed to do it by the
will of God; and as when young he girded himself, others
should gird him when old and carry him whither he
would not. It should be given him by the will of God
to die for the Lord, as he had formerly declared himself
ready to do in his own strength. Now also that Peter
was humbled and brought entirely under grace that he
knew he had no strength—that he felt his dependence on
the Lord, his utter inefficiency if he trusted to his own
power—now, I repeat, the Lord calls Peter to follow Him;
which he had pretended to do, when the Lord had told
him he could not. It was this that his heart desired.
Feeding those whom Jesus had continued to feed until
His death, he should see Israel reject everything, even
as Christ had seen them do; and his own work end,
even as Christ had seen His work end (the judgment
ready to fall, and beginning at the house of God).
Finally, what he had pretended to do and could not, he
would now do—follow Christ to prison and to death.

The portion and ministry of John

Then comes the history of the disciple whom Jesus
loved. John having, no doubt, heard the call addressed
to Peter, follows also himself; and Peter, linked with
him, as we have seen, by their common love to the Lord,
inquires what should happen to him likewise. The Lord's

answer announces the portion and ministry of John, but,
as it appears to me, in connection with the earth. But
the Lord's enigmatical expression is, nevertheless, as
remarkable as it is important: "If I will that he tarry
till I come, what is that to thee?" They thought, in
consequence, that John would not die. The Lord did not
say so—a warning not to ascribe a meaning to His words,
instead of receiving one; and at the same time showing
our need of the Holy Spirit's help; for the words literally
might be so taken. Giving heed myself, I trust, to this
warning, I will say what I think to be the meaning of the
Lord's words, which I do not doubt to be so—a meaning
which gives a key to many other expressions of the same
kind.

The connection with the earth in John's Gospel: Jerusalem's destruction as an earthly centre: the heavenly assembly gathered out

In the narrative of the Gospel, we are in connection
with the earth (that is, the connection of Jesus with the
earth). As planted on earth at Jerusalem, the assembly,
as the house of God, is formally recognized as taking the
place of the house of Jehovah at Jerusalem. The history
of the assembly, as thus formally established as a centre
on earth, ended with the destruction of Jerusalem. The
remnant saved by the Messiah was no longer to be in
connection with Jerusalem, the centre of the gathering of
the Gentiles. In this sense the destruction of Jerusalem
put an end judicially to the new system of God upon
earth—a system promulgated by Peter (Acts 3); with
regard to which Stephen declared to the Jews their resistance to the Holy Ghost, and was sent, as it were,
as a messenger after Him who was gone to receive the
kingdom and to return; while Paul—elected from among
those enemies of the good news still addressed to the
Jews by the Holy Ghost after the death of Christ, and

separated from Jews and Gentiles, in order to be sent to the latter—performs a new work that was hidden from the prophets of old, namely, the gathering out of a heavenly assembly without distinction of Jew or Gentile.

The extent of John's ministry

The destruction of Jerusalem put an end to one of these systems, and to the existence of Judaism according to the law and the promises, leaving only the heavenly assembly. John remained—the last of the twelve—until this period, and after Paul, in order to watch over the assembly as established on that footing, that is, as the organized and earthly frame-work (responsible in that character) of the testimony of God, and the subject of His government on the earth. But this is not all. In his *ministry* John went on to the end, to the coming of Christ in judgment to the earth; and he has linked the judgment of the assembly, as the responsible witness on earth, with the judgment of the world, when God shall resume His connection with the earth in government (the testimony of the assembly being finished, and it having been caught up, according to its proper character, to be with the Lord in heaven).

The scope of the Apocalypse

Thus the Apocalypse presents the judgment of the assembly on earth, as the formal witness for the truth; and then passes on to God's resumption of the government of the earth, in view of the establishment of the Lamb upon the throne, and the setting aside of the power of evil. The heavenly character of the assembly is only found there, when its members are exhibited on thrones as kings and priests, and when the marriage of the Lamb takes place in heaven. The earth — after the Seven Churches—has no longer the heavenly testimony. It is not the subject, either in the seven assemblies, or in the properly so-called prophetic part. Thus, taking the assemblies as such in those days, the assembly according to Paul is not seen there. Taking the assemblies as descriptions of the assembly, the subject of God's government on earth, we have it until its final rejection; and the history is continuous, and the prophetic part immediately connected with the end of the assembly: only, in place of it, we have the world and then the Jews.[74]

The coming of Christ (as spoken of in Chap. 21: 22) and John's ministry

The coming of Christ therefore, which is spoken of at the end of the Gospel, is His manifestation on earth; and John, who lived in person until the close of all that was introduced by the Lord in connection with Jerusalem, continues here, in his ministry, until the manifestation of Christ to the world.

The teaching of John, and the work of Peter and Paul

In John, then, we have two things. On the one hand, his ministry, as far as connected with dispensation and with the ways of God, does not go beyond that which is earthly: the coming of Christ, is His manifestation to complete those ways, and to establish the government of God. On the other hand, he links us with the Person of Jesus, who is above and outside all dispensations, and

---

[74] Thus we have in the ministerial life, and in the teaching, of Peter and John, the whole religious earthly history from the beginning to the end; commencing with the Jews in continuation of the relations of Christ with them, traversing the whole Christian epoch, and finding itself again, after the close of the earthly history of the assembly, on the ground of God's relationship to the world (comprising the Jewish remnant) in view of the introduction of the First-born into the world (the last glorious event terminating the history which began with His rejection).

Paul is on very different ground. He sees the assembly, as the body of Christ, united to Him in heaven.

all the dealings of God, save as being the manifestation of God Himself. John does not enter upon the ground of the assembly as Paul sets it forth. It is either Jesus personally, or the relations of God with the earth.[75] His epistle presents the reproduction of the life of Christ in ourselves, guarding us thus from all pretensions of perverse teachers. But by these two parts of the truth, we have a precious sustainment of faith given to us, when all that belongs to the body of testimony may fail: Jesus, personally the object of faith in whom we know God; the life itself of God, reproduced in us, as being quickened by Christ. This is for ever true, and this is eternal life, if we were alone without the assembly on earth: and it leads us over its ruins, in possession of that which is essential, and of that which will abide for ever. The government of God will decide all the rest: only it is our privilege and duty to maintain Paul's part of the testimony of God, as long as through grace we can.

Remark also that the work of Peter and Paul is that of gathering together, whether it be in circumcision or the Gentiles. John is conservative, maintaining that which is essential in eternal life. He relates the judgment of God in connection with the world, but as a subject that is outside his own relations with God, which are given as an introduction and exordium to the Apocalypse. He follows Christ when Peter is called, because, although Peter was occupied, as Christ had been, with the call of the Jews, John—without being called to that work—followed Him on the same ground. The Lord explains it, as we have seen.

[75] John presents the Father manifested in the Son, God declared by the Son in the bosom of the Father, and that withal as eternal life— God to us, and life. Paul is employed to reveal our presentation to God in Him. Though each alludes in passing to the other point, one is characterized by the presentation of God to us, and eternal life given; the other, by our presentation to God.

The inexhaustible fulness of all that Jesus did

Verses 24, 25 are a kind of inscription on the book. John has not related all that Jesus did, but that which revealed Him as everlasting life. As to His works, they could not be numbered.

Here, thanks be to God, are these four precious books laid open, as far as God has enabled me to do so, in their great principles. Meditation on their contents in detail, I must leave to each individual heart, assisted by the mighty operation of the Holy Ghost; for if studied in detail, one might almost say with the apostle that the world would not contain the books that should be written. May God in His grace lead souls into the enjoyment of the inexhaustible streams of grace and truth in Jesus which they contain!